The Santa Fe Trail

The Santa Fe Trail

A Guide

Hal Jackson
&
Marc Simmons

Foreword by Leo Oliva

 Published 2015

Jackson, Hal (Hal E.)

The Santa Fe Trail, A Guide

ISBN 978-0-9859098-1-9

Cover illustration, chapter start illustrations
by Ron Kil

Book design and type composition by Mike Plantz

This book is in honor of Faye Gaines
who is representative of the dedicated
landowners along the Santa Fe Trail
vital to its preservation.

Contents

MAPS

SIDE TRIPS

SIDEBARS

FOREWORD

The Santa Fe Trail, 1821-1880, was primarily a route of commerce, with caravans of freight wagons passing to and fro between Missouri and New Mexico, an international road between the United States and Mexico until the 1840s. Secondarily, the Trail was a military road, followed by General Stephen Watts Kearny's Army of the West and other troops to capture the Southwest during the war with Mexico (1846-1848), after which military posts were established, with troops and supply wagons going to and returning from field campaigns and forts along the route and in the American Southwest. During the final years the route was also used for migration of families to the Southwest. The wagon road was shortened and then superseded as the railroads built westward. The fascinating history and the network of routes traveled have captured the interest and imagination of travelers who have followed and potential travelers who plan to follow the historic Santa Fe Road, commonly called Santa Fe Trail but also known as the Mexican Road.

There is a special emotion and understanding evoked when one visits a place where history happened. There are many such places along the old Santa Fe Trail. I, for example, am always elated to stand in "Ralph's Ruts" in central Kansas, and think about the many famous people (such as Kit Carson, Susan Shelby Magoffin, Marion Sloan Russell, Stephen Watts Kearny, William Bent, Antonio José Chávez, and Cheyenne Chief Black Kettle), hundreds of merchants, thousands of teamsters, thousands of soldiers, generations of Plains Indians, and uncounted families who passed through and created these impressive trail remnants. This guidebook directs you to scores of such places from central Missouri to Santa Fe, where you may experience those feelings.

Marc Simmons provided the first detailed traveler's guide to the historic trail in 1984 when he published *Following the Santa Fe Trail: A Guide for Modern Travelers*. This was three years before Congress established the Santa Fe National Historic Trail in 1987. As a tour director escorting an annual bus trek over the Santa Fe Road, I found Simmons's guidebook was an essential reading assignment for all participants. The volume helped thousands of tourists find remnants and historic places along the entire route from the site of the original Franklin in Missouri to the plaza in Santa Fe. The second edition was published in 1986, and the third, with Hal Jackson as co-author, in 2001, now out of print.

Hal Jackson has utilized material from these earlier editions and added new information, maps, and photos to create much more than another edition of the original traveler's guide. This is essentially a new guidebook with details and directions not found in previous volumes.

Traveling the trail can become an addiction, as many "trail junkies" know. Fortunately, for those who love this major overland trail, including its romance and adventure, you now have the most informative and detailed guide to the historic trail that has been written. When you venture anywhere near the Santa Fe National Historic Trail, you will rely on this fine book to find and enjoy the places where history happened. It is a dependable guide; use it often and enjoy the journey.

Leo Oliva
Woodston, Kansas

Preface

The aim of this book is to assist travelers in finding their way over the Santa Fe Trail. Paved highways parallel much of the old wagon road, but in some places graded county roads must be followed for short stretches. With the directions we have provided, anyone should be able to retrace large sections of the trail with comparative ease, although we have not tried to describe the route precisely mile by mile.

There will be numerous opportunities for adventure because you will be traveling with a purpose. This should offer you a deep and fulfilling experience, which is seldom the case in random sightseeing, Another attraction is the magic and beauty that persists in much of the landscape through which the Santa Fe Trail passes.

Background reading is essential preparation for any historical trip, and in the bibliography, we give titles of useful and interesting books that will provide basic information on the subject.

The main text briefly describes the chief points of interest along the Santa Fe Trail and furnishes precise directions for finding them while using standard road maps. We have tried to provide sufficient detail so that those venturing have more time to spend at sites worth a prolonged visit. No attempt has been made, however, to recount the full histories of individual trail sites, a task requiring a book many times larger than this guide.

Historic pioneer trails serve as some of the most fascinating links to our nation's past. Retracing them can be an exhilarating and educational experience. An added pleasure, we have discovered, comes from meeting people along the way who are dedicated history buffs and know many obscure details of the trail story in their localities. We have found such individuals, including most private owners of trail sites, unfailingly friendly and eager to share information. They enjoy talking with persons who are retracing the old wagon road, and if you are open and courteous, you will have a splendid chance of becoming acquainted with America at its grassroots.

Numerous changes have occurred since the 1980s. Interest

really jumped when President Reagan signed a congressional bill in May 1987 designating the Santa Fe Trail a National Historic Trail. This placed the National Park Service into the picture making that organization the overseer of the trail for purposes of interpretation and commemoration.

Another landmark event was the 1986 founding of the Santa Fe Trail Association (SFTA), with headquarters in Larned, Kansas. Through its historical and promotional programs, supported by twelve local chapters, the SFTA is engaged in mapping and marking the trail, sponsoring publications, and holding annual conferences. The Association's fine quarterly journal, *Wagon Tracks,* contains recent trail scholarship, news, and a calendar of current events.

There are three websites that are particularly valuable for SFT buffs. The National Park Service ahs a wealth of information about the SFT as does the Santa Fe Trail Association. Another important site is the Santa Fe Trail Research site. The SFTA also has 73 geocache locations along the route of the SFT (*santa fe national historic trail geotour).* These sites have proven to be very popular among those with families. Competition develops to see who can find the most geocaches.

In compiling this guide we have incurred many debts. We will begin in the eastern end of the trail with Don Cullimore of Howard County and Mike Dickey of the Arrow Rock State Historic Site. Both Don and Mike were very helpful with providing pictures and reading early drafts of the first chapter. Mike also was kind enough to write the sidebar for Boone's Lick. Sandy Slusher in Lexington also read the Lexington section to check for errors and omissions. Our thanks to all three.

The Kansas City area always presents special problems for us "country boys." Getting around this urban area is no mean feat and we thank Larry Short, Ross Marshall, and Craig Crease for guiding us through it. The SFTA has a new chapter in Douglas County, Kansas, and Roger Boyd is the president. Roger was very helpful to us and the nice section on Black Jack is a result of his help.

Council Grove was a big problem for us as the Government Land Office surveys show one route while locals claim another. Kenneth McClintock convinced us to place the route where we did. You will see it. Thanks Kenneth. Steve Schmidt was a great help in the Lost Spring to Durham area. His work on the Sibley survey of 1825 was also rewarding for us.

Linda Colle is president of the Quivira chapter of the SFTA and helped us locate all the important sites in the Little Arkansas crossing area. Thanks Linda. Bill Bunyan of Dodge City and Pat Palmer of Lamar, Colorado guided us through their respective sections. Jeff Trotman was instrumental in taking us from Ulysses to Elkhart, Kansas and we have placed this important route in the book.

Last, we thank Pat Macklin for editing assistance, Mike Plantz for computer expertise, and Leo Oliva and Bev Jackson for patience and editing help.

INTRODUCTION

The Santa Fe Trail was the first and most exotic of America's great trans-Mississippi pathways to the West. Its opening in 1821 preceded by two decades the birth of the Oregon and California Trails. Unlike them, the Santa Fe Trail began in the United States and ended in a foreign country, Mexico, at least for the first quarter-century of its existence. The strange customs, unfamiliar language, and breathtaking scenery found at the foot of the trail exerted a strong appeal and filled overlanders bound for New Mexico with special excitement.

The trail to Santa Fe was first and last a highway of commerce. In that, it differed markedly from trails farther north whose traffic consisted mainly of pioneer settlers, ranchers, farmers, and miners pushing toward the Pacific Ocean in quest of new homes and opportunities to be won from the land. The Santa Fe Trail was opened by a merchant, William Becknell, who foresaw profits to be made in transporting American goods across the southern prairies to eager Hispanic customers in the Republic of Mexico's far north. The merchants who followed him with mighty caravans of freight wagons merely enlarged upon a commercial opportunity that Becknell first brought to public attention. Within a short time the Santa Fe trade ballooned into a million-dollar-a-year business, pouring Mexican silver coin and raw products into the state of Missouri and precipitating a minor economic boom in what heretofore had been a depressed area on the American frontier.

The twenty-five years in which Mexico controlled the western end of the trade are generally regarded as the heyday of the Santa Fe Trail. In that period occurred many of the most dramatic events associated with trail history, including noted Indian fights, weather disasters that befell several caravans, the survey of the route in 1825, the first experimentation with military patrols, and the travels of Josiah Gregg, whose book on the subject, *Commerce of the Prairies*, first publicized this chapter in America's far western adventure.

After Gen. Stephen Watts Kearny led a conquering army over the Mountain Route of the Santa Fe Trail in 1846, the first year of the Mexican War, and brought the Southwest under United States rule, the character of the overland commerce changed. With both ends of the trail in American hands, the traffic was no longer of international scope. Forts were added along the route to guard against Indian attack, and the freighting of military supplies became a new business. Stagecoach and mail services were inaugurated. More varied types of travelers put in an appearance. Where once the trail had been frequented only by merchants, their wagon masters, and ox drovers, by the late 1840s one could begin to meet, besides U.S. Army soldiers, newly appointed government officials, gold seekers bound for California, Catholic priests and nuns, a sprinkling of Protestant missionaries, and even a few emigrant families.

The last phase of the trail story unfolded during the 1860s and 1870s as railroads pushed across Kansas and into the Southwest, creating a new railhead with each advance and progressively shortening the Santa Fe Trail. When the train reached Las Vegas in summer 1879, only 65 miles remained of the original wagon route to Santa Fe. In February, 1880, with that last gap closed by rails, newspapers in New Mexico's capital proclaimed in bold headlines: "The Santa Fe Trail Passes into Oblivion."

The Santa Fe Trail may have closed but it certainly is not forgotten. There are many organizations watching over its best interests. The National Park Service through its Long Distance Trails office in Santa Fe is responsible for the trail's preservation, interpretation, and marking. It has developed and installed distinctive signs designating the auto tour route that more-or-less parallel the trail. The official logo shows an ox-drawn freight wagon.

The federal program also works with private landowners who seek voluntary certification of historic sites on their property. To qualify, strict standards must be met.

In 1986, at Trinidad, Colorado, the Santa Fe Trail Council, afterward renamed the Santa Fe Trail Association, was established to promote all aspects of the trail, including preservation, marking, research, publications, and travel. The local chapters of the SFTA develop programs at the local level. In odd-numbered years the

SFTA holds a three-day symposium featuring lectures, tours, and period entertainment. The association's quarterly, *Wagon Tracks* has become a major source of information on both the historic and contemporary trail. The SFTA coordinates its efforts with the National Park Service at all levels.

The administrative, office and archives of the SFTA are located at the Santa Fe Trail Center in Larned, Kansas. Both the SFTA and NPS have extensive web sites for more trail information.

The advent of the Good Roads movement in the early twentieth century led to a recognition of the earlier pioneer roads. As states battled for routes across their states for better roads the Daughters of the American Revolution entered the debate by suggesting that new roads should follow the earlier national historic roads. In addition, to punctuate their efforts they began marking the old roads. Missouri led the way followed by Kansas, Colorado, and New Mexico. The DAR located the old SFT and marked it with handsome incised granite markers. Many of these markers are in their original location but highway departments and individuals have moved others.

A problem or challenge that many first-time SFT seekers have is finding the trail. It sounds easy but is not. These routes are 135 years old now and weather and use has taken its toll on them. Certainly one of the most interesting features of the modern trail are these old ruts or tracks left by the heavy wheels of freight wagons. Newcomers to the trail are looking for well-defined ruts left by the wheels of the wagons. However, oxen or mules pulled those wagons and these were harnessed in a manner that obliterated any notion of a "two track." Many people new to the trail, hearing of ruts, expect to see something resembling tire tracks of a car or pickup truck, sometimes called a "two track."

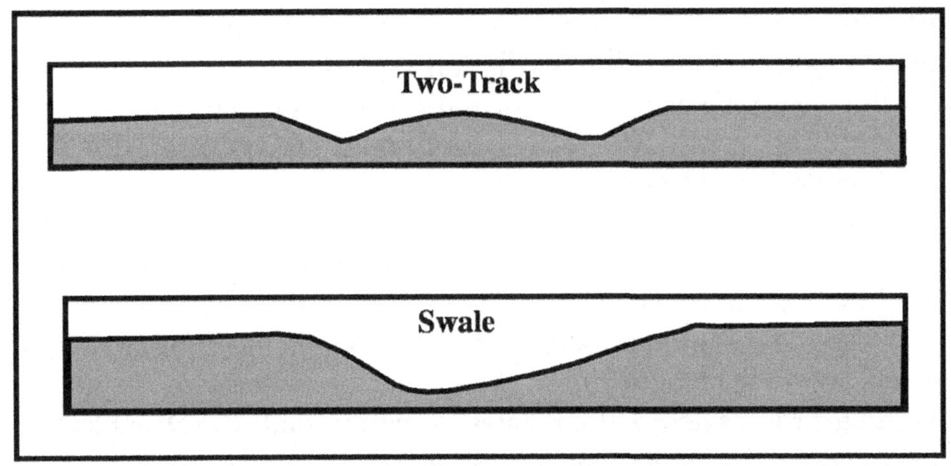

The included diagram shows a two track and a swale, or rut. It is the second of these diagrams that should be your guide. Two other trail features, both produced by erosion so excessive that little semblance of the original trail trace remains, are washouts and blowouts. A washout is caused by heavy water erosion widening and deepening a rut until it resembles a streambed (called an arroyo in New Mexico).

A blowout occurs when wind gouges a relatively deep depression well beyond the limits of the original rut. The best example of a blowout is in the Durham area of Kansas and a pair of photos in Chapter 4 will show these.

Finally, we must advise you about the temporal development of the SFT. Most books on the SFT include a map showing the SFT. The single map might make one think that all those places, towns, and sites were there all along. Remember that when William Becknell left Missouri at Fort Osage he did not see a town, village, or community until he reached San Miguel del Vado in New Mexico. In addition, there was no Mountain Route until the Mexican War in 1846-1848. Trail traffic used the Cimarron Route until after the war and even then did not switch to the Mountain Route until later. There were few communities along the SFT until after Kansas was made a territory in 1854.

It was in the early period that towns like Council Grove and Baldwin City came to life. Most towns along the route of the SFT in Kansas were railroad towns and not trail towns.

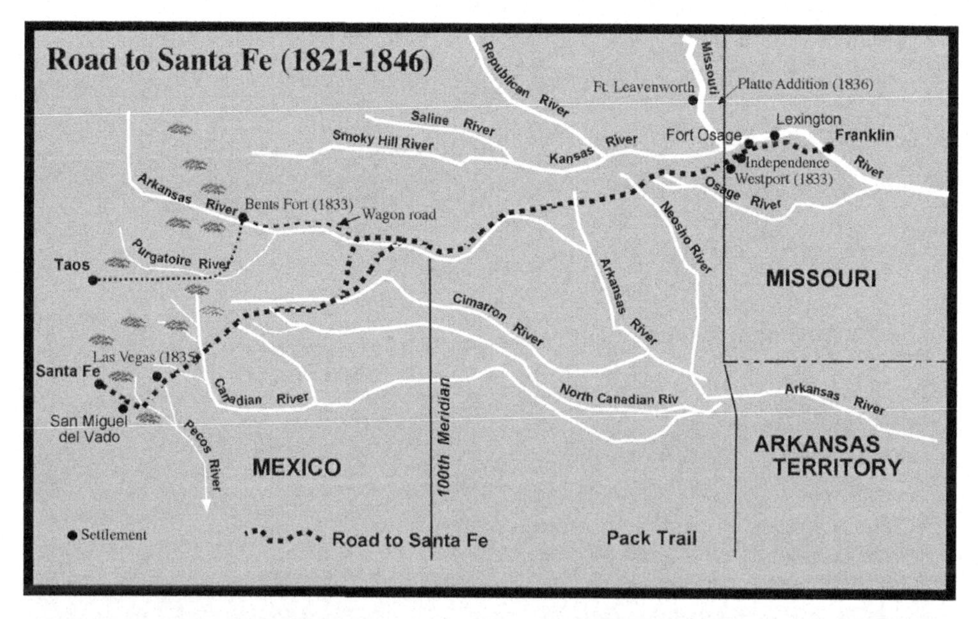

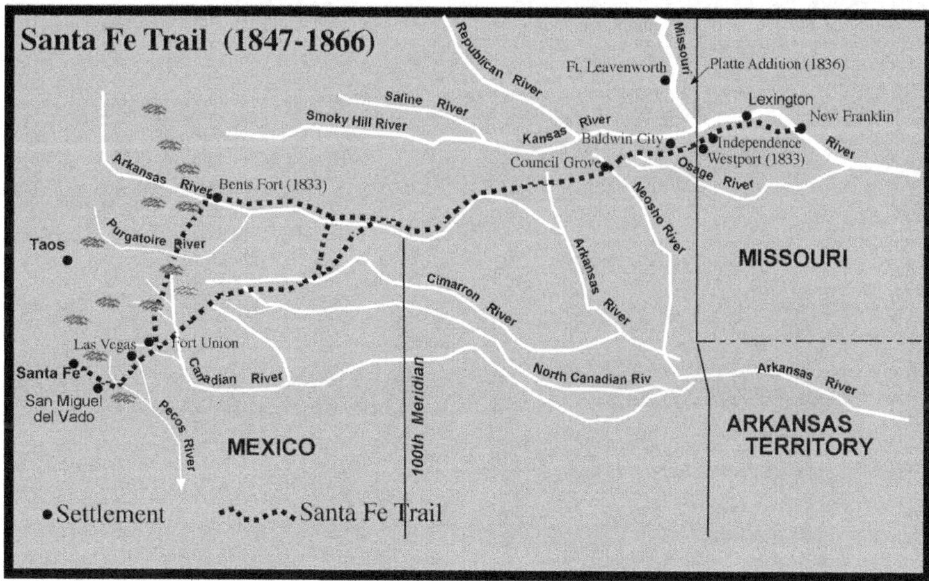

After 1866 the SFT began to shrink as the railroads built west (a map of this period can be found on page 176). So, as you start your trek from Old Franklin keep these facts in mind.

Chapter 1
MISSOURI

FRANKLIN

The Santa Fe Trail (SFT) opened for successful commerce in 1821 when William Becknell and five others departed Franklin, Missouri with pack horses loaded with trade items for Santa Fe in Mexico.

Franklin, platted on a low floodplain on the north bank of the Missouri River in 1816, was the county seat of Howard County. It was a rapidly growing town by 1821 and was not only the county seat of Howard County but also the unofficial capital of the Boonslick Country. The name Boonslick comes from the salt springs in Howard County called Boone's Lick; developed commercially by Nathan and Daniel Morgan Boone, sons of the famous hunter Daniel Boone, in 1805.

Ninety-seven lots were laid out in Franklin in 1817 and this number was soon expanded to 678. There were two ferries along the waterfront and thirteen shops located on or near the town square; there were four taverns, a courthouse, and a strong log prison. A visitor to Franklin in 1818 reported seventy families here. In addition, Franklin had its own newspaper, the *Intelligencer,* which began publication April 1819. In addition, in that year, the first steamboat, the *Independence*, made it up the Missouri to Franklin, leading to a large public celebration. Unfortunately, Franklin was not to have another steamboat visit until 1826.

The previous statement is not quite accurate, as the Western Engineer of the Yellowstone Expedition in 1819, and several supply steamboats for the Upper Missouri trade made their way past Franklin. The town would continue to rely on the several keelboats that regularly made their way upstream to Franklin.

KEELBOATS

Access to the Boonslick country before 1816 was limited to utilization of the Missouri river or a horse trail paralleling the river called the Boone Trace. The principal boat used upriver was the keelboat. These large boats were used for decades on the Ohio and Mississippi rivers, and after the Louisiana Purchase in 1803, their use was expanded to the Missouri river.

An artist's drawing of a keelboat.

Keelboats were between forty and eighty feet in length and seven to ten feet wide. Their draft was only two feet when fully loaded and cargo might be as much as thirty tons. They were propelled by a combination of sails, oars, poles, and ropes. Sails were used when favorable winds were available. Oars were often used and these might be in conjunction with poles. Men would walk on a cleated passageway on both sides of the vessel. When all else failed, the crew would go ashore and use ropes to pull the keelboat along.

These boats could be surprisingly fast as demonstrated in 1811 when Manuel Lisa's party averaged eighteen miles per day ascending the Missouri from St. Charles to the Mandan villages in present-day Montana.

Keelboats were especially well suited in the early period on the Missouri. There simply was not enough to export, as the Boonslick country remained a subsistence economy without products to send downriver. In 1821, Franklin's imports were handled by two keelboats, the *Domestic* and the *Missouri*. It would take a few years before enough migration had occurred, the economy had matured, and, most importantly, the Santa Fe trade had grown before steamboats supplanted keelboats.

Most residents were confident their town would soon rival St. Louis but a few were not so sure. John Bell, visiting in 1820, wrote that "Franklin, but from its situation, and the uncertainty in the stability and permanence of these bottoms in high stages of water, must operate against the advancement of the town to a very considerable size." In short: Watch out for the floods.

Part of Howard County's prosperity was a result of the government land office opening at Franklin in 1818. Before that time it was impossible to buy land in Howard County and the Boonslick. By October 1821, almost 760,000 acres were sold at Franklin. The other Missouri land office, at St. Louis, sold 545,000 acres during the same period. The accompanying map shows the population distribution for central Missouri in 1820 and the westward protuberance of the Boonslick is clear. It was truly the El Dorado of westward migration.

The first flood visited Franklin in 1826, followed by a more dramatic rise in the Missouri in 1828. Most Franklinites moved to higher ground after 1828 and formed a new town, calling it New Franklin. Many rolled their homes up the hill on logs to New Franklin as well. Franklin was no longer the important town it had been.

In 1821, the same year that Missouri gained statehood, the then booming town of Franklin became linked to the Santa Fe Trail.

The national financial crisis, known as the Panic of 1819, caused many economic problems for both Missouri and the Boonslick. The Bank of St. Louis closed in early 1819 and the Bank of Missouri failed in 1821. Currency was in very short supply and bartering became common.

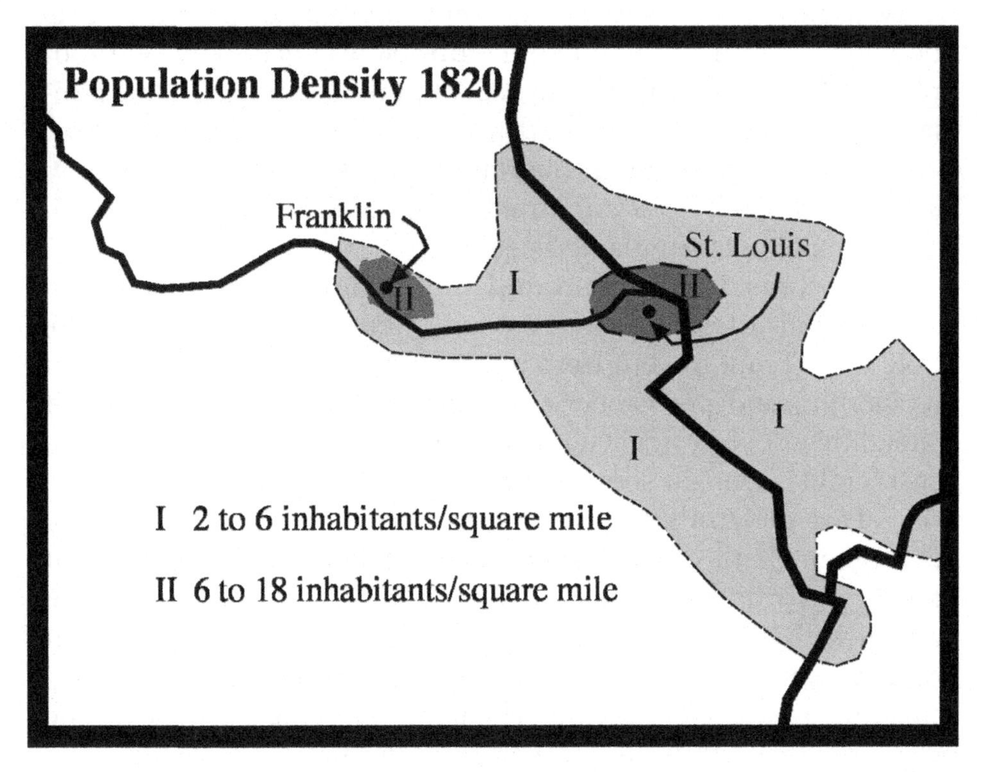

William Becknell moved to the Boonslick in 1817 after having lived in St. Charles County since 1810. He bought a license to operate a ferry connecting Howard County to the Arrow Rock landing in fall, 1817. (Note: there was no town at Arrow Rock until 1829). Becknell had previously worked for the Morrison brothers when he lived in St. Charles County and continued sporadic employment with them at the salt springs near the ferry landing. The Morrisons were wealthy merchants in both Missouri and Illinois. They had supplied Jean Baptiste La Lande with trade goods which he took to Santa Fe in 1804. Pike found him there when he was captured in

1807. For more on the Morrisons see Morrow (2015). In 1821, Becknell was broke. There were five lawsuits against him and he was out of debtor's prison on bond. He left for Santa Fe hoping for the best on September 1, 1821. His timing was auspicious; Mexico achieved independence from Spain the same year and Becknell's party was welcomed to trade in Santa Fe.

VISITING THE FRANKLIN AREA

Begin your visit by driving to the center of Old Franklin. Access to this site is from Interstate 70, the principal highway between St. Louis and Kansas City. Exit at Boonville (Exits 101, 103, and 106), drive north through the center of Boonville on Main St., and cross the Missouri River on a concrete bridge. Do not worry about neglecting Boonville as you will be directed back. You are now on US 40 and just after crossing the river, you should turn left (west) on Missouri 87.

Drive about one-quarter mile west on MO 87 and on your right, near a row of trees, is a turnout with parking **(A).** You are at the site of Kingsbury Siding, a terminal for the Missouri-Kansas-Texas Railroad, known popularly as the "Katy." Here the Katy Trail enters from the north, a walking and biking trail from St. Charles, Missouri that follows the old bed of the railroad.

You have been directed here because this spot is very near the center of Old Franklin, the original starting point for the Santa Fe Trail (SFT). The center of Old Franklin was located two blocks southwest of this park. Careful inspection of the map of Old Franklin shows that you are very near the corner of Boone and Ash Streets in Old Franklin. There are several markers here of interest. They refer to the history and route of the Santa Fe Trail. Especially noted are the sites one should visit to the immediate west. Another marker is for the Boone's Lick Road (BLR), the principal route to St. Charles, Missouri. Referring to the map again, you can see St. Charles Street on the south side of the town square. This was the road to St. Charles, the BLR.

Franklin Area.

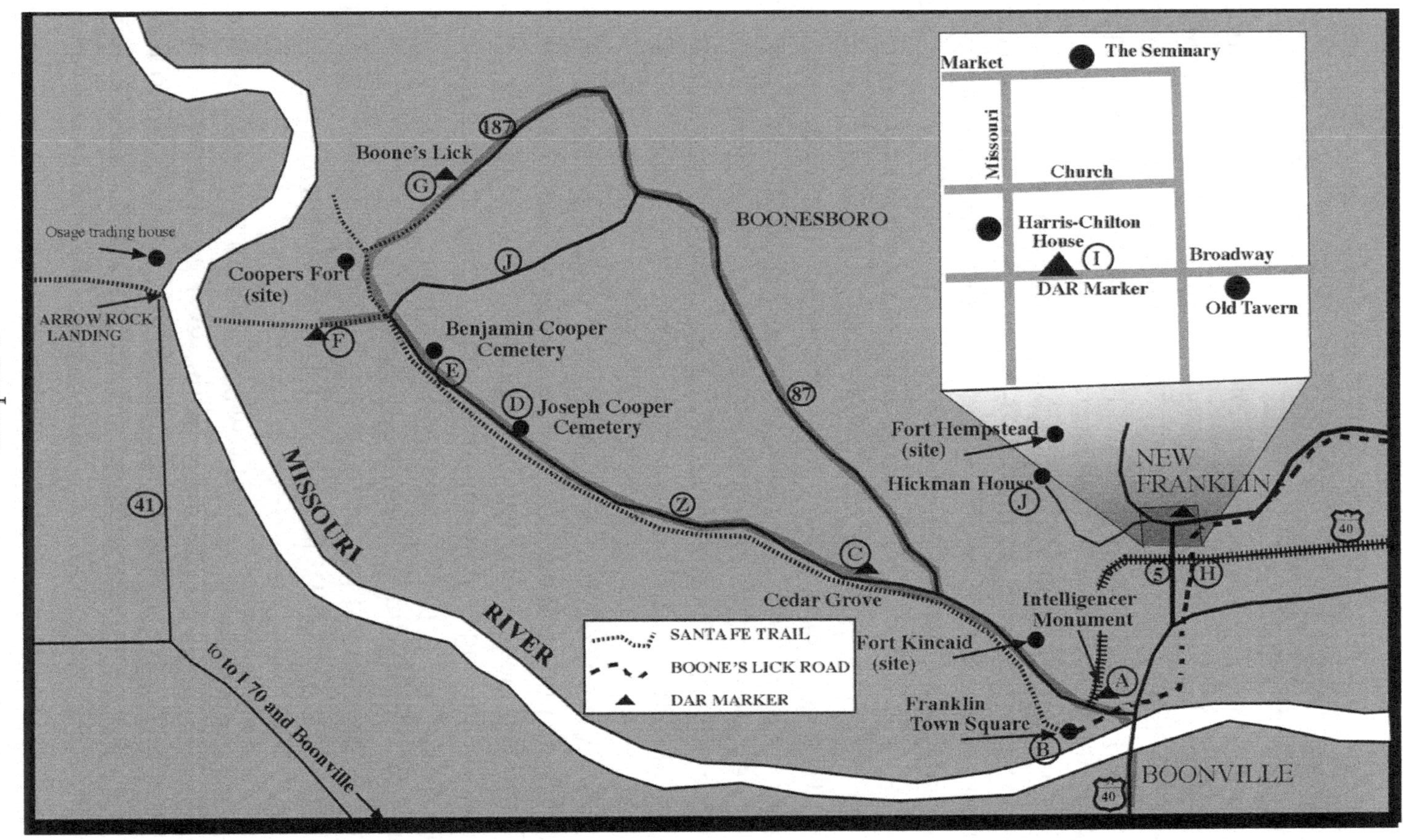

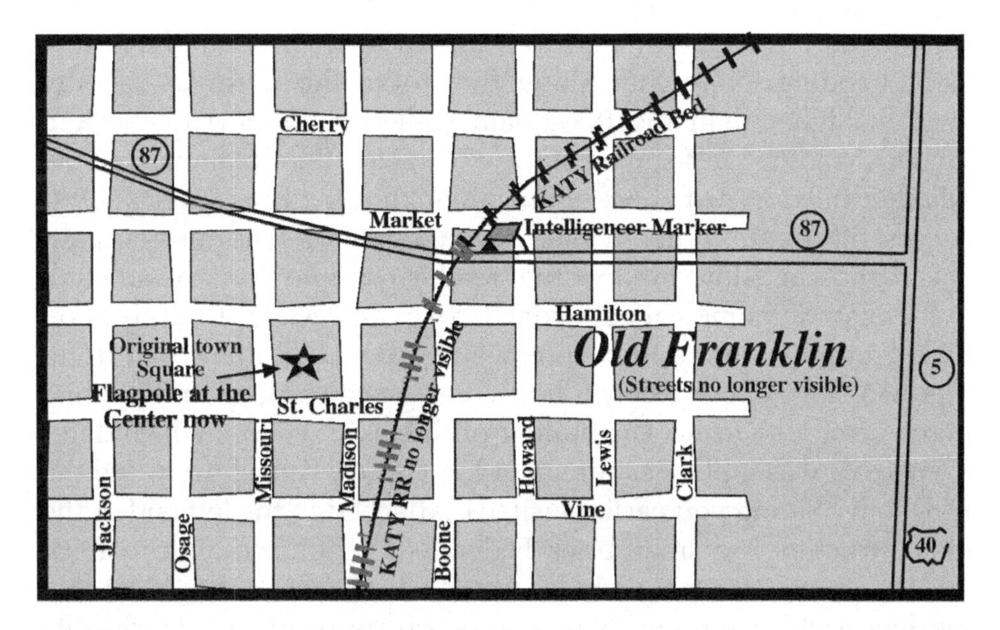

Of SFT interest is a marker with an inscription commemorating two newspapers, one of them the *Missouri Intelligencer*. This marker replaces one lost in the flood of 1993. The *Missouri Intelligencer* was the first weekly newspaper established (1819) west of St. Louis, and today the back files of this paper are a prime source for information about the history of the SFT. Its pages carried the first announcement of Becknell's initial trip to Santa Fe, and on October 12, 1826, a notice that the boy Christopher Carson (better known as "Kit") had fled his apprenticeship. Soon after, the *Missouri Intelligencer* moved its offices 15 miles north to Fayette, the new county seat. The marker notes that the original newspaper office was "500 feet west of this spot," which would be the center of Old Franklin.

Walk a few paces from this site to the highway and then turn west. This will take you to another small turnout with additional markers. One of these markers directs your attention to a pole erected in the field across the highway by the Santa Fe Trail Association. The late Denny Davis, a local historian, had surveyors locate the exact center of the old town square and directed the erection of the pole at this point **(B).**

Now return to MO 87 and turn right (west) where you will follow the Santa Fe Trail. After the SFT left the town square it headed west toward the ferry that crossed the Missouri River to the Arrow Rock Landing. Note that along this route the highway is only slightly higher than the floodplain (called a bottom) to the left. Traders heading west stayed at the edge of the floodplain next to the adjacent hills. At just short of 2.5 miles from the Katy Trail, MO 87 curves right and climbs a hill. Paved Route Z continues straight ahead and you should follow that road. At .8 mile from the junction is the historic home called Cedar Grove, on the right **(C).** It is on high ground behind a low stone wall with a DAR marker in front. The two-story Greek Revival house has green shutters and a white porch across the front. The builder of the main section, which dates from 1856, was a physician named Dr. Horace Kingsbury (note the Kingsbury Siding you earlier visited). Attached to the left end of the main structure is a small brick Federal-style house dating to 1824. Built by pioneer farmer Nicholas Amick, this is one of the oldest area residences still standing. It is now a private residence. During its earliest years of occupation, Santa Fe-bound caravans passed in front.

Continue on Route Z to a small cemetery on your right, about 4.6 miles from Cedar Grove **(D).** This cemetery contains the grave of Joseph Cooper, a son of Sarshall Cooper who was the Captain of all the forts in Howard County during the War of 1812 and for which Cooper County was named. There is a small sign and a stile for easy entrance. It is a short but steep walk to the cemetery. About 1.6 miles past the first cemetery, you come to a second, which contains the graves of Benjamin Cooper and his brother Sarshall. Sarshall was killed in his home at Cooper's Fort in 1815 by Indians shooting through a hole in the wall of his house **(E).**

The Cooper family played a very important role in the early history of the Boonslick. Col. Benjamin Cooper, an officer in the Revolutionary War, came to this area in 1808 with his wife and seven sons. Territorial Governor Meriwether Lewis ordered them out of the area. They went downriver for two years before returning here in 1810, making them the first family of the county. The sons distinguished themselves in many ways. Benjamin Cooper, Jr. led an early caravan to Santa Fe, his brother Steven was along on that trip as well as serving as the pilot on the Sibley survey of the Santa Fe Road in 1825. The land to your left as you drive the SFT was called the Cooper Bottoms.

Continuing on Route Z another .3 mile, you come to a crossroad, which was the hamlet of Petersburg. You should take the road to the left (gravel County Road 330) toward the river. Follow this road (weather permitting of course) for about .8 mile, where there is another DAR marker on the left by a telephone pole **(F).** The marker is inscribed at the base "Cooper's Fort" but can be difficult to read because of silt deposited at the base. Just beyond, on the right, is a commemorative sign placed by the Boonslick Historical Society telling about Cooper's Fort.

Artist conception of Cooper's Fort by Stephanie Witt

Brothers Benjamin and Sarshall Cooper built a fort near here for protection of local settlers during the War of 1812. This was one of four such forts in Howard County and there were two more across the river in Cooper County. The exact location of this fort is not known but it was between here and the hills to the north. Sarshall Cooper was elected captain of the military company overseeing all the forts. There were sixty-four men (males able to be armed) at this fort during this period. Twelve of the sixty-four defenders were named Cooper. Additionally, three were named Gregg including Harmon Gregg, father of Josiah. Josiah, the future author of *Commerce of the Prairies* (1844), was but six years old in 1812 when his family lived at the fort.

The determination of the Coopers and others at the fort is clear from the defiant statement on the commemorative sign. The U. S. government ordered settlers to withdraw at the outbreak of the war and the following was their response:

"We have maid our Hoams here and all we hav is here and it Wud ruen us to leave now. We are all good Americans, not a Tory or one of his Pups among us and we hav 2 hundred Men and Boys that will Fight to the last and we have 100 Wimen and Girls whut wil tak there places wh. makes a good force. So we can Defend the Settlement wh. Gods help we will do. So if we had a few barls of Powder and 2 hundred Lead is all we ask."

Benjamin Cooper, Jr., son of the patriarch who brought the family west, led a party with pack mules and horses to Santa Fe at the same time William Becknell took the first wagons to Santa Fe on his second trip to Santa Fe in 1822. Cooper returned to New Mexico the following year with traders headed by his nephew Steven.

The road beyond the DAR marker formerly continued on to the Missouri River where traders utilized a ferry to cross to Arrow Rock Landing and, after 1829, the town of Arrow Rock. One such trader, John Glover, passed here in October 1826 and wrote: "came on to Airy Rock Ferry at Mr Becknal where I tarried all night. Becknals house stands on the north Bank of Missouria on a Bank of sand 2 small cabbands bad appearance but good fair bill Ferriage and all 87 and one-half cents." (There will be more on the 87 and a half cents later).

Artist conception of an early ferry by Ron Kil.

Return on County Road 330 to the pavement at Petersburg, turn left and left again onto a gravel road, County Road 328. Follow this road and in about one mile, you will come to a corner where the road goes right over a creek and up the hill. Cooper's Fort was sited near the turn and about 100 yards west. Continue up 328, which follows the course of Salt Creek. In 1808 William Clark wrote, "passed thro a butifull small plain Makays about a mile wide and crossed a Cart Road leading from Boons lick to the Missouri." Thus, the first "road" in the Boonslick was a simple cart road used to transport salt from the lick down to the river for shipment to St. Louis.

It is important to tell about William Clark's trip west in 1808 at this point. Nathan Boone, who with his brother Daniel Morgan Boone, was in charge of the lick's operations, guided Clark. After passing by the lick, Clark's group went to the river where a pirogue (small boat) had been left for them. They crossed the river to the Arrow Rock and then continued west to Fire Prairie where Clark established Fort Osage. (His journal is available as *Westward with Dragoons: The Journal of William Clark.*) His description of the trip from the Arrow Rock to Fire Prairie should be read as it is the first description of the country that the Santa Fe Trail traversed, starting in 1821. Becknell's description of his first trip along the same route is much less reliable than Clark's.

Continue on County Road 328 until you reach the entrance to Boone's Lick State Historic Site, then drive into the site and park. You will know when you reach the site because the pavement begins here **(G).**

BOONE'S LICK

Salt was an important commodity in Missouri Territory in the early eighteenth century. It was used for preserving meat, tanning animal hides, sustaining livestock, and seasoning foods. The salt springs at Boone's Lick were well known by 1805 when Nathan and Daniel Morgan Boone began the salt extraction operation. The two men were sons of the famed Daniel Boone, who is often, mistakenly, given credit for the discovery of the salt springs. This mistaken credit for Daniel Boone persisted even after Nathan Boone made it clear in an 1851 interview that his father was not the discoverer of the springs.

DAR marker at Boone's Lick
erroneously crediting Daniel Boone as discoverer.
Entrance signs at the Historic Site. Photo by Don Cullimore.

A very interesting description of the Lick comes from a visit in 1808 by William Clark (of Lewis and Clark fame). Clark was directed to take a military force from St. Charles, across the Missouri River from St. Louis, to the Fire Prairie in present-day Jackson County, Missouri to construct a fort and trading post for the Indians of the Osage nation. Clark chose Nathan Boone as his guide for the trip west. They arrived at the Lick and Clark wrote in his journal "...passed thru a butifull small plain "Mackeys" about a mile wide and crossed a Cart Road leading from Boons lick to the Missouri." Clark went on to write, "...this water is Very Strong 250 gallons to a Bushell of salt." Mackey was a name sometimes used for the salt lick even as late as 1814. James Mackey was born in Scotland and immigrated to North America in the 1770s. He became a Spanish citizen after moving to Missouri about 1790. He led an expedition up the Missouri to the Mandan villages in 1795 and it was on this trip when he saw or heard about the salt springs at Boone's Lick. He was given a Spanish grant for 400 arpents (330 acres) of land around the springs.

To complete the story of the Lick's exploitation one needs to know a little about the brothers Morrison, James, Jesse, and William. The Morrison family was one of the wealthiest in Missouri and Illinois. They controlled much of the trade in this part of the country. They provided the capital necessary to buy the iron kettles and transport everything upriver to the Lick. Therefore, we have Morrison money, Mackey land, and the Boone brothers as site managers at the Lick. The Morrisons paid Mackey $500 per year for the right to exploit the salt at the Lick. This was a great deal of money in 1805, Nathan Boone said the operation would have been profitable but for the troubles and pilferings of the Indians at the works, chiefly in stealing and killing the working and beef cattle. The Morrisons only paid Mackey for four years or so since the U S government did not confirm Mackay's Spanish grant at this time.

Daniel Morgan Boone sold his interest to Jesse Morrison in 1810. Nathan sold his interest in 1812 when he became a captain of the Missouri Rangers at the outset of the War of 1812. Other managers of the salt works include William Becknell and Braxton Cooper.

The operation produced about 25 bushels of salt per day from two furnaces handling 60 kettles each. There were some 20 men working at the site. The salt was sent down river on flat boats or keelboats until the steamboats entered the river trade in the late 1820s. The salt sold for $2.50 per bushel in St. Louis. The estimated value of salt produced at the lick each month was over $1800.

The Lick faced serious competition as other salt works developed in the region. In 1833, the U. S. government confirmed Mackey's Spanish land grant to his heirs and commercial salt manufacturing ceased at Boone's Lick. After that date, salt manufacturing occurred only sporadically. In 1869, there was a short-lived attempt to restart the operation but it failed. In addition, in 1900, there was a plan to raise oysters here. That scheme failed when there was no fresh water in which the oysters could spawn.
Courtesy Michael Dickey, Site Administrator
Arrow Rock State Historic Site

As there is no bridge or ferry across the Missouri to Arrow Rock today, you must return to Old Franklin via MO 87, which is the paved road at the historic site. Follow MO 87 through Boonesboro, past the Kingsbury Siding parking area, returning to US 40. If you cross US 40 you will be on a gravel road which was part of the Boone's Lick Road until at least 1828. This road will take you to Rivercene, which is on the National Register of Historic Places. Now a bed and breakfast, a sign on one of the two stone pillars at the gate reads: "Steamboat Captain's House." A Captain Kinney, who at various times owned nine steamboats on the Missouri River, built the house in 1869.

Return to the intersection of MO 87 and US 40 and turn right (north) toward New Franklin. Turn left on MO 5, and just before New Franklin and just as you leave the floodplain, there is a turnout on the right with parking which provides access to the historical site on the left of the highway **(H).** This is a new site dedicated only recently with markers placed there by the South Howard County Historical Society. This spot is where the KATY railroad crossed until 1986 when it ceased operation. There were eight tracks here and a viaduct was constructed to allow autos to travel to New Franklin safely.

William Becknell as etched in stone.
Photo by Don Cullimore

There are six large panels at the site of particular interest to Santa Fe Trail buffs: William Becknell, Kit Carson, Josiah Gregg, Millie Cooper, Ezekiel Williams, and George Caleb Bingham (a famous portrait painter from Missouri). Millie Cooper was a young girl who went by horse to bring help to the settlers at Cooper's Fort who were under Indian attack. Ezekiel Williams was a resident of Franklin and Boonville who made several trips to Santa Fe, including one prior to 1821.

Continue up the hill on MO 5 to the stop sign, turn right on Broadway, and in the center of the avenue you will find a large red boulder and plaque surmounted by a three-bulb antique streetlight. This is the Beginning of the Trail Monument, placed with much ceremony by the DAR in 1909 **(I).**

For modern travelers intending to drive all the way to Santa Fe, here is one of this trail's high points. From this spot to the End of the Trail Monument on the Santa Fe Plaza, lie almost 1,000 miles, all studded with history. At the New Franklin monument, your adventure into the past officially commences.

The heading on the bronze plaque reads "Franklin, Cradle of the Santa Fe Trail, 1821." At the top, William Becknell's first packhorse train to Santa Fe appears in sculptured relief. (Other Becknell trains in bronze relief can be seen along the road at Pawnee Rock and Wagon Mound.) The full inscription, left to your discovery, will stir all road buffs that respond to the drama and romance of history. Behind the DAR marker, note a separate stone designating the "End of Boone's Lick Road," the road connecting St. Charles with Franklin and the start of the SFT. Actually, these markers properly belong on the square in Old Franklin, but since that site is inaccessible, this location will have to do.

Continue east on Broadway to the two-story house at 207, which may be one of the old taverns originally in Old Franklin. Note that a "tavern" in the 1820s was a place to sleep, eat, and consume beverages, which most likely would have been hard cider as it was safe to drink. We know a tavern was put on logs and moved to New Franklin, and possibly it was this building since locals claim that the upstairs rooms in this house had numbers over the doors before remodeling took place. If it is the old tavern, then it may be the house where the famed Missouri portrait painter George Caleb Bingham, as a boy, watched Chester Harding finish a painting of Daniel Boone. Harding had stopped by Boone's residence in Defiance, Missouri a year before Boone's death and had him propped up for a portrait. Bingham, himself, went on to become one of Missouri's most famous painters. Bingham's image was one of those you saw at the turnout south of New Franklin.

Return to Missouri Avenue and turn right. In the middle of the first block on the left, at 108 N. Missouri, is the two-story, Federal-style Harris/Chilton House built in 1832. Continue another one and a half blocks to Market Street and turn right. In mid-block on the left, at 110 Market, is a two-story white house with a sign next to a wagon wheel, reading, "Seminary, 1832." This old brick building was the first school, or academy as it was called, in New Franklin.

Return to Broadway in New Franklin and turn right (west) on West Broadway. In about .3 mile turn left, following W. Broadway and leaving MO 5, drive .5 mile and turn right toward the Horticultural Center. Follow this gravel road about .6 of a mile to the Hickman House **(J).** Thomas Hickman came to the Boonslick in 1816 and went into business with William Lamme and Company in Old Franklin. He built this house in 1819 and it is now on the National Register of Historic Places after extensive restoration in 2006. Hickman is representative of the group of settlers coming to the Boonslick directly from the East, mainly from Kentucky. This group tended to be better educated and wealthier than the Coopers, Boones, and Coles who came earlier. (The Coles are discussed later in the section on Boonville history). This one-and-one-half-story brick house is one of the oldest such houses west of the Mississippi River.

Thomas Hickman house in New Franklin.

Inspection of the Franklin Area map will show that Fort Hempstead was located near the future site of the Hickman house. There were 112 men in this fort including three named Carson. One of these Carsons was Lindsay, father of Kit Carson. Kit spent three years of his early life in this fort.

Return toward New Franklin and make an interesting side trip to Fayette if you wish. When you arrive at MO 5, turn left and drive 9 miles to Fayette, the county seat of Howard County. The town was established in 1823, and soon after, became the county seat. There are many attractive houses here, but one of interest to trail buffs is that of Joseph Davis, an assistant surveyor on the 1825 Sibley SFT survey and a signer of the treaty made with the Osages at Council Grove, Kansas. Located at 208 South Main Street, half of the house (to the right) is older and was likely built about 1826. Davis's great-grandson, the late Denny Davis, was the owner of the local newspapers and was a dedicated and valuable source of information on local history. It was Denny who helped with the planting of the pole in the center of the square in Old Franklin.

Kit Carson sent his half-Indian daughter Adaline to Rock Springs School here in Fayette. Later Adaline attended Howard Female Seminary (afterward Central Methodist College), which still exists in Fayette. Then, in the 1850s, Carson took her back to Taos, New Mexico.

Return to Old Franklin and cross over the Missouri River to Boonville.

BOONVILLE

Old Franklin, built on the bottoms of the Missouri River on the north bank, had the advantage of being on Boone's Lick Road and having easy access to the river. Opposite Franklin on the south side, steep limestone cliffs rose almost from the water's edge. In 1817, Boonville, named for Daniel Boone, was established atop these cliffs.

In fact, settlement on this side of the river began concurrently with the settlement on the north side. In 1808, the Cole families accompanied the Benjamin Cooper clan to the Boonslick. While the Coopers settled on the north, the Coles built their cabins on the south side. Both Coopers and Coles were ordered to move downriver by territorial governor Meriwether Lewis because the land titles were not cleared from Indian claims. In 1810, the Coopers and Coles returned to claim their homes. By this time, William Cole had been killed by Indians near Loutre Island so it was his wife Hannah and her nine children, and William's brother Steven Cole who returned.

During the War of 1812 settlers here had to take refuge in quickly assembled forts. Hannah Cole's fort was the most important of these. After the conclusion of the hostilities and when Howard County was created by the Missouri legislature in 1816, the fort was the county seat until Franklin was ready to assume that role in 1817.

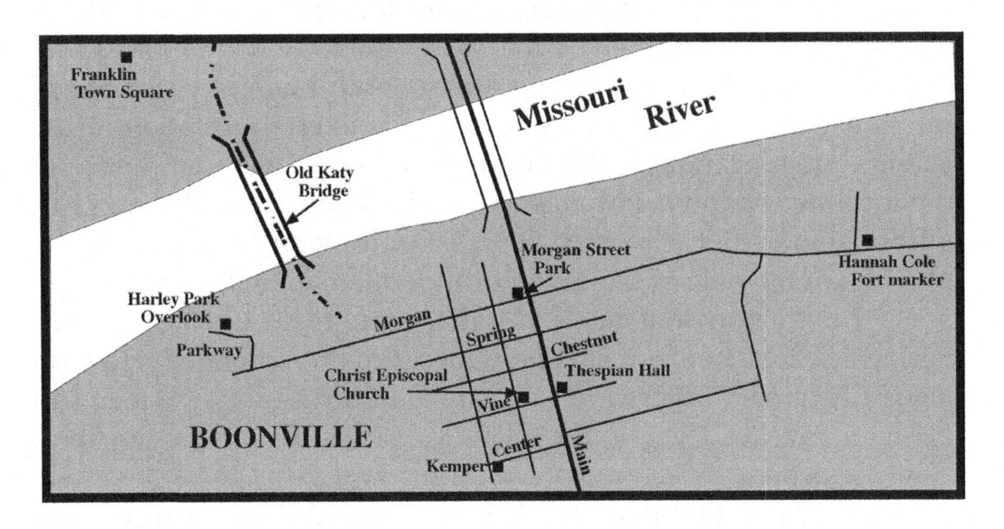

Boonville is mentioned as a starting point for some Santa Fe caravans but its role was minor compared to that of Franklin. Several early Boonville buildings must have been familiar to SFT traders. Christ Episcopal Church (northeast corner of Vine and Fourth Streets) dates from 1846 and is said to be the oldest Episcopal church west of St. Louis. Thespian Hall, at the corner of Main and Vine Streets, was begun in 1855 and is the oldest theater west of the Alleghenies. Kemper Military School (Center and Third Streets) was established in 1844, not closing until 2002. Famed Santa Fe trader Franz Huning of Albuquerque placed his nine-year-old son Arno in this school in about 1878.

Today, Boonville is a thriving community with a great deal of interest in its past. It is certainly worth the traveler's time to pause here.

Of interest downtown is Morgan Street Park where there is a nice statue of Hannah Cole with marker. Driving east on Morgan Street .7 miles will take you to a nice marker for Hannah Cole's Fort on the left side of the road adjacent to a lane. The actual fort was north of here on the bluff overlooking the river and where the settlers could safely draw water from the river.

An artist conception of Cole Fort by Stephanie Witt.

Of special interest is the Harley Park Overlook, where one has a fine view across the river to the site of Franklin. To get to this overlook, drive west on Morgan Street to Parkway, and then turn right. Continue one block on Parkway and turn left on Harley to the overlook. From here, you can see the "bottoms" across the river, the location of the once-thriving town of Franklin, and a long view up the valley, the route of the SFT to Arrow Rock.

SIDE TRIP TO COLUMBIA, ST. CHARLES, AND ST. LOUIS

One of the markers at the Kingsbury siding in Old Franklin is for the Boone's Lick Road (BLR), the road that began in St. Charles and ended at Franklin on the square. One can say that the Santa Fe Trail was an extension of the BLR. A detailed account of the BLR is not appropriate in these pages but such account can be found in the book *Boone's Lick Road* (see Bibliography) that details every turn and stop of that important road from St. Charles to Howard County.

We suggest, however, that before continuing to Arrow Rock you consider making the relatively short drive east to Columbia, St. Charles and St. Louis to visit sites of particular interest to Santa Fe Trail buffs.

Franklin to St. Louis.

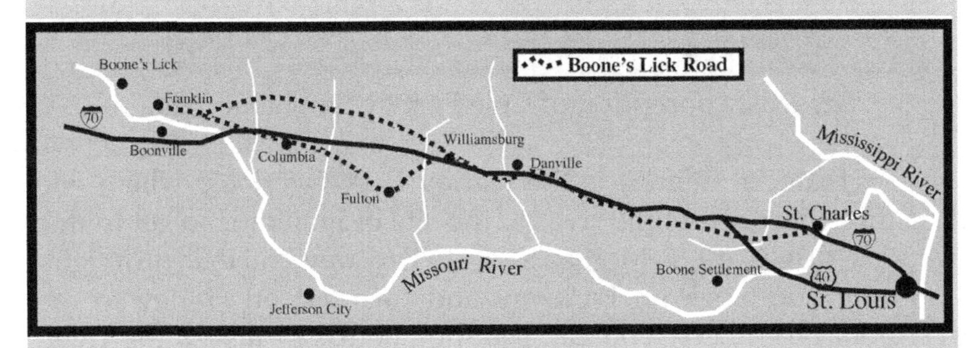

COLUMBIA

After leaving Boonville, drive east on Interstate 70 soon passing over the Missouri River. You can exit the interstate and visit Columbia where you can visit the State Historical Society on the campus of the University of Missouri at 1020 Lowry Street. The University faces Broadway, which was the Boone's Lick Road. The society has a fine library with rare Missouri and western American materials and they have copies of the *Missouri Intelligencer*, published in Franklin in the earliest years of the SFT. Also available is their extensive photo collection with many images of interest.

The Historical Society's web site is: *shs.umsystem.edu*. You can access the *Missouri Historical Review* (MHR) on the same web site with almost all issues (the first issue was in 1906) available for review and downloading. Included in back issues of the MHR are at least thirty scholarly articles on Santa Fe Trail themes as well as many traders associated with the SFT.

ST. CHARLES

Returning to eastbound Interstate 70 you will soon be following the approximate route of the BLR. Exit at St. Charles. This city was founded in the 1760s by the fur trader Louis Blanchette and was the first settlement on the Missouri River. St. Charles is a very interesting small city with numerous buildings from the early nineteenth century. Meriwether Lewis and William Clark visited the town in 1804 on their way up the Missouri on their famous voyage of discovery; Maj. Steven Long also stopped here on his 1819 expedition. George C. Sibley, the leader of the 1825 government survey of the Santa Fe Trail, moved here sometime after completing the survey. He and his wife, Mary Easton Sibley, were instrumental in founding Lindenwood College (now University) in St. Charles. They are both buried on the campus in a small cemetery near the football stadium, in the Easton family plot.

Main Street in St. Charles

When Independence and Westport became the principal starting point for the SFT, there were still many travelers and emigrants using the Boone's Lick Road from St. Charles to Franklin and then west from Franklin on the Santa Fe Trail. The starting point for the Boone's Lick Road is at the intersection of South Main and Boone's Lick Road in St. Charles. If you turn toward the river here, you can drive or walk to the Lewis and Clark Boat House and Nature Center. The lower level houses replicas of the boats used in their journey west including a keelboat. Such boats were much used in the early period of the SFT to ascend the Missouri with supplies for Franklin and later Lexington and Independence. Steamboats did not dominate the river traffic until the 1830s. Also, in a building at 515 South Main was located Eckert's Tavern, where Sibley wrote the final report on his 1825 survey of the SFT. The building has been replaced with the modern Eckert's Tavern, but there is a marker on the building.

Missouri gained statehood in 1821 and chose a new site for its capital, Jefferson City, which was yet to be constructed. While construction was taking place at Jefferson City, St. Charles was the temporary state capital. The building that was used as the capitol is located at 200 South Main Street. It is the First Missouri State Capitol Site run by the Missouri State Park system. The building has a fine museum with many exhibits showing early Missouri. Behind the museum runs the KATY Trail, which you saw earlier in Franklin and New Franklin. This biking and hiking trail can be used to go west to Clinton, Missouri southeast of Kansas City.

ST. LOUIS

Drive to St. Louis on Interstate 70, which will take you to the Gateway Arch. St Louis was the nerve center for western exploration and the fur trade in the nineteenth century. The Gateway Arch at the Jefferson National Expansion Memorial, has exhibits relating to the SFT and today symbolizes its role in the history of the West. This memorial covers much of the original site of St. Louis and is accessible from Interstate 70.

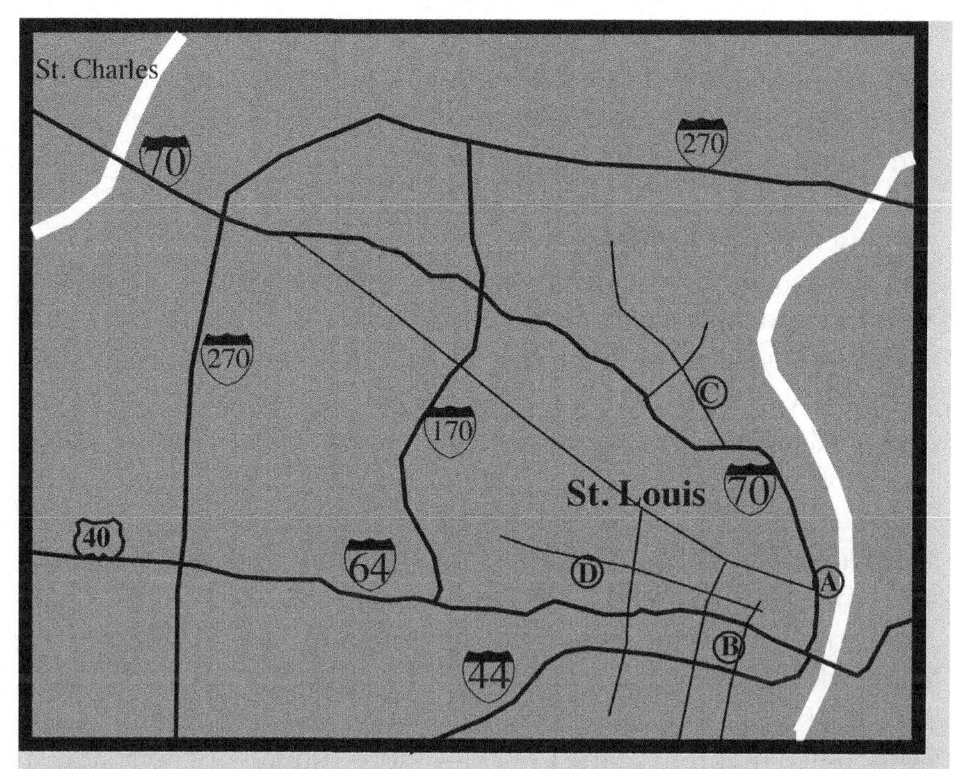

Four St. Louis points of interest associated with the SFT are the following:

A. Gateway Arch

Just off Interstate 70 in downtown St. Louis near the river. This is where you should start your visit to the city. Besides the Arch itself, there are many fine exhibits illustrating the westward expansion.

B. Statue of Missouri Senator Thomas Hart Benton

This heroic statue is located in Lafayette Park, bounded by Mississippi, Missouri, Park, and Lafayette Avenues. The splendid statue of Benton, cast in bronze in Munich and erected in 1868, is a gem. Benton's daughter, Mrs. Jessie Benton Fremont, wife of John Charles Fremont, the Pathfinder, unveiled it. The statue faces west, and at its feet are inscribed the words: "There lies the west, there lies India."

Thomas Hart Benton, elected senator when Missouri achieved statehood in 1821, became the chief spokesman in Washington for Santa Fe traders. He introduced the bill that led to the survey and marking of the trail in 1825 and pressured the secretary of war to provide military protection from the Indians for wagon trains. Surrounding the park are once-beautiful homes, now being restored.

C. Bellefontaine Cemetery

In addition, in St. Louis, you can visit Bellefontaine Cemetery (pronounced Bell Fountain here) located between Florissant and Broadway, adjacent to Interstate 70.

Since it is such a large cemetery with a maze of lanes, visitors will need a map showing notable graves, available free at the office. Many SFT notables' graves are in this cemetery. Of primary interest to trail buffs is the Magoffin family plot. Brothers James W. (d.1868) and Samuel Magoffin (d.1888) were prominent traders well known in Santa Fe, El Paso, and Chihuahua City. Samuel's young Kentucky-born wife Susan Shelby Magoffin (d. 1855) kept an extraordinary diary of her SFT trip in 1846. The plot (in blocks 79-80, lot 1002, behind the elks' statue) has markers for Samuel and Susan. Although a diagram of the grave locations (photocopy available in the cemetery office) shows James located to the right of Susan, in reality, he is buried in San Antonio, Texas, where he died.

A short distance away, under a 15-foot column, rests Gen. Stephen Watts Kearny, who led his army over the SFT in 1846. Before departing New Mexico for California, he entertained Samuel and Susan in the old Spanish Palace of the Governors on the Santa Fe Plaza. Further, Sterling Price, his successor, is buried under another tall column nearby. Early in 1847, Price put down the revolt in Taos, which had resulted in the death of Governor Charles Bent and many others. In addition, you will also want to see the impressive monument marking the grave of Senator Thomas Hart Benton, as well as the graves of Manuel Lisa, a founder of the fur trade, and Gen. William Clark of the Lewis and Clark Expedition.

D. Missouri Historical Society, Jefferson Memorial Building

The Missouri Historical Society is located in Forest Park, at Lindell

Boulevard and DeBaliviere. The History Museum and Research Center is at 225 South Slinker Boulevard, facing Forest Park. The society maintains a web site (www.mohistory.org) which has a map showing how to get to the museum, hours of operation, and other important information. The collections include excellent materials related to the SFT and fur trade.

THE BOONE SETTLEMENT

The connections between the SFT and the Boone settlement are tenuous. Nathan and Daniel Morgan spent considerable time in eastern Kansas between 1830 and 1840 but not directly dealing with SFT issues. These brothers were the first operators of the salt works at the Boone's Lick site. Nathan was Clark's guide to the site of Fort Osage. Daniel Boone moved to Missouri in late 1799 and brought with him a considerable number of families. The included map shows the location of the many Boone-associated families. The old warrior himself never built a house but stayed with family members, especially his daughter near Marthasville and Nathan Boone. When you visit the beautiful "Daniel" Boone home you are actually visiting Nathan's home but Daniel did, in fact, die here.

To get to the Boone settlement drive west on Interstate 64 (U S 40) to Weldon Spring where U S 94 intersects the Interstate.

Boone Settlement.

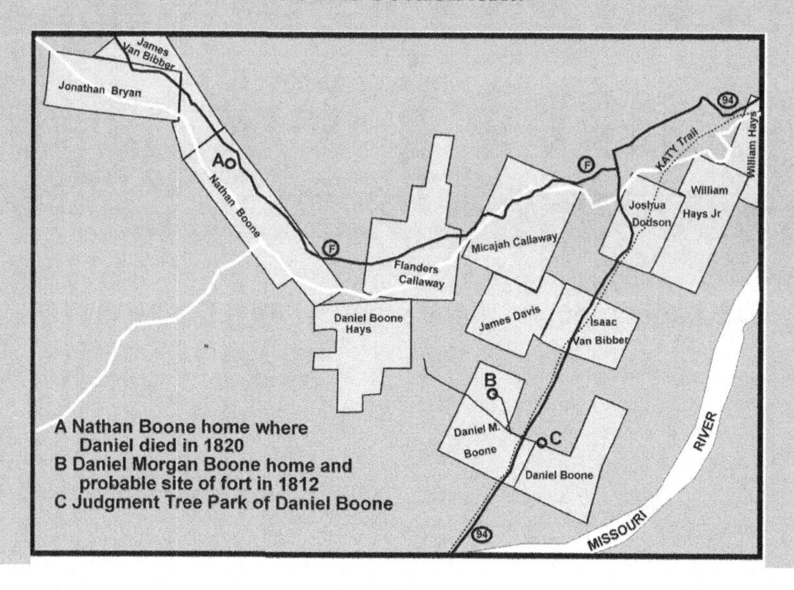

Go west (left) on 94 6.8 miles to where it meets highway DD. Continue on 94 to County Road F which is only one-quarter mile farther and turn right on F. (You could also continue on 94 to visit many interesting sites including the grave of Daniel and Rebecca Boone.) From the intersection of U S 94 and County Road F, it is about 4.8 miles to the Nathan Boone home on the left. It is now owned by Lindenwood University and they "market" it as the home of Daniel Boone. Daniel died there but this was not his home. They have moved many other important buildings to the site so there is much for you to see here.

To return to Interstate 70 turn left after exiting the Boone site and continue on F and the County Road Z which will take you to the interstate where you will want to return to Boonville and, then, Arrow Rock.

The Nathan Boone home where Daniel Boone died.

ARROW ROCK

From Boonville, go west on Interstate 70 to the Arrow Rock/MO 41 Exit. Turn north on MO 41 and proceed 12 miles to Arrow Rock. As you approach Arrow Rock, the first road to the right leads to a campground that is part of the Arrow Rock State Historic Site. Continue to the second road, which leads you to the visitors' center. This center has extensive information about the SFT and the Arrow Rock area, as well as three of George Caleb Bingham's paintings. Mentioned many times are "chains," the instrument used by surveyors to survey the West. Be sure to seek out the chain here at the museum. From the center, it is an easy walk to the village of Arrow Rock. As you enter the village from the visitors' center, you will be heading for Main Street. The Friends of Arrow Rock have a small shop on Main Street and offer guided tours several times daily to all the important sites in town (Tours are curtailed in winter season.)

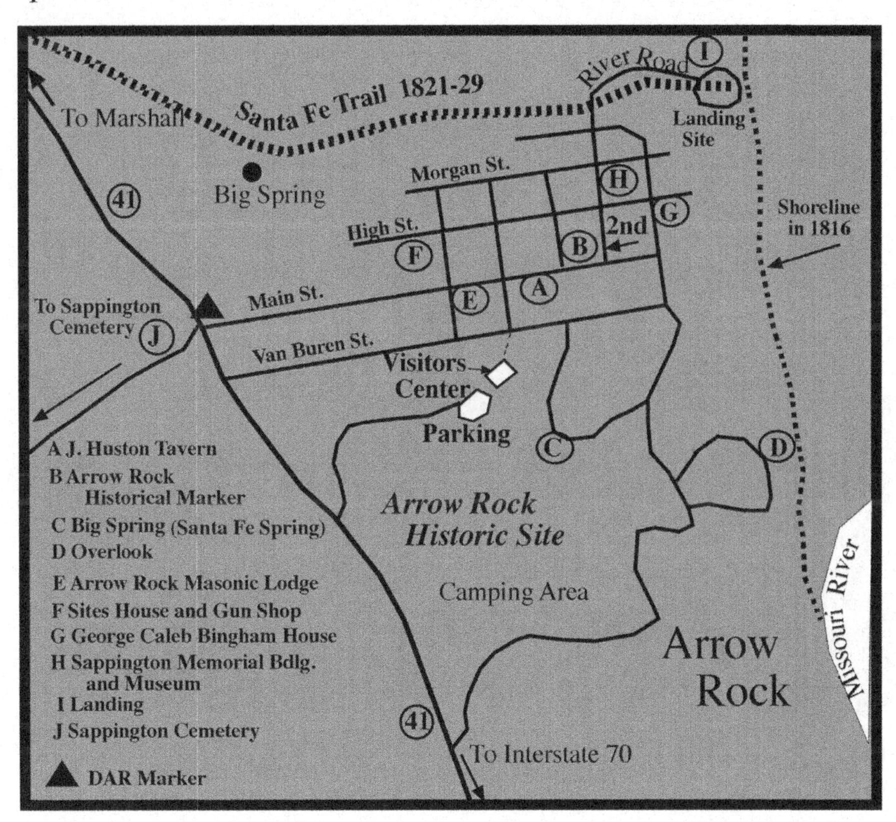

The Arrow Rock site was well known by the time Lewis and Clark traveled by in 1804. They noted it in their journals. When William Becknell passed through here in 1821, he used the ferry that he himself had begun years earlier. The landing is shown on the map and can be visited by a short walk or drive. From the landing, Becknell likely would have gone up the draw and stopped at a spring called Big Spring at the summit of the draw. Meredith Miles Marmaduke did not lay out the village until 1829. By this time the jumping-off point for the SFT had moved west to Lexington and Independence, so Arrow Rock did not play a major role in the trade. Still, people heading for New Mexico continued to pass through Arrow Rock, initially called New Philadelphia, and it remained associated with the trail for the next several decades.

Although there are a number of early homes of historical and architectural importance, only sites related to the SFT follow:

The Arrow Rock Tavern in 1920s. Photo Library of Congress.

Missouri

A. Old Arrow Rock Tavern

A two-story structure built about 1834 by John Huston; the Old Arrow Rock Tavern is the town's most familiar landmark and a major point of interest relative to the SFT. Noted SFT travelers are known to have stopped here. Dr. Glen Hardeman stayed at the Huston Tavern in 1840 and wrote, "I was charged the sum of twelve and one-half cents, or I should say a 'bit.'" We return to the use of the term "bit." This term was mentioned earlier when John Glover passed the Becknell ferry in 1826. U.S. currency is based on the Spanish dollar, a piece of eight. Each dollar had eight "bits," each worth twelve and one-half cents (100 divided by 8). In the United States today the use of the expression "two bits" or "four bits" is old fashioned and destined to leave our vocabulary.

Portraits and relics are on display in the tavern. The State Park System runs the restaurant and fine meals are served. Historical brochures are available too.

B. Arrow Rock Official Missouri Historical Marker

The marker is just past the tavern toward the river. The sign contains a brief history of the town and references to the SFT.

C. Big Spring, also called Santa Fe Spring

To reach this spring, continue two blocks east from the tavern along Main Street (toward the river), then take the second right toward the camping area. This spring was used after the town was developed and the SFT traders came up from the landing and passed through the town. There is a white sign with a SFT marker on top identifying the spring as a watering stop for caravans.

D. Overlook

To find the overlook, continue toward the river. This spot commands a good view across the river toward Boone's Lick. The included map indicates the location of the Missouri River in 1821 and it was directly below the overlook.

E. Arrow Rock Masonic Lodge

The lodge, founded in 1842, is located on the north side of Main Street, one-half block west of the tavern. Today, the first floor houses a craft center. It is known that a number of its members traveled the SFT. The building dates from 1868.

F. Sites House and Gun Shop

Both buildings are behind the Masonic Lodge. These restored structures belonged to John Sites, Jr., who learned gunsmithing in his father's Boonville shop, which was established in 1835. In 1844, he moved to Arrow Rock, where he opened his own business. Thereafter, Sites catered to the needs of local citizens and supplied guns to individuals heading west on the Santa Fe and Oregon Trails.

G. George Caleb Bingham House

The house is located on the eastern end of High Street. George Caleb Bingham lived here intermittently from 1837 to 1845. The house is in disrepair now.

H. Sappington Memorial Building and Museum

The building is located near the end of High Street, next to the Lyceum. For Dr. John Sappington's relation to the SFT, see a later section.

I. Arrow Rock Landing

To get to the landing, drive past the Sappington Museum on Second Street and down the slope and to the right toward the river. There is ample parking and you will find several nice markers describing the landing site, which is now on the National Register of Historic Places. This where the ferries landed with SFT travelers and from here they would ascend the gully to Big Spring. A deep set of swales leads from the landing up the side of the ridge. The trail reached a spring where traders could rest and prepare for the next long segment.

J. Sappington Cemetery

From the parking lot at the Arrow Rock State Historic Site visitors' center, return to MO 41 and turn right, and drive west to Main Street. At the junction of Main Street and MO 41, is a gas station, which was for some time named the Turley Service Station. The Turleys from this area traveled the SFT and were prominent in New Mexico. Simeon Turley operated a distillery at Arroyo Hondo north of Taos. Much of Turley's product went north to satisfy the demands of traders who used it to trade with Indians (illegally, of course). He and his men were killed in the same January 1847 uprising in which Charles Bent perished. (Bent will be discussed later in this guide.)

Drive southwest from this junction on Route TT. At .7 mile, pass the Arrow Rock Cemetery on the right. Buried here is Joseph Huston (1784-1865), founder of the Old Arrow Rock Tavern. Continue another 4.3 miles until the road ends in a T. Turn left, and a short distance beyond (on the left) is a sign and gate for the Sappington Cemetery State Historic Site. A lane leads to the actual cemetery, which is surrounded by a low stone wall topped by an iron fence.

Close to the front on the left as you enter the cemetery is the grave of Meredith Miles Marmaduke (1791-1864); a marble arch connects two square columns over the grave. In 1824, Marmaduke, famed SFT trader and later governor of Missouri, was a member of the first large caravan to Santa Fe, consisting of eighty-one men and twenty-five wagons. His famous journal of the trip was published in the *Missouri Historical Review* in 1911 (Marmaduke 1911). He married a daughter, Lavinia by name, of Dr. John Sappington.

Dr. Sappington (1776-1856) and his wife Jane (1783-1852) are buried toward the right rear corner of the cemetery under the large trees. The inscription on top of their aboveground tombs has almost weathered away. The doctor indirectly played a major role in the development of the SFT. In 1832, he began distributing his famous Sappington's Anti-Fever Pills to western travelers. Intended for the prevention and control of malaria, they contained one grain of quinine compounded with gum myrrh and licorice. Sappington revealed the formula for his pills in his treatise *The Theory and Treatment of Fevers* (1844), the first medical book published west of the Mississippi. The pills were produced by the doctor's twenty-five slaves and distributed by traveling salesmen on horseback, one of whom was William Becknell.

Malaria, called ague, then the most serious disease in western Missouri and eastern Kansas, was the scourge of the SFT. It was especially prevalent at Council Grove and along the Arkansas River, where mosquitoes abounded. It was not until 1895 that someone discovered that mosquitoes were malaria carriers. Before that time the carrier was simply thought to be "bad air," or *mal aria*. Susan Magoffin and many others using the SFT carried packages of Sappington's pills, and every traveler was familiar with his name.

Sappington's large two-story log house, located 0.5 mile southwest of the cemetery, burned in 1871. An 1834 portrait of him and another of his wife Jane, painted by famed Arrow Rock artist George Caleb Bingham, are in the Old Arrow Rock Tavern, along with his medicine case and pill roller.

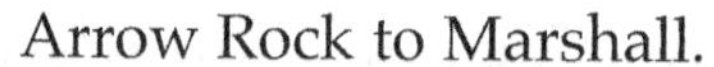
Arrow Rock to Marshall.

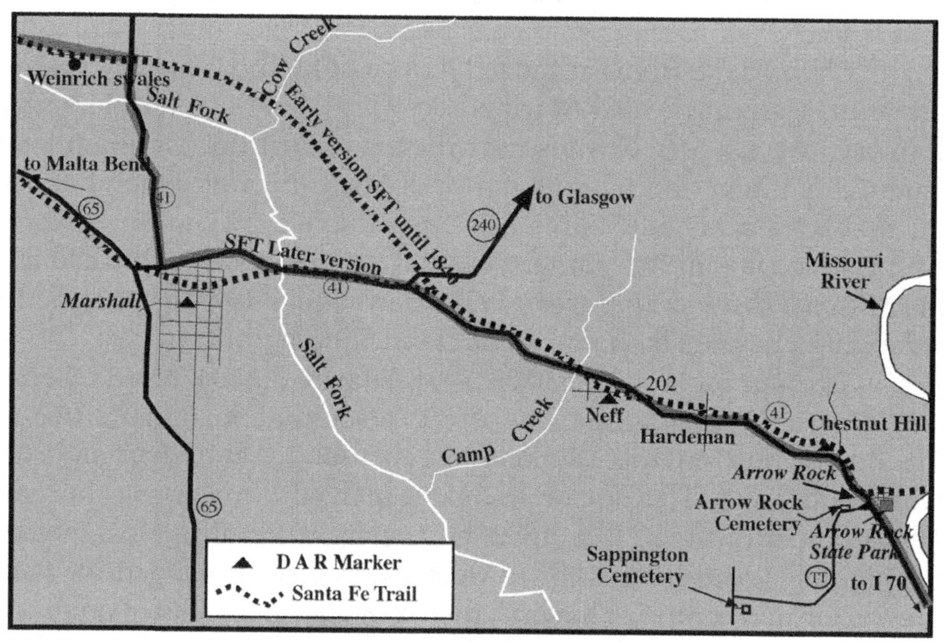

CHESTNUT HILL

From the cemetery, return five miles to the junction with MO 41, on the edge of Arrow Rock. Turn left on MO 41 toward Marshall. At 1.25 miles from the junction, is the Chestnut Hill DAR marker on a bank above the east (right) side of the highway. Behind the marker 200 feet is Chestnut Hill, the white two-story home of Santa Fe trader Phillip Thompson, built in 1844 (now a private residence). One of the area's first settlers, he purchased 1,400 acres of land just west of Arrow Rock as early as 1826. As a result of repeated trips to Santa Fe, Thompson reportedly spoke Spanish better than English.

HARDEMAN CORNER

Continue on MO 41 until you reach a crossroads. This is Hardeman Corner, named after the Hardeman family. John Hardeman came to Howard County in 1817 and created the famous Hardeman Gardens just northwest of Franklin. He was also a Santa Fe trader going on the SFT in May 1828. He died on his return from New Mexico by way of New Orleans. It was his son, Locke, who went to Saline County and built a house in 1844. The house still stands in the vicinity of Hardeman Corners.

NEFF TAVERN

At 4.9 miles from the junction at Arrow Rock, MO 41 crosses a small bridge. At .5 mile past the bridge, turn on to a gravel road (County Road 215) that angles in from the left. Go .5 mile to the Neff Place DAR marker in the yard of a farmhouse on the left. In 1837, Isaac Neff (many sources say it was Nave) built a log tavern here on the old route of the SFT. Apparently, the SFT went between the tavern and the barn, which later became a stage station, then the trail went west a quarter of a mile, bending around the Neff family cemetery and on northwestward down the grade. The tavern was torn down in 1890.

The brick residence behind the DAR marker is said to be on the original site of the tavern. To the left rear of this house and visible from the road, is a two-story stone smokehouse, the only structure remaining of Neff's original complex. It is on the National Register of Historic Places. Continue up road .2 mile to the little Neff Cemetery on the right, marked by a small sign. It contains the graves of Isaac Neff, his wife, and children.

Continue on the road until the next corner, turn right on Nocturne and drive until you rejoin MO 41.

MALTA BEND

Turn left on MO 41 and follow that road into Marshall. The first part of this trip will be almost directly on the SFT when it left Neff's Tavern. You will come to the junction with MO 241 (that road goes to Glasgow in Howard County) and to this point the SFT and MO 41 are close to the same. The early traders wanted to stay on high ground and cross as few streams as possible. Thus, the route they follow here is avoiding crossing the Salt Fork of the Lamine River, keeping it to their left. The included map shows two routes: the early one staying north of the Salt Fork, the later version going through Marshall which was not founded until 1839. The route we suggest is the earlier one so continue on MO 41.

If you choose to go through Marshall, you can see a DAR marker on the southwest corner of Courthouse Square. Taking US 65 you will head toward Malta Bend and there will be another DAR marker at Kiser Spring on your left just before descending to the Salt Fork.

Continue on MO 41 (now also called Santa Fe Trail) entering Marshall on the north and look for the sign directing you to follow MO 41, which turns right. Follow MO 41, cross the Salt Fork, and at the next road turn left (this road is County Road 275 and Santa Fe Trail). As you turn left on County Road 275, you will notice a National Park Service (NPS) sign inviting you to follow this route on the SFT, which the NPS is designating a "signed segment." At the time of writing, there is no notice of this important turn on MO 41 but the Missouri Highway Department will likely place advisory signs soon. This is the first of such "signed segments."

The dramatic Weinreich swales north of Marshall.

At 1.1 miles after the turn you will come to a magnificent set of SFT swales, the "Weinreich Swales." These are the first swales that you have seen on the trip and their location gives you a clue as to what saved them. They are on a hill and location steep enough not to have been farmed. Continuing on the route marked by the NPS you will cross two more locations where the SFT crosses the road before reaching Malta Bend and rejoining US 65. There is a DAR marker on US 65 after you turn, on your left.

Much has been said about the Osage Trace, a horse or pack route that went east west across this area. Some have said that the SFT followed the earlier Osage Trace but this was not the case. The government surveyors noted the trace in their field notes in 1818 as they progressed west. The surveyors found the Osage Trace just south of the later Malta Bend. There was an Osage Indian village a bit north of that town (not open to the public) and the trace led from there to Fort Osage in Jackson County. The Osage Trace is shown on the next few maps in this guide and is always some distance south of the SFT. One government surveyor noted that the trace was "4 links wide, bears NE & SW." A chain is 66 feet long and has 100 links; therefore, a trace 4 links wide is a little less than three feet wide.

Marshall to Waverly.

Continue west on US 65 toward Grand Pass. The highway here is actually on a narrow ridge separating the Missouri River on the north from the waters of the Salt Fork River on the south. At 4.5 miles beyond Malta Bend, is the Grand Pass DAR marker, located slightly below ground level in a landscaped area, framed by wagon wheels, on the northwest corner of US 65 at its junction with Gilham Street. Turn on Gilham and then, at the edge of the cemetery, turn right again. Drive a short distance and, on your right, in the cemetery, you can make out distinct swales passing through the cemetery.

Distinct Swales in the Grand Pass cemetery.

Return to US 65 and turn right. After another four miles, enter the town of Waverly. Turn right to the business district and go two blocks to Kelling Street. A DAR marker is in the middle of the block on the lawn of a house directly across from the post office. Col. John Denis Thomas, a Revolutionary War veteran, built the house behind the marker in 1819. It is a log house and the local citizenry is anxious to have it restored. There was an early road from Fort Osage east to Arrow Rock before the SFT was opened and this house was likely built on that road for the title says it was on the Boone's Lick Road. That may seem strange, but the road did head toward the lick.

Waverly to Lexington.

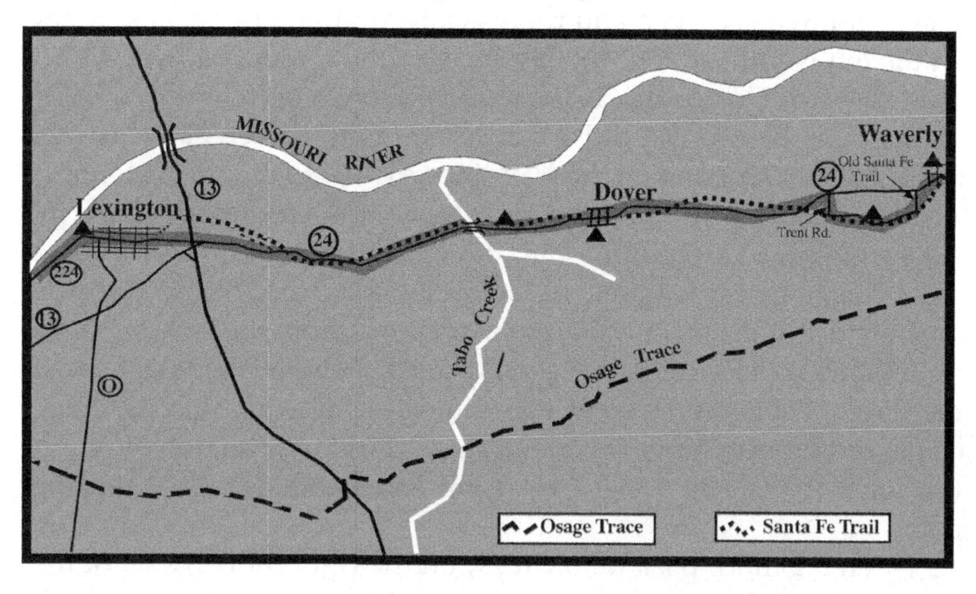

The highway you have been following, US 65, turns north at Waverly and you will now be following US 24, which will be your companion to Independence. Leaving Waverly on US 24, look for a road on your left—Old Santa Fe Trail. Turn on Old Santa Fe Trail and you are entering the second NPS "signed segment." Follow the signs along this short 4.3 mile segment of the SFT and you will return to US 24. You will not see any SFT swales but there is a DAR marker at an old tavern site. Again, the highway department may have placed signs on US 24 advising you of this turn at the time of use.

John Thomas log house in Waverly with MRO marker in front.

DOVER

The next town is Dover, and there is a DAR marker in a small park on the left (south) side of the highway in the center of town. At 2.5 miles west of Dover, the SFT crossed Tabo Creek. There is a DAR marker just before the old road descends to the creek. This was the first water crossing on the trail since Arrow Rock on the Missouri River, and in April 1821, the first ferry was established here by Adam Lightner. Although today the creek does not appear to be a great challenge for wagons, in fact, it lacks a firm bottom and was much wider than it is now. Farmers upstream from the crossing have terraced their fields over the years, which has diminished the flow of the creek. Therefore, a ferry was almost a necessity. Josiah Gregg spoke of this portion of the SFT being "miry" and that avoiding it was one of the advantages of using Independence as a starting point.

At 5.2 miles past Tabo Creek, on the right (north) side of the highway, look for an antebellum house, Hicklin Hearthstone, built in the 1830s. From the highway you can see the fence and gate in front of the house, and to the left, the brick overseer's house, and behind the overseer's house and plantation house, the brick slave quarters. The SFT, undoubtedly, passed directly in front of the gate.

This part of Missouri was strongly proslavery before the Civil War, which can be explained by the labor-intensive crops grown here, including hemp and tobacco. Hemp was used for cordage and for burlap, which was sent down the Missouri and Mississippi Rivers to wrap bales of cotton raised in the Deep South. It can still be seen growing in ditches.

LEXINGTON

This town is seldom mentioned in connection with the SFT but, in fact, was linked with the trail's history in several ways. First, Lexington was the center of the giant mercantile firm of the Aull Brothers-John, James, and Robert. Branch stores in nearby Richmond, Liberty, and Independence made this the largest business enterprise on the Missouri frontier and the first chain store in the state. John Aull built his first store and warehouse here in 1822 and, by the 1830s, the Aulls were leading outfitters for individuals departing on the SFT. After following the American army to Santa Fe and Chihuahua in 1846, the next year James was killed in a robbery at the store he had opened in Chihuahua City.

Second, Lexington was also headquarters for the renowned freighting firm of Russell, Majors, and Waddell, which hauled both civilian and military freight over the SFT in the 1850s. Between April 1860 and October 1861, this company also operated the Pony Express over the central route to California. Alexander Majors, the only one of the partners with extensive trail experience, made his first journey to Santa Fe in 1848.

Formally established in 1822, Lexington, like Boonville, sits atop a bluff on the south bank of the Missouri River. Lexington began life as a small community directly atop the SFT and it was only later, after steamboat traffic began in earnest, that Lexington moved its focus to the river and its landing. Its old steamboat landing at the base of the bluff was once a major shipping point but that was after 1830. Many fine antebellum houses lend the town more of a southern than western air.

In 1837, Alphonso Wetmore wrote in the *Gazeteer of the State of Missouri*: "Lexington is one of the towns which outfits are made in merchandise, mules, oxen, and wagons for the Santa Fe or New Mexican trade. The fur-traders who pass to the mountains by land make this town a place of rendezvous, and frequently going out and coming in with their wagons and packed mules, at the same period of going and coming that is chosen by the Mexican traders. Lexington is therefore occasionally a thoroughfare of traders of great enterprise, and caravans of infinite value" (Wetmore 1837).

For valuable information about the trail in the Lexington area, consult Roger Slusher's article in *Wagon Tracks* (Slusher 1991). In addition, if you stop at the Historical Museum on 13th Street (MO 13 Business), just south of Main Street or west of Franklin Avenue, you can pick up a detailed guide that Slusher compiled for all the local SFT points of interest.

The following are a few of the sites of interest:

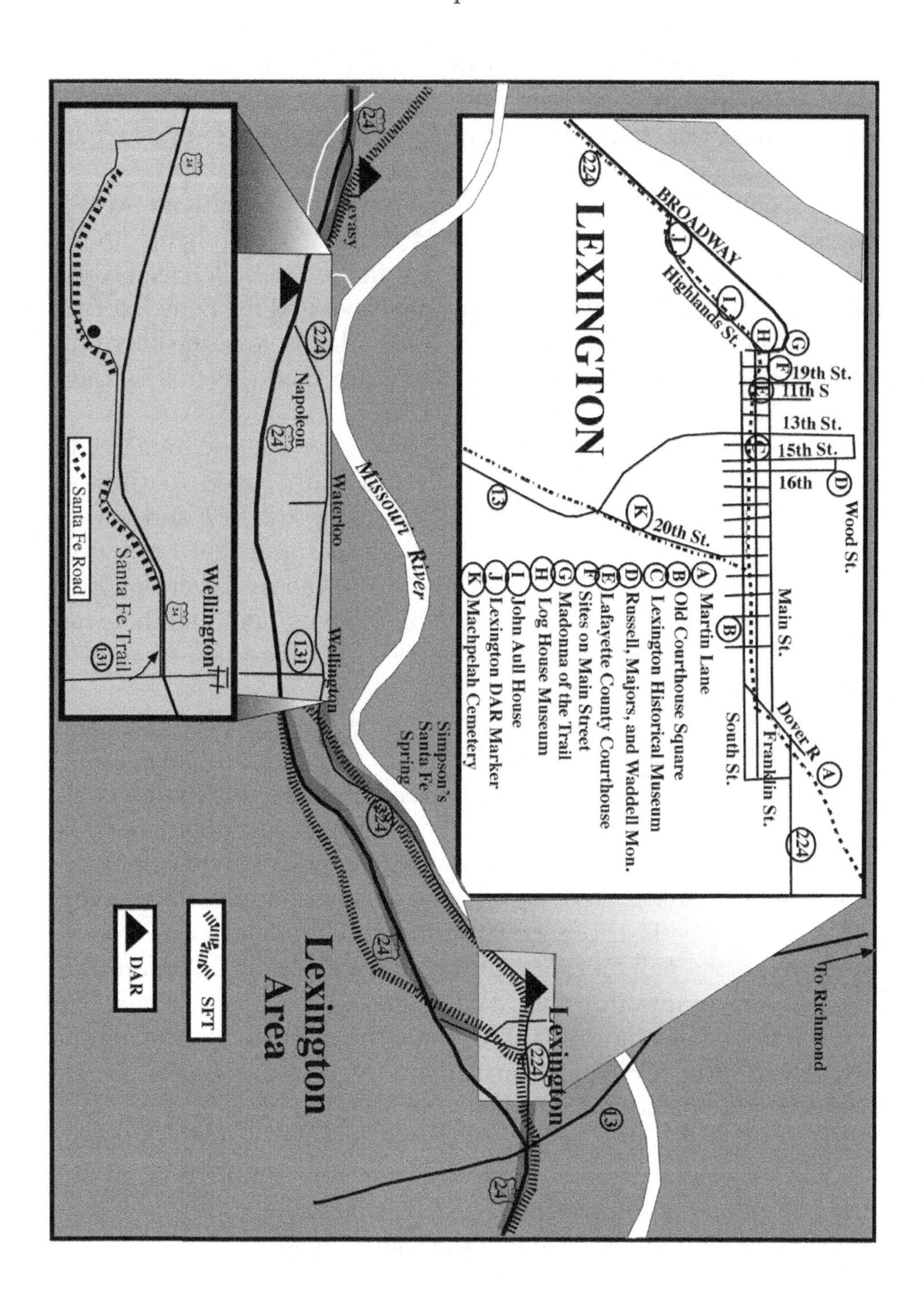
LEXINGTON
BROADWAY
Highlands St.
19th St.
11th S
13th St.
15th St.
16th
Wood St.
20th St.
Main St.
Dover R
Franklin St.
South St.
A Martin Lane
B Old Courthouse Square
C Lexington Historical Museum
D Russell, Majors, and Waddell Mon.
E Lafayette County Courthouse
F Sites on Main Street
G Madonna of the Trail
H Log House Museum
I John Aull House
J Lexington DAR Marker
K Machpelah Cemetery
Missouri River
Simpson's Santa Fe Spring
Wellington
Waterloo
Napoleon
Levasy
Santa Fe Trail
Santa Fe Road
Lexington
Lexington Area
SFT
DAR
To Richmond

A. Martin Lane

As you enter Lexington from the east on US 24, you will come to a new interchange with MO 13 and you should leave US 24 taking MO 224, which will lead you to Lexington's Main Street. About one-half mile from the interchange, you will see Lakeview Drive on your right. Turn right and in just a few feet, turn right again onto Martin Lane. The SFT came directly down this curved street heading for Lexington. The SFT circled north of the interchange to get to this point. Drive a few blocks on Martin Lane to get the feel of the trail here.

B. Old Courthouse Square

To get to the square, follow Main Street (MO 224) to Dover Road, just past 26th Street on your left. Drive on Dover Road two blocks to South Street. At a sharp curve, the large white house to your left is Greystone Park, built in the 1830s, and almost directly on the SFT. It is occasionally open for tours. The Courthouse Square is on the south side of South Street at 24th Street. This is where Lexington began. There are two markers at the site. This was the center of Lexington at least through the 1830s, when the focus shifted to the river. The Aull brothers had a store and a warehouse here.

C. Lexington Historical Museum

Drive west on South Street to 13th Street (MO 13 Business). Along this route are some of Lexington's oldest and finest homes. At 13th turn right and drive two blocks to the museum on the right. Built in the 1840s as the national headquarters of the Cumberland Presbyterian Church, it has excellent exhibits featuring the SFT, the Pony Express, and the Civil War Battle of Lexington. Touring brochures are available here as well.

D. Russell, Majors, and Waddell Monument

Leaving the museum, drive north on 13th Street past Main Street, which will take you directly to the Battle of Lexington Historic Site. The entrance to the battlefield visitors' center is on the left about two blocks past Main. After passing the visitors' center, continue to Wood and 15th Streets, where you will see the Lafayette Regional Health Center. At the corner of the parking lot is the silhouette monument to Russell, Majors, and Waddell. This was thought (incorrectly) to be the site of pastures for the firm's livestock, a misconception that explains the bovine nature of the monument. Return to Main Street and go right for two blocks.

E. Lafayette County Courthouse

The Lafayette County Courthouse is located on Main Street between 10th and 11th Streets. Built between 1847 and 1849, this structure was familiar to local travelers of the 1850s. Holding up the clock tower are four columns, and, in the east column is a cannonball fired during the Civil War Battle of Lexington (September 1861). A sign in front of the courthouse calls attention to the cannonball. On the east side of the courthouse is an official Missouri Historical Marker, "Lexington," with text, while at the northwest corner of the grounds (facing Main Street) is a bronze Pony Express plaque with busts of Russell, Majors, and Waddell.

F. Sites on Main Street

Two minor points of interest lie on Main Street west of the courthouse. At the northeast corner of Main and 10th Streets, is the site (not the building) of the office of Russell, Majors, and Waddell. Two doors west at 926 Main Street, between 9th and 10th (on the north, or right side of the street) is a white sign marking a two-story building that was Sterling Price's headquarters during the Battle of Lexington. Price led reinforcements over the SFT in late 1846 and, in 1847, put down the revolt in Taos, New Mexico.

G. Madonna of the Trail

Continue one block on Main Street to Broadway, which angles to the right toward the river. At the edge of the bluff above the river, Broadway curves and starts downhill to the left. At this point, on the right, is a small park containing the first of four Madonna of the Trail Monuments located along the SFT (there were a total of eleven such monuments placed in states from Maryland to California). Unveiled in 1928, the statue is of cast stone and stands 18 feet high. The four faces of the base contain historical inscriptions, those on the east and west being especially relevant to the SFT. This marker was dedicated by then Jackson County Judge Harry S. Truman. Truman was an important supporter of the Good Roads Movement and served as president of the National Old Trails Road Association in 1926.

The Pioneer Mother statue in Lexington, Missouri.
This monument was dedicated by Harry S. Truman.

H. Log House Museum

Almost across the street from the Madonna of the Trail Monument at Broadway and Highland Streets is the Log House Museum. Built in the 1830s, it served as a tavern and private residence. It was originally located one block to the west overlooking the Missouri River, and the river route the SFT passed directly in front of it.

I. John Aull House

Driving west on Highland Street, you pass by a house at 788 that was used as a temporary bank by Robert Aull in 1845. At 784 Highland, you will see the building that was once part of the Elizabeth Aull Seminary. Finally, at 712 Highland is the home of John Aull.

The John Aull house on Highland Street in Lexington.

J. Lexington DAR Marker

To get to the Lexington DAR marker, continue on Highland Street, which will descend toward the river. At the bottom of the hill, the marker is to the right.

K. Machpelah Cemetery

To reach the Machpelah Cemetery, which is on 20th Street, climb back up the hill, drive east on 20th, and turn right. Drive south on 20th, and as you pass South Street, you are about on the highland route of the SFT. The cemetery, which is on the right about .5 mile farther, was established in 1849 and contains the graves of many families connected to SFT history, such as the Aulls and Waddells.

At this point, you have three choices:

1. You can drive to Richmond using the "Side Trip to Richmond."
2. You can continue west to Wellington on the river route.
3. You can drive to Wellington on the highland route.

SIDE TRIP TO RICHMOND

From the Madonna of the Trail Monument an excursion can be conveniently made to Richmond 9 miles to the north. Return to the interchange where you departed MO 24 to enter Lexington. Take US 13 North, which takes you across the river. Approaching Richmond look for North Main where you should turn left (west). Continue on Main until you reach the Courthouse Square in the center of town. On the west side of the courthouse, is a magnificent 10-foot bronze statue of Colonel Alexander Doniphan, head of the Missouri Mounted Volunteers, who accompanied Kearny on the SFT to conquer New Mexico in 1846. A plaque on the south base of the statue depicts a sword-waving Doniphan leading his troops at the Battle of Sacramento (north of Chihuahua City) on February 28, 1847. Doniphan died in Richmond on August 8, 1887, but is buried in nearby Liberty.

Either go back to Lexington, where you can return to US 24 and drive west toward Wellington, following the highland route, or you can follow the somewhat more picturesque river route. If you choose the river route, simply return to the Madonna statue and go toward the river and turn left (west).

LEXINGTON TO FORT OSAGE

River Route

Backtrack to the DAR marker at bottom of hill on Highland, turn left and follow the river road to Wellington. The river route, which hugs the narrow ledge just above the floodplain and below the bluffs, was likely used only when the Missouri was not too high. Continue to Wellington and turn left (south) at MO 131, which will take you back to US 24. Continue on MO 131 across US 24 and in just a few feet turn right on a gravel road marked "Santa Fe Trail."

Highland Route

Drive south on 20th where you will join 13th (MO 13 Business). Turn left onto 13th Street until you rejoin US 24. Turn right onto US 24 until you reach MO 131 in Wellington, turn left and then immediately right on Santa Fe Trail.

Wellington to Fort Osage

You will be entering the third "signed segment" of the National Park Service. This route is well marked and most of the road is directly on top of the old SFT. You will pass one site marked "Burns Swales," on your left. Just before rejoining US 24, you will have turned north and passed a house on the right with a DAR marker in front. The marker is for the Ish School, which was located at this site. Three-quarters of a mile beyond the Ish School marker you rejoin US 24. At this junction, turn left and drive 1.6 miles to the small hamlet of Levasy where there is another DAR marker close to the old highway and the railroad tracks. Return to US 24 and head west toward Fort Osage.

FORT OSAGE

For a brief period in the 1820s, Fort Osage was the westernmost outpost in Missouri. Established on 1808 by William Clark (of Lewis and Clark Expedition), the palisade walls and log blockhouses sheltered both a military garrison and an Indian trading post run by the government, the latter called a factory. On the summit of a 70-foot bluff overlooking the Missouri River, the fort figured prominently in the fur trade for a time. However, it was abandoned in 1825 by the government and the factory system ended in 1822. In 1827 Fort Leavenworth was established farther up the Missouri for military use.

Levasy to Fort Osage.

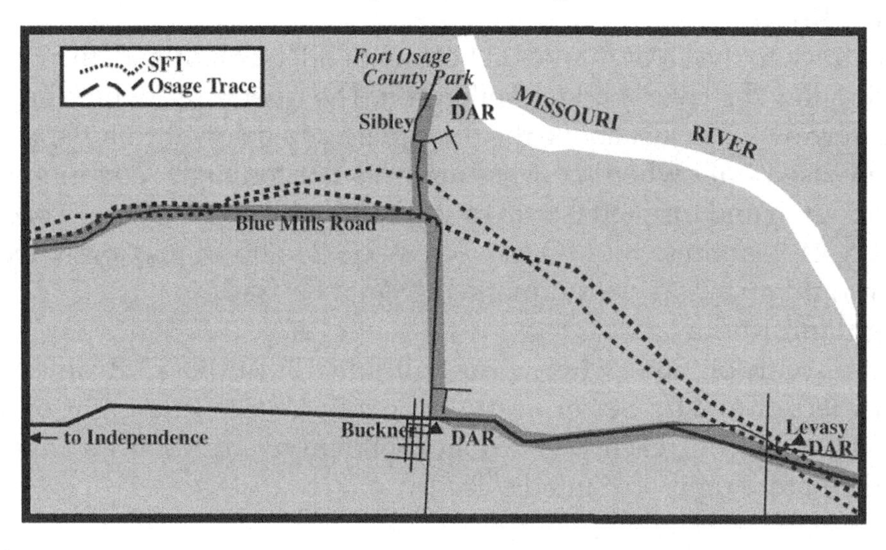

One first-hand account makes it very clear that Fort Osage was barely functioning in 1822 when Major Jacob Fowler and entourage stopped at the end of their year-and-a-half tour of the West. Fowler arrived on Friday, July 5, 1822, and was shown to "Sibley's Porch Wheare We Spent the Ballence of the night." Sibley would have been the fort's factor and would become an important figure in the SFT a few years later when he led the government expedition west to New Mexico. The next day, a Saturday, the group was taken to an empty house where they moved their baggage. Fowler wrote that "the garrisen at this time Was Commanded by one officer of the united States armey-Having two men under His Command Both of them Having disarted a few days ago and Carryed off all His amenetion." So now, the defense of the West was down to one officer and he without any ammunition. Fowler went on to write "We Ware treeted Heare With more Coolness than amongst any Indeans or Spanierds We meet With…" He did have kind words for Mr. Boggs, the assistant factor.

It was from Fort Osage that a party of U. S. government commissioners set out in 1825 to survey the SFT, actually making Taos and not Santa Fe their final destination. They began recording compass directions and chained distances to New Mexico at the west gate of the fort. Because George C. Sibley, the factor at Fort Osage was the de facto leader of the commissioners, the enterprise is usually referred to as the Sibley survey. Sibley is buried in St. Charles, Missouri, on the Lindenwood University campus, and you have visited the gravesite if you took the St. Charles side trip earlier in this volume.

In the community of Buckner, look for the only traffic light on US 24. On the southeast corner of this intersection is the largest DAR marker on the SFT. It consists of three large granite blocks from the old Santa Fe Bridge, which were given to Buckner by the Atchison, Topeka, and Santa Fe Railroad.

Meredith Miles Marmaduke wrote in 1824 that after leaving the "big Sni-a-bar," he "travelled 10 miles and encamped on the Prairie at Camp Rendezvous, about three miles into the wilderness." The campground was likely very near Buckner; going south from Buckner would have put Marmaduke on the Missionary Road, a route connecting Fort Osage with Harmony Mission in Bates County, Missouri (established 1821). From the campground, the traders continued south ten miles to Blue Springs campground and then southwest, crossing the Little Blue near its head and the Big Blue River at about 151st Street and State Line Road. From there, the route continued west to Round Grove campground near where it met the other trail.

The unique DAR marker in Buckner.

From US 24 proceed north on North Sibley Street 3 miles to Fort Osage, following the small signs. The Sibley Cemetery is on the right, where the paved road turns left in front of the new visitors' center and museum.

The only grave here of major interest is that of famed fur trapper Zenas Leonard. After returning from the Rockies and California, he settled at the site of Fort Osage and became an Indian trader and steamboat operator. His *Narrative of the Adventures of Zenas Leonard* (Quaise 1934) is a well-known account of western adventuring. The modern gray granite headstone, flat and level with the ground, is near the center of the cemetery and behind and to the left of the tall Harrelson Monument. In addition, at the far back corner of the cemetery is a DAR marker. It is one of those markers that is not on the SFT.

The cemetery served the community of Sibley, founded in 1836 by Archibald Gamble after the dismantling of neighboring Fort

Osage. He and George C. Sibley had married sisters, a relationship that no doubt helped him obtain the position of secretary to the commissioners on the 1825 SFT survey. In 1837, overland trader Alphonso Wetmore wrote of the new town of Sibley: "It has already been made a point of landing for Santa Fe goods, and it will probably share largely in the increasing advantages of that trade. The landing and harbor of Sibley are excellent, made so by the eddy-water at the base of the bluff" (Wetmore 1914).

A reconstructed building at Fort Osage with palisade walls.

Continue to the entrance to Fort Osage, where there is an explanatory historical marker at the beginning of the sidewalk that leads to the visitors' center. The log fort, reconstructed on its original site in recent years, is today one of the high points at the eastern end of the trail. Blockhouses, soldiers' quarters, and the factory (trading post) can be toured. Shelves in the factory are stocked with trade goods, and the part of the building in which George C. Sibley and his wife lived briefly contains period furnishings. Moreover, a porch at the rear provides a spectacular overlook of the Missouri River.

In 1962, Fort Osage became a Registered National Historic Landmark, and more recently has been certified as a National Park Service Site. Operated by the Jackson County Parks System, a River Days celebration is held here in May. It is well worth the detour to visit the fort.

TRAIL BACKGROUND

Although we think of the Santa Fe Road as a land route traversed by wagons, in reality it was from the onset a combined water and land voyage. In addition, after 1866, much of the merchandise was carried by railroads where possible, moving the eastern terminus of the SFT farther and farther west.

Franklin received much of its merchandise by way of the Missouri River. Keelboats stopped regularly at Franklin throughout the 1820s. The first commercial steamboat on the Missouri, the *Independence,* arrived at Franklin in 1819. The citizens of the Boonslick were ecstatic about the arrival but the next commercial boat did not arrive until 1826. Most boats were going upstream to forts along the Missouri or fur trading posts even farther upriver.

Independence was founded in 1827 on the wagon road and soon Independence Landing was established north of town. This surely was a sign that steam boating was becoming important. Louise Barry wrote that after the steamboat *William D. Duncan* made several trips from St. Louis to Franklin in 1829, "her series of voyages may be said to have ushered in the era of steamboat travel on the Missouri." By 1830, regular steamboat service was maintained on the Missouri and in 1831 there were nine boats in the trade. By 1833, steamboats were also using the Blue Mills Landing northeast of Independence as well as the Independence Landing.

At the same time that steamboat technology and service were improving, there was a dramatic change in the Santa Fe trade. As you can see from the included graph, in the early period the trade was dominated by individuals, Becknell and Cooper for example, who bought trade goods from local merchants and went to Santa Fe to sell them. By about 1830, there was a shift from individual entrepreneurs to capital-intensive merchants who bought their goods in St. Louis, Philadelphia, New York City, or even Europe. Additionally, the market for goods had dried up in a relatively poor Santa Fe and sales to Chihuahua and beyond increased.

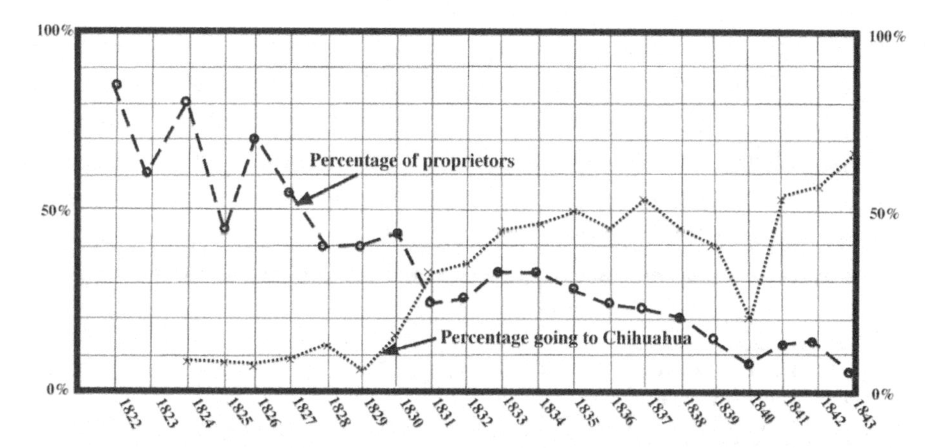

Graph based on Josiah Gregg's research on SFT commerce.

Traders to New Mexico had considerable challenges confronting them in the early years as they departed Lexington. In contrast to the danger of the Jornada, or waterless landscape between the Arkansas and Cimarron Rivers, here at the eastern end of the trail the threat was not a shortage of water but a surplus of it.

Along the route of the SFT in western Missouri, there was a sequence of streams, tributaries of the Missouri River, with considerable water. Bordering the streams' banks were forests (called bottom timber in the diaries). Between the streams on the divides were more or less open prairies. For the most part, traders stayed on the high ground, that is, on the prairies. They would move along the divide and whenever possible "head" the streams, crossing them where they were smaller. When they did cross streams, they would seek a gravel or rocky bottom and approaches that were passable with some effort.

Earliest Period (1821–1827)

In the earliest period, 1821–1827 (see map), there were two routes used. At this time, Independence did not exist, and the last settlement was at Fort Osage, a location not on the SFT and rarely visited by traders. The first route left Lexington going west a few miles south of Fort Osage, crossing the Little Blue River just north of the later Blue Mills. After crossing the Little Blue, travelers headed southwest following the prairie on the high ground between the Big and Little

Blue Rivers. The crossing of the Big Blue was finally made in present-day Swope Park about where 73rd Street would bisect the river. From there the route continued southwest, crossing the present state line nine miles south of the confluence of the Missouri and Kansas Rivers. The trail then continued into Kansas, and passed Round Grove (later known as Lone Elm campground), located a few miles south of today's Olathe.

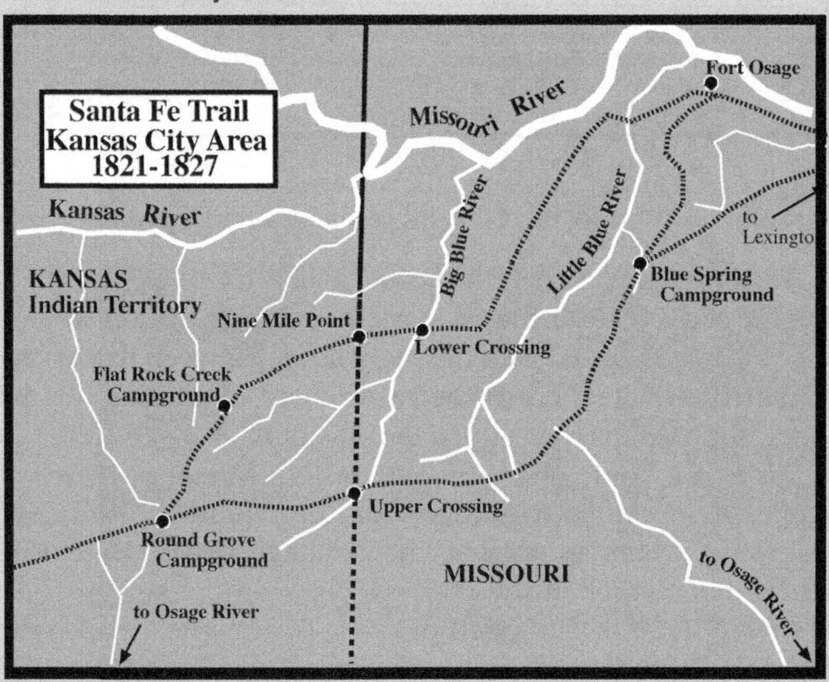

The second early route left Lexington and went southwest, following the road that connected Fort Osage and Harmony Mission (founded 1821 in Bates County, Missouri, farther south). On this route the Blue Spring campground was an important rendezvous point. Meredith Miles Marmaduke was a trader going to Santa Fe when he camped at the Blue Springs in 1824. He wrote in his journal: "Travelled 10 miles to Camp Blue Springs and passed over a prairie country uneven and rolling; but of fine rich soil. We this day travelled the Missionary Road." From Blue Springs traders went southwest to cross a small Little Blue and then at present day 151st and State Line, crossed the Big Blue at the Upper Crossing.

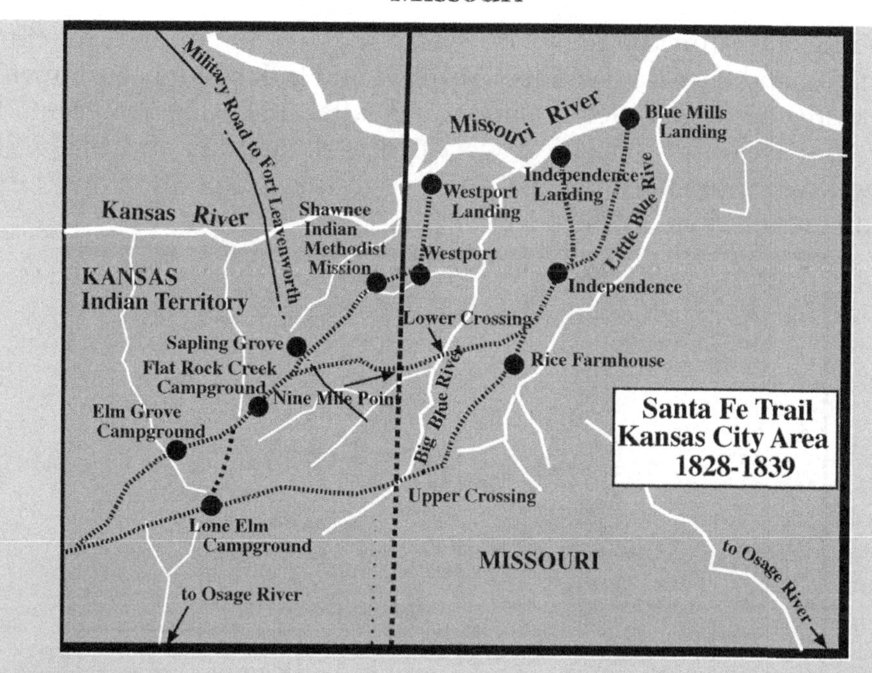

Middle Period

After Independence was founded in 1827, it quickly became the starting point for traders. Transport by water, even on the notorious Missouri River, was easier and cheaper than by land. Consequently, landings were added up the river, and jumping-off points for Santa Fe moved accordingly. As the map of this period shows, the Missouri River, which has been heading west to Independence and upstream, here begins to swing north. However, for travelers going to Santa Fe, the usefulness of the Missouri River ended here. This is about as close as they would get to Santa Fe on the Missouri River.

There were two landings for Independence: Blue Mills Landing and Independence Landing. The latter is almost due north of Independence Square in Independence and only 3 miles away. From Independence, the trail headed south to connect with the earlier two routes described above. Thus, the principal entries into Kansas were at the Upper Crossing (near 151st Street and State Line Road) and Nine Mile Point (near 79th and State Line Road). Another change in this period was the establishment of a community at Westport in 1834. The town was created at a small creek and near the Shawnee Indian Missions just across the state line in Kansas. The community soon grew as it was discovered there was a very good landing site directly north of Westport, which became Westport Landing and later Kansas City. Westport and Independence competed for both the SFT trader business and, after 1841, the emigrants to Oregon. Westport's position west of the dangerous and fickle Big Blue River ultimately proved decisive in the competition and most trade moved there in the 1850s.

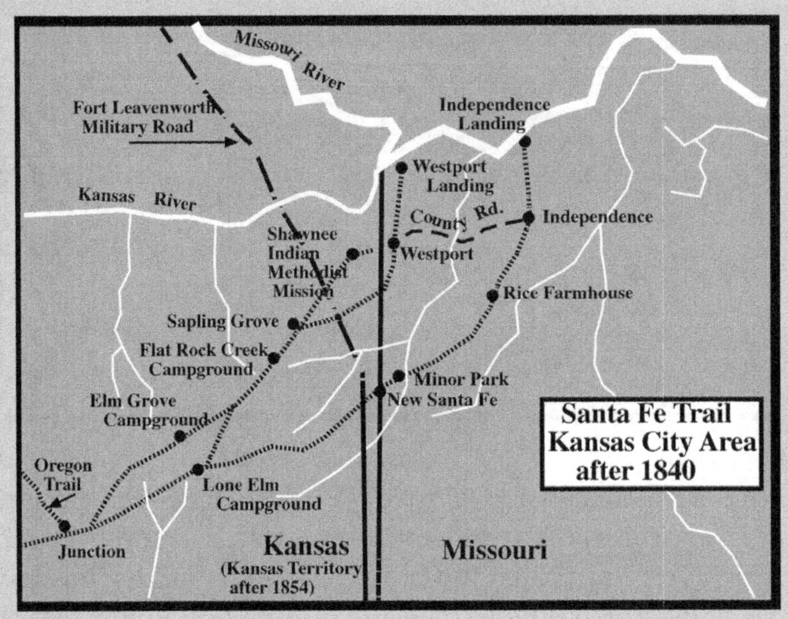

Later Period (After 1840)

During the later period (after 1840), the new trailhead at Westport, west of Independence, began to overwhelm Independence. The Great Flood of 1844, larger than any before or since, sealed the fate of Independence. The flood may have left a large sandbar in front of the Independence Landing and demonstrated that the limestone shelf that served as Westport's landing was superior. After that year, Westport and its landing dominated traffic on the SFT. From Westport the trail turned west into Kansas, then angled southwest to join the earlier trails. These routes emerged as the SFT traffic increased because of emigrants bound for Oregon and California using the SFT as far as Gardner, Kansas. At Gardner, the Oregon and California Trails separated from the SFT and headed northwest.

Drive south from Fort Osage and follow directions in Chapter Two of this book.

CHAPTER 2
Kansas City Area

INDEPENDENCE

Leave Fort Osage driving south toward Buckner and at about 1.3 miles turn right on East Blue Mills Road. Go west on Blue Mills 3.4 miles to a DAR marker for Six-Mile Church. A log church was built here in 1825, just as the Osages ceded this area to the United States. Another two miles and you will be at North Twyman Road but continue another .7 mile to Lentz Road where you turn right. Go .6 mile north on Lentz and you will arrive at the very important site of Blue Mills. A grist mill was constructed here in 1834 followed by a saw mill the next year. The mills were owned by Samuel Owens and James and Robert Aull. The Aull brothers were very involved with the SFT, having outfitting stores in Lexington, Liberty, and Independence. Samuel Owens was among the SFT traders forced to follow behind Kearny's Army of the West as they moved southwest to conquer New Mexico in 1846. Owens went south with Colonel Alexander Doniphan and was the sole U.S citizen killed at the Battle of Sacramento north of Chihuahua, Mexico, a great American victory.

Chapter 2

Fort Osage to McCoy Park.

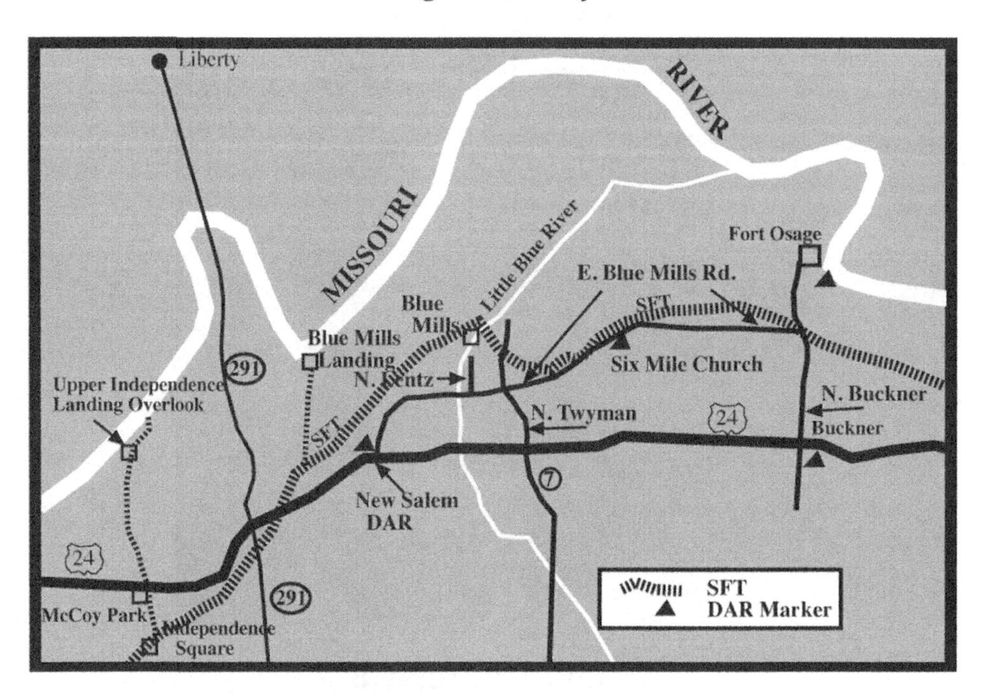

Blue Mills about 1920 before the building was demolished in 1923. Photo courtesy of Jackson County Historical Society.

Only foundations survive of the mills as well as a visible stream channel which powered the mills. The flour from the mill was sold in Independence as well as St. Joseph, St. Louis, and New Orleans. The flour was taken to the landing northwest of the mills, called Owens or Blue Mills Landing, where it was put on steamboats.

This was at a time when communities along the Missouri were anxious to develop products for export. Thus, flour was a welcome addition to hemp and tobacco.

The Little Blue Crossing of the SFT was also nearby. This was an important point and the crossing was about one-half mile north of the site of the mills. The mill site is now on the National Register of Historic Places.

Return to East Blue Mills Road and turn right (west). Continue on Blue Mills until you reach US 24 where you should stop. This is New Salem and there is a DAR marker on the northwest corner, which recognizes the founding of a log church here in 1826. In a short time after this writing, there will be another important collection of markers here for the SFT. There will be a kiosk here modeled after the one you saw in Franklin. The next such kiosk will be in Gardner, Kansas as you leave the Kansas City Metropolitan area.

INDEPENDENCE

From its founding in 1827 until the mid-1840s, Independence served as a main outfitting point for the Santa Fe trade. Here goods bought in St. Louis, Philadelphia, New York, and even Europe were transferred from Missouri steamboats to freight wagons bound for Santa Fe. Blacksmiths, wagon and harness makers, sellers of livestock, and local merchants did a lively business in supplying overland travelers, which by the early 1840s included emigrants on the newly opened Oregon Trail and the later California Trail.

Before the trailhead shifted westward to Westport and Kansas City in the mid 1840s, Independence was a noisy, bustling place frequented by such notables as Kit Carson, Josiah Gregg, Francis Parkman, Samuel and Susan Magoffin, and the long-distance horseback rider Francis X. Aubry. Locals call the town the "Queen City of the Trails."

All sites and markers noted here, with one exception, have some association with the SFT. Information about other places of interest can be obtained from the Chamber of Commerce, 210 West Truman Road, Independence, MO, or from the City of Independence Department of Tourism, 112 W. Lexington, Independence, MO. Both of these agencies have extensive websites.

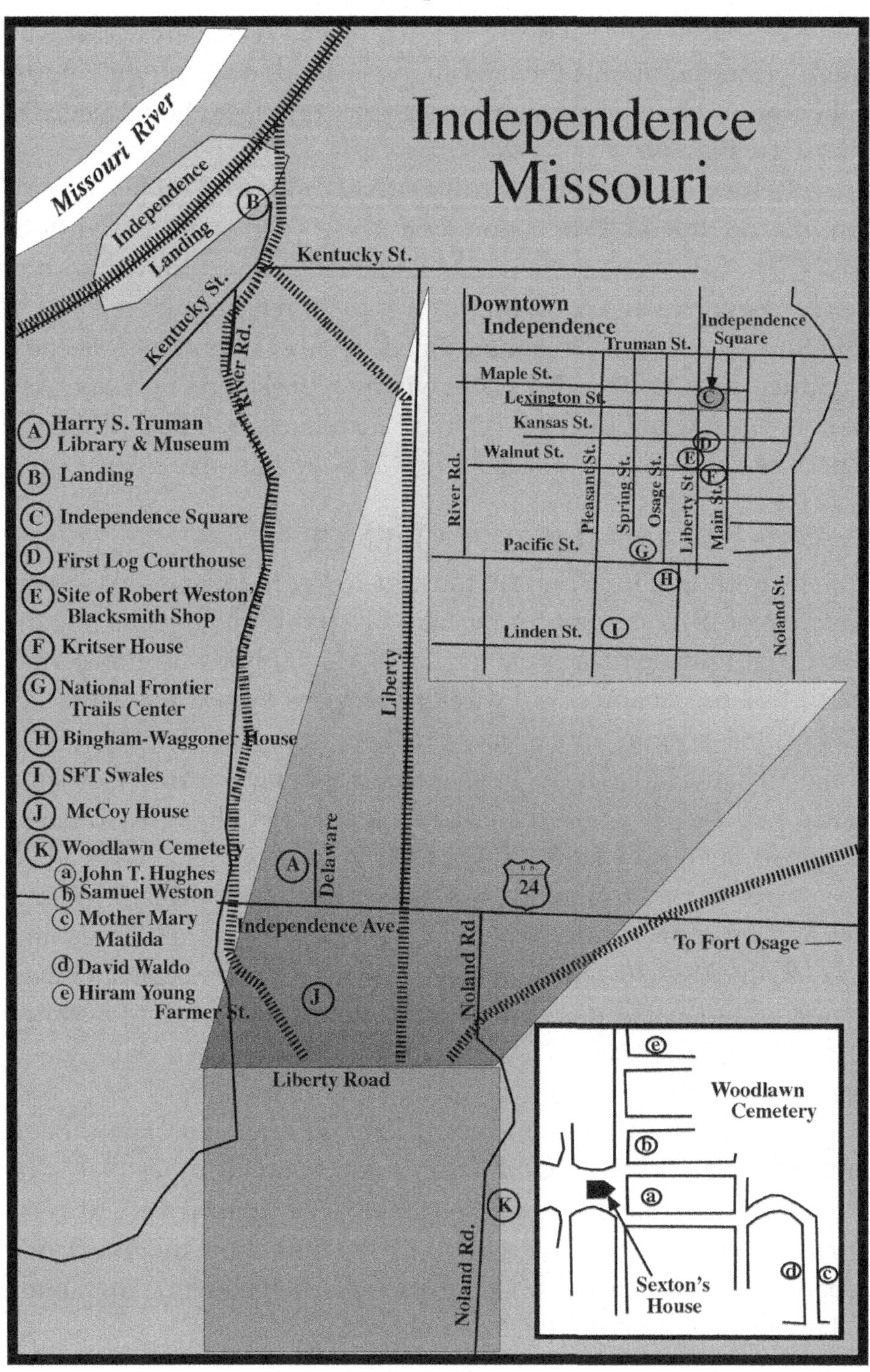
Independence
Missouri
Missouri River
Independence Landing
Kentucky St.
Kentucky St.
River Rd.
Downtown Independence
Independence Square
Truman St.
Maple St.
Lexington St.
Kansas St.
Walnut St.
River Rd.
Pleasant St.
Spring St.
Osage St.
Liberty St.
Main St.
Pacific St.
Noland St.
Linden St.
Liberty
Delaware
Independence Ave.
Noland Rd
To Fort Osage
Farmer St.
Liberty Road
Noland Rd.
24
A Harry S. Truman Library & Museum
B Landing
C Independence Square
D First Log Courthouse
E Site of Robert Weston's Blacksmith Shop
F Kritser House
G National Frontier Trails Center
H Bingham-Waggoner House
I SFT Swales
J McCoy House
K Woodlawn Cemetery
a John T. Hughes
b Samuel Weston
c Mother Mary Matilda
d David Waldo
e Hiram Young
Woodlawn Cemetery
Sexton's House

It is truly remarkable how local organizations, cities, historical societies, and the National Park Service have cooperated to create the many historical markers, kiosks, silhouettes, and panels that we can enjoy along the SFT. These elements go far to help the public appreciate the role their community played in early trail days. The majority of these markers were placed in the last ten years.

A. Harry S. Truman Library and Museum

The library and museum are on US 24 at Delaware Street. At the entrance to the grounds, there is an official Missouri Historical Marker, "Independence," with text referring to the SFT and Josiah Gregg.

Although you may wish to tour the entire facility, the one point of interest for trail buffs is the splendid mural by Thomas H. Benton entitled *Independence and the Opening of the West.* It is located in the main lobby, along with a sales desk that has items of historical interest. The mural depicts scenes typical of the Santa Fe and Oregon Trails. The far right of the mural shows blacksmiths readying wagons for the westward journey. The upper right portrays a caravan heading for Chimney Rock, a famous landmark on the Oregon Trail. The left side is devoted to the SFT. There is a Pawnee warrior with his scalp lock and behind him a Cheyenne chief bartering red fox furs with a trader.

McCoy Park gazebo near the Truman Library in Independence.

Across MO 24 from the Truman Library is McCoy Park that has a new gazebo with five panels telling about the Wayne City Landing, Hiram Young the black wagon builder, and the Archibald Rice house. The park is named for William McCoy, the first mayor of Independence, whose house you will see later.

B. Independence Landing

As you leave the library (and McCoy Park), turn east and drive several blocks to Liberty Road where you should turn left (north). Driving north on Liberty Road will put you directly on one of the branches of the SFT, which is staying on the high ground. You are headed to the Upper Independence/Wayne City Landing. In about two miles, you come to Kentucky Street where you turn left and drive .5 mile before angling right toward the Missouri River on River Road. In .3 mile, there is a parking area on the left with several historic markers at the overlook. You are looking down over the old landing that was so very important for SFT traders and Oregon and California Trail emigrants. The latter two trails began about 1841 and will follow the SFT as far as Gardner, Kansas.

Here we can mention again that there were two landings on the Missouri River north of town. The older, founded before 1832, was the Blue Mills or Owens Landing located 6 miles northeast of the square. The earlier landing was named for SFT trader Samuel C. Owens, who was an active partner in the Blue Mills, which you visited earlier. Independence Landing, several miles upstream, soon overshadowed Blue Mills, as it was only about 3.5 miles north of Independence Square.

From this point return south on River Road which is the second route of the SFT from the river to US 24 and from that corner continue south on River Road one-half mile to Truman Road where you should turn left (east) and drive one-half mile to Liberty. Turn right on Liberty and in one block you are at Independence Square.

C. Independence Square

Early writers often described the bustle and color surrounding the courthouse as wagons formed up for the departure to Santa Fe. None of the buildings on the square date from the heyday of the trail. The last such, the Nebraska House, built in 1849, located at the northeast corner of present Liberty and Maple, was torn down in 1980 to make way for a parking lot. Even more popular than the Nebraska House as a hostelry was the Merchants Hotel, which was operated by Colonel Smallwood ("Uncle Wood") Noland and soon became known as the Noland House. It was situated on what is now the northwest corner of Main and Maple and faced the square. The two-story brick building currently there is believed to incorporate some portions of the original structure. Susan Magoffin, who spent a night under its roof before starting for Santa Fe in 1846, mentions the hotel.

On the southwest corner of the square (at Liberty and Lexington), the three-story Christman-Sawyer Building is on the site of the Aull and Owens store. (For their role in the Santa Fe trade, see "Lexington" and "Blue Mills" above.)

During the period from 1828 to 1839, traders left the square and went almost due south to meet the SFT (the SFT as used from 1821 to 1827) near present-day Raytown. Then they continued southwest to cross the Big Blue River in Swope Park. By 1840, they traveled south, crossing the Big Blue River near today's Red Bridge Road. From Red Bridge, they went southwest and crossed into present Kansas where New Santa Fe was located by the early 1850s. From there, they passed through Lone Elm Campground. By 1840, the crossing at Red Bridge had gained favor over the Upper Crossing (see maps in trail Background sidebar).

The courthouse, inspired by Independence Hall in Philadelphia, is now called the Truman Courthouse since Judge Harry S. Truman had an office there in the 1920s and 1930s. It incorporates the foundations and sections of several earlier Jackson County courthouses dating from trail days. See the restored courtroom on the first floor, which dates to 1852 and was used later by Truman. Offices of the Jackson County Historical Society Archives are also on the first floor. On the west side of the courthouse is a large equestrian statue of Andrew Jackson, for whom the county is named. Flanking the statues are two monuments, one the DAR marker for the SFT and the other marker designating the beginning of the Oregon Trail.

D. First Log Courthouse

The First Log Courthouse, the oldest remaining courthouse west of the Mississippi River, is located at 107 West Kansas Street, one block south of the square. The small structure was built in 1827 to serve as a temporary courthouse until a more permanent one could be constructed.

E. Site of Robert Weston's Blacksmith Shop

The shop was located at the southwest corner of Liberty and Kansas, just west of the First Log Courthouse. This blacksmith shop catered to the needs of Santa Fe traders in the 1840s. The structure was demolished in the 1940s, and the site is now a parking lot. A historical bronze plaque mounted on a red granite monument is on the corner. Robert Weston's father, Samuel, also a noted blacksmith, is honored by a historical marker at his grave site, mentioned in the Woodlawn Cemetery section below.

F. Kritser House

Located at 115 East Walnut, this small residence with a gable roof was built in 1847 by Martin L. Kritser. Reportedly, he traveled the SFT in 1846 and with the profits from his trading venture built this house. A municipal historical marker with text is on the lawn.

G. National Frontier Trails Museum

At 524 South Osage, are the buildings associated with the Waggoner-Gates Milling Company. The mill itself was destroyed by an explosion and fire in the 1960s. The headquarters for the Oregon-California Trail Association (OCTA) and the National Frontier Trails Museum are now located at this site. OCTA's address is 318 West Pacific. The museum has extensive exhibits on the Santa Fe, Oregon, and California Trails, as well as a bookstore with many titles of interest to SFT enthusiasts. The museum is a high point of the trail and should not be missed. In the area north of the remaining mill office (between Osage and Spring Streets), is Emigrant Spring, whose waters in trail days were said to flow in the volume of "about the size of a man's arm." Here wagons once gathered before departing for Santa Fe.

H. Bingham-Waggoner House

The Bingham-Waggoner House is located at 313 West Pacific. The SFT passed by this residence located just a few blocks south of the square. An early owner of the property was Jacob Hall, a prominent freighter in the Santa Fe and Chihuahua trade and operator of stage lines to New Mexico. He and partners received the first U.S. mail contracts, providing mail service to Santa Fe. His letters and business ledgers are preserved in the Historical Society Archives at the courthouse.

The Bingham-Waggoner house in Independence.

A later property owner, John Lewis, built the two-story brick house. He was a saddle maker, also associated with the Santa Fe trade. After changing hands twice more, the estate was purchased by celebrated Missouri artist George Caleb Bingham, who lived there with his wife for six years. In 1879, Peter and William Waggoner bought the house, which was destined to remain in the hands of their descendants for the next ninety-nine years. Today, it is owned by the City of Independence and is open to the public.

I. Trail Swales

Recently a fine set of swales of interest to trail buffs was discovered in a small area in the southwestern portion of the Bingham-Waggoner estate. To reach the swales, park you car in the lot immediately west of the Bingham-Waggoner House. From here, look for a paved path at the back of the parking lot leading to the swales.

J. McCoy House

The McCoy House is located at 410 West Farmer. Samuel Owens, famed merchant and outfitter for the Santa Fe trade, purchased the lot in 1833. He built the rear section of the house in 1840. William McCoy bought the house in 1851 and added the front portion in about 1856. William McCoy arrived in Independence in 1838 and became the town's first mayor in 1849. He was heavily involved in the New Mexico trade, and government freighting. McCoy, along with Jacob Hall, also operated a stagecoach line. A historical marker with text is near the street.

K. Woodlawn Cemetery

The cemetery is at 710 South Noland Road (see included map). Begun around 1837, reportedly on an Indian burial ground, this cemetery contains the graves of several individuals associated with the SFT, as well as Independence pioneers. Unfortunately, the cemetery attendant cannot help you in finding graves of interest because no records are kept of people buried here before 1900. However, the following descriptions of locations and map will guide you.

(a) Grave of John Taylor Hughes. Drive on the right side of the sexton's house and take the first lane leading east, toward the back of the cemetery. Hughes's waist-high stone is on the left next to the lane, with two large cedars just to the north of it. Private Hughes accompanied Col. Alexander Doniphan's First Missouri Mounted Volunteers over the SFT to conquer New Mexico in 1846. Further, he participated in the Navajo expedition to western New Mexico and later was in the Battle of Sacramento north of Chihuahua City. After returning home, he became the official historian for these events when he wrote and published *Doniphan's Expedition,* a book that remains a standard source on the SFT and the Mexican War in the Southwest.

(b) Grave of Samuel Weston. From Hughes's gravestone continue straight ahead (east) to the rear of the cemetery, where the lane curves to the right (south). The 6-foot-high Weston marker of red granite is on the right in front of a large tree. Samuel, father of blacksmith Robert Weston (noted above), had a blacksmith shop on Lexington between Osage and Spring Streets. He was also a carpenter and did interior work on two of Independence's early brick courthouses. His headstone is of recent origin and more in the nature of a historical marker with references to the SFT.

(c) Grave of Mother Mary Matilda Mills. Across the lane from the Samuel Weston grave and a few feet south, Mother Matilda's flat stone, level with the ground, is next to the edge of the pavement. It is in the Stayton family plot. In July 1852, New Mexico's Bishop John B. Lamy was returning to Santa Fe from Kentucky with a party that included a group of Sisters of Loretto. From St. Louis, they sailed up the Missouri River on the steamer *Kansas*. Four days out, Mother Matilda, superior of the nuns, died of cholera, and the others became gravely ill. Because of his fear of the disease, the captain put Lamy's entire company off the boat 6 miles east of Independence, where they found refuge from the rainy weather in an abandoned warehouse. Mother Matilda lay in a hastily constructed coffin on the riverbank. Lamy finally secured a hearse but, because some of his people still suffered from the dreaded cholera, local authorities refused them entrance to the town. Finally, a family named Stayton who learned of the problem offered to let Mother Matilda's coffin be carried to their burial plot in the present Woodlawn Cemetery, There, at night and in secret, Bishop Lamy and Father Donnelly, the local priest, performed the funeral service. Note that in his biography of the bishop, *Lamy of Santa Fe,* Paul Horgan tells of Mother Matilda's death but fails to mention where or how she was buried.

(d) Grave of David Waldo. From the rear of the sexton's house, take the lane leading north and turn right, or east, at the first intersecting lane. The large Confederate monument is immediately on the left, and just past it, on the right side of the lane, is the Waldo monument. David Waldo was a leading Santa Fe merchant, entering the trade as early as 1831. He made numerous trips over the SFT and played a conspicuous role in the conquest of New Mexico in 1846. His younger brother, Lawrence L. Waldo, also a trader, was killed near Mora, New Mexico, early in 1847 during the same disturbance that led to the death of Governor Charles Bent. In the early 1850s, David Waldo was engaged in hauling military freight to New Mexico over the SFT. With Jacob Hall, he also operated the stage line to New Mexico. A brief sketch of his life is included in Ralph E. Twitchell's *The Military Occupation of New Mexico, 1846-1851.*

(e) Grave of Hiram Young. On the next lane north of the Waldo monument is the small Sawyer mausoleum, white with a pitched roof. Across the lane from it, to the northeast, is the chest-high gray granite marker for Hiram Young. In the decade before the Civil War, ex-slave Young gained a reputation as a superb wagon maker. He also carved oxbows by the hundreds for use on the Santa Fe and Oregon Trails. In *Wagons for the Santa Fe Trade: Wheeled Vehicles and Their Makers,* Mark Gardner notes that in 1856 Young had twenty-five large new Santa Fe wagons with 2.5 inch tread, as well as provision boxes, on his lot for sale. During the Civil War, he and his family fled briefly to Fort Leavenworth, and when he returned to Independence, he found that his shops (between present Main and Liberty Streets on the south side of US 24) had been destroyed by Union occupation forces. He is pictured, working at his forge, in the lower right corner of the Benton mural at the Truman library.

Other sites of interest in the Independence area include the following:

Jim Bridger's Grave

Drive west on Truman Road to the entrance of the Mount Washington Cemetery. Upon entering, go straight ahead about two blocks, and after crossing a little bridge, Bridger's tall monument is seen immediately on the right, standing alone in a small triangular lot. James Bridger (1804-1881) had little to do with the SFT, but as a trapper with Kit Carson in the central and northern Rockies and an associate of Jedediah Smith (both closely identified with the trail) Bridger was a leading figure in the history of the West. He did own a store in Westport that served SFT traders.

Santa Fe Trail Park

The entrance to Santa Fe Trail Park is off Santa Fe Road, which was formerly McCoy Street, one block north of 31st Street. Caravans from Independence Square passed through the park, headed in a southwesterly direction. Good swales are visible in the lot just south of the park, and beyond them additional trail swales can be found in the yards of homes, such as behind 3131 Santa Fe Terrace.

Blue Spring Campground and Rendezvous

From Santa Fe Trail Park, drive south on Santa Fe Road to 33rd Street, right on 33rd to Chrysler, and south to Interstate 70. Then go east on Interstate 70 to Woods Chapel Road and turn right. Drive south 1 mile, and when you cross a small stream, you are at the site of the Blue Spring Campground and Rendezvous. This was on the Fort Osage to Harmony Mission Road, important in early trail history. The Mission was established in Bates County in 1821; the road provided a way to get supplies to the Osage Indians at the mission. Some traders from Lexington and Franklin came directly to this campground, bypassing Fort Osage, and later crossing the Big Blue at the Upper Crossing (see map 1821-1827). Of this site Meredith Miles Marmaduke wrote in 1824: "Travelled 10 miles to Camp Blue Springs and passed over a prairie country uneven and rolling; but of fine rich soil. We this day travelled the Missionary road." Traders would meet here before using the Upper Crossing and then head west to Round Grove Campground (later called Lone Elm).

Missouri Town 1855

Continue south to US 40 and drive east to MO 7. Go south on MO 7 about 3.5 miles and then turn west on Cowherd Road. At the end of Cowherd Road, turn north to the entrance of Missouri Town 1855. This fine living-history museum, managed by the Jackson County Parks and Recreation Department, consists of residences and businesses built between 1820 and 1860, which have been moved to the site from various locations in western Missouri. Although the place has no direct connection with the SFT, it is so well put together that it helps visitors catch the spirit of trail days.

After completing a tour of trail sites in and around Independence, Missouri Town 1855 is a good point of departure for Raytown. Return north to US 40 and turn left (west). US 40 is also 47th Street here. Continue west on 47th past Noland Road to Blue Ridge Boulevard. Turn left (south) on Blue Ridge, and you will be directly on the SFT route leading into Raytown.

RAYTOWN

An "Original Route" sign on Blue Ridge Blvd.

The people of Raytown are very conscious of their location on the Santa Fe, Oregon, and California Trails. Blue Ridge Boulevard was the route of the SFT from 1827 through at least 1845 when the Westport route became more important. Entering the city limits of Raytown on Blue Ridge, note the sign "Original Route." The National Park Service placed this sign, and others like it. There were earlier SFT routes (you likely visited Blue Springs on an early route). The Sibley survey team and the Becknell wagons of 1822 used a route a bit to the west of Blue Ridge so, in fact, they were earlier routes. Nevertheless, the route you will be following south on Blue Ridge is an important route and one in which thousands of wagons used. Blue Ridge angles diagonally through the center of town. Here the SFT followd the high ground, or ridge, between the Little Blue and the Big Blue Rivers, which was the easiest travel route for wagons.

At 59th Street, turn right (west) and drive three blocks to the intersection with Raytown Road. The City Hall, on the right, is at the site once occupied by the home of George Washington Rhoades **(A).** He was the Jackson County surveyor (1840-1844), commissioner of roads, and "an advocate of the Santa Fe Trail." According to *Raytown Remembers*, a book written by Roberta Bonnewitz and published in 1975 by the Raytown Historical Society, in May 1839 George W. Rhoades "petitioned the County Court to establish a public highway to Santa Fe." The SFT was already well traveled, but owners of adjacent farmlands often put gates across the road to discourage wagons from crossing their properties. Rhoades may have been engaged in trade to the Southwest because his estate inventory included "five Trading Wagons." A cast aluminum plaque referring to the SFT was placed at his homesite in 1975. It is now set in a concrete monument next to the flagpole in front of City Hall.

Raytown

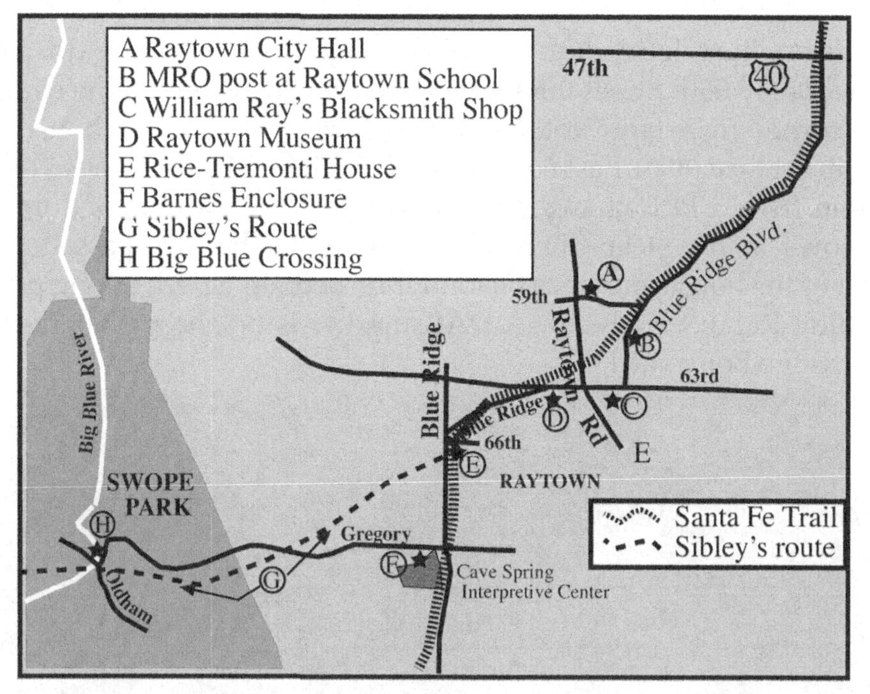

Return to Blue Ridge Boulevard and turn right (south). There will be a Missouri River Outfitters (MRO) post on your left at 60th Street in front of the Raytown High School **(B).** The MRO is one of the chapters of the Santa Fe Trail Association and is very active in researching trail information and preserving trail assets. You will see their markers in other locations along the SFT. Near the corner of 63rd and Raytown Road, on the southeast corner, facing Raytown Road is a historical marker with text commemorating the site of William Ray's Blacksmith Shop **(C).** Ray settled at this spot with his family in the late 1840s, providing wagon repairs for travelers on the SFT. He charged 88¢ to shoe a horse. By 1854, the community that grew up around the shop was known as Raytown, although by that time the smith himself had already migrated westward on the Oregon Trail.

From this intersection drive west on 63rd Street one and a half blocks to the Raytown Historical Society Museum on the left (at 9705 East 63rd) **(D).** Some of its exhibits relate to the era of the SFT.

Continue west on 63rd Street .3 mile to Blue Ridge Boulevard, which veers off to the left and after .6 mile intersects with Blue Ridge Extension. Turn left (south) on Blue Ridge Boulevard. In addition, immediately 66th Street intersects from the left. There on the southeast corner in a large lot, hidden by trees, is the farmhouse of Archibald Rice (8801 East 66th Street) **(E).** The white frame structure, built in 1844, is little changed except for the later addition of dormer windows in the steep-pitched roof in 1929. The SFT passed just north of the house and once beyond it turned left (south) along present Blue Ridge Boulevard. A DAR marker is on the corner facing Blue Ridge Boulevard.

The Archibald Rice farmhouse in Raytown.

New Orleans journalist Matt Field, who made a trip over the SFT in 1839, wrote: "About a day's travel [from Independence] brings the Santa Fe bound traders past the flourishing plantation of Farmer Rice, where leisure travelers often linger to enjoy his sweet bacon, fresh eggs, new milk and other nutritious and unsophisticated luxuries that appease appetite without encumbering digestion." Field must have stopped at an earlier Rice house since he came through here before the present house was constructed.

On the west side of the Rice House, facing Blue Ridge Boulevard, is a small log structure with a stone chimney known as Aunt Sophie's cabin. The restored cabin is said to have been built in 1837 but in fact was probably built later. This was one of several cabins Rice provided as quarters for his slaves. All have disappeared except this one, which housed the slave remembered as Aunt Sophie. Before her death in 1896, at age seventy-seven, she often spoke of the Santa Fe caravans that had passed by in the early days. She is buried in Independence's Woodlawn Cemetery in the colored section. Independence Parks marked her grave a few years ago with a granite marker.

Continue south on Blue Ridge Boulevard about four blocks to the intersection of Gregory. Turn right (west) on Gregory, and almost immediately on the left is the entrance to Cave Spring Park. This is known as the "Barnes Enclosure" after the Barnes family that had a farm here **(F).** Susan Magoffin wrote in June 1846 that, " between the hours of 3 and 4 we left the little village of Independence for the residence of Mr. Barns, a gentleman some ten miles this side of that place."

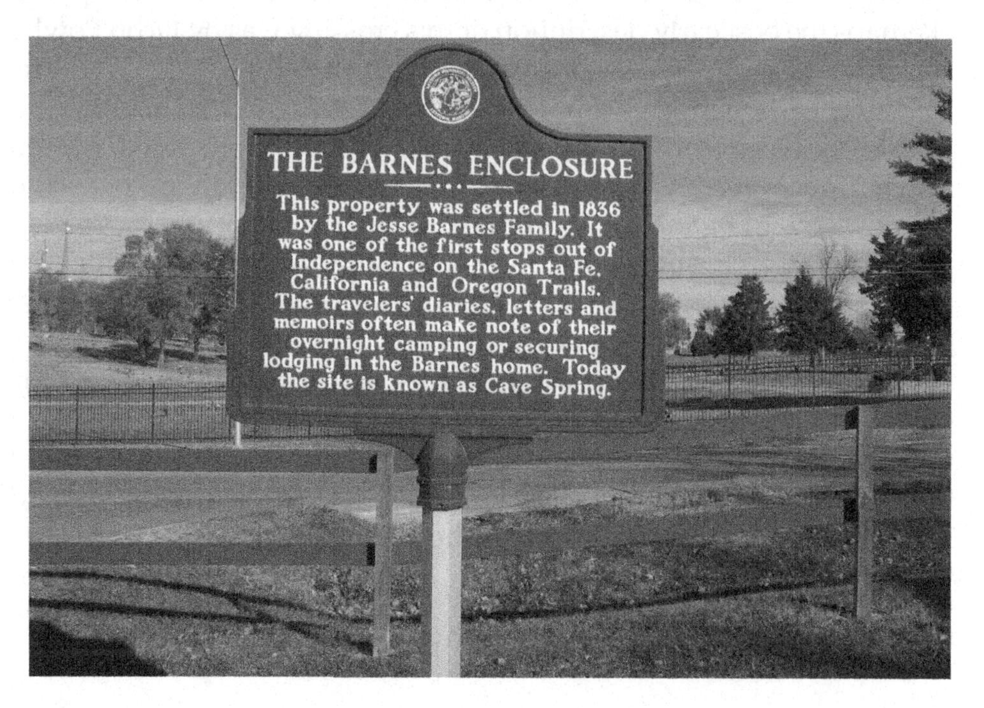

At this point, there are some choices to make for there are three possible routes one might pursue. First, the Sibley survey team and others went west about here to cross the Big Blue River in Swope Park **(G) (H).** The second consideration is the route that continued south on Blue Ridge Boulevard and then southwest through Minor Park. Lastly, one could follow the older route that ended by crossing into present Kansas at the Upper Crossing. All this can be ascertained by inspecting the maps in the Trail Background section.

EARLY ROUTE THROUGH SWOPE PARK

The earliest route of the SFT through this area, the one described by George C. Sibley in the 1825 mapping expedition, left Fort Osage and passed on the east of the site which was to become Independence Square. Then it continued towards the Big Blue River, crossing in present Swope Park. The trace south of Independence was about one-quarter mile west of the later SFT that you have been following.

To get to Swope Park, go west on Gregory. At about the point where Gregory and Oldham meet was the crossing point. Perhaps the best early description of this crossing was by Jacob Fowler (you heard from him at Fort Osage) who on July 5, 1822, wrote: "Sot out early and at five miles Crossing a large Crick [the Blue] 50 yards Wide Runs north the Bottoms and Hill Sides are Well Covered With timber Heare went up a High Steep Hill over some Rocks and Continu over High Roleing ground." Fowler was not a great speller, but no early chronicler is more enjoyable to read. Although no marker exists at the crossing, locals are working to get one. It must have been a very difficult descent from the bluff on the east.

The Sibley route continued west after fording the Big Blue crossing into present Kansas at the "Nine Mile Point." You will visit this point later in this guide. Instead of going to the Nine Mile Point now, it is suggested you go back to the intersection at Gregory and Blue Ridge Boulevard and follow the later trail.

TO NEW SANTA FE

From the intersection of Gregory and Blue Ridge Boulevard drive south on Blue Ridge about two miles to 83rd Street and turn right. Go to Manchester, turn left, and drive to 85th Street (**A**). Here there are nice swales ascending the hill toward the southwest. Today, the name given to these swales is the Wiedevult Swales, crediting the family presently owning the upper portion of the swales. The Barnes Enclosure / Cave Spring Association owns the majority of the swales. These swales are a certified site on the Santa Fe, Oregon, and California National Historic Trails. There are explanatory panels there as well as an MRO column.

The Wiedevult swales.

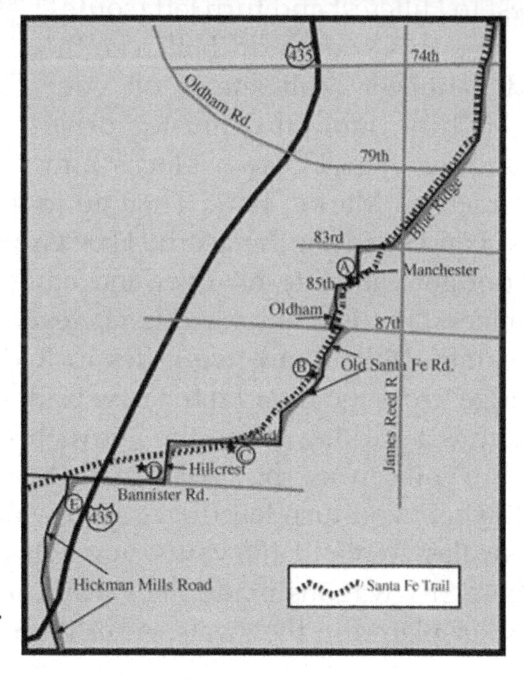

South from Raytown.

Drive west on 85th Street to Oldham Road. Turn left (south) on Oldham and continue to 87th Street. At 87th turn left, go a short distance, and turn right on Old Santa Fe Road. This road is on top of the trail, at least on those portions going southwest. Old Santa Fe Road makes a few turns but in one-third mile, on your right, there will be some silhouettes and NPS panels (**B**). This site is Hickman Mills and the buildings behind the markers are the headquarters for the Hickman Mills School District. You can also see markers for a walking and biking trail that follows in the trace of the SFT here. Edwin Alfred Hickman built a steam-powered mill along Hart Grove Creek in 1854. In addition, it is for him that Hickman Mills is named.

The next stop is Schumacher Park. Continue south on Old Santa Fe Road to 93rd Street and turn right (west). Drive on 93rd until you reach Schumacher Park on your left (**C**) . A DAR marker is here in this small park.

An attractive silhoutte at the Hickman Mills site.

Leave the park and travel west to Hillcrest and turn left (south). As you drive south on Hillcrest, the old Bannister Mall site is on your right. Turn right on Bannister, drive past Interstate 435 two blocks and turn left on Marion Park. Then go to the first right, Hickman Mills Road and head south past the Hart Grove Crossing. (**D**) This was an important campsite for overland emigrants in the 1840s, with the Donner families, among others, resting here. Continue south on Hickman Mills Road two miles to Red Bridge. Turn right on Red Bridge, cross the river on the new bridge to Minor Park on your left. There is a parking lot on the left with several NPS markers. This is where you can see the swales made by wagons climbing the modest hill.where you turn left (E). As you walk you will cross several sets of swales. At about 100 yards, you will see a truly magnificent swale where SFT wagons made their way up the incline. There is a DAR marker placed in the swale. After the wagons had forded the river, they moved up the slope below the present marker, and their wheels sliced a path in the brow at the top. These are some of the most dramatic trail remnants in the Kansas City area.

Schumacher Park

Swale with a marker in the notch
at Minor Park in Kansas City.

New Santa Fe

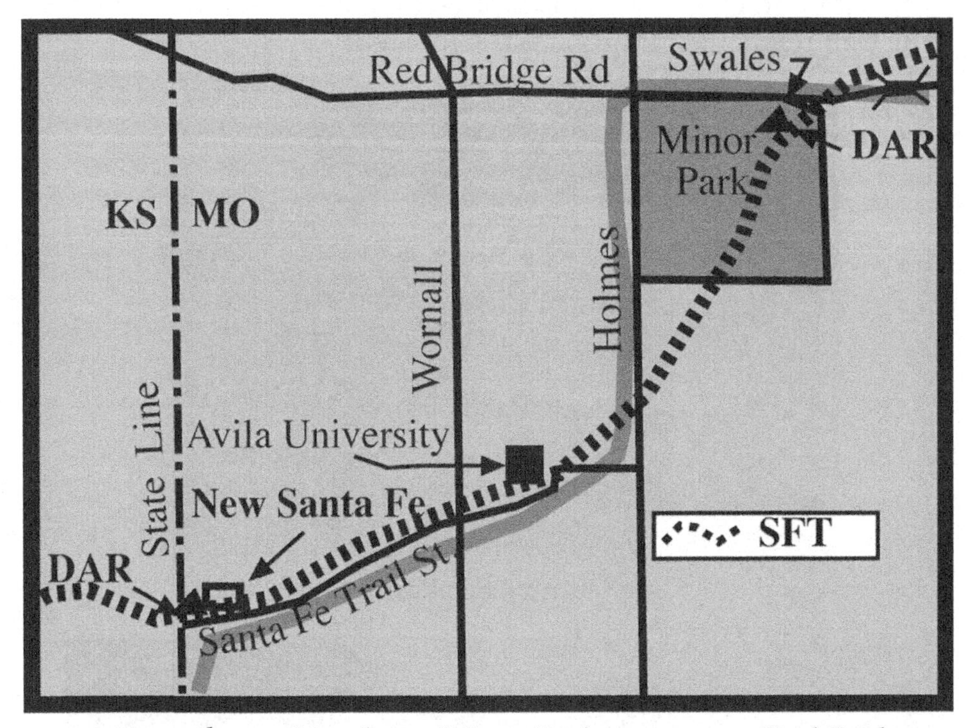

From the parking lot at Minor Park go west on Red Bridge to Holmes and turn left (south). Drive south one mile on Holmes to Santa Fe Trail Street and there turn right and cross Wornall in a few blocks. You will come to the Santa Fe Bible Church on the right side of the street. Enter the parking lot on the west side of the church. Adjoining it in the rear is an old cemetery. At the back of the lot is a historical marker, "New Santa Fe," referring to the SFT, but there are factual errors. The early history of New Santa Fe is somewhat unclear. A tavern may have been on the site by the mid-1840s, selling whiskey to persons who crossed the state line from the "dry" Indian reservation on the present Kansas side. Selling whiskey to Indians, although illegal, was a very big business and a contributing factor to the decline of the Indian population. Bill Unrau's recent book, *Indians, Alcohol, and the Trails to Taos and Santa Fe,* makes clear that alcohol was the most profitable item on the Santa Fe Trail, and this illegal trade with the Indians was enormous.

Faint swale in the New Santa Fe church cemetery.

There are some gentle swales in the cemetery if you look closely. On the northeast corner of Santa Fe Trail Street and State Line Road is last DAR marker you will see in Missouri.

Upper Crossing and the State Line

From the intersection of State Line Road and Santa Fe Trail Street, turn left (south) and drive 1.5 miles on State Line where it veers a bit to the right and continues south as Kenneth. Two miles on Kenneth brings you to West 151st Street where you should turn left and in .2 mile, you will cross back into Missouri. One-tenth mile farther, on your left, is the entrance to Big Blue Park where there is parking. As you enter the park immediately on your left is the Upper Crossing of the Big Blue River (**A**). This was the logical place for traders to cross the Big Blue, since here the riverbanks are less treacherous, and the water level is lower.

There are two choices at this point. First, and the better of the two, is to follow the old SFT north from the Upper Crossing.

The second is outlined below. To find the old route, turn left on Kenneth as you exit the park and continue to Holmes. At Holmes, turn left again (north) and drive to 139th Street where you should continue on this street until, after a few turns, it becomes Arrington. As you drive northeast on Arrington you are directly on the very old SFT, the piece that Marmaduke followed in 1824. Continue on Arrington to Main and turn left. Drive on Main that becomes 129th and then Blue River and, finally, West Blue Ridge. When West Blue Ridge intersects State Line turn right to follow that street north.

Santa Fe Trail Crossings into Kansas.

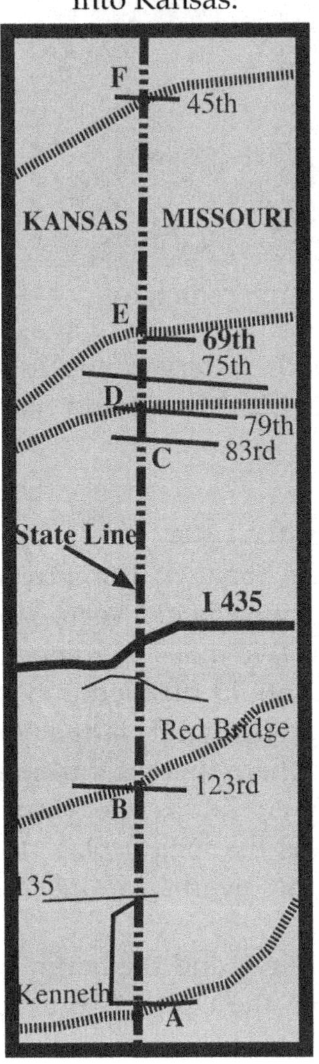

You have been to the Upper Crossing **(A) so** the next goal is to visit other important sites along the Kansas-Missouri state line, which is, of course, State Line Road. Driving north you will pass Santa Fe Trail Road that is where New Santa Fe was located in trail days **(B).** Continue north and stop at the house of Alexander Majors at 8201 State Line **(C).** Amid the trees on a large lot on the north-east corner of 83rd Street and State Line Road is the Alexander Majors House. As noted in the Lexington section, Majors, along with his partners Russell and Waddell, operated the largest overland freighting firm in the early West. In fact, Majors did some freighting on the SFT before the partnership was formed with Russell and Waddell in 1848. This two-story frame house was built in 1856. Majors died in 1900 and is buried in Union Cemetery at 29th and Grand in Kansas City. Also buried in that cemetery is John C. McCoy, the founder of Westport and discoverer of Westport Landing. The Majors House has been restored and furnished. Behind it are a smoke house and a large barn (with exhibits), reconstructed on the original foundation. The site, open to the public, is administered by the Alexander Majors Historical Trust and is a certified National Park Service Santa Fe National Historic Trail Site. Apparently, according to local historian Craig Crease, the state line actually runs through the front porch of the house.

Continue north on State Line. At 79th Street drive around Weltner Park and stop at the north side of the park in a parking area. There are two interpretive panels there for Nine Mile Point, the point that Joseph Brown marked in 1823 **(D).** He was the government surveyor charged with establishing the western boundary of the new state of Missouri. Brown wrote in his notes that he went south 10 chains (660 feet) "to a trace heading from Fort Osage towards Santa Fe." That trace would be the mark left by William Becknell in 1822 when he passed through here on his second journey to Santa Fe. You are at the nine mile point and if you walk to the corner at State Line and look right (south) you will see a McDonalds and that is where the SFT crossed in its earliest days.

Three panels discussing the crossing at the 9 mile point.

Continue north on State Line to 69th Terrace and turn into a little pocket park called Nymph Park **(E)**. This is the point at which the South Branch of the SFT from Westport crossed the state line from the 1840s onward. This crossing eventually supplanted the Nine Mile Crossing, which is about one mile south from here. There is an effort by community leaders to develop interpretive panels for this site.

Driving north on State Line, at about 45th Street you will see the Kansas City Area Historic Trails Association (KCAHTA) brown signs noting the crossing of the state line here; this would be the North Branch of the Santa Fe Trail from Westport **(F).** This was the crossing closest to Westport and the trail here continued past the Shawnee Methodist, Shawnee Baptist, and Shawnee Quaker Missions. This crossing predates the 69th Terrace crossing by several years.

OLD WESTPORT AND KANSAS CITY

Our next stop will be at the site of Westport Landing in Kansas City at the waterfront. From 45th and State Line Road drive north on State Line to 43rd Street. Turn right and drive to Westport Road. Turn east on Westport. Continue to Broadway where you turn left. Drive north on Broadway to 6th Street and turn right on Delaware. Continue on Delaware to 3rd Street, turn right onto Main Street. Follow Main for two blocks and park your car for a short walk to new pedestrian bridge with nine interpretive exhibits. You are now at the location that would serve Westport.

Westport grew up 4 miles south of the Missouri River, the point where the road connecting Independence and the Indian agencies just west in present Kansas crossed Mill Creek. In 1833, John Calvin McCoy built a two-story cabin here to serve as a trading post, the beginning of the new community of Westport. About the same time, a new landing was cleared on the Missouri River where steamboats could unload their cargoes. First called Westport Landing, the landing went by various names throughout the 1830s and 1840s: Kanzas Landing, Kansas Landing, and finally Town of Kansas. It was about 1.5 miles downstream from the junction of the Kansas (or Kaw) and the Missouri Rivers. The site had a fine ledge of rock jutting out into the water. Goods were first deposited in warehouses, and then freighted up the bluff and on to stores in Westport.

McCoy was very successful in luring trail outfitters away from Independence.

The small settlement that grew up around the landing afterward was called Kansas City. As the century advanced, Kansas City expanded and, by 1897, eventually engulfed Westport. In the beginning, however, it was Westport, newly booming as a jumping-off point for the Far West that gave promise of becoming the region's chief population center. By the early 1840s, Independence's monopoly over the Santa Fe trade had been broken, and by the early 1850s, Westport virtually controlled the overland traffic. In the decade before the Civil War, Westport fairly hummed with activity as Santa Fe traders, mountain men, Indians, and Oregon- and California-bound emigrants mingled in the streets.

Westport remained the main eastern terminus of the SFT as long, or longer, than any of the places that preceded it—Franklin, Lexington, Fort Osage, or even Independence. However, guerrilla warfare prior to the Civil War, and finally the war itself in 1861, brought border disturbances and caused most Santa Fe traders to move their business upriver to Fort Leavenworth, which was more secure. After the war, Westport briefly recovered some of its lost trade, but by 1866, the railroad had pushed into Kansas, and the eastern terminus of the SFT moved with it.

A large number of sites and markers exist in the Westport-Kansas City area. Those unfamiliar with the region will need to rely on an up-to-date city map. Gregory Franzwa's *The Oregon Trail Revisited, Silver Anniversary Edition,* is also useful for reaching many of the places noted below.

Beginning in Westport, you will see brown and white signs erected by the Kansas City Area Historic Trails Association, located at points where the trail crossed section lines, extending from McCoy's trading post in Westport to the western border of Johnson County, Kansas.

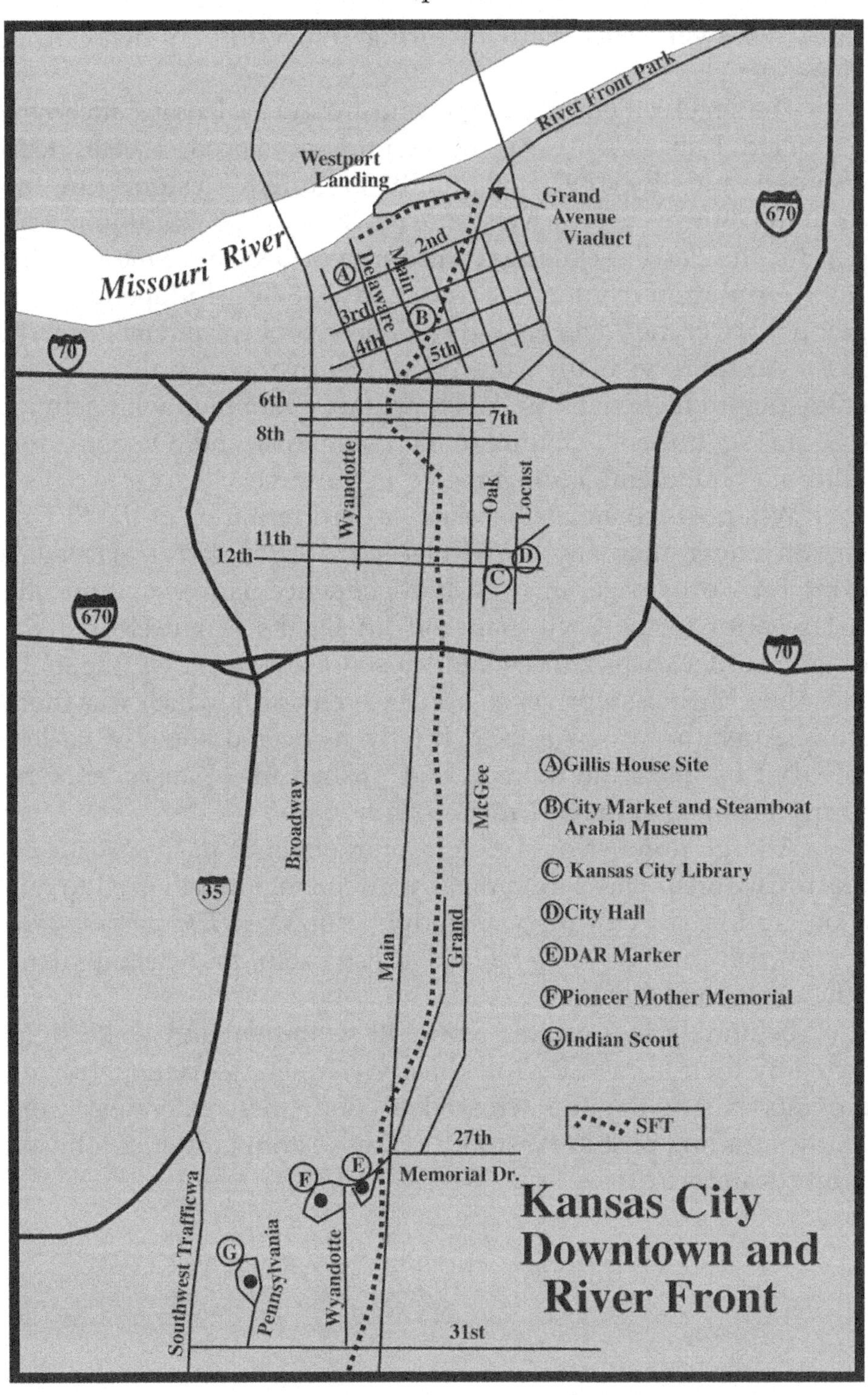
River Front Park
Westport Landing
Grand Avenue Viaduct
670
Missouri River
2nd
Delaware
Main
3rd
4th
5th
70
6th
7th
8th
Wyandotte
Oak
Locust
11th
12th
670
70
Broadway
McGee
35
Main
Grand
Ⓐ Gillis House Site
Ⓑ City Market and Steamboat Arabia Museum
Ⓒ Kansas City Library
Ⓓ City Hall
Ⓔ DAR Marker
Ⓕ Pioneer Mother Memorial
Ⓖ Indian Scout
SFT
27th
Memorial Dr.
Southwest Trafficwa
Pennsylvania
Wyandotte
31st
Kansas City Downtown and River Front

KANSAS CITY

The Kansas City metropolitan area takes its role in the history of the SFT very seriously. The phone directory lists forty-one businesses named Santa Fe Trail. There are also six Santa Fe Trail roads, streets, and lanes, and over a dozen schools called Santa Fe Trail, Oregon Trail, or California Trail. Along with this awareness comes an interest in restoring the riverfront. The original Westport Landing stretched several blocks along the Missouri River from Wyandotte to about Grand. Today's bramble along the old landing will eventually be removed, and foundations of early buildings uncovered as much as possible. This rejuvenation will give us a better idea of the setting along the river.

The city has already developed a park on the Missouri River, which can be reached by driving north on Grand Avenue Viaduct. This will take you to a nice walkway along the river running a mile east of the Town of Kansas site. The landing would have been upstream from the walkway.

The following sites are valuable in gaining an understanding of the SFT from Westport Landing to Westport.

A. Gillis House Site

From Second and Delaware Streets walk north (toward the river) to the foot of the bluff, turn left, and continue one block. On the left is the site of the Gillis House, built by Benoist Troost in 1849. In 1856, it became known as the American Hotel and was also known as the Union Hotel. Many SFT traders stayed here. Other buildings lined this bluff, continuing eastward several blocks. There are no markers here at the time of writing.

B. City Market and Steamboat *Arabia* Museum

From the landing return to 3rd Street and turn east to Main Street. The SFT went directly southwest through today's City Market, arriving here by ascending the bluff along what is the present-day Grand Avenue Viaduct (see map). The market is full of shops, but most important is the Steamboat *Arabia* Museum on the east side, which displays a grand collection of goods recovered from the *Arabia*. In 1856 this boat hit a snag in the Missouri River and sank which, according to museum records, was not uncommon. The average life of a steamboat on the treacherous Missouri was three years. The display includes part of the ship and many of the trade items carried in the hold, providing an opportunity to view the kinds of goods that might have been carried on the SFT during this period.

From the museum, you can trace the SFT south through Kansas City by using the following directions (see map page 98). If you take this route, you will be following the SFT as far as Penn Valley Park.

1. South from the *Arabia* to 5th
2. West on 5th to Delaware
3. South on Delaware to 7th
4. West (right) on 7th to Wyandotte (The SFT made this detour because of local topography.)
5. South on Wyandotte to 8th
6. East on 8th to Main
7. South on Main to 12th
8. East on 12th to Grand
9. South on Grand to Memorial Drive (The SFT in this stretch is immediately to the west.)

If you followed the trail to Penn Valley Park, you missed two important places. The Kansas City Library (**C** on the map) between 12th and 13th Streets and McGee and Oak has some good research materials on the SFT in the Missouri Valley Room. Further, murals around the ceiling depict the early history of the city, including scenes associated with the trail. Also, just outside the room hangs a copy of the Spalding Map of 1855, which shows the area in the heyday of the SFT.

Another place of interest is City Hall between llth and 12th Streets and Oak and Locust (**D** on the map). Here major episodes in the city's history are depicted in a frieze of sixteen panels directly above the sixth story.

As you approach the Penn Valley Park area, turn right on Memorial Drive, which takes you into the park. Across the road to the west on a small hill is the Pioneer Mother Memorial (F on the map). The memorial is a larger-than-life group of bronze figures surrounding a pioneer mother on horseback. This sculpture is unrelated to the series of stone pioneer mothers on the SFT, the first example of which has already been noted at Lexington. To view the sculpture, you must walk up the hill. With the Kansas City skyline rising behind it, this work is beautiful and should not be missed.

Finally, drive south on Wyandotte. At 31st Street turn right (west) and go several blocks to Pennsylvania. Turn right here and look for the Indian Scout statue on the hill to the left (**G** on the map), a location that provides another grand view of the Kansas City skyline.

Two more places of interest in the northern part of the city are the Thomas Hart Benton Memorial and the Kansas City Museum of History and Science. They are located in a part of the city where one should use caution and visit in the middle of the day.

The Thomas Hart Benton Memorial is in a traffic circle at the intersection of Gladstone and Benton Boulevards. (Senator Benton's role in developing western trails was mentioned in connection with his statue at St. Louis.) Here a 7-foot granite monument holds two bronze plaques, one of which bears Benton's likeness.

The Kansas City Museum of History and Science is located at 3218 Gladstone Boulevard, two blocks west of the Benton Memorial. Occasional exhibits concerning mountain men, Indians, the Oregon Trail, and the SFT are some of the best anywhere.

From the Indian Scout in Penn Valley Park, return to 31st Street and turn left to Broadway, then follow Broadway south to Westport.

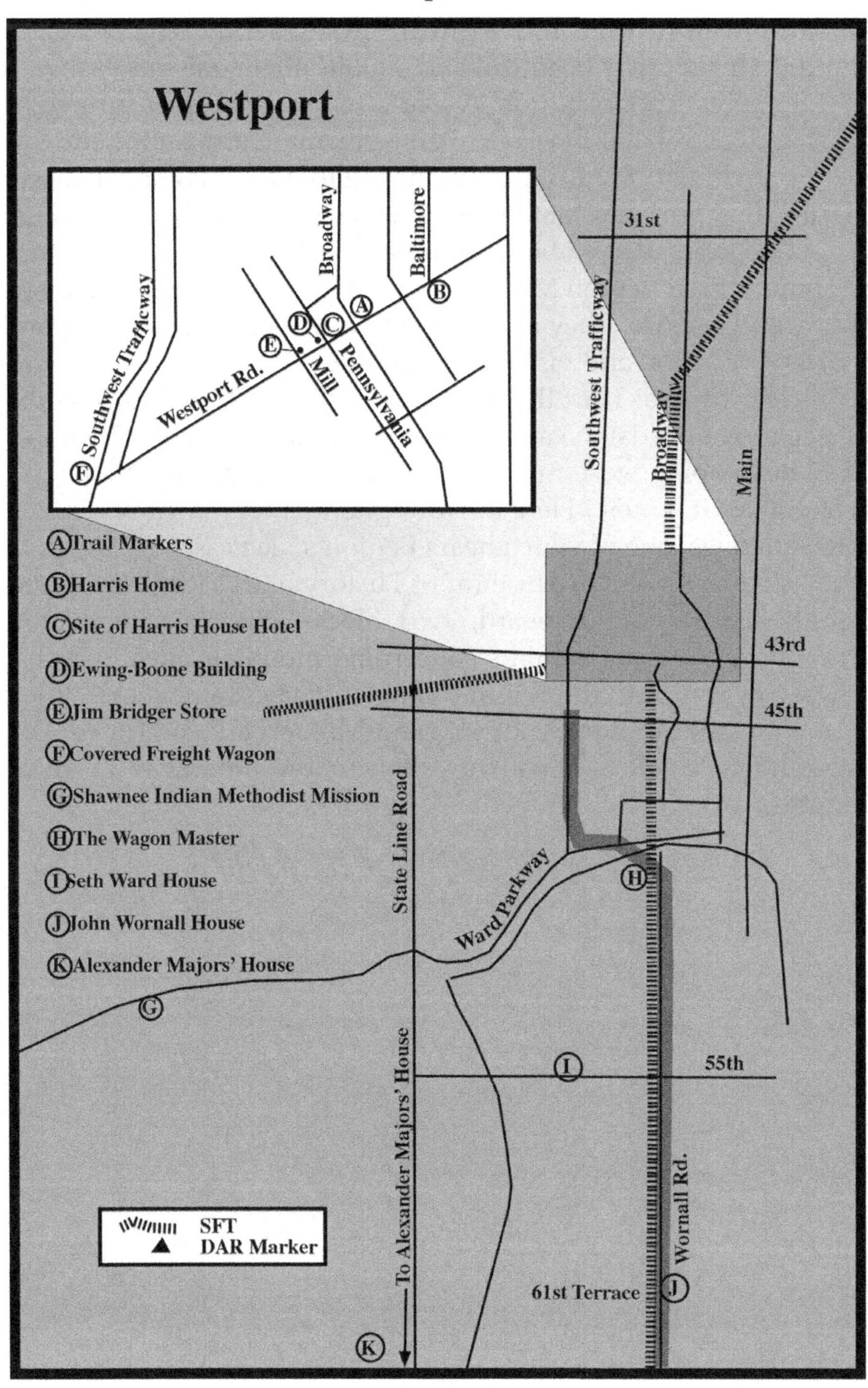
Westport
Broadway
Baltimore
Southwest Trafficway
Westport Rd.
Mill
Pennsylvania
A
B
C
D
E
F
A Trail Markers
B Harris Home
C Site of Harris House Hotel
D Ewing-Boone Building
E Jim Bridger Store
F Covered Freight Wagon
G Shawnee Indian Methodist Mission
H The Wagon Master
I Seth Ward House
J John Wornall House
K Alexander Majors' House
31st
Southwest Trafficway
Broadway
Main
43rd
45th
State Line Road
Ward Parkway
55th
To Alexander Majors' House
Wornall Rd.
61st Terrace
SFT
DAR Marker

Kansas City Area

WESTPORT

A. The Trail Markers

A cluster of trail markers is near Broadway and 40th Street, just north of the Broadway and Westport Road intersection and a block northeast of the center of Old Westport. They are in a small triangular park at Broadway and Westport Road.

(1) A DAR marker placed in 1987 is farthest to the north in the park.

(2) A heroic statue of Jim Bridger (mountain man and store owner in Westport), John C. McCoy (founder of Westport), and Alexander Majors (freighter on the SFT).

(3) A large "Three Trails West" terrazzo tile map on the ground showing the Santa Fe, Oregon, and California Trails.

Statue of Alexander Majors, John Calvin McCoy and Jim Bridger in Westport.

B. Harris Home

The Harris home is at 4000 Baltimore. Built in 1855 by Col. John Harris, who was a participant in the Santa Fe trade, the house was moved to the present site in 1922 from its original location a half-block away at Westport and Main, a spot now marked by a plaque. The beautiful two-story brick house is currently the headquarters of the Westport Historical Society, which has restored several rooms for public view. (Address inquiries to the society at Box 10076, Westport Station, Kansas City, MO 64111.)

C. Site of the Harris House Hotel

The hotel was located at the northeast corner of Westport and Pennsylvania in the center of Westport. In 1846, Colonel Harris bought the log building at this location when it was known as the McGee Tavern and Hotel, or more popularly the Catfish House, catfish being a specialty of the chef. Owner Alien McGee was selling it to enter the Santa Fe trade. When the building burned in 1852, Harris rebuilt a three-story brick structure, which was razed in 1922. A plaque now marks the spot. The Independence to Westport road passed by both the Harris home and his hotel. The McCoys Public House Restaurant is now at this site. John McCoy, Westport's founder, had a log trading post here first in 1833.

D. The Ewing-Boone Building

The Ewing-Boone Building is at the northwest corner of Westport and Pennsylvania. Westport's leading historian, the late William Goff, established that this structure was built in 1850-1851. The owners were George and William Ewing, prominent traders with the Shawnees, whose lands lay just across the Kansas line to the west. Albert G. Boone, a grandson of Daniel Boone, bought the building in 1854, the year the Shawnee lands were opened for settlement and the Indian trade declined. It is now Kelly's Bar.

E. Jim Bridger's Store

Jim Bridger's Store is next to the Ewing-Boone Building on Westport Road. The structure was built in 1850 by Cyprien Chouteau, member of a prominent fur-trading family of St. Louis and Kansas City. Before coming to Westport in that year, he had operated a trading post at Council Grove on the SFT. In 1866, Chouteau sold the two-story store and warehouse to aging Jim Bridger, known in his younger days as "The King of the Mountain Men." Bridger and his son-in-law, Albert Wachsmann, ran a grocery business here for several years. A bronze historical plaque is attached to the outside front wall. A restaurant presently occupies the building.

F. Covered Freight Wagon

The freight wagon is three blocks west of Bridger's Store on Westport Road (which is also 43rd Street) at Southwest Trafficway. This large wagon on the west side of the intersection under the

"Old Westport" sign is a replica commemorating trail days. Look for a shopping center behind the freight wagon. There is a "Citizens Commemorative Plaque" in this center listing one hundred prominent early citizens of Westport and Kansas City designated "Old Settlers of Westport and Kansas City."

THE SANTA FE TRAIL FROM WESTPORT

From Old Westport, one route of the SFT ran almost due south for a few miles, meandering near and on present-day Wornall Road. From Westport the trail crossed Brush Creek, climbed Brush Creek Hill, and continued on to the "great camping ground." At this well-watered and grassy site, caravans organized for their departure on the SFT. That area now lies between Wornall Road and the state line and is bounded on the north by 67th Street and on the south by 71st Street. At about 66th Street, the south branch of the SFT turned toward the southwest, crossing the state line and meeting the north route at present-day Strang Park in the city of Overland Park.

The other original route leaving Westport went almost due west and then turned southwest. This route led traders by the Shawnee Indian Methodist Mission (**G** on the map on page 32) and near the Shawnee Baptist Mission, as well as the Shawnee Quaker Mission. The Methodist Mission, now a Kansas State Historical Site, is on Mission Road at 53rd Street just across the state line in Kansas. The Shawnee Reservation extended 25 miles south from the Kansas (or Kaw) River through these Indian lands. The Delaware Indians had the lands to the north of the Kaw River. Although the Shawnee Methodist Mission dates from 1829, the location on Mission Road was started in 1839 and was maintained as a manual training school for Shawnee children. Santa Fe Trail travelers and emigrants bound for Oregon often stopped here. Three of the original brick buildings on twelve landscaped acres have been preserved, and a historical marker with text is in front of each.

To reach the Shawnee Mission from the covered freight wagon, drive west on 43rd Street to Mission Road. Turn south on Mission Road to 53rd Street, then right (west) to the mission.

H. The Wagon Master

This bronze, 10-foot-tall equestrian statue of a SFT wagon master is impressive and should not be missed. It is located in front of the Fairmont Hotel on the southern section of Ward Parkway just west of where it intersects with Wornall Road. (Ward Parkway is on both sides of Brush Creek here.) Note the authentic detail of the Santa Fe-style saddle and the long rifle across the pommel. Cast in Italy, the statue was dedicated in 1973.

I. Seth Ward House

Drive south on Wornall Road to 55th Street. Turn right (west) and go about .5 miles to 1032 West 55th Street. In the yard of this private residence, is a black historical sign with text in gold letters. The two-story white house in front belonged to Seth Ward, who served as post sutler at Fort Laramie on the Oregon Trail. Ward also traveled for a brief period on the SFT, at least part of the time in the employ of famed merchant Ceran St. Vrain. He was a friend of Kit Carson as well. Later, he became a patriarch of Westport, with Ward Parkway named for him. The only sketch of the life of Seth Ward appears in volume 3 of LeRoy R. Hafen's *The Mountain Men and the Fur Trade of the Far West*.

To the rear of the beautiful Ward residence, is a second house that was owned for a time by William Bent, one of the founders of famed Bent's Fort on the Mountain Route of the SFT. Bent commuted between this house, which was the center of a farm, and his fort via the trail. His daughter was married here in 1860. Most of the wording on the historical sign refers to the Civil War Battle of Westport, which took place in the area in October 1864.

J. John Wornall House

Return to Wornall and drive south to 61st Terrace. On the northeast corner of this intersection, is the handsome antebellum residence of John Wornall, built in 1858 by one of the area's most prominent citizens. It was the center of a 500-acre farm. From Westport, the SFT passed nearby going south to the great camping ground just beyond. The home was briefly used as a hospital during the Civil War Battle of Westport. Now restored, it is administered by the Jackson County Historical Society and open to the public.

K. Alexander Majors House

(You may have visited this house earlier as you followed crossings along the state line.)

From the Wornall house, drive west to State Line Road, turn south, and continue to 8201 State Line. Amid the trees on a large lot on the northeast corner of 83rd Street and State Line Road is the Alexander Majors House. As noted in the Lexington section, Majors, along with his partners Russell and Waddell, operated the largest overland freighting firm in the early West. In fact, Majors did some freighting on the SFT before the partnership was formed with Russell and Waddell in 1848.

This two-story frame house was built in 1856. Majors died in 1900 and is buried in Union Cemetery at 29th and Grand in Kansas City. Also buried in that cemetery is John C. McCoy, the founder of Westport and discoverer of Westport Landing. The Majors House has been restored and furnished. Behind it are a smokehouse and a large barn (with exhibits), reconstructed on the original foundation. The site, open to the public, is administered by the Alexander Majors Historical Trust and is a certified National Park Service Santa Fe National Historic Trail Site.

ENTERING KANSAS

A little over half of the total length of the SFT fell within the present boundaries of Kansas. US 56 (and beginning at Kinsley, Kansas, US 56/US 50) generally follows the original route of the trail. US 56 will be your companion as far as Dodge City, Kansas. Scattered along it are nearly one hundred DAR markers and other monuments in Kansas.

The SFT used five separate routes, evolving over a forty-year span, to enter Kansas (see maps pages 58, 59, and 60). This guide will direct you to Lone Elm Campground by way of the route that utilized the Lower Crossing of the Blue River in the earliest period (1821-1827). The traders passed into Kansas at Nine Mile Point, went on to Flat Rock Creek Campground, and finally, Round Grove/Lone Elm Campground south of Olathe.

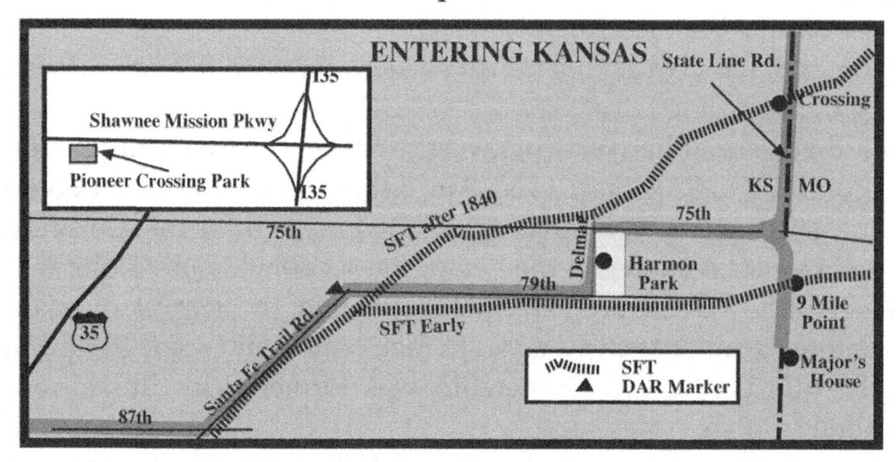

Drive south on State Line Road past 69th Street. This intersection is about where the SFT, by way of Westport and Wornall Road, crossed into Kansas after 1840. Continue south on State Line to 75th Street. At this location, you are .5 mile north of Nine Mile Point. Turn right (west) here, continue west to Delmar, and turn left to Harmon Park, which can be spotted by its tall water tower. Near the pavilion is a parking lot, southeast of which is a good set of swales. This is actually on the later route of the trail, after 1840.

From Harmon Park, drive south to 79th Street, turn right (west), and continue past Metcalf several blocks to Santa Fe Drive. Turn south on Santa Fe Drive. At 80th Street and Santa Fe Drive on the northeast corner is a DAR marker, the first one in Kansas.

From the DAR marker continue southwest on Santa Fe Drive to 87th Street. At this point, you are about .5 mile southeast of Sapling Grove and .25 mile northeast of the junction of the two SFT routes out of Westport. Sapling Grove was an important rendezvous for SFT traders and Oregon Trail emigrants. If you wish to visit the site; it is in Comanche Park at 83rd Street and Grant.

Pioneer Crossing Park Side Trip

A side trip from this point to the Pioneer Crossing Park is well worth the trip. Drive north on Interstate 35 exiting at Shawnee Mission Parkway (see inset map in the Entering Kansas map). Go west on that road to 1040 Shawnee Mission Parkway where there is located a very nice small park containing wagon replicas and other items of trail interest. This small park demonstrates the strong interest the local communities have in trail history.

The very impressive statue depicting a wagon train on Shawnee Mission Parkway.

Drive west on 87th Street, passing Interstate 35, and about 1 mile beyond turn left (south) onto Pflumm. Continue on Pflumm until you pass under the interstate and turn left at 103rd Street. Follow 103rd east for .33 mile and turn left into Flat Rock Creek Park (**A**). The Flat Rock Creek Campground was near the small stream (Indian Creek) in the park. In later trail days, this site was called Indian Creek Campground.

Flat Rock Creek was the site of an important Santa Fe Trail camp ground.

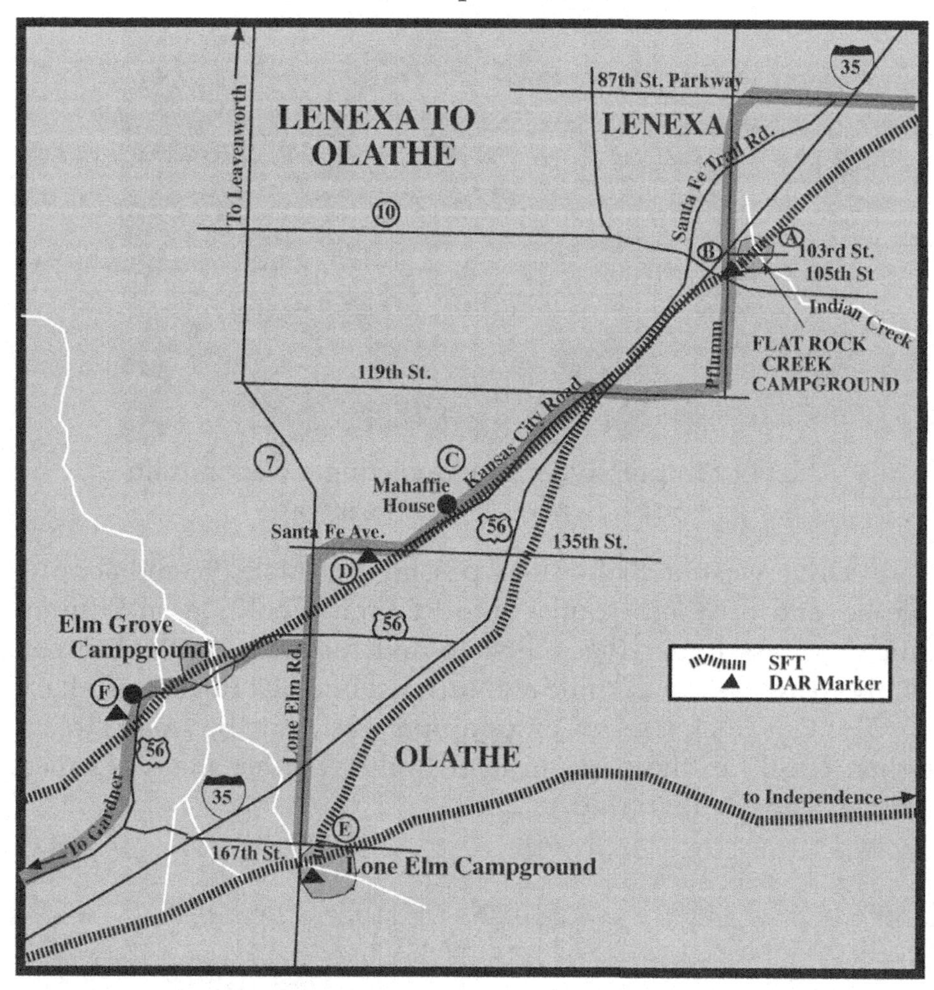

Return to Pflumm and drive south to 105th Street. There should be a DAR marker on the west side of Pflumm, moved here from its original location 1.5 miles north (**B**). This is the second DAR marker (Lenexa) in Kansas.

From the DAR marker, go south on Pflumm to 119th Street and turn right (west). Go over the interstate, and just beyond turn left onto Renner Road, which becomes Kansas City Road. Continue south on Kansas City Road. This road is directly on top of the SFT from here to 135th Street. (If some places are being skipped, you can drive south on Interstate 35 and take the Olathe exit to arrive at this same location.)

OLATHE

Continue southwest on Kansas City Road toward Olathe. This road becomes Old Kansas City Road as you enter Olathe. Immediately beyond the intersection of Old Kansas City Road and Ridgeway, on the right, is one of the white oval SFT markers of the American Pioneer Trails Association, actually one of several replicas placed along the SFT by Michael Duncan, formerly director of the Mahaffie House.

One block beyond the Ridgeway intersection on the right (1100 Kansas City Road) is the Mahaffie House and Farmstead (**C**), a Registered National Historic Landmark. The fine two-story residence was built in 1865 as a farmhouse, but it soon served as the first noon stage stop beyond Westport. It is the only remaining stage station on the SFT that is open to the public.

Continue southwest on Old Kansas City Road about 1 mile to the intersection with Santa Fe Avenue. Turn right (west) four blocks to the Johnson County Courthouse on the left (**D**). On the southeast comer of Courthouse Square, is a fine SFT monument. At the top is an oxbow carved in the stone, while below is a bronze plaque with an ox-drawn covered wagon in relief, like the one noted earlier in Penn Valley Park.

In the Kansas Room of the Olathe Public Library, a good collection of SFT materials and maps is available for researchers and trail hounds. Its location is one block east of the courthouse, at Park and Chestnut Streets.

SOUTH OF OLATHE

Several locations of interest can be visited on roads south and west of Olathe. From Courthouse Square in Olathe, drive west on Santa Fe Avenue to Lone Elm Road, also the intersection with KS 7. Turn left (south) on Lone Elm and drive about 4 miles to the intersection with 167th Street. On the southeast corner is the DAR marker for Lone Elm Campground (**E**). First known as Round Grove, this site came to be called Lone Elm by 1844 when all the surrounding timber had been cut by travelers for firewood and only a single tree remained.

By the end of the decade, the lone elm itself had fallen to the ax. The campground encompassed forty acres behind the marker. Many caravans from Independence made this place their second stop on the trail. Lone Elm Campground was confused with another campground, Elm Grove, on the same creek until recently. Elm Grove Campground will be detailed in the next chapter. There is an extensive site developed at Lone Elm today. The NPS has provided several very informative markers here and there are picnic facilities available too.

The new shelter at Lone Elm Park.

Return north on Lone Elm Road (to reach KS 7) to Olathe. This is the last opportunity to make a side trip to Fort Leavenworth. To get to Leavenworth, continue north on KS 7 about 33 miles to the town and fort.

FORT LEAVENWORTH

From anywhere in the Kansas City area, a convenient side trip can be made up the Missouri River to Fort Leavenworth. Established in 1827 by Col. Henry Leavenworth, several branches of the Santa Fe and Oregon Trails crossed its grounds.

There were two principal routes from the fort to the SFT. One followed the Military Road south, crossing the Kansas River at Grinter's Ferry and connecting with the SFT in Lenexa at about present-day 90th and Barton Streets (see maps on pages 46 and 47). The second branch went more directly west and crossed the Kansas River near its confluence with the Wakarusa River in Douglas County. This branch continued and met the main srem of the SFT at Willow Springs near present-day Overbrook. Gen. Stephen Watts Kearny's Army of the West, as well as the celebrated Mormon Battalion, used this route when they marched over the SFT in 1846 to conquer New Mexico. Later, after Fort Riley was established in 1853, there was a route from Fort Leavenworth to Riley that carried SFT traffic, first south from Riley to join main trail near Lost Spring and later southwest to Walnut Creek to join main SFT.

Border disturbances concerning slavery issues several years before the outbreak of the Civil War disrupted the Westport and Kansas City markets, and many Santa Fe traders began to use the safer protected routes from Fort Leavenworth southwest to the SFT. By the late 1850s and early 1860s, traders and emigrants heading for New Mexico or California increasingly debarked at Fort Leavenworth from Missouri River steamboats and organized caravans for a crossing of the SFT or the Oregon-California Trail. There are two clusters of sites associated with the SFT, one in the town of Leavenworth and another on the grounds of the fort immediately to the north

THE TOWN OF LEAVENWORTH

Entering the south side of the town of Leavenworth, watch for the junction of KS 7/US 73 with KS 5, which enters from the right (east) along the south side of the large Veterans Administration Hospital. Turn right at this intersection onto KS 5 (which is also Muncie Road) and go two blocks to the entrance of Leavenworth National

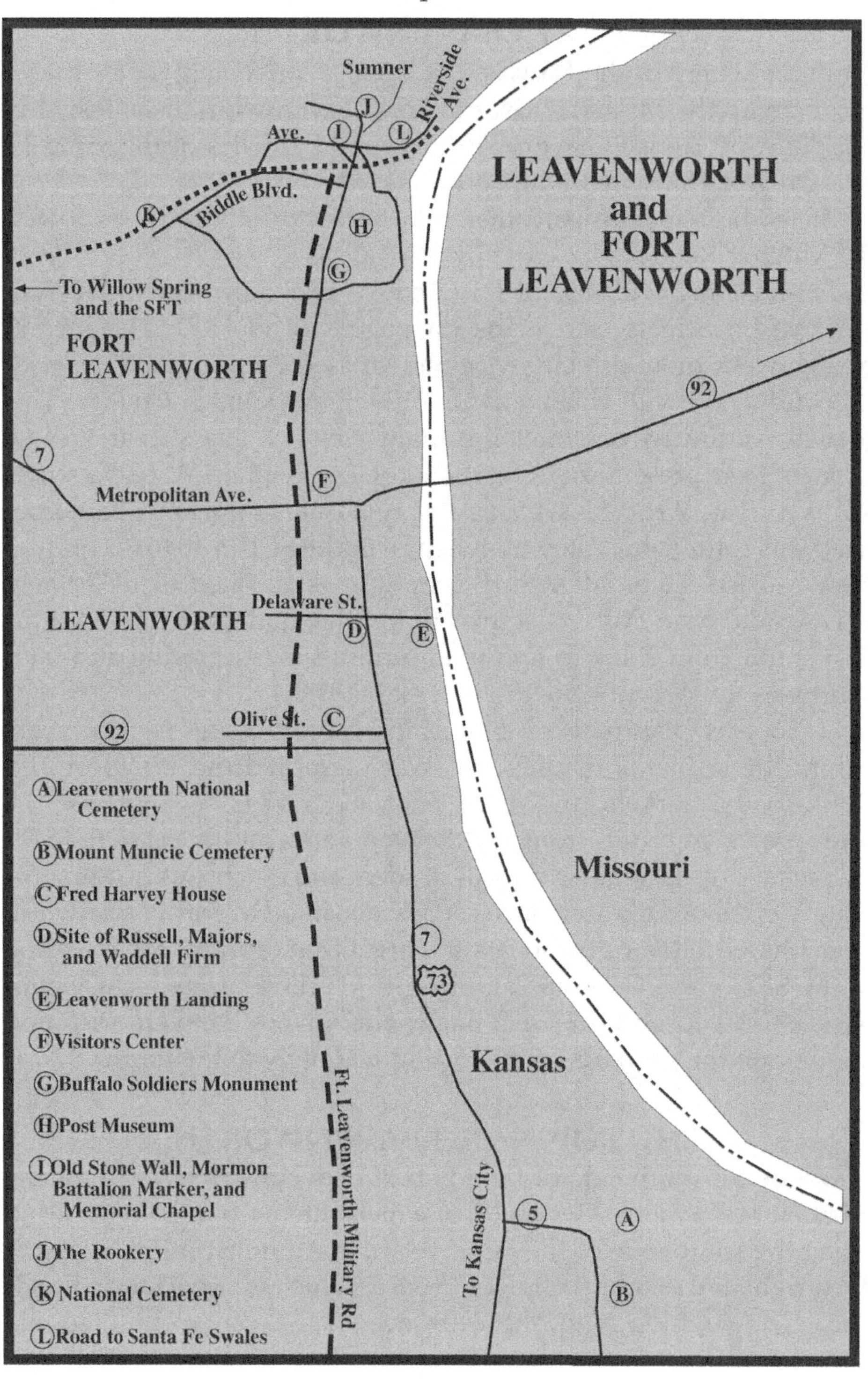
LEAVENWORTH
and
FORT
LEAVENWORTH
Sumner
Riverside Ave.
Ave.
Biddle Blvd.
To Willow Spring
and the SFT
FORT
LEAVENWORTH
Metropolitan Ave.
Delaware St.
LEAVENWORTH
Olive St.
Missouri
Kansas
To Kansas City
Ft. Leavenworth Military Rd
92
7
73
5
A Leavenworth National Cemetery
B Mount Muncie Cemetery
C Fred Harvey House
D Site of Russell, Majors, and Waddell Firm
E Leavenworth Landing
F Visitors Center
G Buffalo Soldiers Monument
H Post Museum
I Old Stone Wall, Mormon Battalion Marker, and Memorial Chapel
J The Rookery
K National Cemetery
L Road to Santa Fe Swales

Cemetery on the left (A on the map on page 78). (Note: This cemetery is distinct from the Fort Leavenworth National Cemetery on the fort grounds, described below.)

Here is buried William Sloan who, as a boy in the 1850s, accompanied his mother Eliza and sister Marion on several SFT crossings. True trail buffs, addicted to Marion Sloan Russell's memoirs *Land of Enchantment*, will want to visit the grave of her brother, who figured prominently in the narrative. He served as a corporal in the Civil War, which entitled him to be buried here, and he died at the neighboring Veterans Administration Hospital in 1917. Sloan's marker is in Section 30, Row 14, Grave 7, near the flagpole. (Directions to his sister Marion's grave west of Raton Pass near Stonewall, Colorado, are given later.)

Back at the cemetery entrance, turn left (east) on KS 5, which quickly curves to the right. Beyond the curve on the left (east), is the gate to Mt. Muncie Cemetery (B on the map on page 78). It is .4 mile between the gates of the two cemeteries. Enter and take the first lane to the right. The Fred Harvey family stone, the largest in the immediate vicinity, is on the left about 50 yards up this lane. The Harvey name is on the back of the stone and thus not visible from the road.

Beginning in the 1870s, Frederick Henry Harvey (1835-1901) began developing a chain of famous restaurants and hotels along the Santa Fe Railroad, the successor of the SFT. His splendid company encouraged tourists to travel the "new Santa Fe Trail" by rail. Harvey's name remains legendary in the Southwest, with much written about his career. We usually associate Harvey with the SFT, perhaps the Judy Garland movie helped do this. However, the first Harvey Houses were on the Kansas Pacific which followed the Smoky Hill Trail—one at Wallace KS and the other at Hugo CO.

Return to KS 7/US 73, turn right, and continue north into Leavenworth. Approaching the center of downtown, turn left (west) on Olive Street and go four blocks to the Fred Harvey House on the northeast corner of Olive and 7th Street (C on the map on page 78). The beautiful two-story mansion, once the residence of Harvey, now is a private residence but can be visited by appointment. Appointments can be arranged through Parker Carousels at 913 682 1331. A metal historical sign on the front lawn has a text concerning Harvey.

Again, return to KS 7/US 73 (that is, 4th Street) and turn left (north) toward downtown. On the northwest corner of 4th and Delaware Streets, is a two-story brick building now occupied by the Guarantee Land Tide Company. Originally, the freighting firm of Russell, Majors, and Waddell, whose association with the SFT is described under "Lexington," maintained general offices here in the late 1850s and 1860s (D on the map on page 78). Two plaques are attached to the side of the building facing 4th Street, one commemorating the freight company, the other its famous Pony Express line.

Drive east four blocks on Delaware toward the Missouri River to the Riverfront Community Center, and then turn right one block. On your left is a parking lot. This is the site of the Leavenworth Landing, where steamboats docked for the town of Leavenworth (E on the map on page 78). It has a nice view of the river and picnic facilities. In addition, there is an interpretive marker near the river, a good round map of the Leavenworth area, and some stylized cement sculptures of covered wagons.

Return to 4th Street (KS 7/US 73) and continue north until it ends at a T at Metropolitan Avenue. Turn left (west) and proceed to the entrance of Fort Leavenworth on the right.

FORT LEAVENWORTH

F. Main Entrance

Visitors enter the fort on Grant Avenue. On the right is the information building, where it is possible to obtain maps and a self-guiding tour booklet of the fort. Here, behind the building, is the official Kansas Historical Marker for Fort Leavenworth with reference to the SFT.

G. Buffalo Soldiers Monument

Continue on Grant to the new Buffalo Soldiers Monument on your right, an impressive monument not to be missed. The tenth U. S. Cavalry, or Buffalo Soldiers, was organized at the fort in 1866. These black soldiers saw extensive service at various locations along the trail.

H. Frontier Army Museum

Go north on Grant past the lakes to Reynolds Avenue and turn right one block to the Museum. Here are displayed objects of pioneer and army life, "emphasizing the drama of westward expansion." One of the largest collections of pioneer vehicles in the world can be seen, including a freight wagon and army vehicles of the type that traveled the SFT.

I. Old stone wall, Mormon Battalion marker and Memorial Chapel

Continue north on Grant to the intersection of Keamy Avenue. Here in a traffic circle is a statue of President Ulysses S. Grant. Behind it and across the street is a section of the Old Stone Wall, which formed part of the original defense line of the fort. Two plaques are mounted on it, one placed by the DAR. In addition, there is a Mormon Battalion marker at Kearny and Sumner Place nearby. The Memorial Chapel is just to the east of the Grant statue. The walls of this building, made of Kansas's stone, are lined with memorial plaques honoring soldiers killed in the line of duty on the western frontier.

A statue of a Buffalo Soldier in Ft. Leavenworth, Kansas.

J. The Rookery

One block northwest of Grant's statue at 12 Sumner is the Rookery. Constructed in 1832, this is the oldest building in Kansas, in use as the post headquarters during the heyday of the SFT. Rookeries are where eagles live; the post commander was a Colonel whose emblem of rank is an eagle. Another explanation for the "Rookery" name is provided by Leo Oliva who has written widely on Kansas forts. He says: "My understanding is that the building served briefly for the commanding officer until a new CO home was built next door, and the Rookery became the bachelor officers' quarters. It was at this time it became known as the Rookery (because the young lieutenants and maybe a captain or two made so much noise—like the nesting area for birds—a rookery; just as the bachelor officers' quarters at Fort Laramie was known as Old Bedlam)."

K. National Cemetery

Go west on Pope from Grant Avenue to Biddle Boulevard and the cemetery entrance. Civilians and soldiers killed on the SFT were buried here. Near the flagpole is a tall column over General Leavenworth's grave. Another interesting monument is the one for Col. Edward Hatch, once commander of the Department of New Mexico, who pursued Apaches led by Chief Victorio. Graves of Tom Custer (brother of Gen. George Armstrong Custer) and other soldiers killed at the Little Bighorn are also here. Ask at the cemetery visitors' center for the location of individual graves. It should be noted that the remains of soldiers originally buried at SFT Forts Harker, Larned, and Dodge, were removed to Fort Leavenworth National Cemetery after those posts were abandoned, as well as those from other frontier Kansas forts such as Hays and Wallace. Unfortunately, most of those remains were buried in common graves and marked "unknown." Fort Larned erected a plaque at the National Cemetery a few years ago, with a similar plaque at Fort Larned NHS, listing all the known military burials moved from Larned to Leavenworth.

L . Santa Fe Trail ruts and monuments

Beginning at Grant's statue, follow Riverside Avenue's loop down to the Missouri River. A deep rut running from what was once a boat landing on the river to the top of the hill is the track left by ox-drawn covered wagons. In the 1830s, the river swept along the base of the hill, and the landing was at the location of a present-day warehouse. Stone columns with brass plaques designating the Oregon and Santa Fe Trails are located at the top and bottom of the cut. Military supplies for most western military posts, until the construction of railroads, came through Fort Leavenworth via boats on the Missouri River and were freighted westward by wagons—millions of tons of freight traveled up this hill to supply troops in the field and at military posts along the Santa Fe, Oregon, California, and other trails.

A swale with notch ascending from the Missouri River at Ft. Leavenworth, Kansas.

After completing a tour of the Leavenworth area, return to Olathe via US 73 and KS 7 and pick up US 56 leading to Gardner.

Chapter 3
KANSAS EAST

GARDNER

On US 56 at 1 mile west of the junction with KS 7 are two houses on the right. The first is a two-story red brick structure and the second a long white bungalow. Just past the bungalow on the right side of the highway is an open field leading down to Cedar Creek, the site of a major SFT campground, Elm Grove. Originally an Indian campground, it was the location of George C. Sibley's "Caravan Grove." Elm Grove was long confused with Lone Elm, but we know now they were two distinct sites (see Crease 1991). The trail wound along the foot of the slope that rises to the present highway.

About .9 miles west of the creek, US 56 curves to the left. Here, 151st Street, really just a section line road, continues straight ahead. In the small triangle formed where the two roads split, is a DAR marker, which has been moved here from its original site 100 feet away.

A. Santa Fe Trail Monument

At the main intersection in the center of Gardner, turn right (north) off US 56 onto Elm Street, which has no street sign. Drive one block to the SFT monument in the schoolyard located on the northeast comer of Elm and Shawnee. This handsome marker with a bronze plaque is like the one in Olathe. Continue another block north on Elm to a fine Oregon Trail DAR marker on the right in the schoolyard.

The information kiosk near the junction of the SFT and Oregon Trails.

B. Junction of the Santa Fe and Oregon Trails

Two miles west of Gardner on U S 56 there is a small roadside park on the right (north). The historical markers in the park tell the story of the parting of the Santa Fe and Oregon Trails (**A**). This complex of markers sets the tone for the many other similar locations along the route of the SFT. Visitors here will know what to expect east and west of this spot. Just before the park there is a gravel road leading west. Continue on that road for about .25 mile past a farmhouse and row of trees on the right. The actual fork in the trails was about 200 yards to your right on the small rise. The Oregon Trail continued just north of west, while the SFT went west heading for Lanesfield.

C. Lanesfield DAR marker

To find the Lanesfield DAR marker, continue west on the gravel road past the fork in the trails to the next road to your left—Dillie Road. Drive south on Dillie Road for .5 mile to the old Lanesfield School on your left (**B**). There is a museum on the south side of the school, a DAR marker in the southwest corner of the grounds, and a patch of land being restored to a tallgrass prairie. Lanesfield School was placed on the National Register of Historic Places in 1988.

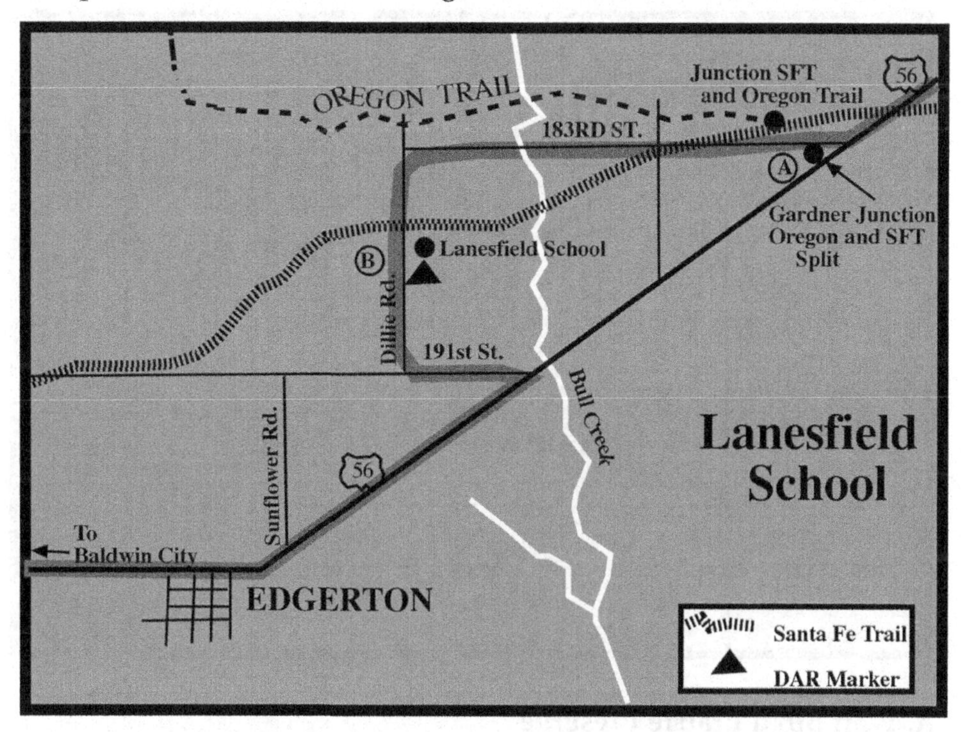

The SFT passed diagonally north of the Lanesfield School grounds from northeast to southwest heading toward the Narrows. Drive south on Dillie Road to the first intersection and turn right (west). Continue to the next corner and go left, returning to US 56 at Edgerton. Then go west on US 56 toward Baldwin City.

BALDWIN CITY

Just east of Baldwin City begins the Narrows, a ridge or divide separating the waters of Wakarusa River on the north from those of the Marias de Cygnes (pronounced locally Mara du Seen) on the south. Scarcely noticeable today, it is nevertheless an important divide since the Wakarusa River flows to the Kansas River, while the Marias de Cygnes flows into the Osage River. The SFT caravans kept to this ridge (this is very clear when you look closely at the included map) because it was the easiest way with no streams to cross, at least in dry weather. When it rained, wagons sunk to their axles in the deep mud.

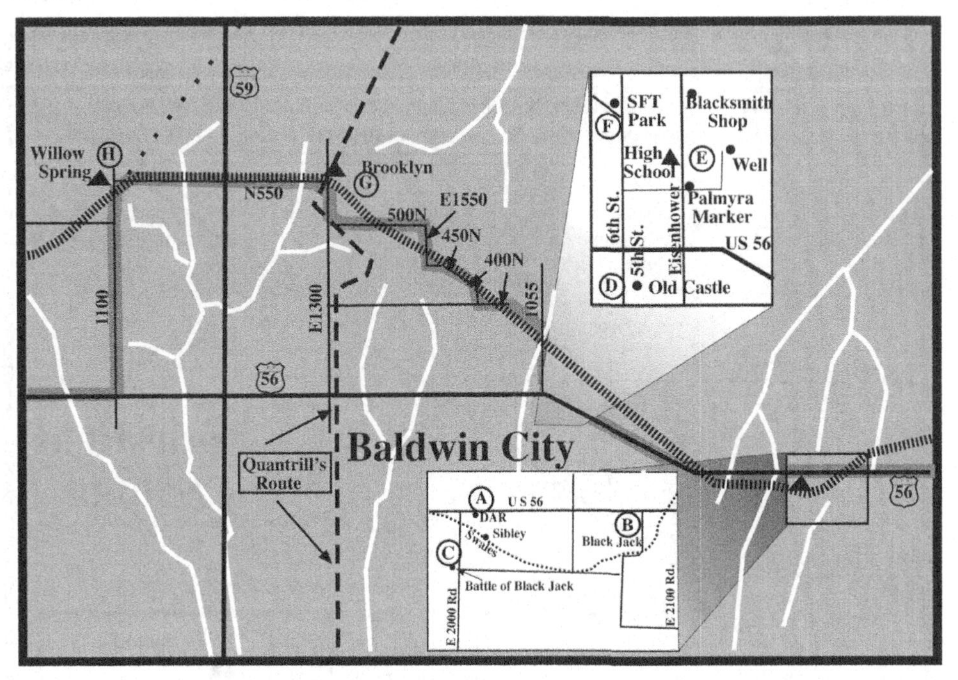

A. Ivan Boyd Prairie Preserve

On the south side of US 56 about 3 miles east of Baldwin City is the Ivan Boyd Prairie Preserve, a small roadside park near the beginning of the Narrows (**A**). Coming from the east, it is 2.8 miles from the intersection of US 56 and KS 33. A halfcircle drive enters from the highway at the east end of the park and exits at the west end. Near the entrance on the left is a Pioneer Meeting House of native logs, a replica dedicated in 1971. The meeting house is called the Black Jack Cabin and was built by members of the local Santa Fe Trail Historical Society.

To visit the site of old Black Jack return .7 miles to E2075 Rd., turn right and consult the inset map which can be found on the Baldwin City map (**B**).

THE VILLAGE OF BLACK JACK

There are many towns and villages along the Santa Fe Trail that owed their existence to the old road. The village of Black Jack was built directly on the SFT and was meant to serve the needs of the traders using the road. The first settlers came here in 1852, two years before the Kansas-Nebraska Act permitted white settlement in Kansas.

The early settlers built log cabins and eventually, in 1857, formed a company and petitioned the government to be a town. The town's main street was the Santa Fe Trail. (See inset map on the Baldwin City map). The name Black Jack came from the nearby crossing of Captain's Creek, which was lined with Black Jack oaks.

Black Jack cemetery.

The town originally was a rest stop and repair stop on the SFT. One old timer recalled there were two blacksmith shops, two stores, a hotel, a wagon shop, a stage barn, a doctor's office, and a cemetery. It also had a tavern, boarding house, and two churches.

The villagers were antislavery and this position brought about two raids by pro-slavery gangs. Dick Agarese led the first, in May 1863. The second occurred in August 1863 and this gang's leader was the notorious William Anderson. Both raids saw the town's stores broken into and the citizens robbed.

By the end of the Civil War, traffic had slowed on the SFT here and in 1866 the opening of the railroad to Junction City spelled the end for Black Jack. The SFT had remained its only source of income.

[Information for this sidebar came to us from Roger Boyd of Baldwin City. He thought the information originally came from Mrs. Van Tries whose ancestors lived in Black Jack from the town's beginning.]

There are three markers here. One, an official Kansas Historical Marker, describes the Battle of Black Jack, a clash that took place .25 mile south of the park. This small clash, which occurred on June 2, 1856, was the first battle between free-state and pro-slave militia forces, an early prelude to the Civil War, sometimes called "the first battle of the Civil War." By this interpretation, the Civil War began on the SFT. John Brown was the leader of the free-state forces which defeated the pro-slavery unit led by Henry Clay Pate. The second marker, a DAR marker for the SFT, is located nearby. The late Amelia Betts and Katharine Kelley, dedicated women of nearby Baldwin City, painted the worn, incised inscription on this marker (and the other six DAR markers in Douglas County) so that it is easily read by visitors. The third marker is a handsome metal one for "Black Jack Park," with reference to the SFT.

If you wish to visit the site of the Battle of Black Jack, continue on the gravel road along the west boundary of the park about .12 mile to the entrance to Battle of Black Jack Park on the right (**C**). This park has blow-by-blow markers allowing you to follow the course of the battle.

B. Trail Swales

Enter the gravel road that leads south from the highway along the west boundary of the roadside park. Behind the row of trees along the back of the park is an eighteen-acre field containing fine traces of the SFT, seen as wide swales and ridges in the sod. They are directly behind the large wooden sign facing the gravel road.

The ease of viewing the swales depends on the time of year. In April, the dead grass is burned off, and they are clearly visible in the blackened field. Later in the summer when vegetation is thickest, they are difficult to see, but on the ridge to the right rear of the sign they show as Indentations against the sky. During June, wild strawberries can sometimes be found growing in the depressions. Wagon travelers mentioned their pleasure in collecting the fruit in this area.

Swales at Black Jack Park.

The best way to experience this site is to leave your car at the roadside park and walk south over a small bridge, from which you can ascend the hill. At the top are two modern stone monuments commemorating the Sibley survey of 1825, the easternmost with an inscription.

MEASURING THE LAND

Accurate records of where the Santa Fe Trail crossed Kansas are available as the result of the Public Land Survey System. Established by law in 1785, most land transactions in the American West are covered by this law. A very brief description of the survey system follows. Note that this system did not help locate the SFT in Missouri because the surveys were completed in that state before 1821, the date the SFT began.

The Kansas-Nebraska Act of May 1854 defined the boundaries of Kansas and Nebraska. To survey these bounds and, later, the interior lines, required that an initial point be established. This would be a spot where all surveys in Kansas, Nebraska, eastern Colorado, eastern Wyoming, and part of South Dakota are referenced. It began on the Kansas-Nebraska boundary, the fortieth parallel, called the baseline. Surveyors located where this parallel met the Missouri River, the eastern boundary of Kansas. They measured west from that point 108 miles and established the new initial point, the Sixth Prime Meridian, for all subsequent surveys.

To save time in the surveying process a line, First Guide Meridian East, was surveyed so the lands in very eastern Kansas could quickly be surveyed, as settlers were impatient to get their land. From that guide meridian, land was surveyed into six-mile squares called "townships." All townships surveyed were designated by numbers from the established point on the fortieth parallel, with the first row of townships across northern Kansas designated as Township 1 South and those in Nebraska designated Township 1 North. They were identified by "ranges" east and west of the Sixth Prime Meridian, with those townships east of the line designated as Range 1 East and those west of the line designated Range 1 West. These townships were further subdivided into thirty-six one-mile squares called sections, each containing 640 acres, numbered from 1 to 36.

Township Range

6	5	4	3	2	1
7	8	9	10	11	12
18	17	16	15	14	13
19	20	21	22	23	24
30	29	28	27	26	25
31	32	33	34	35	36

Section Divisions

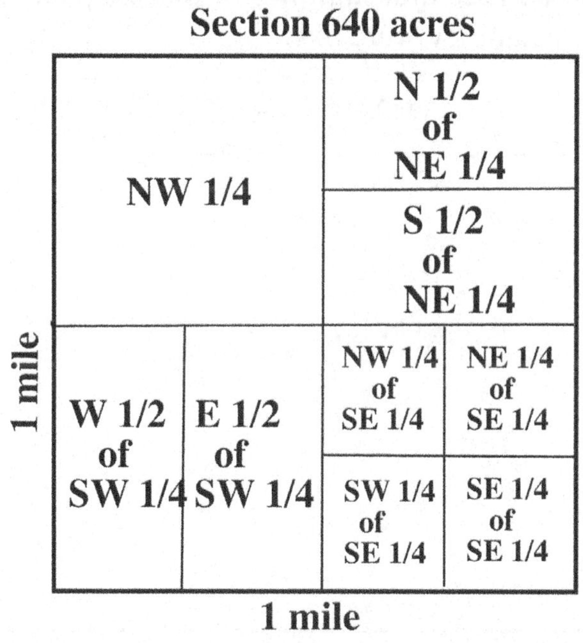

Section 640 acres

NW 1/4

N 1/2 of NE 1/4

S 1/2 of NE 1/4

W 1/2 of SW 1/4

E 1/2 of SW 1/4

NW 1/4 of SE 1/4

NE 1/4 of SE 1/4

SW 1/4 of SE 1/4

SE 1/4 of SE 1/4

1 mile

1 mile

Surveyors walked and measured every section line twice, making detailed notes on their observations.

To measure distance they used a "chain." These chains were 66 feet long and had 100 links (80 chains equal one mile). When surveyors crossed a creek or the Santa Fe Trail, they noted that fact and these notes are available today. There is part of one such chain on exhibit at the Arrow Rock State Historic Site museum, which you may have noted.

The field notes tell us where the SFT crossed a section line. The plat maps were later (later may have been 30 or 40 years) drawn based on these initial observations. The person drawing the plat map only had the field notes to rely on so the lines he drew showing the route between the section lines may not be accurate.

When using this guide you will read about "crossing markers," markers set precisely on the points the surveyor marked when he was in the field. You may or may not see the SFT at these points but we assure you that the surveyor did see the spot where the SFT crossed the section line.

Included here are examples of plat maps and field notes so you can see what they were like.

Plat Map 15 south 20 east.

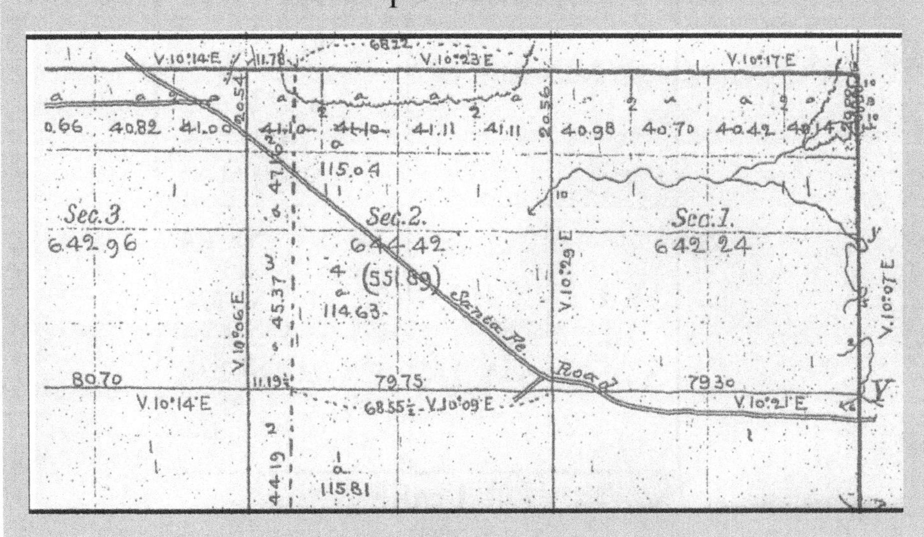

Field Note.

Township 15 S. R 20 E.

Chains

62.00 Road from Santafe to Westport

80.54 Intersected Northern Boundary of Town-
-ship 1.30 chs East of the corner to Sections 2, 3, 34, & 35, from which corner I ran
South on a true line between Sections 2 & 3

The field work was led by surveyor Thomas Connelly and was begun October 20, 1855 and completed December 12, the same year. The plat map was done in October, 1859, apparently in Nebraska City. We will lead you through the process. Connelly started in the southwest corner of section 2 and went north between sections 2 and 3. He noted the 'Road from Santafe to Westport" at 62.00 chains from that corner. Sixty two times 66 feet (a chain is 66 feet in length) is 4092 feet. The Road, then, crossed the section line 4092 feet north of that corner and you can go to that starting point and go north to find the exact spot where the SFT crossed.

Today's road does not follow the route of the SFT as shown on the plat map. Highway US 56 matches the plat in the southeast corner but goes a liitle south of the original mapped route.

Almost every property today is described using the township/range system. Roger Boyd in Baldwin City provided us with the property description for Black Jack Park also known as the Ivan L. Boyd Memorial Prairie Preserve. The deed description is as follows: The West Half of the West Half of the North Half of the Northwest Quarter of the Section Seven, Township Fifteen South, Range Twenty-one East containing 20.0 acres more or less.

C. Official Kansas Historical Marker, "Baldwin"

This marker, referring to the SFT and local history, is located on US 56 at a turnout on the north (right) side of the highway about 2 miles west of the roadside park as you approach the limits of Baldwin City.

D. Old Castle

On 5th Street, five blocks south of US 56 in Baldwin City is the Old Castle (**D**). Built in 1858 during trail days, this three-story native stone structure was the initial building of the first college in Kansas Territory. Now a museum, it is open afternoons. A bronze marker in front has an interesting relief of a SFT wagon.

The first building of the first college in Kansas located in Baldwin City.

E. Palmyra Town Site

On the northern edge of Baldwin City, is the Palmyra Town site (**E**). Palmyra, founded in 1854 near the beginning of the Narrows, was known as a "repair stop" during the latter days of the SFT. Here blacksmiths and wheelrights maintained shops for the benefit of travelers. After entering Baldwin City on US 56, turn north (right) on Eisenhower Street (a sign here points to the high school) and go one block to the first intersection. A "Palmyra" sign on the northeast corner indicates the center of the old town (**E**). The SFT passed through the grounds of the high school on the left.

At this intersection turn right (east) and go one block, then turn left (north). In the middle of the block on the right, is a modern blue house, the site of Palmyra's Santa Fe Hotel, which burned a few years ago. Continue past it to the sign on the right marking the Palmyra Well, a watering place for Santa Fe caravans. The restored well now has a new base and old bucket and hand crank with a new sign describing the purpose and depth of the well and when it was used.

Return to Eisenhower Street and turn right (north). About one-half block beyond the end of the high school parking lot is a metal sign on the east (right) side of the road indicating the site of the original Palmyra Blacksmith Shop. To view the route of the Narrows from this location, climb the grassy ridge behind the sign and look back toward the southeast, in the direction of the roadside park and ruts visited earlier.

Palmyra well.

Go back south about a block to the junior high school, and note the markers on the grounds in front of the school. One is a DAR marker, moved here from the site of the blacksmith shop, while another is a Palmyra historical sign, referring to the SFT, installed through the efforts of the late Amelia Betts and Katharine Kelley.

From here at Palmyra the SFT headed in a northwesterly direction to present-day Trail Park. To get there, return via Eisenhower Street to Quayle St. and turn west (right). Go west two blocks to the intersection of 6th Street (also marked County Road 1055). Turn north on 6th and go .5 mile to Trail Park.

F. Trail Park and DAR Monument

Trail Park is a small park on the west (left) side of County Road 1055 where County Road 358N comes in from the left (**F**). Originally, the

DAR monument here had a fine bronze plaque like the ones in Olathe and Gardner, but it was stolen long ago. In its place, the local Santa Fe Trail Historical Society put a marble replica of the plaque on the monument in 1969. Recently, two new SFT historical signs have also been added to the park. The gravel road that intersects with County Road 1055 and runs along the southwest side of the park is the actual route of the SFT. Follow this road west about .75 miles to the point where it curves to the left. On the right, just before the curve, is a farm, and in the open areas around it are traces of SFT swales. The swales just beyond the curve have grown up in trees, as the owner did not want to risk damaging the swales by mowing over them.

The marker replacing the stolen DAR marker.

G. Brooklyn

After the gravel road curves to the left, continue on it about .5 mile, turn right (north) on County Road 1600E and climb the steep hill. Then take County Road N450 to the left (west), and you are now back on the SFT. Then descend into a small valley. At about .5 mile, turn right on County Road 1550E and drive .25 mile to County Road 500N, then turn left (west). Continue west for about .25 miles and there is a sign on your right identifying the area as Hickory Point. It was not an organized town but a loose community. Look ahead and back to the southeast, which will provide you with an impressive view of the "Narrows." You are on top of that ridge that the SFT traveled. Between this sign and the next intersection are some SFT swales out in the field to the left. Follow this road west a little over a mile to County Road 1400E and turn right (north).

Drive .5 mile to an intersection. At this point, you are a few hundred feet west of the old community of Brooklyn (**G**). Here there is a DAR marker and another for the Quantrill Raiders Trail. On the morning of August 21, 1863, William Quantrill and a gang of 450 bushwhackers entered Lawrence and spent four hours burning, looting, and killing two hundred men and boys. Quantrill then left for Missouri through Brooklyn, destroying it as well.

From this corner drive west on County Road 550N for 2.5 miles. At 1.5 miles, you will cross over US 59. The trail will be on your immediate right as you drive. At a point, .5 mile farther west is Willow Springs (**H**). Col. Stephen Watts Kearny passed through here in August 1845 on his return from a 2,200-mile trip over the Plains. From here, he decided to head directly back to Fort Leavenworth instead of following the longer route of the SFT. In June 1846, he sent out a party from Fort Leavenworth to blaze this trail in reverse for the use of his Army of the West and the Mormon Battalion, making it the principal Military Road. There is a DAR marker and an information sign.

H. Sibley Hill

From Willow Springs drive south .5 mile and turn right (west), then continue 5.5 miles on County Road 500N. At the corner of County Road 1029 and County Road 500N, turn left (south). There is a DAR marker 1 mile after the turn. This is where the SFT crossed the road coming from Willow Springs heading toward Flag Springs.

Continue south to US 56 and turn right at the old Globe Rock Store. From there drive west on US 56 and just past E 400 Rd. to a rounded hill with a tall red and white relay tower on your right (north). The deteriorating remains of a house can be seen just east of the hill, back 200 yards from US 56. This is the old Simmons House, built in 1870. Although according to tradition the house was a stage station on the SFT, the SFT had stopped serving this area several years before 1870. The very next road is E 300 Road and turn right (north). Go 250 yards and look for the single swale to the right.

Willow Springs.

Continue west on US 56 to E150 and turn right. Drive 150 yards north and look across the ravine to the west and you will see several sets of swales ascending the far hill. Continue west .5 miles to E100 rd. On the south (left) side of US 56 is another DAR marker, this one telling you that the SFT crossed the highway here headed for Overbrook

OVERBROOK

Continue west on US 56 toward Overbrook. As you approach the town, notice the fine sheet-iron silhouettes on the right side of the road, showing a SFT caravan as it might have looked 150 years ago. Ed Harmison, the local trail expert, is responsible for installing these dramatic images and convincing the town of Overbrook to change the name of a street to Santa Fe Avenue since it was directly on the old trail.

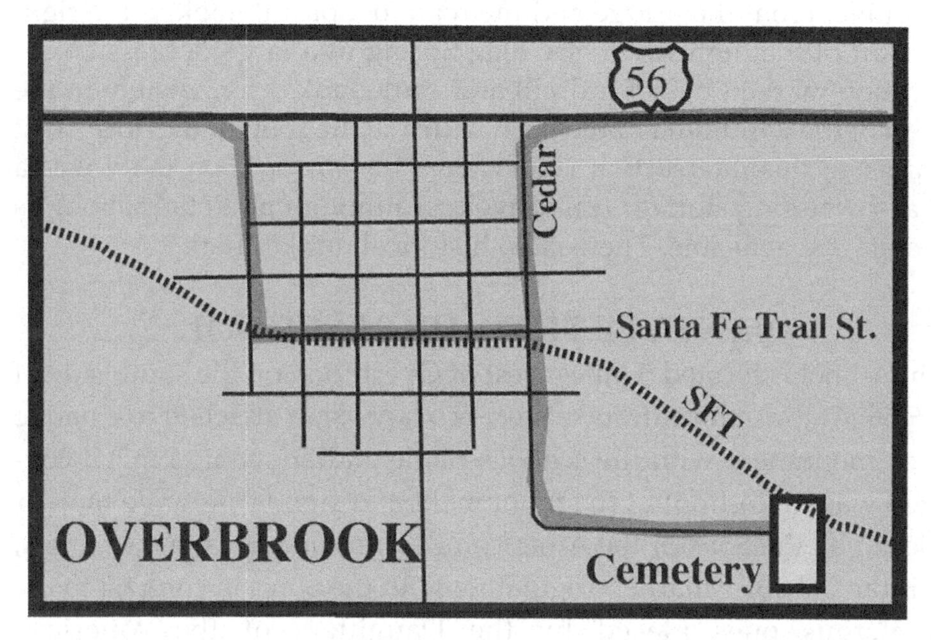

The trail approached present-day Overbrook on the south side of US 56. About 1.5 miles east of town was Rock Springs Campground. Another mile beyond that the trail passed through the current cemetery. To get to the cemetery, take the first street to the left as you enter Overbrook, which is Cedar, and go south several blocks. As the street turns left toward the cemetery, there are several houses. Under one of these houses is an old spring used by traders.

A short distance beyond, drive straight ahead after the lane enters the cemetery gate. The graves on the immediate left lie in the faint ruts of the SFT, which heads toward the old spring. At the back of the cemetery where the gravel road turns left, is a 1.5-foot gray wooden post in the ground marking the center of the trail ruts.

From the cemetery return to US 56, and continue several blocks west to the intersection of Overbrook's one main commercial street. Turn left (south) to the DAR marker in front of the town post office. Here the city street called Santa Fe Trail is the route of the trail.

Continue west on US 56 and about 1 mile from Overbrook watch to the right for a tall water tower on legs. Just beyond it cross a bridge. From the bridge and the road just past it, look to the right (north) of the highway to see Flag Spring in a large depression, its location marked by a windmill and cattle tank. Immediately to the west of the windmill is a red barn with a white roof. In the northwest corner of this intersection is a swale. This spring reportedly was a major watering stop for trail travelers, although no details about its history are available. There is no historical marker here.

SANTA FE TRAIL HIGH SCHOOL

The school is located 5 miles west of Overbrook on the south side of US 56. At the main entrance, there is a large sign attached to a native rock monument with the school's name and above it, a metal covered wagon. In front of the monument and sign is a granite marker placed by the Sons of the American Revolution. As far as we know, it is the only SFT marker originating with the Sons, in contrast to the numerous ones placed by the Daughters of the American Revolution. The school grounds lie atop the ruts of the trail.

McGEE-HARRIS STAGE STATION AT 110 MILE CREEK

Continue west from the high school on US 56 to an intersection with a sign pointing left (south) to Osage State Fishing Lake. (A cement silo is on the southeast corner.) Drive south .2 mile to SFT swales in an unplowed field on the left (east), which show as indentations on the skyline. Here the trail, coming from the school grounds, is going toward the crossing at 110 Mile Creek.

From here, take the road heading west, which goes along the north side of the lake to US 75. As you are about to enter US 75, pause and look northwest across the highway to see the remains of the McGee-Harris Stage Station in the distance. The remains are about .5 mile away.

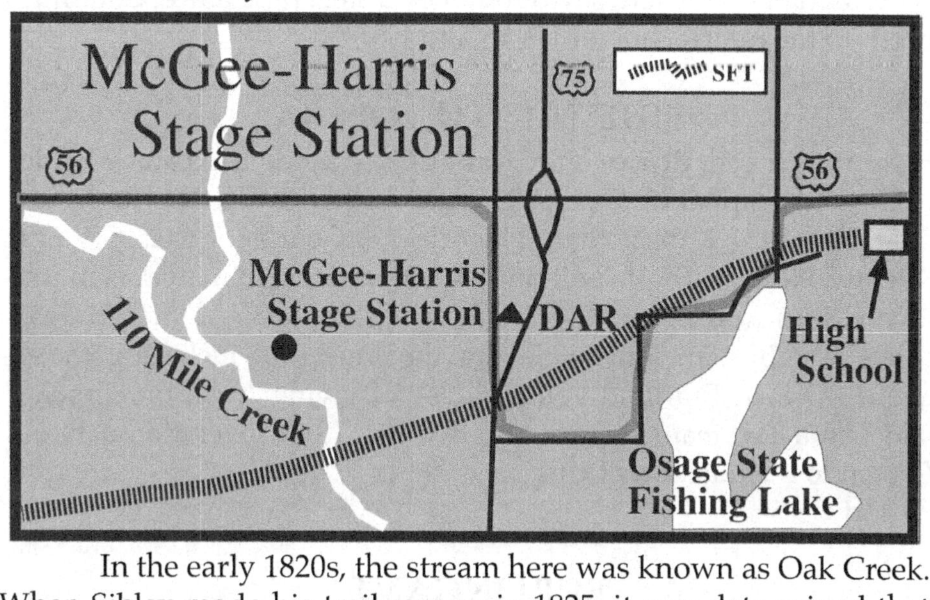

In the early 1820s, the stream here was known as Oak Creek. When Sibley made his trail survey in 1825, it was determined that the crossing was 110 miles from Fort Osage on the Missouri River (the start of the survey). Consequently, the stream soon became known as 110 Mile Creek, retaining that name to the present day.

About 1854, Fry McGee, an early proslavery settler in Kansas Territory, who had been over the Oregon Trail and back, settled with his family on the east bank of the creek at the SFT crossing. He farmed, built a toll bridge, and provided overnight accommodations for wagon travelers and stage passengers. The bridge toll was 25 cents per wagon, and in the late 1850s the coach for Santa Fe stopped twice a month.

Subsequently, William Harris married McGee's eldest daughter, who had the unlikely name of America Puss. Harris then built a residence and store adjacent to his in-laws, and after McGee's death in 1861 operated the stage station until the SFT closed here in 1866 (see Stocking 1971). Today, one major building of stone and frame remains, apparently a residence and station. Ruins of other structures nearby may include the blacksmith shop that was part of the original complex. Traces of the trail are visible at the creek crossing about 100 yards west.

Turn right (north) on US 75, and go a short distance to a DAR marker on the left, surrounded by a steel pipe fence. Continue north to the intersection of US 56 and US 75.

SIDE TRIP TO TOPEKA

From this intersection of US 56 and US 75, a side trip can be made to the state capital of Topeka 15 miles north on US 75. The headquarters of the Kansas State Historical Society is at 6425 SW 6th Avenue. Here SFT buffs will find excellent research materials in the archives, as well as rare books and early newspapers. Superb historical exhibits are on display in the museum, including those about the SFT. Featured is the oldest surviving Atchison, Topeka and Santa Fe steam engine, used in the 1880s over Raton Pass. Return to the junction of US 75 and US 56.

BURLINGAME

At 2.5 miles beyond the McGee-Harris Stage Station, US 56 leads to the town of Scranton. The SFT passed through its southern limits, and formerly there was a sign on the outskirts that greeted visitors with the words "Welcome to Scranton on the Santa Fe Trail," but it has long since disappeared. In the center of town, turn left at the first street past the post office (Boone Street) and go one block to Jones Park on the right, which has a DAR marker moved here in the 1970s.

Five miles beyond Scranton, US 56 reaches the edge of Burlingame. Just after the highway passes under a railroad trestle, cross a bridge over Switzler Creek. Here was a major trail crossing. Originally called Bridge Creek, the creek was later named for John Switzler, who built a log toll bridge at this point in 1847. Switzler had married an Indian woman and thus became a member of her tribe, allowing him to circumvent the prohibition on white settlement.

Burlingame's main street sits directly on the Santa Fe Trail. Photo courtesy of Kansas State Historical Society.

After crossing the highway bridge, Santa Fe Avenue leads two blocks to the center of town. Just past the bridge, there is a stone house on the left that was used during trail days. Burlingame claims to be the only town in Kansas whose main street was once a part of the SFT, and on it are numerous businesses named for the trail. The community was founded in 1857 as Council City and later renamed for Anson Burlingame, a famous minister to China and an anti-slavery advocate. It is said blacksmiths here shod thousands of oxen and mules destined for New Mexico. In 1869, tracks of the Santa Fe Railroad arrived here, and Burlingame now calls itself the place where "Trail Meets Rail."

DAR marker honoring Fannie Geiger Thompson who suggested marking the old trails.

In the center of Burlingame, US 56 reaches a main intersection and turns left (south). Instead of turning, continue straight ahead one block on Santa Fe Avenue (which is also KS 31) to a schoolyard on the left. In the northeast corner of the yard, is a special DAR marker honoring Fannie Geiger Thompson, the woman who initiated the DAR marking of the SFT in 1906.

From Fannie Thompson's marker, continue west on KS 31 about 3 miles to the bridge over Dragoon Creek. According to Stocking (Stocking 1971), the creek was named by a Lieutenant Fields, who brought a company of dragoons (mounted infantry) over the SFT in 1852. Cross the bridge and go 1.5 miles to a DAR marker, next to a wire fence on the north (right) side of the road, commemorating the nearby Dragoon Creek Crossing. The trail here was actually another branch road leading down from Fort Leavenworth to join the main SFT not far to the south.

From the DAR marker, look across the road to the southeast, and in a field about 100 yards from the pavement, you will see the ruins of the Havanna Stage Station. German and French settlers founded the small community of Havanna in 1858. In addition to the stage station, there was a store and hotel, both of which have disappeared. To reach the site, return east .2 miles to a primitive road that leads to an old cattle-loading chute next to the highway. Park here. Next to the chute is a fence and beyond that a field. Toward the back of the field are the fine limestone walls of the station reaching up to roof level, often obscured by brush and trees in summer. Behind it is a more recent weathered gray barn, and to the left rear is a red barn with a tin roof. Both are easily seen from the road and will serve as landmarks to find the station. The Flint Hills Chapter of the SFTA has placed a nice interpretive marker at the site.

Return to the DAR marker and continue west on KS 31 another .2 mile to a wide highway maintenance pullout, that extends along the north (right) side of the road. Recently there have been piles of gravel and dirt and a black portable water tank on legs in this long pullout, but these features can change. At the back of the pullout, in the field just across the wire fence, surrounded by a pipe railing, is the grave of Pvt. Samuel Hunt of Kentucky, who died on the SFT in 1835. The information on the modern gravestone was supplied by the War Department when a new marker was installed a century after Hunt's death.

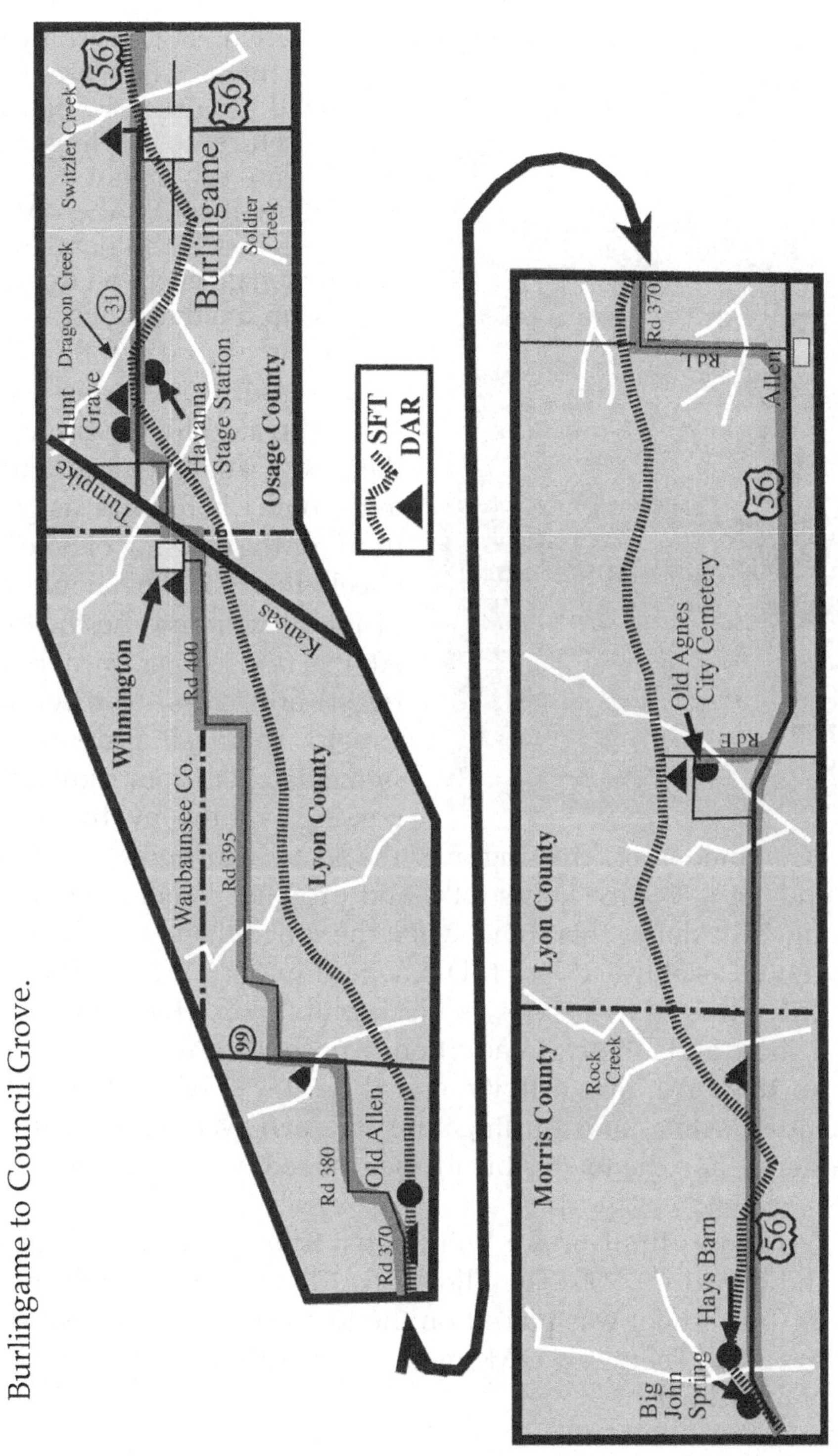

Burlingame to Council Grove.

From Private Hunt's grave, you have two choices. You can opt to follow the trail west by way of gravel roads, which are well maintained but require caution if it has rained recently. Or you can opt to return to Burlingame, where you can rejoin US 56 and follow it south, then west until you reach the hamlet of Allen, then go north on Road L to pick up the trail again.

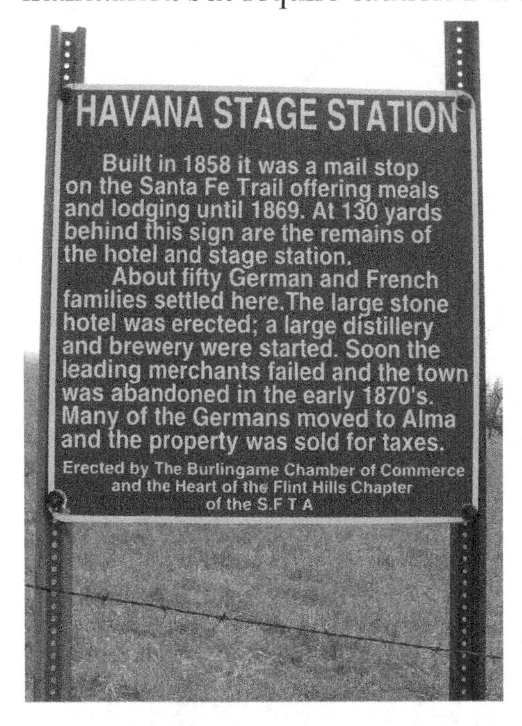

If you choose to follow the gravel-road route, drive west from Private Hunt's grave to the next road, Crawford. Turn left (south) here, and as you head for the crossing of Soldier Creek, the trail ruts should be visible as you descend the hill. At the first corner turn right (west) and cross over Soldier Creek. The trail crossing is immediately to your right after passing over the low bridge.

Continue west (crossing over the Kansas Turnpike) until the road ends in a T. Turn left (south) and proceed .1 mile, then turn west again. Along this road was the once-thriving town of Wilmington, established by H. D. Shepard in 1856. At one time, it had thirty houses, two stores, a blacksmith shop, two doctors, a wagon shop, and a hotel. In addition, a post office was established here in 1858. All this activity ended in 1879, when the MAB (Manhattan, Alma, and Burlingame) Railroad was built north of Wilmington, and the town's businesses moved north to be near the tracks.

At about .4 mile is the Wilmington School, which opened in 1870 and closed in 1950. The Flint Hills Chapter of the SFTA now owns it. This school was placed on the Register of Historic Kansas Places in 2008. There is a DAR marker and an interpretive sign in front of the school.

The Wilmington School was built
on the Santa Fe Trail.

After leaving the Wilmington School, turn south. At County Road 400, turn right (west). Continue on County Road 400 2 miles to an intersection. The SFT crossed the road just south of this intersection. Turn left (south) here and continue .5 mile to the next corner, then turn right on County Road 395, following it west for 4 miles. The SFT is almost directly under the road here.

Turn left (south) and drive .5 mile, then turn west again on County Road 390. About 1 mile straight ahead is KS 99, where you turn left (south).

At .8 mile, there is a DAR marker on your right, before you cross Elm Creek. This is where an Overland Stage Station was established in 1855 by Jacob Hall. Continue past the DAR Marker and then turn right (west) to cross over Elm Creek. As you drive west on County Road 380, you see the William Burch "dug-out" on the right side of the road. In 1874, Burch created a home in the ground here. He first dug a hole and built the walls, then filled in the hole and built a stone arched roof over the dirt, and, finally, excavated the dirt again.

Continue past the "dug-out" to the next intersection and turn left (south). Drive south about .7 miles and take the road approaching from the right on the diagonal, Rd. 371. You will come to One Hundred Forty Two Mile Creek, which is the distance from Fort Osage as measured by George Sibley in 1825. In 1854, the original town of Allen was sited on the east side of the creek by Charles Hall Withington, station agent for Waldo, Hall & Co. stage and mail service in Council Grove for previous two years. He operated a stage station at Allen and served as first postmaster. He made six or seven one-room additions to his original cabin, which he rented to travelers along the trail. A saloon and store quickly followed nearby. Withington built a toll bridge over 142 Mile Creek.

The William Burch dugout.

Although Withington was a free-stater, elected as such to territorial legislature but not seated because proslavers controlled the "bogus legislature, the town was robbed and burned by "Free Staters" in 1856. Later, the rebuilt town had a blacksmith shop with ten forges where repairs were made on trail wagons. The wooden toll bridge, located about 150 feet downstream from the present bridge, had a fee of 25 cents per wagon. It is claimed that a primitive sail-driven "wind wagon" crossed this bridge in 1859. The wagon had a sail which provided power and there was a tiller to turn the wheels for steering. The wind wagon allowed forward movement under a stiff breeze. In 1862 Bloody Bill Anderson's proslavery gang destroyed part of Old Allen, set fire to Withington's home and store, and would have killed Withington had not William Quantrill intervened and saved Withington's life.

Old Allen moved to its present location on US 56 (2.5 miles south) in 1886 when the railroad bypassed it.

KANSAS EAST

As you leave the site of Old Allen, there is a DAR marker on the west side of 142 Mile Creek. At the intersection with Road L, turn left (south) and drive to Allen. At Allen, on US 56, turn right (west) and go 6 miles to Road E. Turn right (north) at Road E and drive about 1.8 miles to the Agnes City Cemetery on your left. A DAR marker is in the cemetery, which is all that remains of Agnes City.

It was near this location where Judge A. I. Baker was murdered by Bloody Bill Anderson in 1862. Anderson stole some horse earlier that year and Judge Baker issued a warrant for his arrest. Anderson bided his time but eventually ambushed Baker at Baker's store. This was not a case of free state versus pro-slavery but a simple case of murder by the thug Bill Anderson.

Return south to US 56, and then turn right (west).

Continue to the next road (Road 200) and turn right again. A short distance on the right (.2 mile) is another DAR marker. The trail crossed in this vicinity as it headed to Council Grove. Return to US 56 and turn right toward Council Grove.

On your left along US 56, you will see on the hill black metal silhouettes of "Indians on the Move," placed by the Community Arts Council of Council Grove. Unique silhouettes mark all four highways into Council Grove. The Flint Hills Chapter of the Santa Fe Trail Association is also very active in locating sites, restoring buildings, and protecting the trail in this area.

Approaching Council Grove, travelers enter the region of the Flint Hills and the prairie grasslands. Here is one of the largest remaining tracts of tallgrass prairie (consisting mainly of bluestem grass) in the Midwest (actually, in the world). In trail days leaves of the bluestem grew 3 feet tall, and the seed stems reached 8 feet. In 1846, Susan Magoffin compared the grass to "a waving sea of green" (Magoffin 1982).

At 1 mile from Council Grove, turn off US 56 into the Morris County Fairgrounds. Big John Spring is located under the berm on the south side of US 56 here. Big John Walker, a member of the Sibley survey team, discovered the spring, no longer visible, in 1827. The explorer John Charles Fremont stopped here in July 1844, as did Stephen Watts Kearny and his army in 1846.

Continue driving in the fairgrounds until you see a beautiful large, stone barn built in 1871 by Seth Hays, Council Grove's first white settler, it is on the National Register of Historic Places. The Flint Hills Chapter of the SFTA is supervising the barn's restoration.

Return to US 56 and continue west toward Council Grove.

COUNCIL GROVE

Council Grove, on the Neosho River, is one of the most historic places on the SFT. It was a natural stop on the route to New Mexico, well watered with plenty of pasture and timber. Past this point no hardwood trees grew on the plains so spare axles were cut along the Neosho and stored under the wagons for later use. Here caravans also organized their military defenses, for they were now on the edge of Indian country. Indians in this part of Kansas weren't hostile until provoked but travelers perceived a threat here. Modern visitors should read Josiah Gregg's description of Council Grove during the heyday of the Santa Fe trade (Gregg 1990).

Commissioner George Sibley named the site in 1825 when he signed a treaty with the Osage Indians guaranteeing safe passage for wagon trains and providing a right of way to Santa Fe. During the Mexican War, the army built a wagon repair depot here. A few years later, when stagecoach service began on the SFT; the firm of Waldo, Hall and Company operated a station, shops, and corrals.

Much of the traffic on this portion of the SFT ended about 1866 with the building of the Kansas Pacific Railroad 50 miles to the north. From Junction City, the railhead moved westward to Ellsworth in 1867 and Hays later in 1867, From Junction City freight went by wagon to Lost Spring or the Walnut Creek Crossing. At either location, the new road would connect with the SFT.

The following places can be located on the included map.

A. Council Oak Stump

On the right just beyond the junction of Main and 3rd Streets, a jagged stump is all that remains of the famous Council Oak, which blew down in 1958. The tree was purported to be the one under which Sibley signed his treaty with the Osage.

Indians. The "stump shrine" is now covered by a roof and surrounded by an iron fence. An interpretive historical sign, a special DAR marker, and the Registered National Historic Landmark plaque for Council Grove are also at the site.

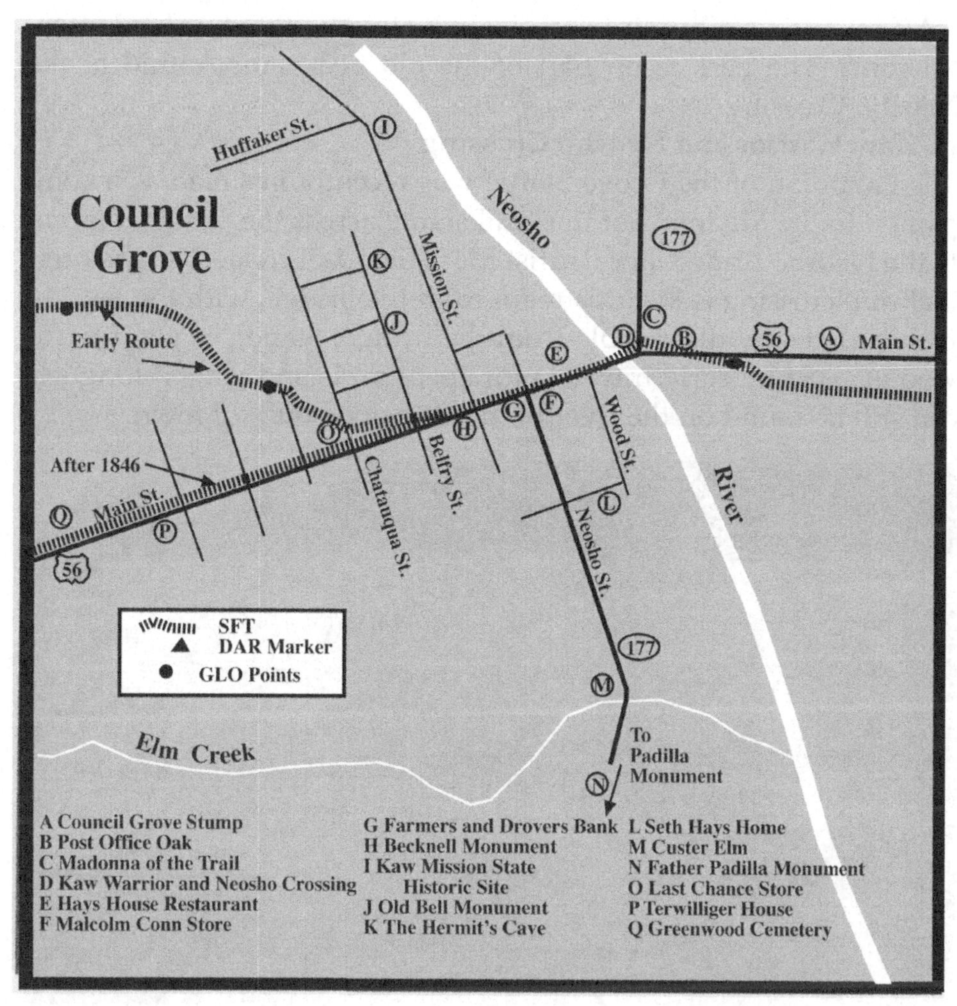

B. Post Office Oak

Located on Main Street one and a half blocks past the Council Oak stump on the right (north) is Post Office Oak. SFT travelers are said to have left letters in a crevice at the bottom of the tree, which were picked up and carried back to the States by returning caravans. This is likely more legend than fact. A nice museum is located behind the stump, all that is left of the Post Office Oak.

C. Madonna of the Trail

Kansas's Madonna of the Trail is located in Madonna Park on the right of U S 56/Main Street just beyond Post Office Oak and facing the Neosho Bridge. This statue of the Pioneer Mother, placed by the DAR in 1928, is a duplicate of the one already noted in Lexington, Missouri. The park is on part of the old SFT campground at the Neosho Crossing.

D. Kaw Warrior and Neosho Crossing

The Guardian of the Grove Statue was recently installed as a companion to the Madonna of the Trail statue across the street, adjacent to the Neosho Bridge. Local artist Mark Sampsel created it. The original trail crossing is just upstream from the bridge, with the natural rock bed clearly discernible from the bridge. Stands of giant hardwoods, used by early travelers for spare axels and wagon tongues, can still be found on the river both north and south of town.

The SFT crossed the Neosho River here in Council Grove.

E. Hays House Restaurant

Hays House Restaurant is located one-half block west of the Neosho Bridge at 112 Main Street. Seth Hays, a great-grandson of Daniel Boone and a cousin of Kit Carson, in 1847 became the first white settler at Council Grove. He established a trading post for the neighboring Kaw Indians, and, in 1857, built this tavern and hostelry to serve wayfarers on the SFT. According to a popular story, he hired a bagpiper to play from the outside balcony of his place to draw customers. The building was also used as a district court, a place for church services, and the site for publication of an early newspaper.

This is one of the original American Pioneer Trail Association markers placed in 1948.

Although it has been remodeled, some of the interior fabric is original, including stone walls and a large walnut beam that can be seen in the basement, and a hand-hewn beam mantelpiece in the dining area. On the wall near the outside entrance, is one of the oval SFT signs of the American Pioneer Trails Association, as well as an ox yoke. The Hays House is a fine restaurant, open six days a week (closed Monday at the time of writing), and a boon to modern travelers on the trail. It claims to be the oldest eating establishment west of the Mississippi.

F. Malcom Conn Store

Across the street from the Hays House Restaurant at the corner of Main and Neosho Streets is the old Malcolm Conn Store. Built in

1858 by a local merchant of that name, it was one of the two most important stores in Council Grove. It has been modified, but the west side of the structure will give you an idea of its original shape.

The Malcolm Conn store built in 1858 has been much modified.

G. Farmers and Drovers Bank

Across the side street from the Conn Store, on the southwest corner of Main and Neosho Streets, is the Farmers and Drovers Bank. This building occupies the site of Waldo, Hall and Company's log depot and warehouse for its mail wagons to Santa Fe.

H. Becknell Monument

At the southwest comer of Main and Mission Streets on the library lawn is the Becknell Monument, a monument and plaque commemorating the 100th anniversary of the Santa Fe Trail. The monument is not mentioned in local historical guides. Behind it, a large cornerstone set in the library building has an inscription about the SFT Indian treaty of 1825.

I. The Kaw Mission State Historic Site

From the corner of Main and Mission Streets, drive north five blocks to Huffaker Street. The Kaw Mission is on the right. This beautiful two-story native stone structure was built in the winter of 1850-1851, and it first served as a school for children of the Kaw (or Kansas)

Indians, upon whose reservation Council Grove was founded. After 1854, it became the school for local white children. As the most imposing building in Council Grove, the mission often accommodated prominent travelers in the later days of the SFT. Now a state museum, it has some trail relics on display.

Sketch of the Kaw Mission by artist Roger Balm.

On the grounds is a stone house built by the government for Kaw families. The house was moved from its original site 3.5 miles southeast of Council Grove on Big John Creek, while other houses and a commissary building for the Kaw Indians are still there. Directions to that site can be obtained at the Chamber of Commerce (212 West Main Street in Council Grove). It is said that the Kaw stabled their horses in the stone houses, preferring to live in their native lodges. Also on the mission grounds is one of the new Mormon Battalion markers.

You might find it a pleasant walk to use the "River Walk" from Main Street to the Kaw Mission. This walk is lined with informative markers.

J. Old Bell Monument

Go west on US 56, turn right on Belfry, and continue two blocks to the Old Bell Monument. The bell was brought to Council Grove in

1863, and was erected on a tower at this site in 1866. It served as an alarm, school, and church bell for nearly thirty years.

K. The Hermit's Cave

Two blocks north of Main on Belfry Street, just past the Old Bell Monument is the Hermit's Cave. In this small cave for a brief period in the early 1860s lived a religious mystic, Giovanni Maria Augustini, who was closely associated with the SFT. Born in Italy in 1801, the son of a nobleman, he lived in caves in South America and Canada before coming to Council Grove. In 1863, the hermit approached the wagon train of wealthy merchant Don Eugenio Romero of Las Vegas and asked to be allowed to accompany it to New Mexico, subsequently walking beside the caravan the entire 550 miles over the SFT. (His fate in New Mexico is described later under "Las Vegas.")

L. Seth Hays Home

Another interesting building is Seth Hays's residence, located two blocks south of Main on Hall Street, just across the railroad tracks on the right. Built in 1867, this neat brick house is now the museum of the Morris County Historical Society, open in the summer and by appointment. Hays never married, but he did adopt a daughter in 1867. Hays's slave, Aunt Sally, lived in the basement of the residence and cared for the family until her death in 1872. She is buried in Greenwood Cemetery. There is a bronze plaque on the corner of the building.

The Seth Hays house built in 1867 is now a museum.

M. Custer Elm

Five blocks south of Main, on Neosho Street at the bridge over Elm Creek is the Custer Elm. At one time, the tree was 100 feet high, but it lost its top some time ago, and only the trunk remains. In 1867, George Armstrong Custer reportedly camped under this tree while pursuing hostile Indians. Events in Custer's life were associated with the SFT at several locations in Kansas. Later, he and his wife may have purchased property near here that was part of his estate at the time of his death. Many local accounts have Custer being places and doing things along the SFT that are not factual. We'll see more of these stories later.

N. Father Padilla Monument

Go south on Neosho Street from the Custer Elm. After three blocks, the road starts up a hill. Halfway to the top of the hill turn right on a small gravel road and go .7 mile. At the third turn in the road, is a gate on the right, and beyond the fence is the tall pyramidal Father Padilla Monument on a hill. A member of the Coronado Expedition of 1540-1542, which visited present Kansas in 1541, Father Juan de Padilla returned to Kansas to minister to the Indians but was soon killed. This is the first of at least five monuments and markers scattered along the SFT to commemorate his passing. Although this monument claims to be the site of his death and burial, the exact site is not known.

0. Last Chance Store

The Last Chance Store is located on the northwest corner of Main and Chautauqua Streets. A small stone building erected in 1857, and the oldest commercial building in Council Grove, it later served as a post office and government trading post. Closed now, its name derives from the fact that for a time it claimed to be the last place where supplies could be obtained between Council Grove and Fort Union. An interpretive historical sign is on the grounds.

P. Terwilliger House

Located at 803 West Main Street, the Terwilliger House was built in 1861 and would have been the last house the SFT traders viewed as they departed Council Grove. It now serves as a café and museum with an owner who serves as the town history expert.

The Last Chance Store in Council Grove, Kansas, with interpretive marker in the foreground.

The Terwilliger house was built in 1861 and would have been the last house traders would view on their way west.

Q. Greenwood Cemetery

The Greenwood Cemetery, established in 1862, is located on West Main Street past the Terwilliger House on the north side of Main Street. After entering the main gate, go straight up the lane to a small house. Seth Hays (1811-1873) is buried under a tall white column to the right. Next to his grave is the broken tombstone of Sarah Taylor (Aunt Sally), Hays's ex-slave, who after her liberation remained with his family.

Council Grove was near the Kaw Indian Reservation and the interaction between these Indians and the white settlers is interesting. The reservation lasted from 1846 until 1873. For a detailed account of this period you should read the fine book *The Darkest Period: The Kanza Indians and Their Last Homeland 1846-1873* by Ronald Parks. Parks is the former administrator of the Kaw (kanza) Mission State Historic Site near Council Grove.

Chapter 4
WESTERN KANSAS

From the Terwilliger House, drive west on US 56 4.4 miles to a DAR marker on the right, about where the trail crossed the highway from the north headed for Diamond Spring. Continue on US 56 about 1.2 miles to County Road 1400. Turn left (south) and drive .6 mile. The trail crossed the road here, and ruts can be seen on the west side. Spring is likely the best time to view them.

Return to US 56, turn left (west) and drive 8 miles to Road 2200.

DIAMOND SPRING

This famous spring, a day's wagon journey from Council Grove was mentioned in the accounts of many trail travelers, including Josiah Gregg, Susan Magoffin, and Marion Russell. In 1825, Commissioner Sibley likened the rushing water to the "Diamond of the Desert," a celebrated spring in Arabia. There may have been a mail station here by 1858. Both Kearny's army and the Mormon Battalion camped here on their way west.

To get to Diamond Spring, not to be confused with Diamond Spring Post Office and community shown on some maps, drive west on US 56 3 miles. KS 149 is to your right here, but turn left (south) on County Road 2200 and drive just over 2 miles. There is a road coming in from the right just past the section road that will take you to the Diamond Spring Ranch headquarters. From the entrance of the ranch, drive about 1 mile to a large house, where permission should be sought to visit the spring.

Diamond Spring.

To the right of the house are a barn and a road that turns left in front of it. Just after the turn, on the left, are Diamond Spring and a DAR marker a few feet above it on a knoll under a tree. The spring has been contained in a concrete housing. Kate Gregg in *The Road to Santa Fe* commented on how disappointing it was that the spring was "contained" by concrete and pipes, stating that the most famous spring in Kansas ought to be a state shrine. We cannot argue with her.

However, the spring is still worth visiting. Given the amount of water flowing from this spring, it is no wonder most travelers commented on it. Sibley wrote: "It is uncommonly large and beautiful, and the water very pure and cold. I have seldom seen so fine a Spring anywhere" (Gregg 1995).

In 1857, when the Government Land Office surveyor came through here, he mentioned in his notes that there was a corral immediately to the west of the spring and the Diamond Hotel 100 feet to the north, which would place the hotel just north and west of the present-day barn. The base of a stone corral was visible until a few years ago when it was covered over with dirt.

Return to US 56 and continue west. Past Delavan is a paved crossroad, County Road 2800 that leads south to Burdick. Turn left towards Burdick and go 4.1 miles to a bridge over Six Mile Creek. At .1 mile past the bridge on the left (east), is a DAR marker. The site is on private property and the owners do not welcome visitors.

The next stream to the east is Three Mile Creek, and east of that, One and A Half Mile Creek. The names, given by wagon masters, were based on distances from Diamond Spring. The Six Mile Creek Post Office was established here in 1863. In 1865, brothers Frank and William Hartwell bought the station for $2,000. Later, in 1866, Charlie Owens established his Six Mile Ranch here, but two years later a war party of Cheyennes burned it to the ground while he and his wife were absent. If you walk though the ruins and cross the creek, you can see nice ruts to the north of the dirt track.

Return to US 56.

FORT RILEY

Continue west on US 56 to the junction with US 77. From here, a side trip can be made 25 miles north on US 77 to Fort Riley and Junction City. One of the functions of the fort, founded in 1853 at the junction of the Republican and Smoky Hill Rivers, was to provide military protection for the SFT to the south. It was named for Gen. Bennet Riley, a Mexican War hero and leader of the first military escort along the SFT in 1829.

Fort Riley remains an active post. An official Kansas Historical Marker, with reference to the SFT, is in a roadside turnout on the grounds. Of chief interest at the fort is the U.S. Cavalry Museum, which includes some SFT exhibits. Associated with the museum is the Custer House, dating from 1854. It was long thought that Custer resided in this house, but recent research has shown that he, in fact, lived in a sister house that was later destroyed by fire. Lt. Col. and Mrs. George Armstrong Custer were stationed at the fort in 1866-1867. This is the only fort in Kansas commanded by Custer.

In addition, in 1866, the Union Pacific Railway, Eastern Division, which became the Kansas Pacific Railway in 1869, reached neighboring Junction City, which then became the railhead and starting point of the SFT for a brief period. The Woolworth and Barton Overland Transportation Line built a large warehouse next to the railroad depot and in January 1867 dispatched its first wagon train to Santa Fe, the shipment destined for the Spiegelberg Brothers. The wagons angled southwest from Junction City to meet the SFT at Lost Spring in Marion County or followed the Smoky Hill River to Fort Harker and then angled southwest to meet the SFT at Walnut Creek. The Barlow & Sanderson Overland Mail stagecoaches also left from Junction City and followed the route via Fort Harker. As the Union Pacific, Eastern Division, advanced westward across Kansas, the starting point of the SFT moved with it, to Ellsworth in spring 1867, Hays in autumn 1867, and Sheridan in 1868. The Kansas Pacific reached Kit Carson, Colorado, in 1870, and was completed to Denver the same year.

HERINGTON

Return to the junction of US 56 and US 77 on the main route of the SFT. Here US 56/US 77 turns south. Before taking it, however, go west on the highway to Herington. When a main thoroughfare (Broadway) crosses the road, turn right (north) on it. Drive .7 mile along Broadway, which has a grass median strip, past the swimming pool, and before a bridge turn left into Father Padilla Memorial Park. At the back of the circle drive, is a tall sandstone obelisk commemorating the death of Father Padilla (see section "Council Grove" for another Padilla monument).

Return to the junction of US 56 and US 77, and then go south 1.5 miles to a turnout on the right. Here is an official Kansas

Historical Marker with text on the Coronado Expedition, which is believed to have followed part of the route of the later SFT.

LOST SPRING

About 5 miles south of the Coronado marker on US 56/US 77, a SFT crossing sign is on the right (west), marking the spot where the SFT, connecting Diamond Spring to Lost Spring, crossed the highway. On the left (east) side of the highway, is a DAR marker, while a tall silo with a red and white top is just beyond on the right (**A**).

Lost Spring.

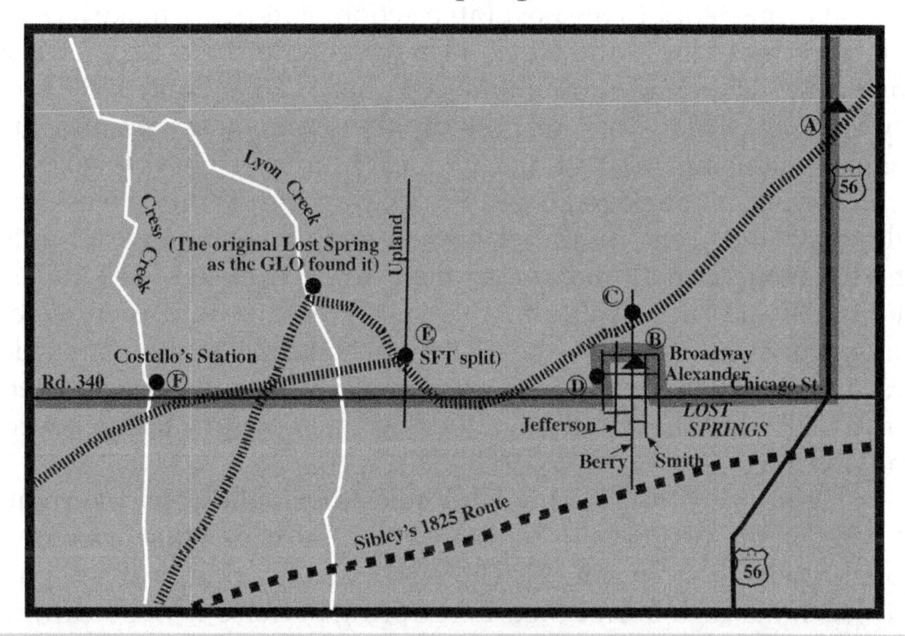

You are now in Marion County, which is part of the Cottonwood Crossing Chapter of the SFTA. The Chapter has been very active in researching the SFT and important sites on that trail. Steve Schmidt, especially, has worked on clearing up the stories of Lost Spring. Our thanks go to Steve and the chapter members for allowing us to draw on their efforts in the county. They have printed a very informative brochure that you can find at the Lost Spring Station pull out.

Continue south on US 56/US 77 to a sign pointing to a paved county road leading 1 mile to the modern community of Lost Springs.

Turn right (west) on this road, called Chicago. Entering the small community, turn right on the first gravel street (Main) that intersects from the north. Drive one block to the municipal park. On the west side of the park, is a DAR marker (**B**) with a bronze plaque like the ones noted at Olathe and Gardner.

Return one block to the paved county road and turn right (west). Continue along that street to Berry Street. At Berry turn right (north) and drive several blocks toward the railroad tracks. Just before the tracks, a sign on the right indicates where the SFT crossed the street (**C**). Return to the paved county road and again turn right (west).

Go one block to the next intersection (Jefferson), make a right turn, and drive north one block. Here on the northwest comer is a waist-high limestone monument (**D**) that reads "Santa Fe Trail, July 4, 1908." This is one of possibly five homemade monuments installed in the area on that date by local resident Dan McNicol.

Return to the paved county road, turn right, and go west one mile to Upland. Turn right (north) here and drive one-quarter mile where there is a small marker on the right (**E**) labeled "SFT 1908." Shallow swales are visible to the east after the field is mowed. This is the location where the SFT branched, one route going due west and the other going northwest about .5 mile to the spring noted in the 1857 GLO survey (the real Lost Spring). Return to the paved road, Rd 340.

Drive west on 340 about 1.5 miles to a pullout on the right. This is the site of Lost Spring Station and is near what was long thought to be Lost Spring (**F**). There is a small spring near the pull out which has also been called Lost Spring because it was near the station (water for the station was supplied by a well dug for that purpose). The station was established in 1859 and was run by Jack Costello after he won it in a card game from George Smith. This is a National Park Service site and has an informative wayside marker. Brochures prepared by the Cottonwood Crossing Chapter of the SFTA are in a small box on a pole here. There is also a large DAR-like marker here originally placed south of the road by the Marion County Old Settlers. Also north of the road is a blue and white interpretive sign that says erroneously that the Pony Express used this spring and has other incorrect information as well.

In 1859, George Smith built a stage station, hotel, and tavern here. The station, with its sod roof, was on a knoll southeast of the present county road. Late the same year, a soldier, Jack H. Costello, returning from New Mexico on the SFT, won the station from Smith in a card game. The place subsequently became a haven for gamblers and outlaws, and, supposedly, eleven men died in shootouts and were buried near the station. The SFT crossed the county road near the Old Settlers marker and angled southwest down to a creek crossing.

The real Lost Spring located a mile to the northeast is still gushing water, which then flows into Lyon Creek. Unfortunately, the spring is on private property and not open for viewing.

COTTONWOOD CROSSING

From the Lost Spring Station site, continue west on the paved county road to the next road, Sunflower (sign may be missing). Turn left here and in one-quarter mile there is a SFT crossing sign and a small limestone marker on the west side. This would be a later version of the SFT, after 1859 and through about 1867.

Go back to Rd. 340 and turn left and drive two miles to Quail Creek Rd. where you turn left (south). On Quail Creek Road just north of 330th Road is a stone marker placed there by the Ramona school children and School District No. 90. The SFT crossed the road here and swales are sometimes visible.

Drive to Road 330, turn right, and go five miles to the village of Tampa. The SFT crossed the road just before the intersection of 330 and Limestone. Good ruts can be seen in the cemetery on the right. Just beyond the cemetery, on the southwest corner is a large marker with extensive text, which looks like a DAR marker but was placed here by the Marion County Old Settlers.

Continue straight ahead on 330 (west) 4 miles to join KS 15, then turn left (south) toward Durham. At 1.4 miles after turning onto KS 15, the SFT, coming from Lost Spring and heading for Cottonwood Creek, crosses the highway, marked by a small sign. Long ruts of the trail can be seen in the grassy field on the west (right) side of the highway.

Continue south on KS 15 to Road 310, turn right (west), and in .4 mile is a SFT crossing sign and swales can be seen running to the northeast of the sign. Drive west on Road 310 to the next corner,

Durham to the Southwest.

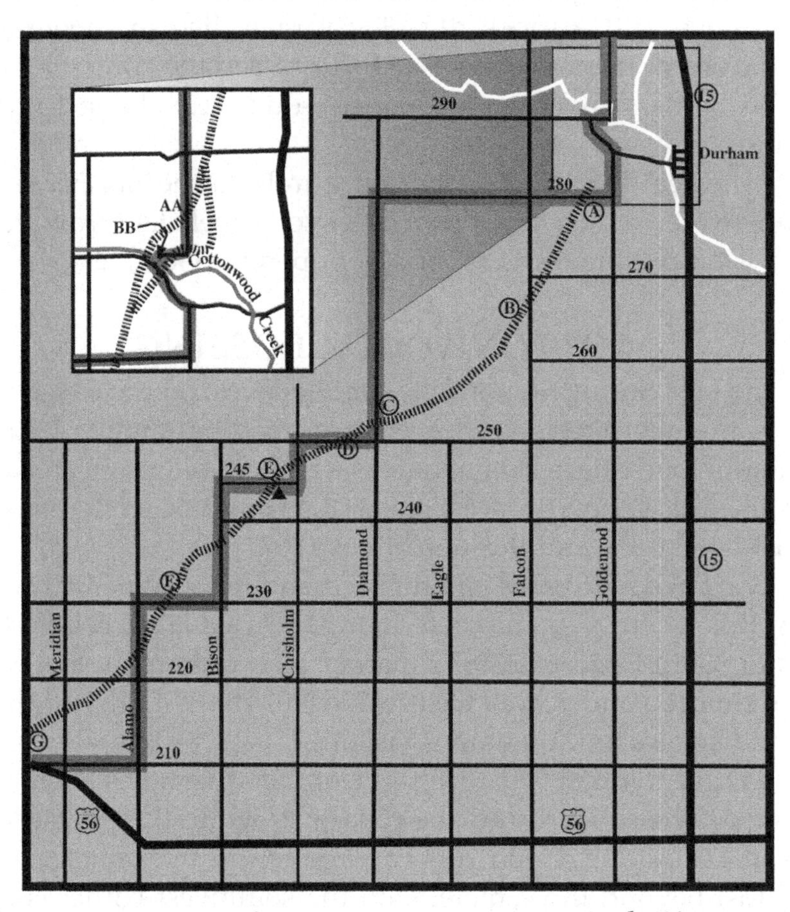

Goldenrod, and turn left. In just over a mile and a half, you will see a monument marking the SFT that was placed in 1906 by School District No. 57 (**AA**). There was a road ranch near here in the late 1850s and early 1860s, which had a mail station. Most important SFT water crossings had such ranches in the same time period. Many proprietors also constructed bridges and charged tolls for their use.

Following Goldenrod south, at 290th Road, you will be at the SFT's crossing of Cottonwood Creek of the SFT (**BB**). At this site are a DAR marker and a kiosk with three interpretive plaques. One plaque tells about the visit here of Zebulon Pike who stopped here on his way to visit the Pawnee village in present-day Nebraska in 1806. It was Pike's journal, published in 1810, that spurred the opening of the SFT in 1821.

There were two groups using Pike's book as a guide before 1821. In 1812 Robert McKnight and James Baird led a small trading group to Santa Fe and were captured and imprisoned in Mexico until 1821. The second group to meet misfortune was the Jules de Mun- Auguste P. Chouteau party in 1816-1817. They were captured by Spanish forces on the Arkansas and taken to Santa Fe. They were released after 48 days and sent back to Missouri. They had likely followed much of the later SFT. In 1820 David Meriwether and his slave Alfred traveled to New Mexico, seeking a wagon route to Santa Fe. They were captured and briefly imprisoned in Santa Fe. Years later, in 1853, Meriwether returned to New Mexico as the territorial governor.

Cottonwood Crossing.

The trail crossed Cottonwood Creek just northwest of the DAR marker. Several parties of travelers were hit by blizzards at this spot. Susan Magoffin mentions it at length in her diary. Across the road to the south is a limestone SFT marker.

At this point, you have a decision to make. The SFT heads off to the southwest from here and directions will follow so that you can follow close to the route. It will be mostly on improved gravel roads and these should not present any problem except in a rain or immediately after a rain. The second choice is to drive the short distance to Durham to your east, then drive south on KS 15, and then turn onto US 56, which will take you to the Marion County line where you will rejoin the tour.

From the kiosk, drive southeast toward Durham and turn right on Goldenrod. Go south on Goldenrod a short distance and turn right on 280th. One half mile west on 280th you will see a crossing sign and SFT swales are visible to the north-northeast (**A**). Do not let it bother you if you cannot detect the swales here or at other crossings. We know it is a crossing because the surveyors for the Government Land Office (GLO) noted them here. Whether one can actually detect the swales depends on time of day, time of year, and ground cover.

If you inspect the included map, you will note a long stretch of the SFT passing through an area without roads (**B**). That land is owned by the Scully family. William Scully came to the United States from Ireland in the late 1800s and purchased large amounts of land in Kansas, Illinois, Nebraska, and Missouri. He was a progressive farmer and made the best use of each piece of land; the land here was best suited for pasture so it was not plowed and the SFT is clearly visible for many miles. Unfortunately, the land is not open to the public.

After leaving the crossing sign on 280th, drive west almost three miles to Diamond where you should turn left and continue south to 250th. Just after crossing the RR is another crossing sign, where you might be able to see swales to the southwest (**C**). Turn west on 250th and in one-half mile, you will come upon a SFT marker (**D**). Swales are visible running to the northeast.

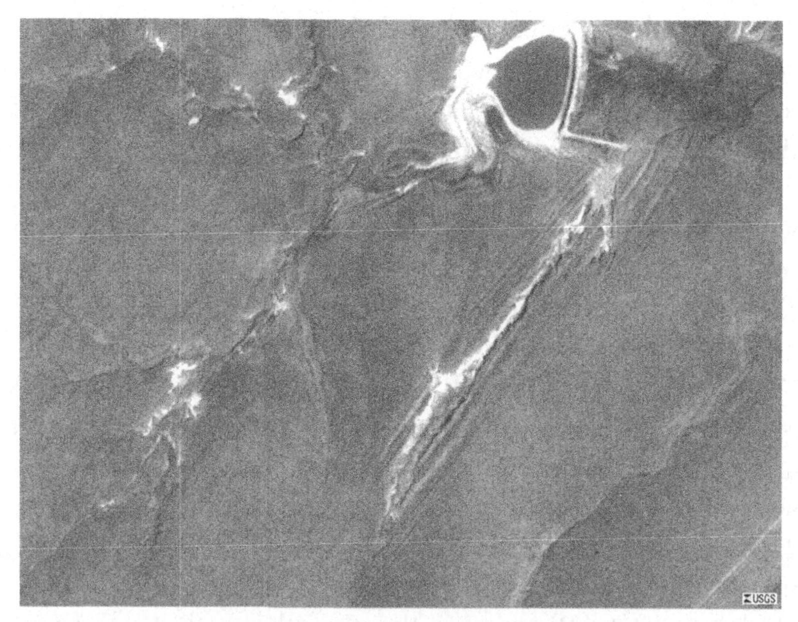

Aerial photo of Durham blowout.
USGS photo.

SFTA members inspecting Durham blowout swales.
Photo courtesy of Steve Schmidt.

Turn south on Chisholm and then, in .5 miles, turn right on 245th. At one-quarter mile west of Chisholm, there is a DAR marker and a crossing sign (**E**). There is also a NPS identification sign and wayside for French Frank's Trail Segment. Swales can be seen running across the land to the southwest. There are five sets of two parallel swales here created as traders chose a variety of routes, perhaps to avoid mud. These are the best swales that you will see in this area and will give you some idea of what you missed in the Durham swales on the Scully land.

This spot is along French Creek and it was named for Claude Francis Laloge (French Frank) the earliest settler in the area. It was not much of a creek but some water would be captured in small depression along its course. Laloge established a road ranch here in 1861. The location was about half way between Cottonwood Creek and Fuller's Ranch on Running Turkey Creek.

Drive west to Bison and then south on that road to 230th where you should turn right. Six tenths miles west of Bison is another SFT sign (**F**). Drive to Alamo Rd, turn left and go to 210th, turn right there and continue to U S 56. On US 56 at the Marion-McPherson county line (on the north side) is a large stone marker (**G**) placed by the Cottonwood Crossing Chapter of the SFTA depicting the locations of the SFT and the Chisholm Trail. The marker is not located on either of these trails. The Chisholm cattle trail passed just east of here intersecting the SFT at French Frank's Trail Segment; there is a concerted effort to make the Chisholm Trail a National Historic Trail.

At .5 mile beyond the Marion-McPherson County line, the SFT crossed US 56. At 1 mile from the county line, turn right (north) on a gravel road (29th Ave). Go north on the gravel road .5 mile to an abandoned railway bed. Just before that track, turn east (right) on a dirt lane (in fair weather only). Park here and walk about .25 mile to the Jones Cemetery (driving there is not allowed) on a rise surrounded by trees and hedges. In the center of the cemetery is a DAR marker, and next to it the gravestone of eighteen-year-old Ed Miller. Miller was a young man sent to the Fuller Ranch to deliver a message (not a Pony Express rider). He was killed on the SFT in 1864 by Cheyennes. Return to US 56 and continue west.

In seven miles (just before Galva) you will see 22nd Avenue on your left. Turn south here and drive 2 miles where you will see a monument erected to show the approximate location of Fuller's Ranche, established in 1855. This ranch is close to Big Turkey Creek.

Return to US 56 and turn left toward McPherson.

Approaching the eastern limits of McPherson, leave US 56 and drive 7 miles north on Interstate 135 to a roadside park located in the wide median of the highway. There are two separate units of the park, one for northbound traffic and the other for southbound. Turn left into the first unit, drive to the rear, and take a small road that leads to the second unit which serves southbound traffic. Here is one of the newly installed Mormon Battalion markers. These soldiers left Council Bluffs, Iowa and marched southwest to join the Santa Fe Trail during the War between Mexico and the United States. They followed the SFT to Santa Fe where they went south on the Camino Real and then west to San Diego, California. Also, note the trail map, "Historical Kansas," on the building adjacent to the marker.

Return to US 56 at McPherson, turn right (west) and make the short drive into that city. Follow US 56 to the McPherson Museum at 1111 East Kansas (Highway 56) **(A).** There are some nice exhibits in the museum but little of interest to SFT buffs. Note the new (2015) informational panels on the west side of the museum. Also, the Quivira Chapter of the SFTA has provided trail brochures in the museum. They are a very good source for guiding you on the SFT from here to Great Bend.

From the museum drive west on US 56 (Kansas Avenue) to Main Street and turn left on Main Street (also called Business 81). Continue south past the refinery on your right and follow it due south as it turns into 14th Avenue. Once you reach the stop sign at the intersection of Old 81 Highway, continue south approximately 3/4 mile. On the east side of 14th you will see a DAR marker moved there from another site, Santa Fe School, nearby **(B).** The school is no longer there. This is near the Dry Turkey Creek crossing which is about one-half mile east of the DAR marker.

Continue south on 14th to Comanche and turn left (east). In about one-half mile you will cross over Dry Turkey Creek and in another quarter mile the small gray marker for the signing of the Kaw Indian Treaty. Site will be on the left side of the road **(C).**

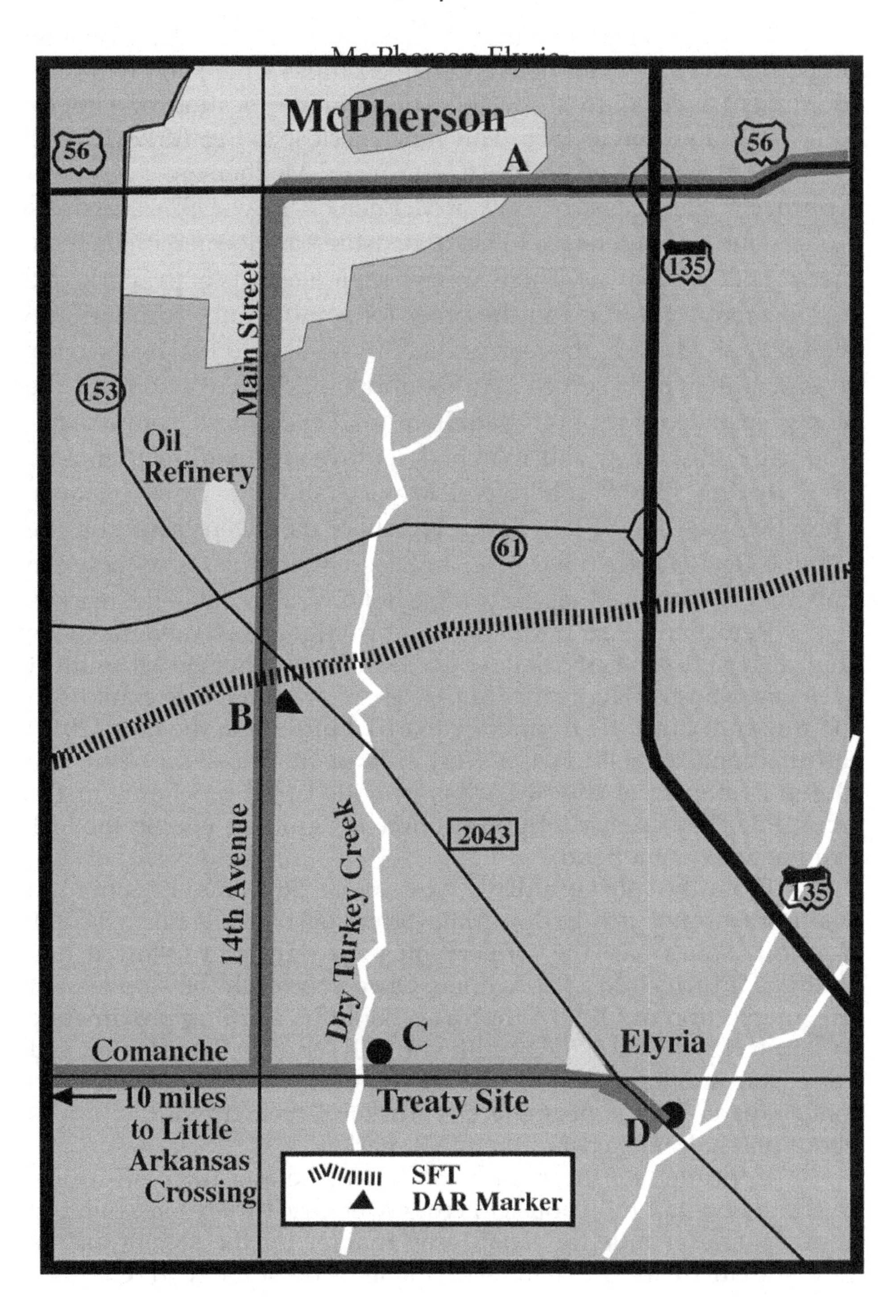
McPherson-Elyria
McPherson
A
56
56
135
135
153
61
2043
Main Street
Oil
Refinery
B
14th Avenue
Dry Turkey Creek
C
Comanche
Elyria
10 miles
to Little
Arkansas
Crossing
Treaty Site
D
SFT
DAR Marker

George Sibley met the Kaw Indians here on August 16, 1825 to get them to agree to allow traders to pass through their lands safely. Sibley made a similar arrangement with the Osage Indians at Council Grove.

Indian Treaty Site.

Continue east on Comanche about 1.5 miles to Elyria where you intersect Old Highway 81. Turn right here and drive .5 mile to a Kansas State Historical marker on your right **(D).** Also present at this site is a DAR marker for Sora Kansas Creek, the earlier name for Dry Turkey Creek. On the front is the usual DAR inscription, but the back is the following: "Sora Kansas Creek. Near this spot August 16, 1825 the Treaty was made with the Kansas Indians for the right of way of the Trail." You have already visited the actual treaty signing spot. This DAR marker was moved here from its original location near the actual treaty site.

LITTLE ARKANSAS CROSSING

The crossing of the Little Arkansas River was a spot well known to early teamsters and merchants for, although it was comparatively small, it had a muddy bottom and steep banks. There were actually two crossings about .5 mile apart. The SFT split several miles to the east, drivers taking the fork leading to whichever crossing their scouts reported was in the best condition.

A short distance beyond the Little Arkansas the two branches came together to form one trail again. The north crossing, or what we call the Upper Crossing, was the older and more important. In trail days there was no thick lining of timber as now, but there was one large "marker cottonwood" that could be seen far out on the plains that guided wagons to the Upper Crossing. The cottonwood stood on the east side of the ford, with a huge trunk that forked into two smaller trunks at about the height of a man. The Marker Cottonwood succumbed to drought and ice storms and fell in late 2012.

About 1865, a notable landmark, the Stone Corral, was built on the west bank near the Lower Crossing. The structure, which was 200 by 400 feet (some accounts say 200 by 300) and had 30-inch-thick walls 8 feet high, not only held livestock but doubled as a fort. Nearby was a stage station and a toll bridge, erected in 1858. In the 1880s, after abandonment of the SFT, local residents hauled away the quarried stone from the corral, and no trace remains today.

To get to the Little Arkansas Crossing, which Stocking described in *Road to Santa Fe,* go west from Elyria and at Main (called 14th here) note your odometer and drive 13 miles to 1st Avenue.

Little Arkansas Crossing.

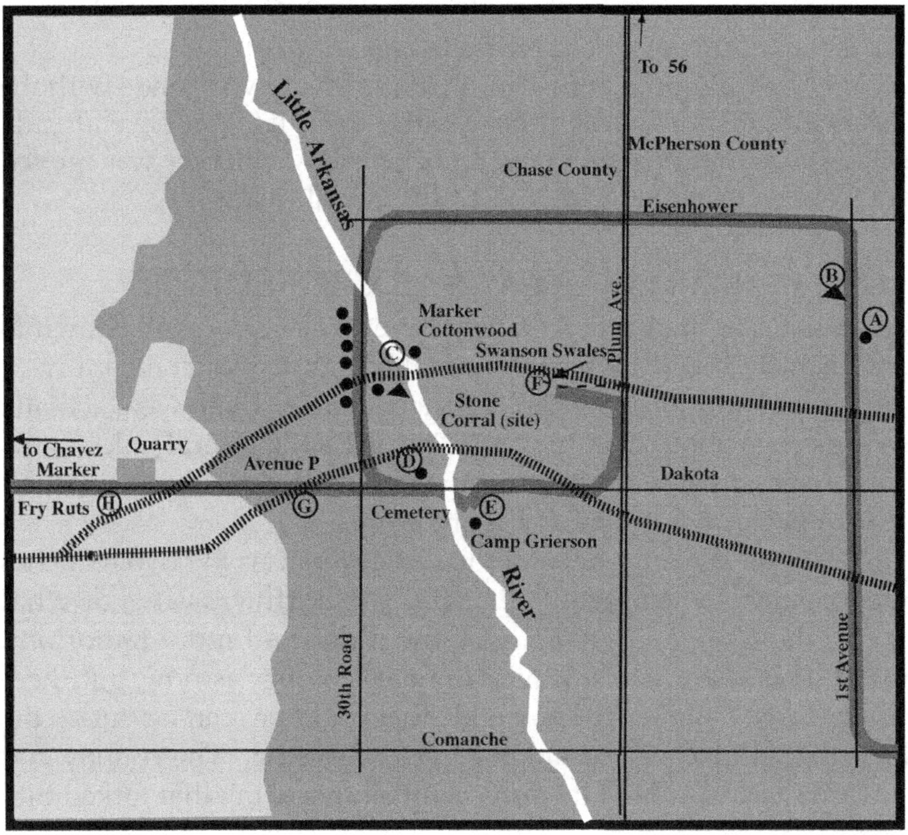

At this intersection turn right (north) 1.5 miles. During this drive you will have passed two branches of the SFT which split two miles east of 1st Avenue. Just past Dakota, on the right, was the Berg homestead and this area was a popular campground for SFT traders (**A**). If you look carefully you can see a very large cottonwood on the east side of the road and this would be about where the traders camped.

Continuing north on 1st you can see a DAR marker on the left (**B**). This marker concerns the point where the road from Fort Harker intersected the SFT. Camp Grierson was a satellite of Fort Harker. At the next intersection, 1st and Eisenhower, turn left and drive two miles to 30th Road. You have passed into Rice County and the naming of the roads has changed.

At 30th Road turn left and go over the Little Arkansas stopping at a DAR marker the "Stone Corral" on your left (**C**). There is a new NPS marker here as well. The DAR marker is a replacement for an older one that had a bronze plaque, which was stolen. The original one was placed in 1929 by the Sterling Chapter of the DAR. The plaque eventually turned up at a farm sale and is now preserved in the museum at Lyons. You are very near the crossing of the river here and the location of the famous Marker Cottonwood that died in 2012. There is another DAR marker closer to the river that you may be able to see from the road.

Drive south on 30th to the next intersection (with Avenue P now that we are in Rice County). In the field to the northeast, near the oil well was the location of the aforementioned Stone Corral (**D**). Stone for the construction of the corral was likely quarried about 1 mile west of the site. When the corral no longer had a use, the corral's rock was sold to locals for a variety of purposes, including the construction of a nearby school.

Drive east on Ave. P, cross the river once again, and look for a small dirt road on your right. Turn in here and park (**E**). A hand-lettered sign on a pipe frame (put up by the property owner) says "Stone Corral" and gives a brief history. However, the corral was not here but across the county road and west of the river. Behind the sign are some depressions reputed to be the remains of trenches dug by troops of Col. George Armstrong Custer when he was here guarding the ford briefly in the 1860s. This is just another location where Custer wasn't! Instead, a troop of the 10th U.S. Cavalry (the Buffalo Soldiers) stationed here fought several skirmishes with Indians and maintained what was called Camp Grierson, named for Colonel Benjamin Grierson, 10th Cavalry.

This is the site of Camp Grierson. Never a major fortification, the camp was originally called Station Little Arkansas and was established in 1864. There were some Buffalo Soldiers stationed here in Summer 1867 when the Franz Huning party passed through. Huning asked for an escort as he was aware of some threats to traders nearby. The troops refused his request and Huning went west and was attacked near Plum Buttes.

There is also a small cemetery as some of the soldiers died of disease and were buried here. Continue down the small dirt road a short distance to a sign on the right: "Cottonwood Grove Cemetery." Depressions behind the sign are remains of graves of soldiers who died of cholera or were killed by Indians while stationed at the crossing. Later their bodies were removed to Fort Leavenworth National Cemetery.

Return to the county road (Ave P) and go east to Plum Avenue (also known as 31st Avenue). Turn left and drive north approximately 0.5 mile to the driveway on your left. Turn into the driveway and follow it along the hedgerow until you reach the

"Swanson's Swales" sign, installed as part of a Boy Scout Eagle Scout Project. Turn left along the field and drive to the hedgerow to the south. Here you will find a small pasture with an excellent set of swales preserved by the Joe Swanson family.

Return to Plum Street (31st Avenue) and turn right. Return to the county road (Ave P) and go west crossing the river again to the next intersection. Continue straight ahead .4 mile to a DAR marker on the left (south) side of the road, the marker is on the approximate site of the Trail (**G**).

Approximately .5 mile west of the DAR marker are the Fry Ruts on your left. The Fry Ruts are in a pasture owned by Steve and Jodene Fisher. There are very nice sets of swales in the pasture traveling to the southwest from the east side of the pasture along the south side of the pond. The Boy Scouts installed the Fry's Ruts sign and also a limestone marker on the actual Trail. The upper and lower portions of the Trail which split prior to the Little Arkansas Crossing appear to meet up in the west end of this pasture.

Chávez Marker

You have a choice here. It is suggested that you continue west 9.5 miles on Avenue P to the Chávez marker. Or, you can drive north on Plum, west on US 56, and drive to 22nd Road, south 2 miles to Ave. M, west 2 miles to 20th Road, and south 2.5 miles to the DAR marker for Chávez crossing. The first is shorter and simpler.

Lyons to Plum Buttes.

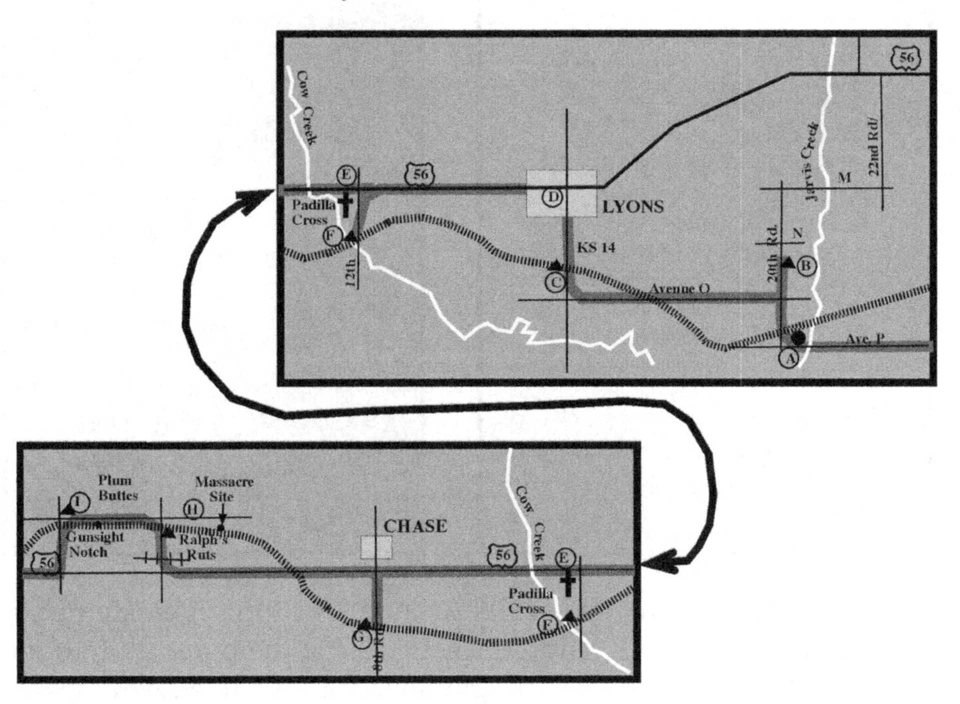

Continue 9.5 miles to Jarvis (Chávez) Creek and just past the creek, on the right, is a stone marker commemorating Antonio José Chávez **(A).** The name Jarvis is a corruption of Chávez. There was also a short-lived town near here called Jarvis View. In 1843, Antonio José Chávez was traveling east on the SFT with five servants, one wagon, five mules, and a considerable amount of money ($10,000). Fifteen men from Missouri under the command of John McDaniel intercepted Chávez somewhere east of here (likely near the crossing of the Little Arkansas). These bandits had come west specifically to

rob Mexican merchants, and after robbing Chávez they marched him west and killed him somewhere near this spot. Most of the fifteen men were eventually apprehended, and two were hanged for his murder.

From the Chávez marker drive .5 mile west to 20th, turn right and go about 1.5 miles north to view a DAR marker for the Chávez Creek crossing of the SFT (**B**).

Return .5 mile to Avenue O and drive west to KS 14. Drive north on KS 14 .6 mile and there will be a DAR marker on the left which is directly on the SFT (**C**). It is likely the second DAR marker placed in Kansas.

LYONS

Drive north rejoining US 56 in Lyons. Turn left on US 56, drive one block to the Courthouse Square. The Coronado-Quivira Museum is located at 105 West Lyon, one block south of the courthouse (**D**). This excellent facility contains exhibits relating, among other things, to the Coronado Expedition and the SFT.

FATHER PADILLA CROSS AND COW CREEK CROSSING

Four miles west of Lyons on the south side of US 56 is a small roadside park with a 30-foot marble cross honoring the Coronado Expedition's well-traveled friar, Father Padilla **(E).** Also in the park is an official Kansas Historical Marker with a text describing Coronado's search for Quivira and, next to it, a Rice County Historical Society sign for the Cow Creek Station on the SFT. In the plowed field behind the cross was once a huge Quivira Indian village.

BEFORE BECKNELL

It is important to know that William Becknell had many explorers and traders precede him. The area that Becknell was to pass through was no "terra incognita," an unknown land. Don Francisco Vazquez de Coronado was the first European explorer to visit central Kansas and his presence is noted in many markers along the SFT. The included map shows a number of others. The map is missing dozens of additional groups that experienced the Great Plains.

Plains Exploration.

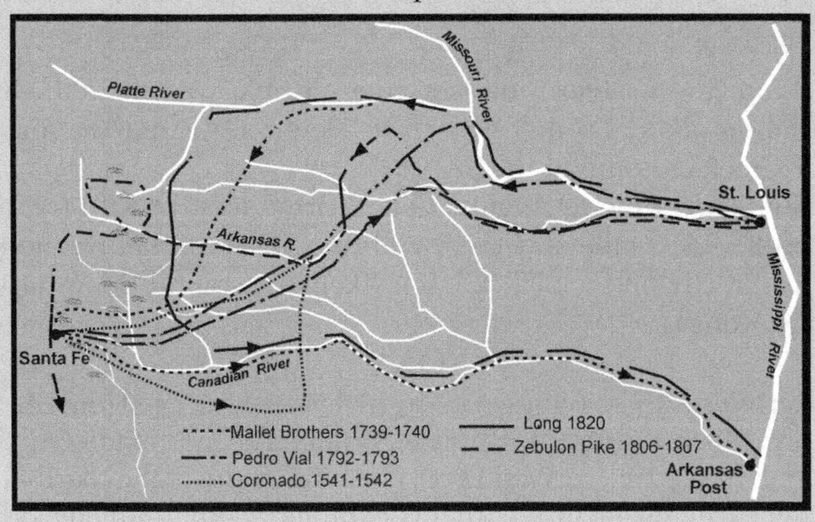

Zebulon Pike's route is shown but the Spanish officer sent to find Pike (and Lewis and Clark), Facundo Melgares, is not shown.

Melgares had a force of over 500 men and went as far as the Pawnee villages to intercept Pike. Pike was four weeks behind Melgares so they did not meet until later when Pike was arrested in Colorado. The map shows that Pedro Vial made a trip in 1792 but does not show the half dozen trips made from St. Louis before that, some led by Vial.

It is clear that many had trod on these lands and some of this information was in Becknell's hands.

On the east edge of the park is a gravel road (12th Road) running south to Buffalo Bill's Well and Cow Creek. Follow this county road 1 mile to the well-marked site **(F).** Next to the well, which is covered by a shelter, is an interpretive sign and a DAR marker. Just beyond, the bridge over Cow Creek is very near the original crossing of the SFT.

Cow Creek marked the boundary between the tallgrass country on the east and the shortgrass prairie stretching westward, the latter being the prize range of the buffalo. Because the site was also on the margin of hostile Indian country, beginning in the 1850s soldiers were often stationed at the crossing to protect passing caravans. Their flagpole is said to have been placed on a low hill just north of the well.

Asahel Beach and his brother built a trading ranch at the Cow Creek Crossing in 1858. William Mathewson was one of Beach's hired hands at that time. Mathewson took over the ranch in the early 1860s and became known as "Buffalo Bill" during the 1860 drought when he hunted and killed thousands of buffalo to feed Kansans reeling from the effects of the drought. A bridge was constructed here in 1859-1860. Mathewson was at Cow Creek ranch until 1866 or 1867. (Louise Barry 1972) Some stories have William Cody

here at the ranch too. There is no evidence to support this and Buffalo Bill Cody likely received his name the same way Mathewson did, by killing large numbers of buffalo, which he did under contract to feed the construction crews of the Union Pacific Railway, Eastern Division.

In July 1864, this was the site of a three-day siege by Kiowas, which ended when Mathewson discharged a small cannon in their direction.

Return to US 56 and turn left (west). At 4 miles the town of Chase is to the right of the highway. Turn left (south) here on 8th Road. Drive south 1 mile, and you will see a DAR marker on the west side, directly on the trail **(G).**

Return to US 56 and turn left (west).

RALPH'S RUTS AND PLUM BUTTES

Midway between Cow Creek and Fort Zarah was the Plum Buttes noon stop. The so-called buttes were really sand hills surrounded by plum thickets. About 100 feet higher than their surroundings and easily noted by travelers, they could be seen shortly after the crossing at Cow Creek. Wagons paused here for lunch, even though there was no water or firewood. Today, the buttes are still in evidence, although difficult to recognize.

Four miles west of Chase on US 56, a blacktop road crosses the highway. Approaching the intersection, a sign points south (left) to the town of Raymond. At the intersection is a small white sign pointing north to Salem Methodist Church and a sign for "Ralph's Ruts." Here, turn north (right) on the blacktop. At about .25 mile cross a railroad track, and after another .5 mile watch for a small sign on the right reading: "Original Santa Fe Trail Crossed Here." Beautiful ruts in the form of deep swales are visible on the east (right) side of the road. They have been carefully preserved by the owner, the late Ralph Hathaway **(H).** Ralph's daughter and son-in-law now maintain a bed and breakfast (Ralph's Ruts Retreat) in the family home. They also have space for horses. Call 620-267-8155 for more information and reservations. They maintain a library of SFT interest as well. There is a new DAR marker at the site (**G**).

It was on the Hathaway farm that the famous Huning, or Plum Buttes, Massacre occurred in September 1867. Franz Huning of Albuquerque was traveling west on the trail with a wagon train, escorting his mother-in-law and others to New Mexico. Apparently, the train was a single column caravan traveling through tall grass when Indians attacked, cutting off the last four wagons, murdering Huning's mother-in-law and her son, and taking mules, which they packed up with stolen goods. As they left they set fire to the prairie, forcing Huning's remaining wagons to flee. Huning knew of the danger here and had requested an escort from the Buffalo Soldiers stationed at the Little Arkansas Crossing, but he had been turned down. Someone rode to Fort Zarah for help and troops were dispatched to help Huning. Help was too late for some of the party.

Continue straight ahead (north) to the next intersection. Turn left (west) and go 1.5 miles to a high point in the road. The trail is visible to your left along this road with many parallel swales. From this high point you can see "Gunsight Notch" to the left, which is the route of the trail as it skirted the buttes. This high point may be on one of the remnants of the Plum Buttes, unmarked but recognizable as low sand hills. Originally, the buttes were over 100 feet high, with no timber to obstruct the view as is the case now. Look for the wild plum bushes still growing along the road and at the base of the buttes. After passing the Buttes, in a half mile or so, stop and look back a the Buttes and you will see the "Gunsight" path clearly.

Drive to the next intersection, where you will see a DAR marker on the northeast corner, returned to this site in 1996 **(H)**. Turn left (south), continuing 1 mile past a grain elevator, to rejoin US 56. Turn right (west).

FORT ZARAH AND WALNUT CREEK CROSSING

The next town after Plum Buttes is Ellinwood. Two blocks past its one traffic light is a DAR marker on the right. This site is very near the trail, on the route from Plum Buttes to Fort Zarah. This is where the trail joined the Arkansas River and a very important campsite was located south of the highway.

Continue west on US 56 about 5.5 miles to a road (NE 40 Ave.) just west of the point where KS 156 comes in from the right (north).

Turn left here, cross the railroad tracks, and drive to the next intersection. It may be possible to continue a short distance straight ahead, depending on the road condition (**A**). Off to the right front was the first Fort Zarah, established in 1864 and abandoned in 1866. The Allison-Boothe Trading Post was to the southeast of that point. The SFT crossing is almost due south. A toll bridge over Walnut Creek was established here in 1859-1860. This trading post was made of logs. After Allison died in 1858 the trading post was taken over by George Peacock. Chief Satank of the Kiowa tribe killed Peacock in 1860. Charles Rath was the next operator of the trading post and he had a very poor reputation. He sold weapons to the Indians as well as whiskey. For details of this crossing see Louise Barry (1971). Her article is available online.

Fort Zarah.

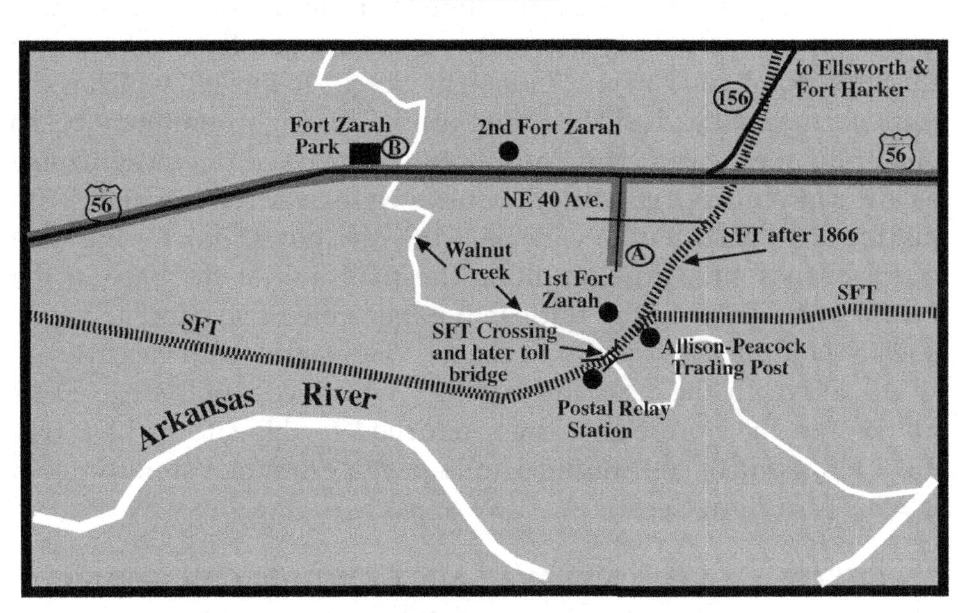

Return to US 56 and turn left (west).

Continuing west on US 56, cross a highway bridge over Walnut Creek and stop in the spacious Fort Zarah Park adjacent to Walnut Creek commemorating Fort Zarah and Walnut Creek Crossing. Near the entrance is an official Kansas Historical Marker, "Fort Zarah," with reference to the SFT. This marker may be replaced in the near future.

The second Fort Zarah with stone buildings was established in 1866 and located in the field across the creek from the park (**B**). For a brief period (1864-1869), the forts guarded one of the most dangerous sections of the SFT. Fort Zarah troopers provided escorts for the stagecoaches that passed through the area on their way between Westport and Santa Fe. However, no trace of the old sandstone fort or mail station remains today. The fort was abandoned in 1869.

Note on the included map that a new Santa Fe Trail is shown. When the railroad reached Junction City in 1866, a new route was developed that went from that city to Fort Harker and then met the SFT at Fort Zarah. The SFT east of Fort Zarah basically ceased to function after that. There was also a trail developed from Junction City to Lost Spring where it joined the SFT before continuing west. It was this route that Huning followed in 1867. He and his family utilized the railroad to Junction City. There may have been the occasional New Mexican trader using the old route but most freight went by railroad as far as they could go.

THE TRAIL SHORTENS

We saw how the introduction of steamboats on the Missouri River led to the migration of the starting point for the Santa Fe Trail from Franklin to Independence by 1830. After the conclusion of the Civil War, another innovation, railroads, led to further Trail shortening.

In 1857, the Baltimore and Ohio Railroad reached St. Louis [actually no, because there was no bridge across the Mississippi there until 1873 or 1874], Another line; the Hannibal and St. Joseph began laying tracks west in 1847 but did not reach St. Joseph until 1859. Impacting the SFT was the Union Pacific Railway, Eastern Division, which worked west from Kansas City beginning 1863. It really began service in 1866 when its tracks reached Junction City near Fort Riley.

A series of wagon roads developed, leading from successive railheads as the rails progressed west. Each of these north-to-south Trails shortened the SFT. From Junction City, a new Trail went south to Lost Spring (on the SFT) or west to Ellsworth and then to Fort Zarah

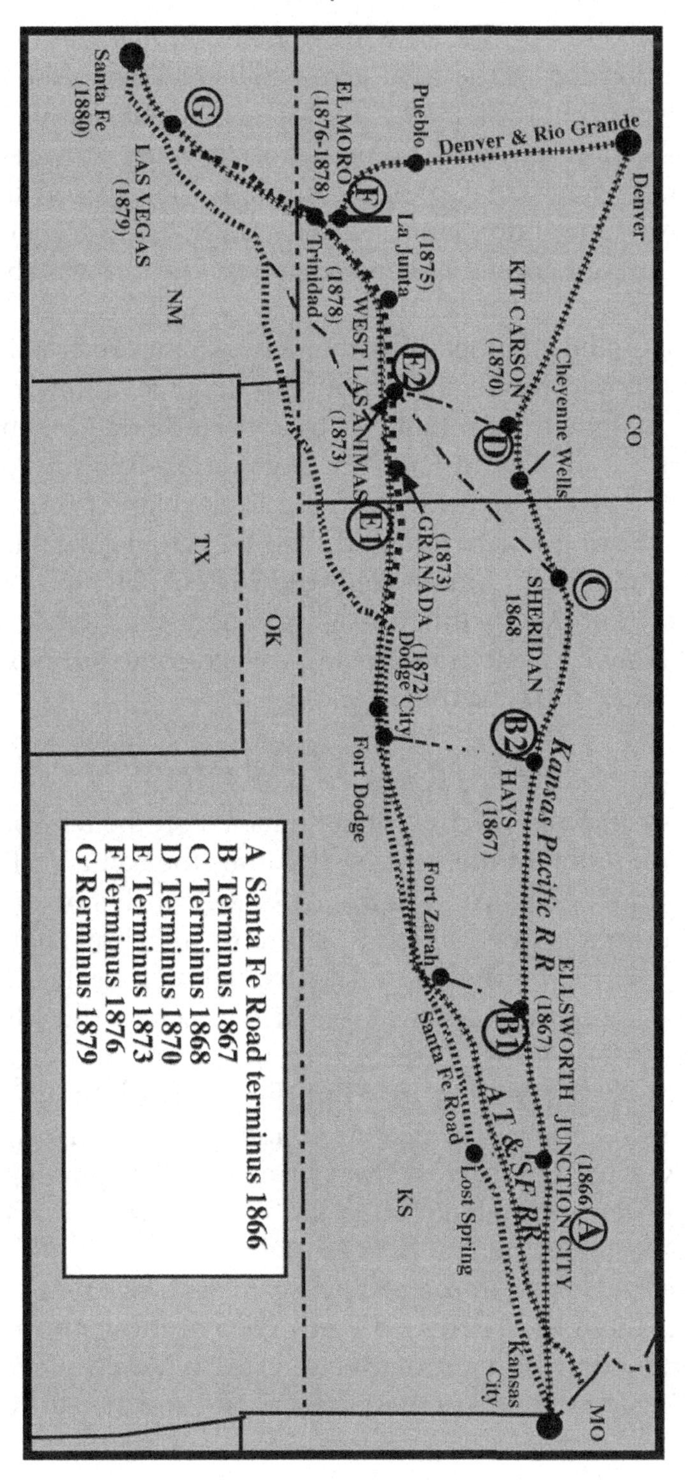

The Trail Shortens.

on the SFT on Walnut Creek. crossing. That ended the SFT east of Walnut Creek.

Ellsworth became the trail head in the spring of 1867, and in October 1867, the rails reached Fort Hays and, again, a wagon road went south connecting Fort Hays with Fort Dodge on the SFT. Next stopping point was Sheridan, Kansas, near Fort Wallace, 1868. From Sheridan a road angled southwest to Fort Lyon on the Arkansas River. Sheridan remained an important railhead until the rails (now named the Kansas Pacific) pushed into Colorado Territory at Kit Carson in 1870. The trail head remained at this point for about two years, although the Kansas Pacific was completed to Denver in 1870, with the southbound wagon Trail going to Fort Lyon. The Kansas Pacific eventually built a spur from Kit Carson to West Las Animas on the Arkansas River.

A competing railroad, the Atchison, Topeka, and Santa Fe (A T & S F), was organized in 1859 and reached Dodge City in 1872. It became a threat to the Kansas Pacific when it reached Granada, Colorado, in 1873. This terminus was important because a new route, the Granada to Fort Union Military Road, began here. This Trail did not follow the established Mountain Route but instead headed for Emory Gap and then on to Fort Union. Huge wagons were used here to transport material to Fort Union, which was the entrepot for the many forts of New Mexico. This route was heavily used in the period 1873 to 1875.

In 1875, both the Kansas Pacific and the A T & S F moved up the Arkansas River to La Junta. In 1876, the A T & S F followed the Mountain Route of the SFT to Trinidad, a town at the northern end of Raton Pass, a route that had to be used to get to Santa Fe.

A third railroad company entered the competition at this time, the narrow gauge Denver and Rio Grande. The D, R and G was at El Moro near Trinidad in 1876. The A T & S F reached Trinidad in 1878, having already secured the right to cross Raton Pass from Uncle Dick Wootton who owned the toll road over the pass. December 1878 found the A T & S F over Raton Pass on switchbacks (the tunnel was completed the next year) and at the Clifton House (renamed Otero) in December.

Las Vegas was reached on July 4, 1879, and from there the A T & S F pushed toward Santa Fe, reaching Lamy in 1880. There was no easy route into Santa Fe so Lamy was used instead and at a later date a spur was laid to Santa Fe. Thus, in 1880, commercial traffic stopped on the old Santa Fe Trail and moved to the rails.

There were forwarding houses at the end of each move west and south. These houses would accept the rail shipments and then transfer the freight to wagons to be sent on to Fort Union, Santa Fe, or other locations. One of the largest and most important of these forwarding houses was the firm of Otero, Sellar, and Company. Miguel Otero moved his headquarters west eleven times in seven years. Another forwarding and commission house that followed the railroads westward was Chick, Browne & Company

GREAT BEND

The SFT joined the Arkansas River at its great bend at Ellinwood. sometimes called the north bend, and followed its broad valley toward the southwest and Pawnee Rock. The present-day town of Great Bend was not founded until 1872, when the AT&SF Railway built through, after the SFT had closed in this area. Entering Great Bend from the east on US 56, a DAR marker can be seen on the left side of the road, next to some evergreens adjacent to a motel.

Continue to the center of Great Bend. At Main Street (US 281), turn right (north). Drive to the courthouse, where there is a DAR marker on the west side of the building, moved here from the railroad depot in 1993. The SFT ran south of US 56 here and likely the original site of the DAR marker was directly on the trail.

Return south on Main Street, crossing US 56 and going past the railroad and the Arkansas River to the Barton County Museum on the right. The museum contains extensive displays of Fort Zarah and the Allison-Boothe, or maybe another Walnut Creek Trading Post. Return to US 56 and turn left (west). Continue west toward Pawnee Rock.

Note: On the west side of Great Bend, US 56 has a stop sign. At this point US 56 turns left. The turn is easy to miss.

PAWNEE ROCK

Pawnee Rock, the most famous natural landmark along the SFT in Kansas, was well known to all trail travelers and described by almost everyone who wrote about the trail. Stocking (1971) wrote "At Pawnee Rock, the Dakota is a deep red-brown soft sandstone, a landmrk to all men, red or white, passing this way." Merely a small hill now with a rock face, it would pass unnoticed anywhere but on the flat plains of Kansas. From its summit there is a view over many miles east and west of the Arkansas Valley.

Pawnee Rock.

Modern visitors with a copy of Susan Magoffin's diary should read her description of the place in the entry for July 4, 1846. As many other passersby, she carved her name here, but those priceless inscriptions were lost in later years when Pawnee Rock was heavily quarried for building materials. Now it is a state park and protected. There are several interpretive signs in this park.

Entering the small community of Pawnee Rock on US 56, turn right (north) at the sign in the center of town which points to the historic site. Go about .5 mile to the park entrance. On the right side of the gate, almost hidden by a lilac bush, is a DAR marker.

The road passes through the gate and leads to the base of Pawnee Rock. Embedded in its face are two bronze plaques. One shows William Becknell's first pack train of 1821 in relief. This plaque, and an identical one at Wagon Mound, New Mexico, were designed and cast by Harold Rosner of Larned and placed in 1971 to celebrate the 150th anniversary of opening the SFT. The Becknell plaque here erroneously claims that he passed by Pawnee Rock. In fact, Becknell traveled along the south side of the Arkansas River on both of his trips. He left the Arkansas in 1822 with the wagons at or near Walnut Creek and never followed the Arkansas west of that point. The second plaque at Pawnee Rock commemorates the SFT. Inscriptions seen on the rock are from post-trail days.

The road makes a circle to the top of the rock, where there are a stone shelter and a tall white marble SFT monument with inscriptions on four sides. This is the only marker we know of on the trail that mentions the women as well as the men who ventured forth on the SFT. Look south across the town to the line of trees marking the Arkansas River. The SFT ran about 100 yards south of the rock, which had a caravan campground at its base.

Return to US 56 and turn right toward Larned. Leaving the western outskirts of the community of Pawnee Rock, stop at an official Kansas Historical Marker in a roadside park on the left. This marker tells the story of Pawnee Rock and the SFT.

About 1 mile past the roadside park, look to the right (west) of the highway about .25 mile to a long ridge. The feature is most conspicuous at this point, although it extends all the way from Pawnee Rock to Ash Creek, paralleling the trail. It might well be called Kirwan's Ridge, after Pvt. John S. Kirwan, 4th U.S. Cavalry. In 1859, he was with a small patrol from Fort Riley operating on this section of the SFT. Escorting a party of eastbound Pike's Peakers (returning Colorado gold seekers) and their families, the patrol encountered hostile Indians, who the day before had attacked the Santa Fe mail coach, killing the driver and conductor. Kirwan says in his journal: "Pretty soon we came in sight of the Indians scattered along the bluff as far as we could see, moving up and down the sides of the slope. They did everything possible to draw us on, and away from the wagons, but Lt. Otis gave positive orders that we were not to fire . . . and under no circumstances to leave the wagons. The women were brave and even the children were plucky" (Kirwan 1955). The strategy was successful, and the wagon train escaped without a fight. Several farm structures can be seen on the low bluff. Try to imagine the same scene with menacing Indians, as Kirwan and his companions saw it in 1859.

THE WET AND DRY ROUTES

The route of the SFT from Pawnee Rock to Dodge City has been researched thoroughly by the Wet and Dry Routes Chapter (W/DRC) of the Santa Fe Trail Association. This group, led by David Clapsaddle of Larned, has placed well over one hundred attractive limestone markers at important sites along the several branches of the trail. The serious trail buff should head for the Santa Fe Trail Center in Larned for a copy of the book *Wet and Dry Routes Self-Guided Auto Tour*, which is very useful for finding the SFT in this area.

One branch, the Wet Route or sometimes called the Water Road, stayed close to the Arkansas River, approximately the route of today's US 56 as far as Kinsley. This route was the primary one until the early 1830s, when a shortcut was developed that was about 10 miles shorter than the Wet Route. This shortcut, the Dry Route, left the Wet Route east of present-day Larned and went directly to the Caches west of today's Dodge City. As its name implies, this route was devoid of water most summers during the travel season but nevertheless remained the road of choice until the mid-1840s. The Dry Route did cross several streams that may have had some water but the primary advantage was it avoided the sand of the route close to the river.

A later variant of the Dry Route developed after the establishment of the Hall and Porter Company mail station in 1859. This station was on the south bank of Pawnee Fork west of present-day Larned. After 1859, the eastern terminus of the Dry Route moved to a point just north of Larned, where wagons headed southwest for Fort Larned, which was established in 1859 **(B).** By 1866, a third variant left the Wet Route as before (north of Larned) but went along the north bank of Pawnee Fork, crossing it just west of Fort Larned. (For a complete description of the Dry Route, see Clapsaddle 1999.)

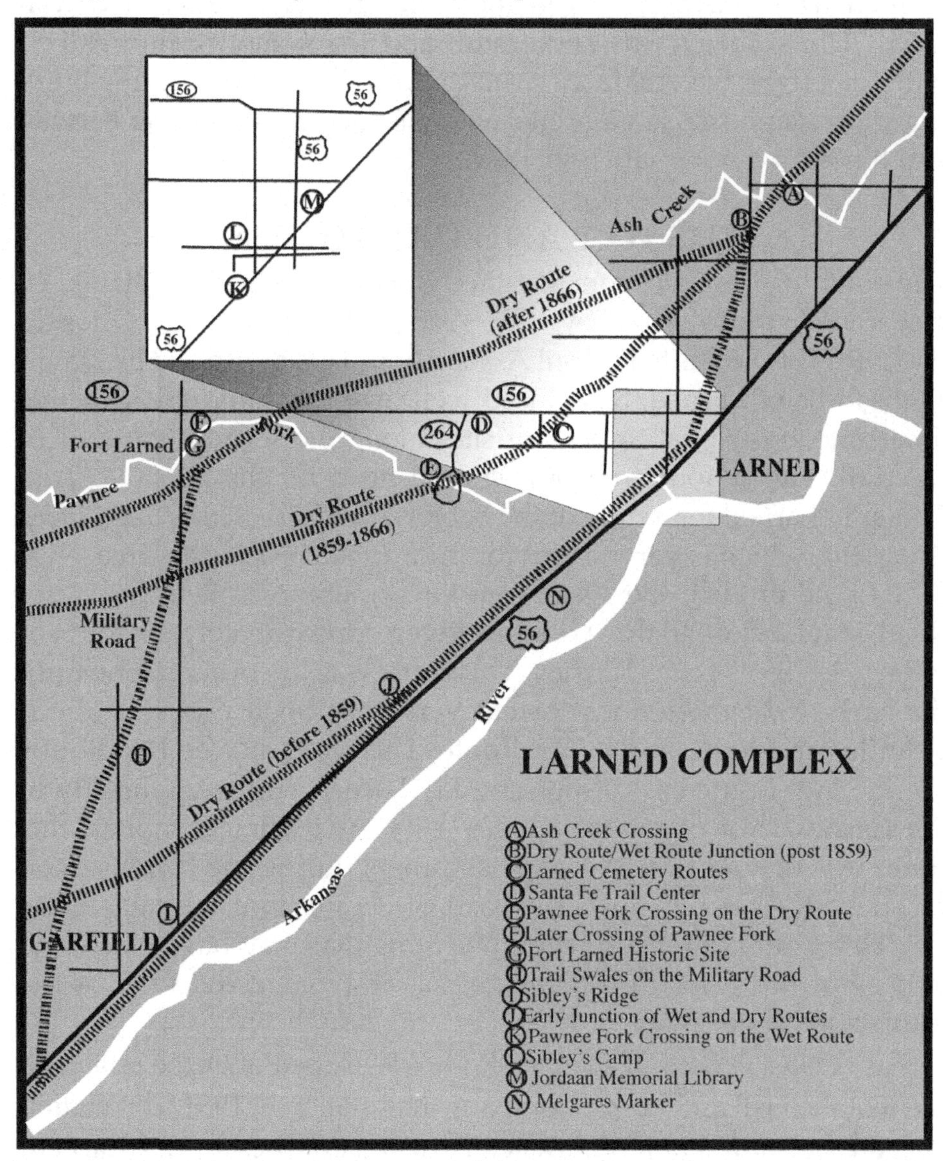

Just as the eastern ends of the Dry Route changed, so did the western end. From its terminus at the Caches (just west of Dodge City)

in the 1830s, it retreated to a point 1 mile east of present Fort Dodge. In 1867, the SFT in the Larned area ended service because the Union Pacific Railway, Eastern Division, had reached Hays City, Kansas. From that railhead, a new road was developed connecting Fort Hays and Fort Dodge, meeting the trail at the latter location. However, even the Fort Hays-Fort Dodge Road was short-lived, as railheads were established farther west on the Union Pacific, and later, on the Santa Fe Railroad as it laid tracks up the Arkansas Valley, reaching Forts Larned and Dodge in 1872.

THE LARNED COMPLEX

In the vicinity of Larned, are a variety of SFT points of interest, probably enough to warrant designating the area a complex. The only complex formally established thus far is the Clayton Complex comprising a cluster of trail sites in eastern New Mexico. At Larned a fairly substantial river, Pawnee Fork, flows from the west and joins the Arkansas River on the southern edge of town. (When you visit the river today it is much reduced because of farmers' terraces and irrigation upstream which cuts the flow somewhat.) The crossing of Pawnee Fork was an important one, and many a wagon train had to wait here for high waters from sudden cloudbursts to subside. The first settlement was at the crossing, and it was near here that George Sibley's survey team camped in 1825.

In late May, 1844 a large trading party on their way east finally was able to cross the swollen Pawnee Fork. Some of these traders had been waiting since April 23rd. The traders included a Bent, St. Vrain and Company train with proprietors Charles Bent, William Bent, and Ceran St. Vrain. The several trading parties crossed the Pawnee Fork and traveled east to Walnut Creek where they were forced to wait until mid-June to cross that stream. The high waters were also at Westport Landing and St. Louis.

The complex consists of the following sites:

A. Ash Creek Crossing

Just over 3 miles past the above roadside park in Pawnee Rock Road R crosses US 56. Turn west (right) and go 2 miles to the Ash Creek Crossing, about 50 yards past the second bridge (**A**).

Immediately to the right (north) of the road is the brush-filled bed of Ash Creek, usually dry. Here there is a Kansas sandstone marker at the site inscribed "Ash Creek Crossing " placed by the Wet Dry Routes Chapter (W/DRC) of the SFTA.

Across the creek due north, is a white farmhouse and a silo with a silver dome. Wagons coming from Pawnee Rock crossed here and camped in the plowed field just to the south of the road. If you know where to look you can see the line of trees marking Ash Creek from the top of Pawnee Rock.

In the context of trail history, this unspectacular crossing is significant because it was here that young Susan Magoffin's carriage turned over. She was thrown to the ground unconscious, resulting in injuries that caused her to suffer a miscarriage later at Bent's Fort. Read the account of the incident in her journal. There is a photo of the crossing at the Santa Fe Trail Center west of Larned.

B. Dry Route and Wet Route Junction (Post 1859)

Continue from the crossing to the next road (about .5 mile) and turn left (south). At about .4 mile on this road, there is a W/DRC marker indicating the junction of the Wet Route and the Dry Route after 1859 (**B**). Following the establishment of the mail station and the fort, this became the preferred way for the Dry Route. At this point the Wet Route continued toward the Lower Crossing of Pawnee Fork, while the Dry Route angled southwest toward the Upper Crossing. From here continue south until the road meets US 56 on the eastern edge of Larned.

This small city was founded officially in 1872 as the Santa Fe Railroad pushed up the Arkansas Valley. We will return to Larned after visiting sites west and southwest of town.

C. Larned Cemetery Route

Continue on US 56 (also KS 156 here) to the first traffic light (actually a 4-way stop) at Broadway. Go straight, leaving US 56 and continuing on KS 156 for 1.7 miles to a road coming in from the left (130 Ave.). Turn left (south) and drive .5 mile to the cemetery, passing the entrance to the southeast corner (**C**). There is a W/DRC trail marker just inside the fence labeled "Dry Route Crossed Here." The wagon trains came this way headed for the crossing of Pawnee Fork about 1 mile ahead. If you look closely under the fence, you can see the faint undulations of the several tracks of the trail. And from the cemetery you can see Jenkins Hill, which is close by the crossing. Return to KS 156 and drive west.

D. Santa Fe Trail Center

On the south side of KS 156 at 2.5 miles west of Larned, is the Santa Fe Trail Center (**D**). Built in 1974, the beautiful center interprets both the trail story and Kansas pioneer history with a series of fine exhibits. For researchers there is a small but growing library and archive. In addition, various trail-related special events are held during the year. One of the Mormon Battalion markers is located near the northeast corner of the building. This center is one of the high points of the modern trail. It also is the headquarters of the Santa Fe Trail Association. Information about this important association and its many chapters along the SFT can be obtained at the center.

Serious trail buffs will want to join the Fort Larned Historical Society, which established the center and issues a newsletter called Trail Ruts. Requests for information can be addressed to: Director, Santa Fe Trail Center, 1349 K-156 Hwy, Larned, KS 67550.

E. Pawnee Fork Crossing on the Dry Route

At .5 mile beyond the Santa Fe Trail Center, turn left (south) off KS 156 onto KS 264 and drive 1 mile to the Larned State Hospital. Entering the hospital grounds, Jenkins Hill, surmounted by a large water tower, can be seen on the right.

Take KS 264 to a T, turn right, and follow the road a short distance until it begins to curve left at the foot of Jenkins Hill. On the right at the curve, is a DAR marker designating the Dry Route Crossing of the Pawnee Fork (**E**). The W/DRC also has a marker here. The river is through the trees immediately behind and below the markers. The cutdown is evident if you walk around to the right and look down through the second-growth trees lining the creek.

In 1865, Samuel Parker established a ranch just south of this crossing. The first Parker Ranch was built in 1864 in Larned near the Wet Route Crossing of Pawnee Fork. In 1868, the ranch at the Dry Route Crossing was acquired by A. H. Boyd, who built the first permanent civilian buildings between Fort Union and Council Grove. The site became known as "Boyd's Crossing" or "Boyd's Ranche," and soldiers from Fort Larned patronized the saloon for drink and entertainment.

Just past the DAR marker is a red brick building, boarded up. On its south side, a dirt lane leads right, off the paved road down to a concrete bridge over the Pawnee Fork. It is best to walk down to the bridge. If you continue across the bridge and take the left fork in the dirt road, you will soon come to a W/DRC marker for "Boyd's Ranche" (the spelling at the time).

F. Later Crossing of Pawnee Fork

Return to KS 156 and turn left (west) toward Fort Larned. At 2.5 miles from the Santa Fe Trail Center is a junction. Here, turn left (south) and drive .8 mile. Across a field to the right, a line of woods marks the course of the Pawnee Fork. The tallest tree is near where a wooden bridge was built in 1859-1860 (**F**). In 1864, it was burned by Kiowas, who ran off some horses and mules, and was never replaced. The crossing was used primarily by military forces at Fort Larned. Once across, the trail continued along the bank of the river about .5 mile to a civilian mail station, built by the firm of Hall and Porter, which had the mail contract in the 1850s. About .1 mile beyond the station was Fort Larned, which was established when the mail station was built. The crew and material for the mail station accompanied the troops that established Fort Larned. The fort was established specifically to protect this mail station and, of course, the travelers using the trail. Jacob Hall, mail contractor, asked the postmaster general to request the Secretary of War to establish this post, and the orders were issued. It had been recommended as a possible site for a fort for several years.

Return to KS 156 and drive west to Fort Larned.

G. Fort Larned National Historic Site

Located west on KS 156 about 6 miles from Larned is the Fort Larned NHS (**G**). The first military establishment in this immediate area was called Camp on Pawnee Fork, established in 1859. In February 1860, its name was changed to Camp Alert, followed by the permanent Fort Larned in May 1860. The fort's function was to protect the mail station, caravans, stagecoaches, and travelers on the section of the SFT between Cow Creek to the east and the several "Cimarron" crossings of the Arkansas River to the west. Protection to the west along the Cimarron Route was shared and coordinated with Fort Union in New Mexico until additional forts were added at the end of the Civil War. Troops at Fort Larned coordinated with soldiers at Fort Wise (Lyon) on the Mountain Route.

Two modern scenes of Ft. Larned.
Photos courtesy of Linda Revello.

Today, the nine surviving stone buildings around the parade ground have been restored and contain military and SFT exhibits. Books pertaining to the SFT are sold at the information desk, and a film about the trail is shown in the theater. Also ask for the brochure entitled Fort Larned History Trail, which provides directions for a walking tour of outlying points of interest, including the site of the stage station mentioned above. Moreover, special historical events, including living-history programs, are scheduled periodically. Direct inquiries to: Superintendent, Fort Larned National Historic Site, 1767 KS Hwy 156, Larned, KS 67550-9321.

At the fort entrance alongside KS 156, is a roadside park, National Park Service interpretive sign, a DAR marker, and a SFT map. Follow the entrance road to the parking lot, walk across the bridge, and enjoy a tour of this historic site, the best-preserved frontier military post on the SFT. [The entrance road does not cross the Pawnee, the walking bridge does that.]

H. Trail Ruts on the Military Road

Go west from the Fort Larned entrance on KS 156 .25 mile to a paved county road that intersects from the left (south). Drive 4 miles, then go right (west) 1 mile, then left (south) on a gravel farm road .5 mile to a well-marked parking area on the left. From the small, elevated observation booth out in the field, visitors can observe excellent SFT ruts that have been preserved in an undisturbed forty-acre pasture

(**H**). The ruts were carved by wagons on the Military Road that connected Fort Larned to the Wet Route southwest of Garfield. An interpretive historical sign is in the booth. A sharp eye can also discern shallow oval depressions about 10 feet in diameter which are old buffalo wallows where the big animals rolled in the dust seeking relief from biting flies. The ruts are now administered as a detached unit of Fort Larned.

Swales at the Larned Military Road site.

I. Sibley's Ridge

From the Military Road site, continue south to the small town of Garfield, where you rejoin US 56. Turn left (back toward Larned) and drive about 1 mile to where US 56 runs adjacent to a small ridge on the north (left) side (**I**). The road that intersects US 56 here goes north to Fort Larned.) This ridge should be called Sibley's Ridge. The Sibley survey team passed by this point, and George Sibley climbed this ridge to get a better view of the surroundings. His account included the following statement: "The Waggons passed round the point, still keeping in the bottom about half a mile from the River. I rode upon the ridge, from the top of which I could distinctly trace the course of the Pawnee River for a great distance by the fringe of trees along its banks" (Gregg 1995). There is a W/DRC marker on the southwest corner on the hill.

J. Early Junction of Wet and Dry Routes (pre-1859)

Continue north on US 56 from Sibley's Ridge 5.1 miles to a marker on the left (**J**). This is the junction of the Wet and Dry Routes called the "Forks in Santa Fe Road" during the earliest period. From here wagons angled off to the southwest toward the Caches. This route began in the early 1830s and was in general use until the late 1840s. A W/DRC marker is on the west side of the road.

K. Pawnee Fork Crossing of the Wet Route

Continue toward Larned until you reach the bridge on the edge of town. Just past the bridge turn left into the nearby park, called now the Pike Plaza (**K**). There are several markers here. The first and second (both placed by the W/DRC) are for the "Pawnee Fork Crossing," although the actual crossing was downstream from this point. The last two markers are the gravestones of Pvt. Robert Easley and Pvt. Arthur Hughes, soldiers who died during the Mexican War. The marker for Zebulon Pike is one of only three Pike markers in Kansas. Pike was such an important figure in the history of the Southwest and it is shameful that his story has gone untold for the most part.

Pike Plaza.

L. Sibley's Camp

From the park drive toward downtown Larned and turn left (north) at State Street. Continue on State to the intersection with Second Street. On the northwest corner is where George Sibley and his survey team camped the nights of September 1 and 2, 1825 (**L**). The site was purchased by David Clapsaddle, Bob Rein, and Mildon Yeager, who placed information signs on the property. Sibley's Camp was donated to the Fort Larned Old Guard in 2014. The original Parker Ranch (see "E" above) was located two blocks west of this site.

M. Jordaan Memorial Library

From Sibley's Camp, go back to US 56 (2nd Street intersects US 56 if you go east on it). Continue on US 56 until it turns left at Broadway. To the right at this corner is the old railroad station, with a DAR marker directly in front. At 8th Street and Broadway, is the Jordaan Memorial Library (**M**), which contains excellent materials on local history and the SFT.

N. Facundo Melgares Expedition Marker

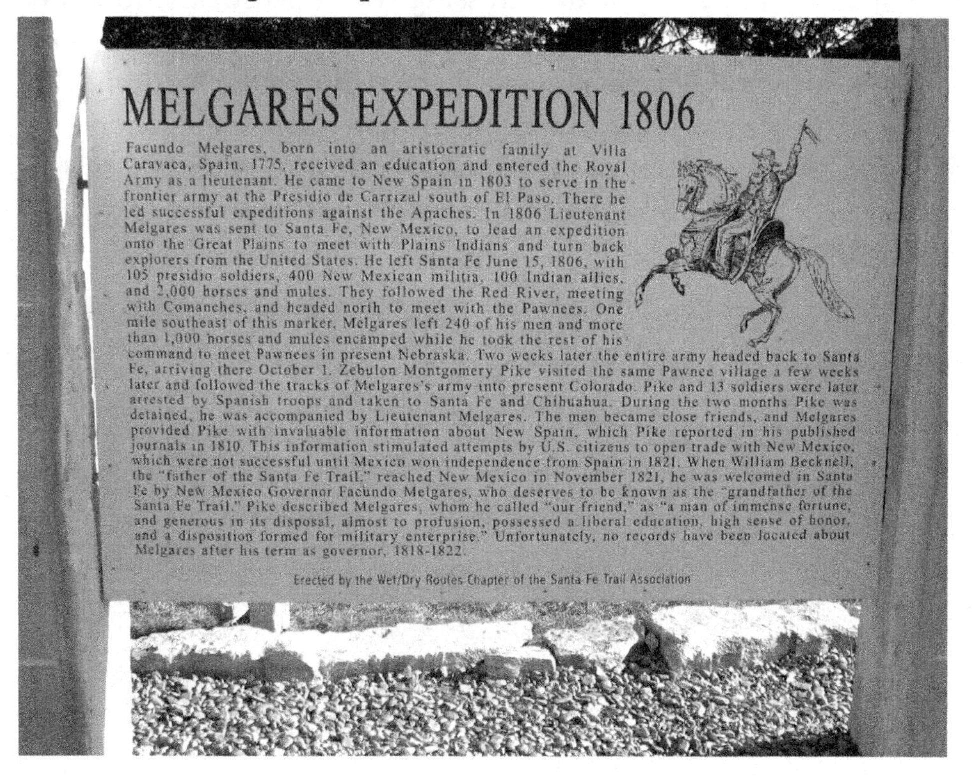

Now drive south on US 56 toward Kinsley and Dodge City and look for a marker on the left at 4.3 miles. This recently-placed marker honors the efforts of a Spanish officer, Facundo Melgares, who led a force of over 500 men from Santa Fe to Nebraska in 1806. Melgares was looking for American explorers such as Lewis and Clark and Zebulon Pike and was under orders to stop them as they were traveling in Spanish territory. The Spanish force camped near this marker before returning to Santa Fe. Melgares later provided information to Pike, recorded in Pike's journal (1810), which spurred efforts to open the SFT. If William Becknell is "father of the Santa Fe Trail," then Facundo Melgares and Zebulon Montgomery Pike should be considered "grandfathers of the Santa Fe Trail."

Continue southwest on US 56.

LARNED TO DODGE CITY

Retrace your route southwest on US 56 to Garfield. A DAR marker is in the northeast corner of the town park, on the right side of the highway near the grain elevator opposite the post office. From this marker continue on US 56 .9 mile to Coon Creek Crossing on the Wet Route of the SFT. Approaching the highway bridge over Coon Creek, a faint dirt road turns right into a field, with a tree at the junction. Stop under the tree after entering the road. There is a W/DRC limestone marker on the fence line for "Coon Creek Crossing-Wet Route." The field behind the marker was the site of a wagon campground. To the left, is the crossing where the Military Road from Fort Larned approached the Wet Route. To reach it, you must cross a fence. Just beyond, several indentations in the cut-bank are wagon ramps leading down to the crossing.

About 400 yards past Coon Creek on US 56 at the right, you can see a set of ruts visible at times, depending on the condition of the grass. This was where the Military Road from Fort Larned met the Wet Route. There is a pullout with a W/DRC marker on the right.

Continuing on US 56 4.3 miles past the bridge over Coon Creek, there is a W/DRC marker on the left for "Plain Camp," which is across the railroad tracks and closer to the Arkansas River. This campsite apparently lacked any defining characteristic, hence its name.

At 7.4 miles past the Coon Creek Bridge on US 56 is a DAR marker on the right, between mile markers 162 and 163. There is also a W/DRC marker here for "Love's Defeat." Lt. John Love's company was attacked here in 1847 by 300 Comanches, resulting in a loss of five soldiers and 130 oxen.

At 4.8 miles past the last marker, turn left to the marker on the left side of the road. On June 18, 1848, the famous Battle of Coon Creek took place here. Lt. William Royall's detachment was attacked by some 700 Comanches and Apaches, but he was able to rout the Indians without losing a single soldier. There is a W/DRC marker at the site.

You have now passed Coon Creek which is the last perennial stream traders would see entering the Arkansas until they reached the Purgatory River in Colorado.

Continue on to Kinsley. The state of Kansas has placed an interpretive marker, "Battle of Coon Creek," on the south side of the Arkansas River along US 50 3 miles east of Kinsley. Since the actual battle site, as noted, was on present-day US 56, this marker can be ignored.

On the western limits of Kinsley, back on US 56, is a large roadside park, where a DAR marker stands beside a black railroad engine, moved here from its original site. The Sod House Museum is also in this park. Just past the park you will join US 50 at a stop sign.

Continuing on US 56/50, at 4.7 miles from the roadside park is a pullout on the left side of the highway with another DAR marker. Three miles beyond is the town of Offerle. On the west side of the town and to the north of the highway, is a small park with a DAR marker. There is also a W/DRC marker there with interpretive text.

The early Dry Route crossed US 50/US 56 at about Offerle. We left the Wet Route at Kinsley, and it is now about 10 miles to the south following the Arkansas River floodplain. Since there is no easy way to follow either route in this area we will continue southwest on US 50/US 56 to its intersection with US 283, just beyond the hamlet of Wright.

On the northeast corner of this junction, is a large roadside park with an official Kansas Historical Marker "Road to Santa Fe."

Its interpretive text on the SFT is one of the most detailed of any found in Kansas, although unfortunately the explanations for the names Wet and Dry routes are incorrect.

SIDE TRIP TO LOWER CROSSING

Go south on a paved county road that leaves US 50/US 56 at the intersection with US 283. Continue 4 miles to join KS 400. At this point you are on the Wet Route, only a few hundred yards east of its junction with the late version of the Dry Route. We will turn here and briefly go east down the valley of the Arkansas River but return to this junction later.

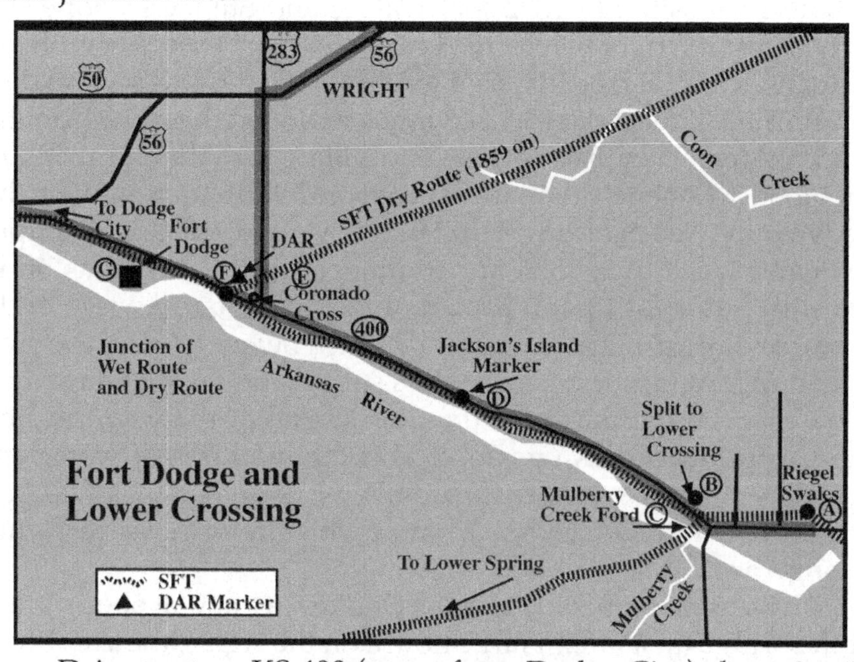

Drive east on KS 400 (away from Dodge City) about 9 miles. There is a large feedlot on the left, and KS 400 curves to the right. As it curves take the paved county road entering from the left. After .5 mile the paved road turns left (north) but continue straight ahead on the gravel road about 1.2 miles.

In the vicinity of a windmill on the left, you will see some excellent SFT ruts (**A**). These are the "Riegel Ruts," and there is a W/DRC marker near the windmill. The Wet Route left the river bottom just east of a drain. A short distance before the brick farmhouse, the trail crosses the county road and goes into a field on the right.

Return to KS 400 and turn right (north) to the entrance of the Ford County Feed Yard. About .7 mile after meandering through the feedlot you will see a W/DRC marker describing the point where the traders using the Lower Crossing left the Wet Route to ford the Arkansas River at Mulberry Creek (**B**). Few, if any, traders used the Lower Crossing as it was far too dangerous.

Return to KS 154, and immediately south of the highway intersection there look for another W/DRC marker identifying the "Mulberry Creek Ford (**C**)." Travelers crossed the Arkansas River behind the marker but we know of but one group of traders using this Lower Crossing. In 1822 Joel Walker and Stephen Cooper led a party across the river here at the lower crossing. They met with one disaster after another, nearly died for lack of water, and several days later returned to the Arkansas, having abandoned the route from the lower crossing. They had to resort to killing buffalo and drinking their blood to quench their thirst. For a detailed account of this misadventure, see Stocking (1971). Sibley's survey team camped here September 6 to 9, 1825 but continued up the Arkansas on its north side. Surveyor Joseph Brown of the Sibley party wrote of the Lower Crossing in 1825: "It would be much nearer to cross the river here and ascend Mulberry creek to its source and then go directly to the lower spring on the Semaron; but on trial of the way travelers have discontinued it as unsafe. It is incommodious of water and timber for fuel and wants such prominent land marks as will be a sure guide. On this route has been much suffering in a dry time; 'tis dangerous."

Drive west on KS 400 toward Dodge City and at about 1 mile past the bridge (just after a large house on the right), the Wet Route descended from the high ground back to the Arkansas River floodplain. Five miles beyond the Mulberry Creek marker on the left is the W/DRC marker for "Jackson's Island (**D**)." This was a commonly used campsite on the Wet Route and the scene of an 1843 confrontation between Capt. Philip St. George Cooke and a group of raiders from the Republic of Texas. The Texans under Col. Jacob Snively had come north to rob Mexican traders on the SFT, and were disarmed by Cooke's forces which had been sent from Fort Leavenworth to protect Mexican traders following the murder of Antonio José Chávez earlier that year.

Continue west on KS 400 about 5 miles to the junction with the road from Wright, where you first joined KS 400. About .25 mile west of the junction, there is a small park on the right. Behind it on a hill is the large Coronado Cross, a 38-foot cross of prestressed concrete erected in 1975 as a bicentennial project (**E**). It commemorates a religious service believed conducted in this vicinity on June 29, 1541, by Father Padilla after the Coronado Expedition successfully crossed the Arkansas River. There is a new informative sign here as well.

At .3 mile west of the park, on the right side of the highway, is a W/DRC marker telling about the western terminus of the Dry Route as it merged with the Wet Route (**F**). This was the later version of the Dry Route, after abandonment of the earlier Dry Route to the Caches. There is also a DAR marker here. Looking up the hill and slightly to the right, you can see ruts leading down toward the marker, a trace of the Dry Route. The deep depression is not part of the trail but a "trench silo."

Drive west 1 mile to the Fort Dodge Soldiers Home (**G**). Just west of the entrance is a marker on the south side describing Fort Dodge as the western terminus of the Fort Dodge-Fort Hays Road. That road came down the hill from the north to meet the Wet Route.

Company Barracks at Fort Dodge. Photo courtesy of Dave Webb.

Fort Dodge was established in 1865 to provide protection for this section of the SFT. Its location was well chosen as it was close to the junction of the Wet and Dry Routes. Because the place has been adapted to modern use, little remains among the remodeled structures to suggest the primitive life of frontier days. Although Custer passed through Fort Dodge and camped nearby, he was not stationed here. The building in the southeast corner of the fort is an original barracks [actually two barracks connected as one today], although greatly modified. In addition, the post hospital and quartermaster's storehouse [military used storehouse, not warehouse] date from trail days. We recommend a visit to the museum. They sell a nice history of the fort. There are several historic markers around the fort identifying original fort structures, including the post commander's quarters and quartermaster's quarters.

From the fort drive west on KS 400 (also called East Trail Street) to Dodge City, 5 miles away. (Note: If you follow this side trip, you will miss an official Kansas Historical Marker, "Dodge City, the Cowboy Capital," which refers to the SFT. It is located on US 50/US 56 3 miles east of Dodge City at an overlook of a giant cattle feedlot and stockyards. The turnout for the sign is on the south side of the highway.)

DODGE CITY

Dodge City is much more interested in its Wild West image of cowboys and shootouts than it is in the SFT. The town was not founded until the railroad arrived in 1872, long after SFT traffic had moved farther west from Kansas Pacific railheads at Sheridan and Kit Carson. However, there are some points of interest in the area for trail buffs. From Fort Dodge continue west on KS 154 to the edge of Dodge City, where KS 400 intersects US 56 at a stoplight. At this intersection continue straight ahead. This is Trail Street and is directly on top of the SFT. In the center of town, turn left at 2nd Street and go south one block to a DAR marker just inside the entrance of Wright Park on the right (**A**). This park was named for Robert M. Wright, who donated the land. An early freighter on the SFT, he also contracted to supply hay to the army posts and served as post sutler at Fort Dodge. In addition, Wright served as mayor of Dodge City and wrote a book, *Dodge City: The Cowboy Capital,* which contains useful trail information. A monument to him is in the center of the park.

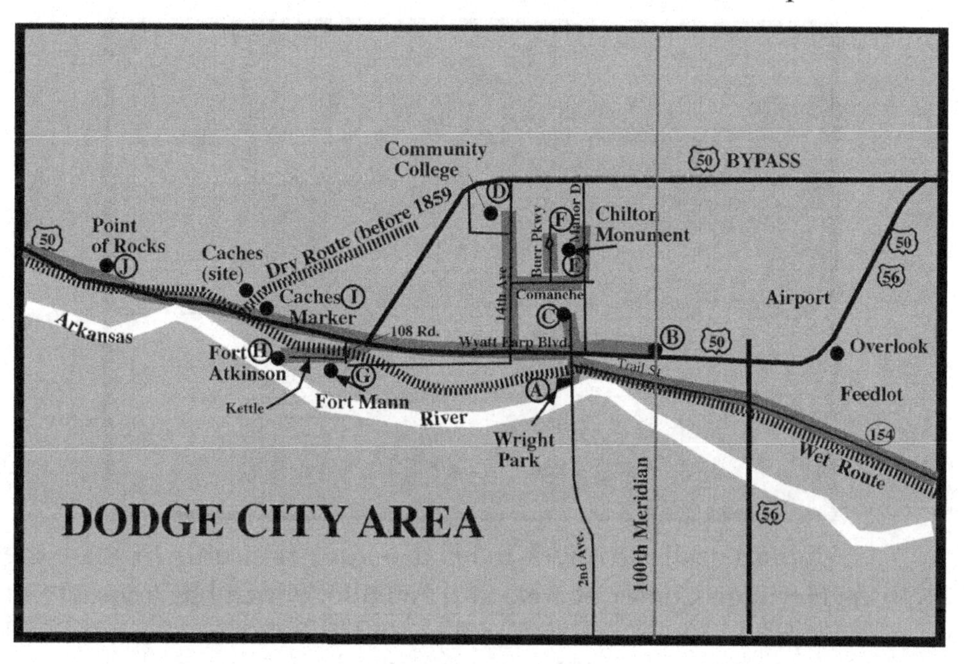

Return north on 2nd Street, cross the railroad tracks, and turn left on Wyatt Earp Boulevard. On the northwest comer of 3rd Street and Wyatt Earp, is the Visitors' Information Center/Convention and Visitors' Bureau, which provides a great variety of information about Dodge City and the surrounding area. Behind and to the west of the Visitors' Information Center is Boot Hill. Front Street, at the foot of Boot Hill, is Disneyesque but does commemorate Dodge City's hey-day in the mid-1870s when it was a shipping point for cattle driven up from Texas. The Boot Hill Museum at the west end of Front Street has excellent exhibits relating to the SFT, Fort Mann, Fort Atkinson, and Fort Dodge.

Drive east on Wyatt Earp to M Street where you will see a marker on the north side of Earp marking the 100th meridian (**B**). When the early traders arrived at this point, Mexico began beyond the meridian south of the Arkansas River. From here on west, traders looked across the Arkansas into Mexican territory, until the Mexican War pushed the international boundary far to the south. Return on Wyatt Earp to the downtown area.

Spanish, and later, Mexican Territory until 1848.

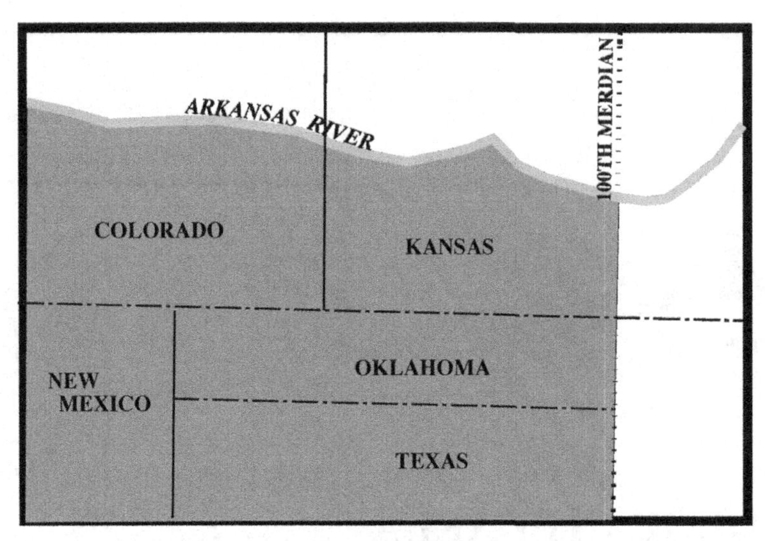

Modern trail travelers may also find it useful to visit the Kansas Heritage Center at 1000 2nd Avenue, which has a variety of historical publications and services provided by a very friendly and helpful staff **(C)**. One of the center's books is *West by Southwest: Letters of Joseph Pratt Allyn, a Traveler Along the Santa Fe Trail in 1863*, edited by David K. Strate.

Another point of interest in town is the modernistic metal statue The Plainswoman, erected in 1972 on the campus of Dodge City Community College to honor early pioneer women (**D**). To reach the campus, drive west on Wyatt Earp Boulevard and turn north on 14th Avenue. After approximately 1 mile the campus is on the left. After turning left into the campus, the statue is at the end of the road.

Returning south on 14th Avenue, watch for a major intersection with traffic lights. Turn left (east) here on Comanche and go about five blocks to Chilton Park. Turn left (north) on Manor Drive and proceed two blocks along the east side of the park, watching for a 6-foot-high light-colored stone monument in the center (**E**). The inscription on it honors Maj. Robert H. Chilton, commander of Fort Atkinson, which was located on the SFT just west of present Dodge City. In 1853, Major Chilton assisted Indian Agent Thomas

Fitzpatrick's efforts at a large council with the Comanches, Kiowas, and Plains Apaches, resulting in the Treaty of Fort Atkinson, designed to provide safe passage for travelers on the trail.

A new sign commemorating Chilton and Thomas Fitzpatrick is prepared and awaiting installation in Chilton Park at the time of writing, a project of the Dodge City SFTA chapter. (Chilton later served in the Confederate Army as aide to General Robert E. Lee). A vivid description of the treaty event is given by Sgt. Percival G. Lowe in his book *Five Years Dragoon* (Lowe 1965).

Return to Comanche, turn right and drive one block to Burr Parkway where you turn north. At about one-quarter mile from Comanche you will see a small "island" in the center of the Parkway. Park nearby and view the very impressive swales in the island (**F**). These traces are part of the earliest Dry Route from the Larned area. The wagons were headed for the Caches which you will visit soon.

The Burr Parkway swales in Dodge City.

Return to Wyatt Earp Boulevard and turn right (west) headed out of town. At about 1 mile, there is a roadside turnout with a DAR marker and an official Kansas Historical Marker, "Dodge City, the Cowboy Capital." The text refers to Fort Mann, Fort Atkinson, and to the SFT.

From the above marker, drive 1 mile west on US 50 and turn left (south) on 108 Road just beyond the point where the US 50 Bypass comes in from the right. Drive .2 mile (one block) and turn right on Kettle Way Street. At .6 mile is the W/DRC marker for Fort Mann (**G**), which was located .4 mile south of the marker. Established in 1847 as a wagon repair depot during the Mexican War, Fort Mann was headquarters for a volunteer Indian Battalion of Missouri Volunteers, commanded by Major William Gilpin, which brought an end to Indian resistance along the SFT in 1848. Following the Mexican War, Fort Mann was abandoned in 1848.

Continue west .4 mile on Kettle Way to a W/DRC marker for "Fort Atkinson," which lies at the end of the road but may be difficult to find because of weeds (**H**). Originally established as Camp Mackey in 1850, at a location farther west, it was soon relocated here and named Fort Atkinson. The fort was built of sod and housed regular military troops, who called it "Fort Sodom." It predated Fort Union, New Mexico, by a year and was abandoned by 1854. It had a small garrison and was very expensive to supply; and it could claim few accomplishments beyond the Treaty of Fort Atkinson, 1853. Katie Bowen stayed overnight in the commanding officer's quarters at Fort Atkinson and left a fine description of her visit there, published in *Kansas History* magazine.]

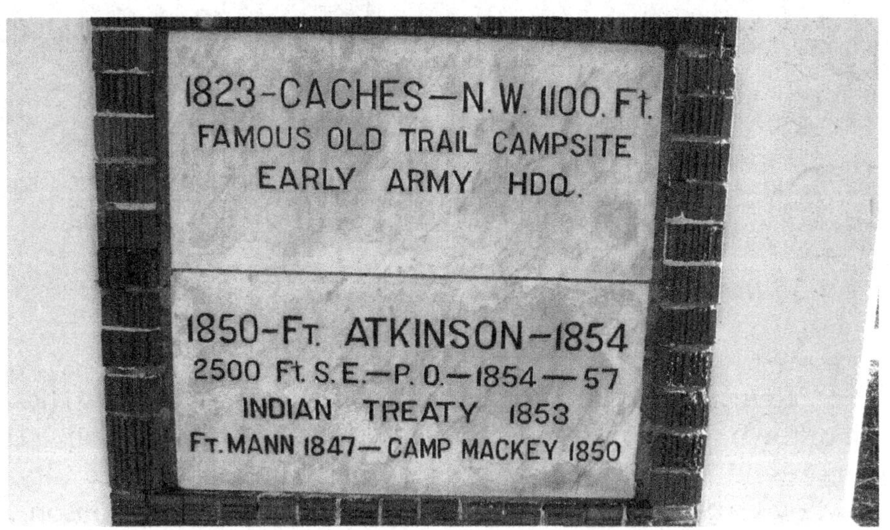

The marker for the famous Caches on the SFT.

Go back to US 50 and turn left 1 mile. At the intersection of a dirt section line road, there is a large white monument for the Caches. Turn right just beyond the monument on the dirt road and go .2 mile. A W/DRC marker for the Caches is on the left (west) of the road **(I).** This spot was where the earliest Dry Route joined the Wet Route. The Caches are named for some pits dug near here by the Baird-Chambers party in 1823. The party had left Missouri late (too late in fact) in 1822 and was hit by a blizzard at this spot. The men lost most of their pack animals and hid (cached) their trade goods in the pits. Then they continued to Taos, New Mexico, purchased mules, and eventually returned to retrieve their goods. The open pits, The Caches, remained a landmark for trail travelers, many of whom wrote about this spot.

Return to US 50 and continue west 2 miles to a W/DRC marker on the right side of the highway, "Point of Rocks." This is the first of several such features by that name on the trail **(J)**. It is here we leave the series of W/DRC markers. The Dodge City chapter of the SFTA is preparing a new marker for Point of Rocks to go in when the expansion of the highway is completed.

Two of the earliest trading expeditions, the Walker-Cooper party on its way to Santa Fe and the Fowler-Glenn party returning from Santa Fe and Taos, met near here on June 12, 1822. Until 1846, individuals standing on top of Point of Rocks could look south across the Arkansas River to Mexican territory on the other side since there was at that time no timber along the river. However, today its banks are marked by a line of trees seen to the left of the highway.

Four and a half miles beyond Point of Rocks is a fine and well-marked set of SFT swales. The trail was compelled to leave the flat floodplain here because the river was hard against the cliffs. The swales are on the right side of the highway, near a sign that reads: "Historic Point of Interest." At the site is a turnout and parking area. These trail remnants are being protected by the Boot Hill Museum in Dodge City. There is also a DAR marker and extensive signage by the National Park Service.

The SFT swung up this hill and made a 2-mile arc before once again returning to the valley farther west. The splendid set of swales here should not be missed. The Soule Canal passed through this area and is sometimes confused for trail ruts. The canal was a failure.

RIVER CROSSINGS

Continue west on US 50 to the town of Cimarron. At the traffic light and main intersection, turn left (south) on KS 23. Four blocks south, just before the bridge over the Arkansas River, is the entrance (on the right) to Cimarron Crossing Park. The park is one of the most pleasant spots on the SFT today in western Kansas. Just inside the entrance on the right is a large red granite marker with text and map showing the two main branches of the SFT. Behind the marker stands a white brick pavilion and beyond it a new official Kansas Historical Marker, "The Santa Fe Trail." Its extensive text includes reference to William Becknell's inaugural trip. To the right of this marker is a covered wagon.

Another, newer, marker is located in the park. This one was placed there by the SFTA and shows a drawing of the mail and stage station, or ranch, at the Cimarron Crossing. The drawing is based on the published reminiscences of the builder of Cimarron Ranch in 1866. We think his memory was a bit faulty as there was no ranch this size at this site in 1866. As shown, it is larger than Fort Union in New Mexico and would have occupied twenty men cutting sod for years to complete. In viewing the Arkansas River directly south of the park, you can get a feel for what a crossing of that river would have entailed.

The Cimarron Crossing of the Arkansas River was a major landmark for trail travelers since it was the midpoint of the journey, roughly halfway between Independence and Santa Fe. Here the SFT split into two great divisions—the Cimarron Route, or Desert Route, and the Mountain Route, also called the Bent's Fort Route. The Cimarron Route forded the river here (or at other crossings 6 miles up the Arkansas River as far as present-day Ingalls) and continued in a southwesterly direction 50 miles across the waterless desert (or Jornada), which ended at the

Lower Springs on the Cimarron River. In addition to the lack of water, there was a threat of attack from Comanches and Kiowas. However, since this was the shortest route to Santa Fe, and much easier than taking the Mountain Route over Raton Pass, it was preferred by most traders. The Mountain Route did not come into general use until the Mexican War, and freighters preferred the Cimarron Route through the Civil War.

This area of the river was called the Middle Crossing, and the fords here were often used. The Lower Crossing (the least utilized) was downriver at present-day Ford, Kansas (14 miles east of Dodge City), while the Upper Crossing was near modern Lakin (roughly 60 miles upriver from the town of Cimarron). All the crossings eventually led travelers to the Cimarron River.

The Mountain Route did not cross the river in Kansas but continued up the north bank of the Arkansas to Bent's Fort in southeastern Colorado, where it forded the river and then headed for Raton Pass. Although it was about 90 miles longer, there were fewer concerns about water and Indian attacks along the Mountain Route. The two branches finally converged at La Junta (present-day Watrous), New Mexico, with a single route continuing the last 75 miles to Santa Fe. Taos was also a goal for traders and it could be reached by several routes.

Continue west on US 50 up the Arkansas Valley and in about one mile you come to the start of Nine Mile Ridge. As Stocking writes "the Dakota sandstone pushes close to the Arkansas and nine miles west, swings back from it." The SFT had to leave its usual course on the edge of the floodplain and climb to the high ground. In Ingalls, the old railroad depot two blocks south of the railroad tracks on the left has been converted into the Santa Fe Trail Museum. Although there are good displays of pioneer artifacts, none actually relates to the trail. There is a DAR marker in front of the museum and another directly across the street to the west on the corner in a small park. All the towns along this stretch were established as the railroad advanced and the SFT was closing down.

Continue on US 50 about 12.5 miles from Ingalls where you will cross into Finney County. Just after the county line there will be a road toward Pierceville. Drive to Pierceville and just after passing over the railroad tracks turn right on Mansfield Road. Continue on Mansfield 3 miles until you see a hill jutting out from the north. This is another Point of Rocks. The SFT barely had space to go between the "Point" and the floodplain. The GLO surveyor shows the SFT a few yards south of the railroad here. This means you have been driving directly on the SFT.

It was somewhere very near this point that the bishop of Santa Fe Jean Lamy and his large caravan was attacked by Indians on July 17, 1867. Lamy had brought five nuns with him from St. Louis. Sister Mary Alphonsa Thompson died of cholera in this area at about the time of the attack. She was buried in this vicinity and her grave has never been found.

From here drive on Mansfield 7 miles to the edge of Garden City at S. Jennie Barker Road. Turn right at Barker and go to US 50 (Business 50)/KS 400 where you should turn left. Drive on US 50 west passing the relatively new US 83. At Campus Drive there is a small roadside park (on the left) with a DAR marker and an official Kansas Historical Marker, "The Indian and the Buffalo," with an interesting text.

GARDEN CITY

Enter Garden City on Business US 50 and proceed to the intersection of Business US 83 in the center of town. Turn left (south) on US 83 (which is also Main Street) and drive three blocks to Maple Street. Turn left (east) on Maple and go two and a half blocks along the north boundary of Finnup Park to a DAR marker in the park on the right. Continue past the marker to Maple and 4th, then turn right (south) into the park.

On the right is the Finney County Historical Society Museum, which contains exhibits and a small research library with items pertaining to the SFT. The facility is open afternoons only.

Return on Maple to US 83, turn left (south), and drive about 2 miles to the bridge over the Arkansas River, which is dry here much of the year. Just beyond the bridge on the right is the information office for the Garden City Buffalo Refuge. Operated by the Kansas Fish and Game Commission, it contains the largest buffalo herd in the state. Late in the last century, a local resident, C. J. "Buffalo" Jones, helped save these animals when they were on the verge of extinction.

Return to the center of Garden City and continue north until you rejoin US 50. In the center of town, note on the left side of the street the imposing four-story Windsor Hotel, built in 1887. Although constructed after the close of the SFT, it is interesting. On the courthouse lawn behind the Windsor Hotel, is a statue of Buffalo Jones.

The next town west of Garden City is Holcomb. The highway now bypasses the town, so you must turn left off US 50 and continue to the center of town. Just past the elementary school is a DAR marker on the right, set directly on the SFT.

TO LAKIN

Continue west on US 50 to the small community of Deerfield. Turn left (south) at the main intersection and drive five blocks to a park on the right. A DAR marker is on the southeast comer of the park, almost directly on the original trail.

Back at the main intersection, go 3 miles west on US 50 to a highway bridge, where you will see a sign advising you of a "historical marker." At a small pullout on the right, is the site of "Charlie's Ruts," which should not be missed. This land was donated to the local Kearny County Historical Society by the late Paul Bentrup of Deerfield. Charlie's Ruts are named for Paul Bentrup's father Charlie, who preserved them. Here you can walk across the small dam and experience the ruts close up. There are some very pronounced ruts behind the marker.

Drive on to Lakin and the intersection of US 50 and KS 25. Turn left (south) on KS 25 and go two blocks to the Kearny County Courthouse on the left, where there is a DAR marker on the lawn.

Continue south two blocks to Waterman and turn right (west) two blocks to Buffalo Street. The Kearny County Historical Museum, a complex of five buildings, is on the left. Turn left on Buffalo and go one block to the entrance, which faces the railroad tracks. This excellent museum has a number of trail-related exhibits, including one of the finest original Conestoga freight wagons to be seen anywhere. In addition, superb railroad memorabilia is displayed in the restored Atchison, Topeka and Santa Fe depot. If you only stop at one museum, this should be it.

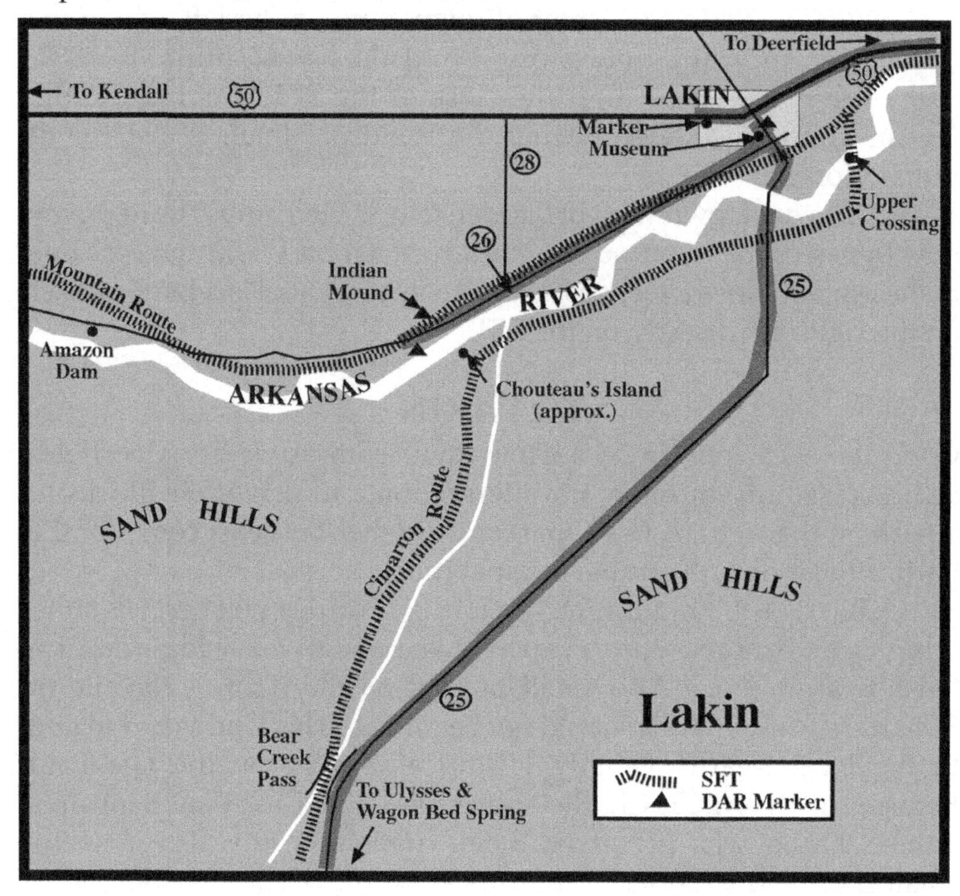

Lakin was in the vicinity of the Upper Crossing of the Cimarron Route. There may have been several places used for crossings. The late Paul Bentrup told us that you can drive a pickup truck across the river at a point just downstream from the bridge. Another likely crossing point was Chouteau's Island upstream from Lakin. Early travelers mention crossing the Arkansas about nine miles below Chouteau's Island and following along the south side of the river to turn south toward the Cimarron near Chouteau's Island. Available documentation shows that the Upper Crossing was the most used by trail travelers in the 1820s, superseded by the Middle Crossings in the 1830s, but used through the Civil War.

Motorists wishing to follow the Mountain Route should continue west on US 50 consulting Chapter 6 in this book. The Mountain Route was a much later version of the SFT beginning during the War with Mexico in 1846. After Bent's Fort was established in 1833, there was a wagon road along the north bank of the Arkansas as far as the fort. From there, if someone wanted to go to New Mexico, they would most likely have used pack animals and gone there by way of the Sangre de Cristo Pass taking them to Taos.

Chapter 5
CIMARRON ROUTE

Lakin is in the general vicinity of the Upper Crossing of the Arkansas River. You recall that the Lower Crossing was near Ford, Kansas on the south bend of the Arkansas where Mulberry Creek enters. The Middle Crossing, really a series of crossings, was located near present-day Cimarron and Ingalls, Kansas. However, it was the Upper Crossing that was utilized in the early days of the SFT.

It was an easy crossing and generally made at Chouteau's Island (**A**), or any number of places downstream from that island. Traders could cross the river and follow along the river on its south side until they reached Bear Creek. A marker for the Creek was Indian Mound, earlier called Chouteau's Mound. The Mound is almost exactly across from the confluence of Bear Creek and the Arkansas. You will visit Indian Mound later when you follow the Mountain Route of the SFT in the next chapter.

From the island landmark, traders headed due south for the lower spring on the Cimarron River. All of the crossings, Lower, Middle, and Upper led immediately to a long line of sand hills on

Cimarron Route.

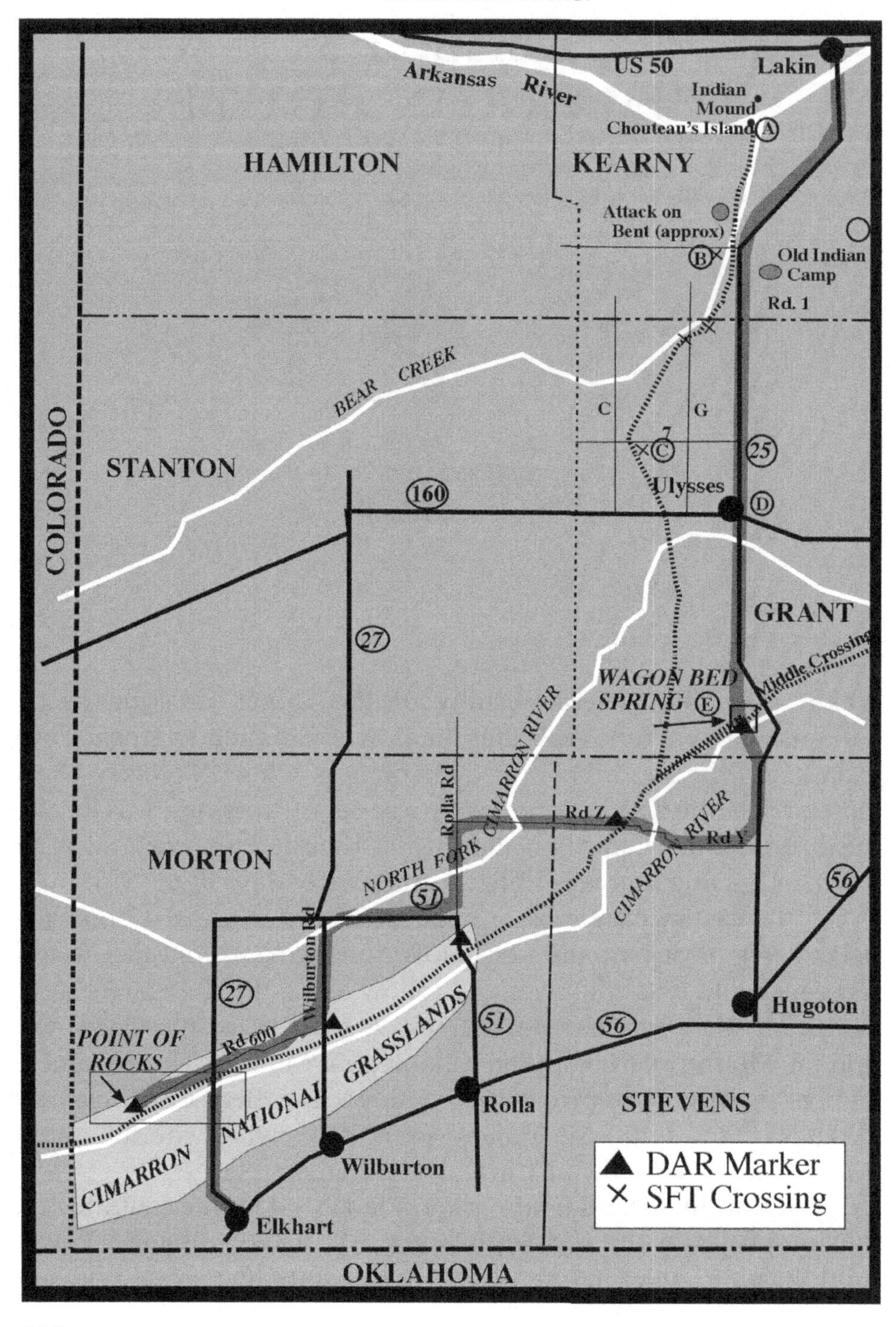

the south bank of the Arkansas. The advantage of the Upper Crossing for the traders was that an ephemeral stream, Bear Creek, cut a path through the sand hills. This creek heads in Colorado but rarely has water in it, however, over the centuries it has had enough flow to provide a path south cutting through the sand hills. George Sibley in his government-sponsored survey in 1825 followed Bear Creek south to the Cimarron, as did Dr. Rowland Willard a few weeks before him (Poole 2015). This was the shortest route between the Arkansas and Cimarron rivers, approximately 40 miles, compared to approximately 60 miles from the Middle Crossings.

Attack at Bear Creek

In the summer of 1829, Bvt. Major Bennet Riley and two hundred infantry soldiers camped on the south bank of the Arkansas near Indian Mound after escorting the annual westbound caravan, captained by trader Charles Bent. The river at this time was the international boundary and separated the United States and Mexico. The troops did not have permission to cross the Arkansas River into Mexico. Bent's caravan headed up Bear Creek and at about six miles was attacked by a large Indian force. Bent sent word back asking for Riley's assistance. Riley sent his soldiers to help and Bent was able to safely go on to Santa Fe with the help of Anglo trappers and Mexican citizens who came to their aid.

Riley's soldiers were infantry and the Indians were mounted on horses, Shortly after, dragoons (mounted infantry), were incorporated into the U. S. Army and then, finally, cavalry. Another important part of the story is that Riley used oxen to pull his wagons, a first; by 1830 traders were also beginning the switch to oxen.

Mexican troops accompanied the return caravan in the autumn and spent a couple of days near the Upper Crossing visiting with U.S. troops and traders. On October 12, 1829, there were gathered on the north side of the Arkansas River in present Kearny County, Kansas, over 500 people, including Anglo-Americans, Mexicans, Spaniards, Frenchmen, and Indians of several tribes, with more than 2,000 animals, including oxen, horses, mules, and donkeys. Lieutenant Philip St. George Cooke declared it was "the strangest collection of men and animals that had perhaps ever met on the frontier of the United States."

Drive south from Lakin on KS 25 toward Ulysses. Just after crossing the Arkansas River Bridge, you are on the floodplain. One branch of the SFT passed here, continued upriver to the crossing at Chouteau's Island, then turned south to head for Lower Spring on the Cimarron. The traders followed Bear Creek until they climbed out of the sand hills at Bear Creek Pass, about 11 miles from the Arkansas River crossing on KS 25 (**B**). As you reach the pass, the cross road is called Menno Road; you should stop to view the swales coming up the creek valley. There is a "crossing" marker on Menno Road.

Traders usually began their journey from the Arkansas River in late afternoon, continuing until midnight. Resting for 3 or 4 hours; then made the push for the Lower Spring arriving mid-morning perhaps. The water situation varied greatly from year to year. Sibley, in 1825, had no problems while M. M. Marmaduke the year before (1824) wrote "I never in my life experienced a time when such general alarm and consternation pervaded every person on account of the want of water." The route from the Arkansas to the Lower Spring and beyond was called the "Waterscrape" by the traders.

From the intersection of Menno and KS 25, continue south toward Ulysses to Road 1, the county line separating Kearny and Grant counties. Turn right here and drive 1.3 miles to a crossing marker on the left. The government land office surveys noted most SFT crossings of section lines south of the Arkansas and this marker is on one of the crossings. It is just before the dry bed of Bear Creek. Continue on Road 1 to Road G where you should turn left and drive 1.7 miles to another crossing marker. You will have passed back over Bear Creek here. Drive south 4 miles on Road G to Road 7 and turn right. Go about 3 miles and look for more crossing markers on your left (**C**). This is a remarkable site for there are a series of parallel swales plainly visible.

Note: At this location you should imagine yourself a trader in 1830. Remember that there are no trees here and as you look at the line where earth meets sky, the horizon, it is identical in all directions. You know you must continue south to reach water and by this time you may begin to worry.

From here, drive west to the next intersection, Road C, and turn left and drive to U S 160. Turn left here toward Ulysses and drive to that town, going beyond the intersection of KS 25 to the Grant County Museum (**D**), a large white building set back on the left. It has excellent SFT exhibits with special reference to the nearby Wagon Bed Spring site.

Return to the intersection of U S 160 and KS 25 and turn left on 25 (south) toward Hugoton. Continue on KS 25 about 8 miles to a point where the paved highway veers slightly left. Here is a sign directing you straight ahead to Wagon Bed Spring.

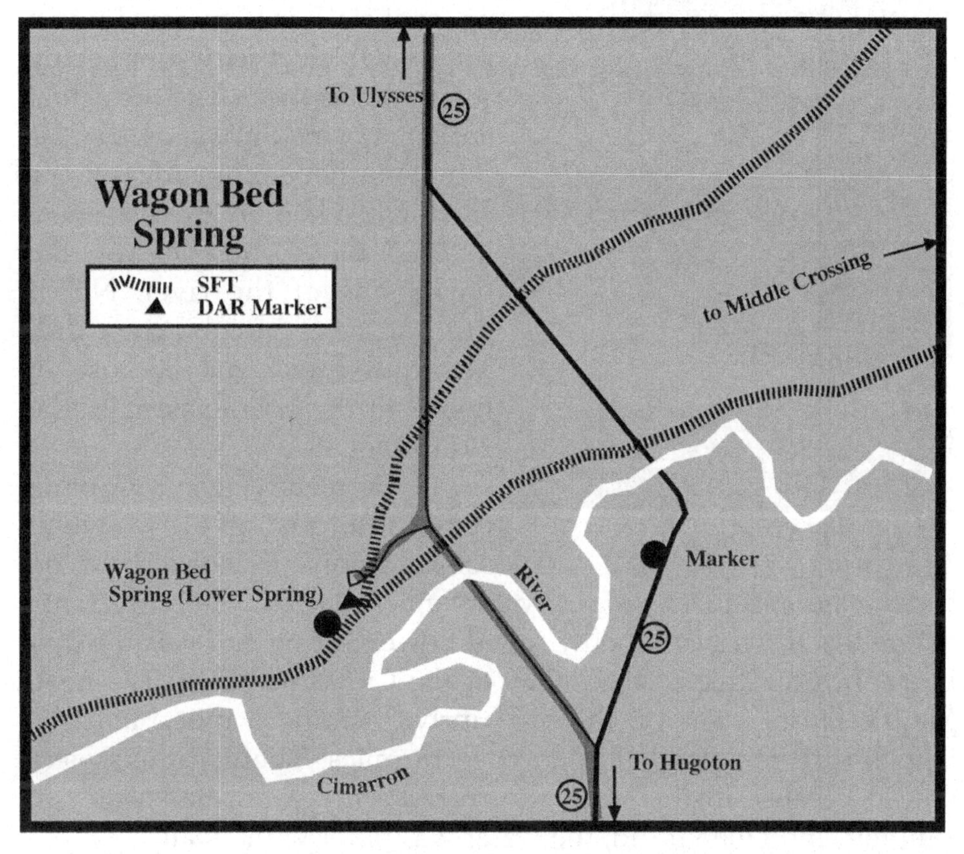

Continue south on that road about 3 miles and turn right on a dirt road to Wagon Bed Spring, about 1 mile from the turn. The road to the spring site is just before the ford at the Cimarron River. There is a small parking lot at the location of the spring (**E**). Initially called Lower Spring, it was the first reliable water source after leaving the Arkansas River. The stretch between Lakin and the

Cimarron represents part of the infamous Jornada. This section was also called the Waterscrape because of the water uncertainty.

At the site is a DAR marker, near the river enclosed by a white railing, as well as a Kansas State Historical Marker reading "Wagon Bed Spring." This spring is a National Landmark.

DAR marker.

Near the parking area is an enclosed space with a hole containing upwelling water. This is not the actual spring but an artificial one operated by a pump with electricity supplied by solar panels nearby. The actual spring, Lower or Wagon Bed, is now on the south side of the riverbed. When Sibley came here in 1825 the spring was on the north side of the river. No, it did not move but the river did. The course changed because of floods in the past, especially the 1914 event.

The name Wagon Bed Spring came into use in 1847 when someone sank a wooden wagon bed in the spring to collect water and serve as a holding tank. Before that, it was commonly called Lower Spring and was the first in a series of three in the valley of the Cimarron River. The next, Middle Spring, was on the SFT upriver about 36 miles, and the Upper Spring beyond that another 18 miles. These springs were crucial because in this area, the river itself seldom had water in summer, and when it did, the water was bitter with alkali.

From Wagon Bed Spring the SFT follows the Cimarron River on its north bank. You will need to do a little wandering to pick up the trail again.

Return to the gravel road that led from KS 25 and turn right to the ford of the Cimarron River. In some very rare instances you will need to go back north to KS 25 because of water in the

Cimarron. Yes, it does occasionally happen. If you choose to come this way, you will miss a marker for Jedediah Smith located on KS 25 where it crosses the Cimarron River.

Lower Spring GLO.

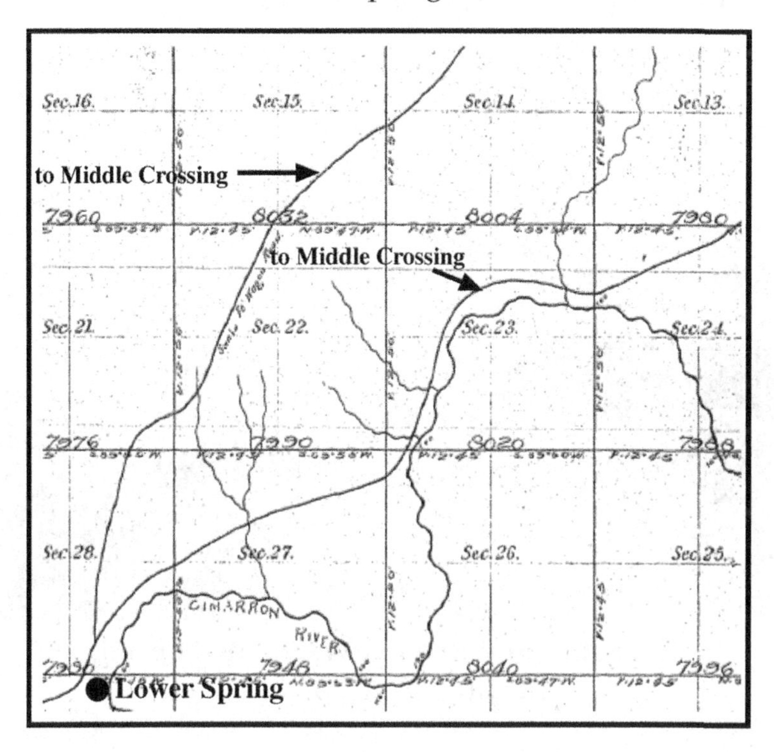

The actual story of Smith's death will never be known. He was ahead of his caravan looking for water when he was killed by Indians, probably Comanches. Many believe Smith's death occurred here at the Lower Spring. It is more likely that he died near Fargo Spring in today's Seward County. Smith was far out in front of his caravan which was desperately seeking water. Smith, of course, was an important figure in this period as he was a renowned mountain man and explorer.

Drive south on KS 25 to Road Y (about 5 miles from the point you join 25) in Stevens County (refer to included map). Turn right here and drive 8.5 miles on Y and it will turn right, left, right, and finally, left (west) again. After you cross over the Cimarron, .5 miles will bring you to a DAR marker on the left. Continue about two hundred feet past the DAR marker; the SFT crossed the highway here. Continue about 9 miles to where you turn left at Rolla Rd., marked as Road 23 here, and continue south on Rolla to the intersection with KS 51. There is a DAR marker 2 miles south of this junction and you will need to return to this spot after viewing the marker.

The Cimarron River at Wagon Bed Spring.
A rare sight with water flowing in the river.

Drive west on KS 51 7 miles to Wilburton Rd., turn left and go 6 miles south to another DAR marker. Now you can begin to look for limestone markers set directly on the trail. At this point you should look for a well-maintained gravel road about .8 miles coming in from the right. This is a Cimarron National Grasslands road and is Rd 600. Take this road west and you will be paralleling the SFT the entire way to the Middle Spring. Note the many limestone posts along the corridor, some to the right, some to the left. These markers are set directly in the path of the SFT.

You will eventually arrive at the paved KS 27. Here you can turn right, climb the nearby hill and turn into the overlook; you will have a grand view of the valley with waysides explaining the role of the springs and Point of Rocks for the SFT.

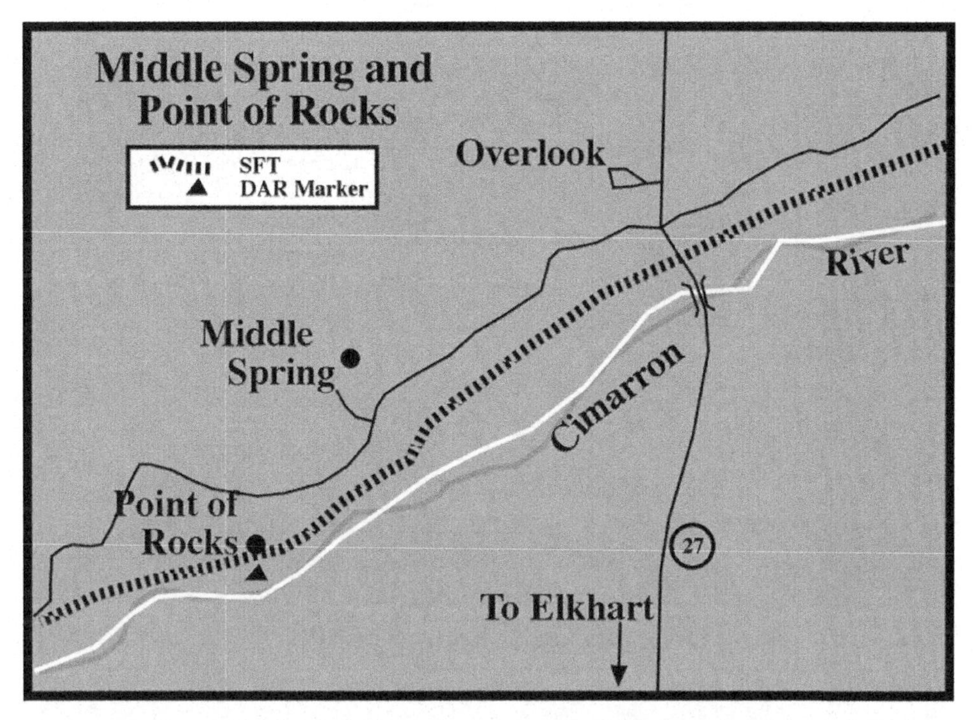

Go back to the road leading to Middle Spring. About two miles after leaving the paved highway, a small road intersects from the right (north). Immediately after turning on it is another cattle guard and just past it the Middle Spring historical sign with excellent text. Immediately behind the sign the spring forms a pond surrounded by a grove of trees where there are several picnic tables and restroom facilities.

Return to the main dirt road and turn right (west) toward Point of Rocks. You can see more limestone SFT markers along here. At about 1.5 mile from Middle Spring, the road divides at a Y. Take the left-hand fork a short distance to the top of Point of Rocks. At the small parking area are several interpretive markers. The SFT passed between the foot of the bluff and the river. From the top, you have an excellent view of the Cimarron River snaking southwestward about 5 miles, where it clips the extreme southeast corner of Colorado before continuing into Oklahoma. It is possible to hike a steep trail from the parking area down slope toward the river to a DAR marker. Rededicated here in 1997, the marker had been moved to nearby KS 27 before it was returned.

Point of Rocks, Kansas.
DAR marker at bottom of hill.

Return to KS 27 where you should turn right and drive to Elkhart crossing the Cimarron on the way. Elkhart has a fine museum, Morton County Museum, with many SFT artifacts. It will be on your left (south) as you enter town on the highway. The headquarters for the Cimarron National Grasslands is just before the museum and the folks here can provide maps and information about the grasslands and the SFT route therein. There are hiking trails along the ruts in the grassland and these are the longest continuous ruts of the SFT in Kansas.

THE OKLAHOMA PANHANDLE

Soon after entering the present state of Oklahoma, the SFT crossed to the south bank of the Cimarron River at a well-known site called Willow Bar, which got its name from a stand of willow trees growing on a sandbar in mid-stream. At that point the trail left the river, but for approximately the next 20 miles it remained in the Cimarron "breaks," the rough country comprised of hills and mesas lying in the wide valley of the river.

Cimarron Route

The SFT route through Oklahoma.

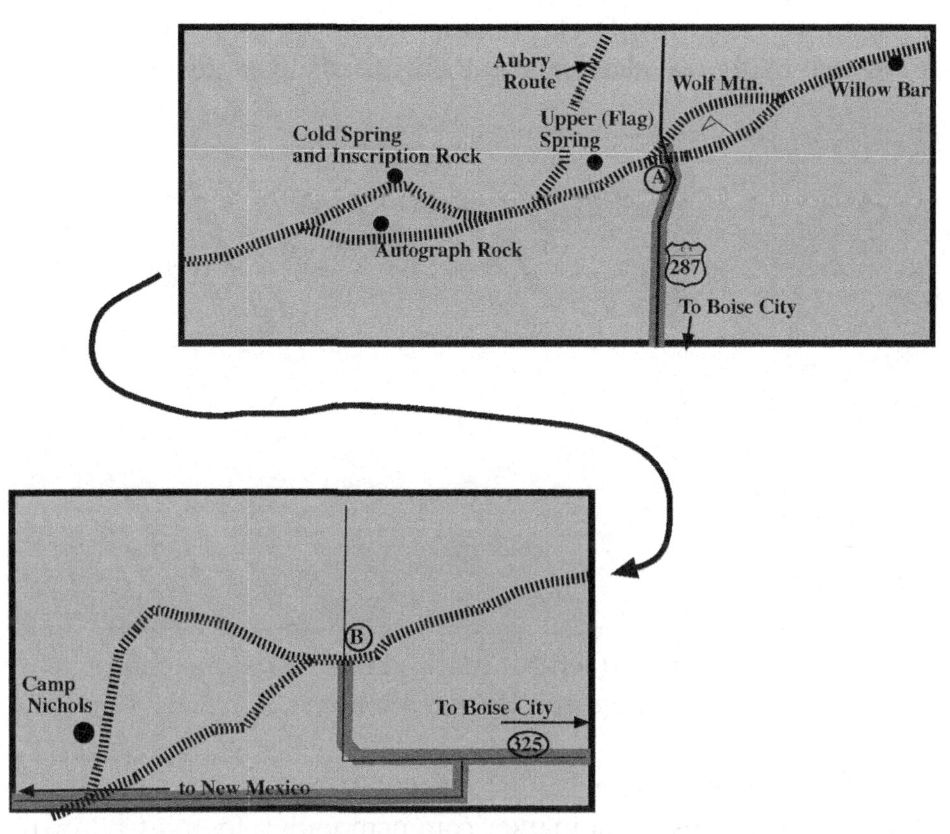

The next campsite after Willow Bar was Upper Spring (or Flag Spring), followed by Cold Spring and then Camp Nichols, occupied for five months in 1865. Camp Nichols was established to guard the southern end of the Aubry Route which came south from the Arkansas River near the camp. About 5 miles beyond Camp Nichols, the trail entered what is today the state of New Mexico. Unfortunately, all of these sites are on private ranch land and not easily accessible. However, several good markers and some fine trail ruts can be seen.

In the center of Boise City, is the Cimarron County Courthouse. On the grounds on the north side is a Mormon Battalion marker dedicated in summer 1983. From here follow US 287/US 385 north and stop at the museum that is part of the Heritage Center, on the left with a large metal dinosaur in front.

The museum has some SFT exhibits. But, more importantly, the museum staff can give you directions and permission to visit fascinating Autograph Rock, an important stopping place on the SFT where many travelers carved their initials in sandstone cliffs.

Trader F.B. Delgado left his mark in the sandstone cliff of Autograph Rock, Oklahoma.

Continuing north on US 287 at about 9.6 miles is a pullout on the left (west) with a historical marker commemorating Joseph C. Brown, the surveyor for the Sibley party of 1825 (**A**).

The SFT crossed the highway here, and swales can be found on both sides of the highway. Excellent swales begin directly behind the pullout; walk west beyond the railroad tracks to view them. Also, look northeast, across the highway, and observe prominent Wolf Mountain, around both sides of which branches of the SFT passed, angling up from Willow Bar on the way to Upper Spring. Upper Spring is about 1.5 miles due west of this location, only a thirty- to forty-five minute walk, although individuals unfamiliar with the country are apt to miss it.

A few miles beyond Upper Spring was Cold Spring near where the Aubry Route joined the Cimarron Route. The Aubry Route was pioneered by Francis Aubry in 1851 and was used by most traders on the Cimarron Route. They would head northeast from a point just west of Cold Spring and then join the Mountain Route east of Syracuse near Fort Aubry. This shortcut was used from 1851 through the Civil War. You will visit the northern junction in Chapter 6, the Mountain Route. For some unknown reason the National Park Service did not recognize this route as part of the SFT so it is not included in the National Historic Trail. This decision should be revisited.

Jose´ Librado Gurule´

One of the more interesting accounts of travel on the SFT was that of the young New Mexican man from Placitas, New Mexico. He was 88 years old when he told his story about leaving New Mexico in February, 1867 for "los estados," the United States. The caravan in which the seventeen-year old traveled had over 50 wagons and carried wool for the U S market. The caravan left Placitas (near Albuquerque) and went through Cerillos and Las Vegas, N.M. before using the Cimarron Route to Cold Spring, Oklahoma. There they left the Cimarron Route and followed the Aubry Route to the Arkansas River. For the entire story one should consult Marc Simmons in *On the Santa Fe Trail*, 1986.

Return to Boise City, and on the west side of Courthouse Square pick up a paved state road (OK 325) that leads to Kenton. At 15 miles, the paved road to Wheeless intersects from the left (south). This is the road that goes to New Mexico, but for the moment continue straight ahead another mile where the highway makes a sharp turn to the right (north). At about 3.5 miles from the curve, is a pullout on the left (west).

Here is one of the choicest spots on this section of the SFT, with no fences and unspoiled prairie stretching toward the western horizon (**B**). The trail crosses the highway coming from Upper Spring and Cold Spring heading for Camp Nichols, 7 miles to the southwest. An official Oklahoma Highway Marker refers to the founding of the fort in 1865 by Kit Carson. During its few months of existence, it guarded this section of the trail from hostile Indians. A second handsome marker refers to Sibley's surveyor Joseph C. Brown.

Behind the markers, thick vegetation in the trail swales appears as a discoloration in the prairie. And, there is a new DAR marker at this site.

The official name was Camp Nichols.

Return 4.5 miles to the Wheeless junction, then go south 1 mile and turn right. The New Mexico State line is 12 miles from this point. As you turn onto this road, ahead to your left you will see the distant Rabbit Ears, the first elevations of any prominence that traders saw on the Cimarron Cutoff.

McNEES CROSSING

At the New Mexico State line, the Wheeless Road makes a sharp left turn. At this turn is a new DAR marker. The SFT passed directly over the marker site and into New Mexico. You can see the swale to the west just behind a sign on a fence stating "Santa Fe Trail Ruts, New Mexico." After turning left at the DAR marker, drive about 1 mile south on the state line and then right again, entering New Mexico. Straight ahead is the distant mountain Sierra Grande, another familiar trail landmark. At 2 miles inside New Mexico, is an intersection and stop sign. Here you join NM 406 and go west and then southwest on that highway.

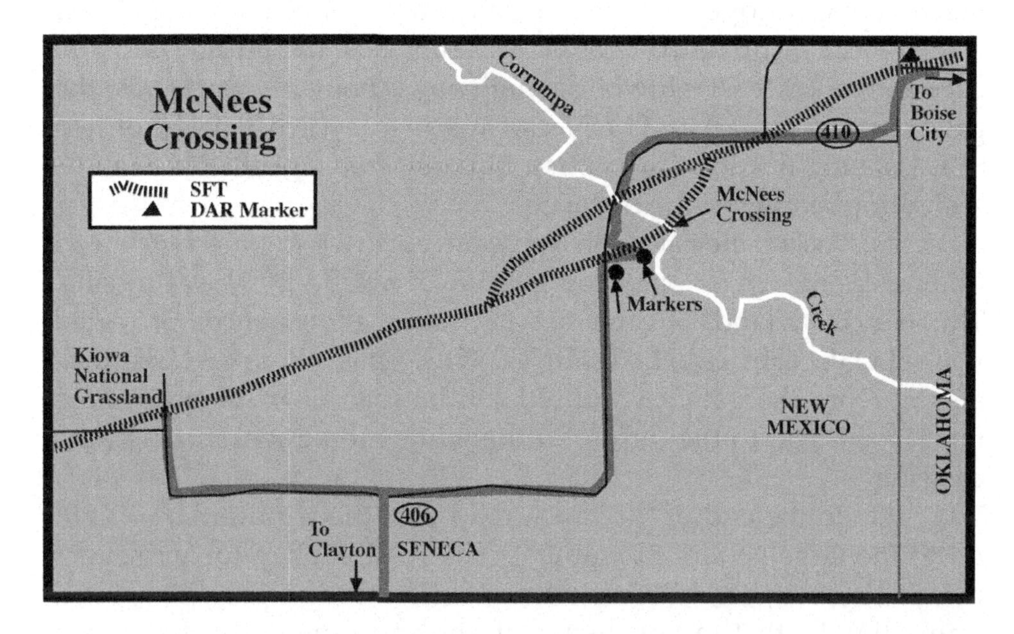

At the intersection with NM 406, you can see the SFT in the fenced pasture on the east (right). It is represented by a wide swale, or cut, that makes a conspicuous indentation on the horizon. Following this trail takes you back to the DAR marker previously noted in Oklahoma. In late summer, because of extra moisture, the trail depression is marked by a thick stand of bright green rabbit weed.

From the high ground at this intersection, the renowned trail landmark Rabbit Ears can be seen in the distance to the southwest. They are a mountain and a butte of unequal size lying close together, but from certain places on the trail they vaguely resemble a pair of rabbit ears. According to one story, however, they did not get their name from their appearance but from Chief Rabbit Ears of the Cheyenne, who was killed in the vicinity by the Spaniards. In any case, all travelers on the Cimarron Route were familiar with the twin peaks, which remained in sight for many days. The main SFT passed along their north flank, while a less-used branch skirted them on the south.

From the intersection go west toward Clayton, noting swales on the left of the road, then curve south on NM 406 for 2.4 miles to the highway bridge over the usually dry North Canadian River (called locally Corrumpa Creek). At .8 mile past the bridge, is a wire gate on the left (east) side of the highway. About 100 yards past the gate, there is a marker, "McNees Crossing," which is right on the SFT. Looking toward the western horizon, traces of the trail can be seen disappearing in the distance.

Go back to the gate which gives access to a two-track ranch road leading east across an open cow pasture .5 mile to McNees Crossing. This is private land, but the current owner allows entry, provided you CLOSE THE GATE BEHIND YOU, since there are livestock inside. From the gate a windmill can be seen near the end of the ranch road, and to the right of it the white monument marking the crossing.

Go to the end of the ranch road past the windmill and right up to the large square monument. The road is okay for passenger cars in dry weather, but in summer the center is high with weeds. Immediately to the southeast of the monument, a dirt ramp (the original trail) leads down to the crossing of the North Canadian. Both upstream and downstream the bed is loose sand, but at this one spot is a rock shelf in the bottom of the riverbed, making a natural crossing for wagons. On the east and west banks are traces of caravan campgrounds.

The cutdown at McNees Crossing.

From the monument or ramp, look east across the North Canadian, where tracks of two branches of the trail can be seen coming down to converge at the crossing. The beginning of this short split is approximately 8 miles back, in the vicinity of Camp Nichols, Oklahoma.

At this crossing, in autumn 1828, two young traders named Robert McNees and Daniel Monroe rode ahead of their eastbound caravan, stopped to take a nap, and were shot by Indians. When the caravan arrived, McNees was dead and was promptly buried on the spot. The wounded Monroe was carried on to the Cimarron River, where he died. These deaths contributed to the clamor for military escorts, the first of which was Major Riley's in 1829. Josiah Gregg records an Independence Day celebration here on July 4, 1831, the first such observance In New Mexico. The white monument was placed by the American Legion in 1921 to commemorate that event.

The monument at McNees Crossing commemorating a Fourth of July celebration noted by Josiah Gregg.

Return to NM 406 and continue south toward Clayton. The highway makes a sharp right and continues for about three miles, where it turns left. Instead of following the highway at this point, continue straight ahead (west) on the gravel road 3.3 miles, then turn right and go 1 mile to an intersection, which is at the corner of the Kiowa National Grasslands. This is a good place to get out and walk the ruts.

At the northwest corner of the intersection is a parking lot, and you can enter the walking area through a gate. Once inside the gate, there are fine ruts about .1 mile from the lot coming from right to left. You can also drive north from here down the arroyo and up the other side through a gate on the right, continuing for about .25 mile. This is also Kiowa National Grasslands property, and you can walk the trail here as well. Moreover, in the arroyo to the right, about .5 mile from where you parked, are many large exposed rocks, and on one there are some dinosaur tracks.

Return to NM 406 and turn right toward Clayton. At 1 mile you will see the deserted Seneca School on your left. This part of New Mexico was homesteaded early in the 1900s, and this school served the homesteaders' children, at one time accommodating ninety-eight youngsters.

THE CLAYTON COMPLEX

In 1964, New Mexico State Senator William Wheatley of Clayton was instrumental in having the Clayton Complex designated a Registered National Historic Landmark. It includes an assembly of SFT campsites and geographical features beginning at McNees Crossing and extending for about 35 miles southwest along the trail to Round Mound. (A description of the various sites is supplied by William E. Brown in *The Santa Fe Trail,* 1988.) Unfortunately several sites,like Turkey Creek Camp and Rabbit Ears Creek Camp, are on private land and not easily accessible to the public.

From Seneca School follow NM 406 south to its junction with US 56 4 miles east of Eklund. There turn right (west) on US 56. At .1 mile on the right (north) is a pullout with an official New Mexico Highway Marker, "Rabbit Ear Mountain."

In the center of town is the old Eklund Hotel, founded in post-trail days by a Swedish-born Clayton pioneer, Carl Eklund. The hotel has been completely refurbished and is open for business. There is a restaurant in the hotel as well. One-half block east of the Eklund Hotel take US 64/US 87, which leads northwest toward Raton. At the city limits just beyond a motel , in a pullout on the left (south) side of the highway, is an official New Mexico Highway Marker, "Clayton," with reference to the Cimarron Route. One mile farther is the Union County Feed Lot (on the right) with plenty of cows. Just past it is another official New Mexico Highway Marker, "Rabbit Ear Mountain," with a text about the SFT that differs from the one east of Clayton with the same title. This location offers a good view of the Rabbit Ears just to the north.

At 18 miles from Clayton, US 64/US 87 goes through the small community of Mt. Dora. The large, round mountain from which the town takes its name lies to the right (north) of the highway. The SFT coming from McNees Crossing passed along its north side and then headed southwest to intersect the highway straight ahead.

Five miles beyond Mt. Dora is a roadside park with picnic table on the right (north). Here, alongside its tracks, the Colorado and Southern Railway has erected a SFT marker (a bronze plaque set in a white monument) designating the place where the trail crossed the tracks and the highway. Directly to the south and slightly west is Round Mound (today often called Mt. Clayton), a major trail landmark recognized by all wagoners, who often scaled the summit for a view of the surrounding country. In Josiah Gregg's *Commerce of the Prairies,* there is a lithograph showing the view from the top with a wagon train passing below.

The "March of the Caravan"
lithograph from Josiah Gregg's book.

From the park and railway marker, rejoin US 56, which is some 20 miles to the south. The longest way is to return to Clayton and pick up US 56 on the west side of town. You can continue ahead on US 64/US 87 another 3.5 miles to the nearly deserted community of Grenville. There NM 453 intersects on the left (south) and leads 22 miles south to US 56. After turning onto NM 453, Round Mound is straight ahead. Note your odometer reading, the SFT crosses the road in 5.7 miles.

At 2.5 miles from Grenville the road turns sharply to the right (west). At this point the SFT is off to the left of the road between you and Round Mound. The trail can be seen from the top of the mound, but if you stop and look carefully you can see it from the road. Those wishing to make the climb should park here. Allow at least half a day, as the distance across the flat prairie to the base and the height of the mound are deceiving.

Two miles from the first turn is a second one to the left (south), which goes along the west side of Round Mound. Soon after the second turn, the SFT crosses NM 453 headed southwest toward the next major landmark, Point of Rocks. The crossing of the road is unmarked, however, and we have not located swales. Continue south to the junction of US 56, located 29 miles west of Clayton, and turn right (west) toward Springer.

TO POINT OF ROCKS

At about 18 miles west of the above junction, US 56 crosses the western boundary of Union County into Colfax County. From this point look north to a long sloping mountain in the far distance. This is 8,720-foot Sierra Grande, which first became visible to wagon travelers as they crossed the Oklahoma Panhandle and remained a prominent landmark for many days thereafter.

From the same location also look north and west (to the front right of the highway) at the corner of a mesa jutting onto the plains. This is the dark outline of New Mexico's Point of Rocks, which caravans used as a guide as they traveled westward after passing Round Mound. There was a fine spring at the site, but it was also a place Indians used for ambushes.

At 31.5 miles from the aforementioned junction (US 56 and NM 453), is a roadside park on the right (north) and an official New Mexico Highway Marker, "Point of Rocks."

A gravel road, County Road 52, intersects with US 56 at the east end of the park, while a power transmitter is on the northeast corner. Look north and a bit east of County Road 52 to a cluster of ranch buildings and trees about 5 miles away on the plain. The round mountain (behind and to the right of the ranch) with the mesa at its base marks Point of Rocks.

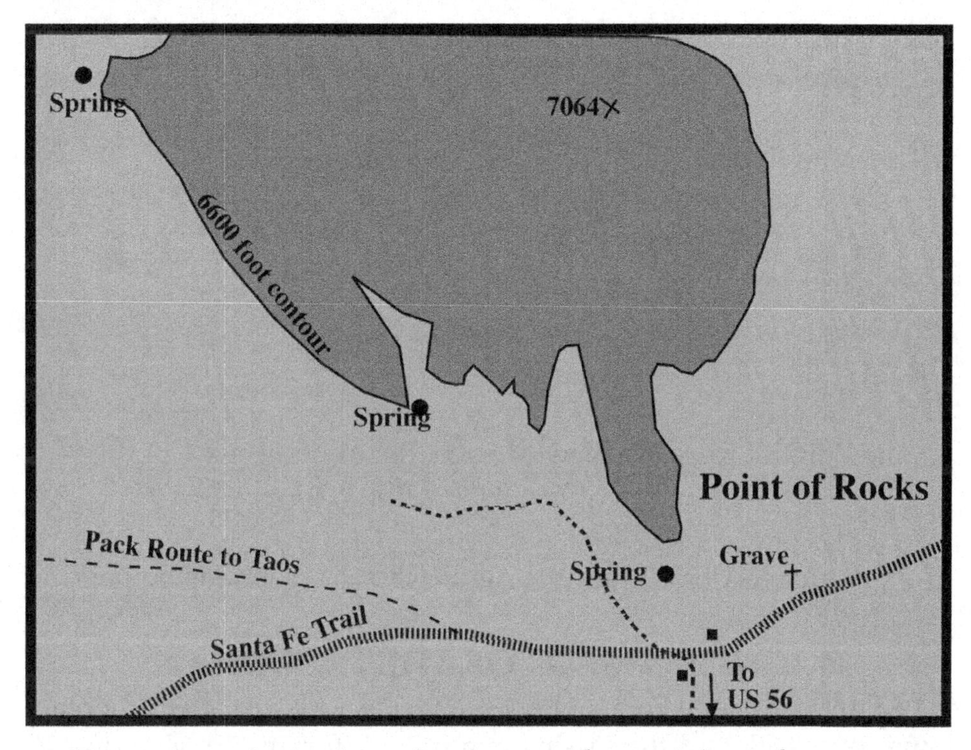

For a closer look, drive (in dry weather only) north on County Road 52 about 7 miles. Between 6 and 7 miles the deep swale of the SFT crosses the road. The Soil Conservation Service has placed low earth dams across the swale to check erosion. At 7 miles turn right (east) at the intersection onto County Road 53, go 2 miles, then turn left (north) and drive on Point of Rocks Road 1 mile toward a ranch house near the base of Point of Rocks. This is the Gaines Ranch, and the owners welcome visitors. A toilet is available for site visitors, and there is a mailbox with trail information that will show you the way to the historic grave and the spring.

The main SFT stuck to the flat plain about 1 mile to the south, but many caravans made a swing here because of the availability of water. Return to the park and continue west on US 56. There is also evidence of the pack train route to Taos which left here and headed almost due west. Sibley used this route in 1825 as did Dr. Willard a month before Sibley (Poole 2015).

The Point of Rocks in New Mexico. For another view of this scene see the cover of this book.

Return to US 56 and turn right (west) at the roadside park.

ROCK CROSSING OF THE CANADIAN

At 14.5 miles from the Point of Rocks roadside park, just after dropping down to a creek and then rising again, look for an old, abandoned stone house. The house is a partial dugout with a weathered shingle roof, on the left (south) side of US 56. A telephone pole is directly behind it. The SFT coming from Point of Rocks crossed from the right to the left side of the highway, although the ruts are not in evidence close to the road. (They can be seen, however, at another point .25 mile down the highway to the left.) There are some new SFT crossing markers here. This location is also near the junction of the Cimarron Route and the Granada to Fort Union Military Road.

To see the well-known Rock Crossing of the Canadian, look southwest past the house and down a natural trough between the mesas about 2 miles away. The mesas form the edge of the

Canadian River Valley, while the river itself is at the bottom of the trough, marked by a line of trees.

The SFT descended the trough to the river. Here was the famed Rock Crossing of the Canadian (*El Vado de las Piedras*). A natural rock bottom at the ford (similar to the one at McNees Crossing on the North Canadian) aided the passage of wagons. Below this point was the impassable Canyon of the Canadian, and above it the river bottom was of sand.

Once past the crossing, the SFT went in a southwesterly direction to the wagon mound. The actual site of the Rock Crossing is on a private ranch, accessible only by a jeep road. Thus visitors will have to settle for this distant view. Hobart Stocking gives a historical sketch of the site in *The Road to Santa Fe.*

SPRINGER

Continue 8 miles on US 56 to Springer, In Springer there is a nice museum about two blocks to the right at the stop sign. At Springer you will join Interstate 25 and go south toward Wagon Mound, which can be seen in the distance. The SFT will be on your left the entire way to Wagon Mound.

WAGON MOUND

Wagon Mound, the village, is a railroad town, chosen for its access to water at the nearby Santa Clara Spring. That spring was of great importance to traders as well for this was their last pause before heading on to the Mora River. Fort Union would be established near the Mora River in 1851. The Mountain Route and Cimarron Routes met at about Fort Union.

From Springer, Interstate 25 goes almost due south 26 miles to Wagon Mound. About halfway there, at the Colmor exit, the silhouette of the mountain that gave the trail name "Wagon Mound" becomes clearly visible on the horizon to the left of the highway. Early Santa Fe traders thought the mountain's shape resembled a high-top shoe. Later someone decided the profile looked more like a covered wagon pulled by oxen, so the feature became known as the Wagon Mound.

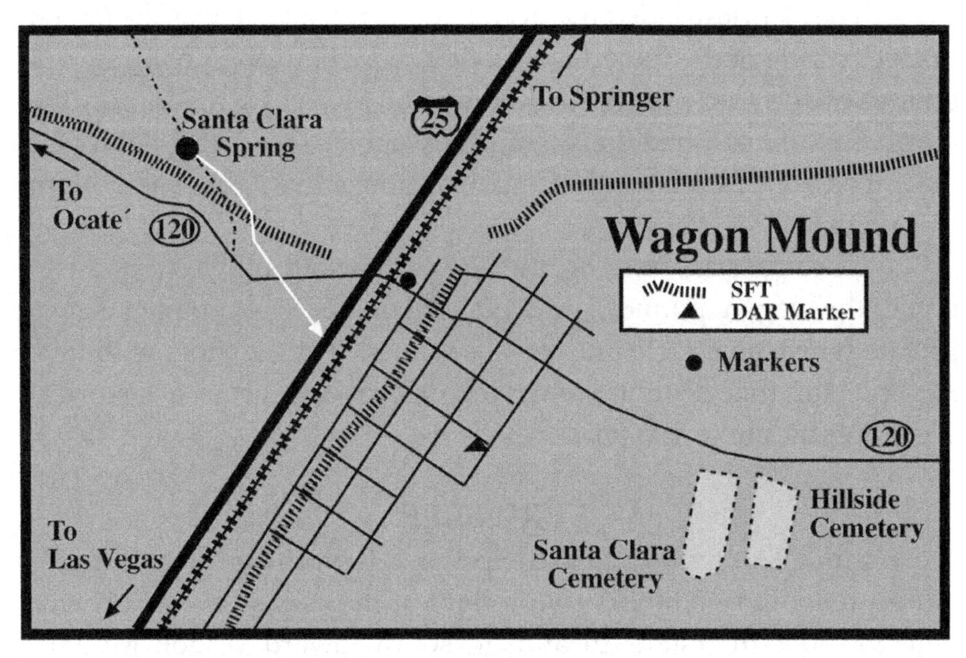

The last great landmark on the westward journey across the plains, it was as renowned as Pawnee Rock and the Rabbit Ears. To the right (west) of the Wagon Mound, are two elevations known to trail guides as the Pilot Knobs. The left one is a narrow flat-topped butte, while the right one is a wider mesa. In former days the term pilot knob was applied rather indiscriminately to any natural feature serving wagon masters as a point of reference. The Rabbit Ears and Round Mound, for example, were both referred to by some diarists as "pilot knobs." The SFT, like today's Interstate 25, threaded a narrow pass between the foot of the Wagon Mound and the Pilot Knobs.

Although from a distance the Wagon Mound appears to rise isolated from the plains, nearer one sees the small town by the same name that hugs its base. Approaching the community's one interchange, look right (west) from the highway up Santa Clara Canyon, a deep indentation in the edge of the plains that stretches westward. At the head of this canyon, about 2 miles away, is Santa Clara Spring, now covered over and serving as the source of the town's water supply. Since there were several smaller springs about where the town is now, it is likely that few traders climbed the mesa to use Santa Clara Spring.

After exiting, turn left (east) and drive under the overpass. Immediately beyond on the left behind the service station note the marshy pond, which shows that water is close to the surface and probably accounts for traders utilizing this area instead of Santa Clara Spring on the mesa.

Continue straight ahead one-half block on NM 120 to the junction of old US 85. In front of the service station on the northwest corner facing US 85, in a small park area, are two plaques set in a low red sandstone monument. One is a bronze marker designating the Wagon Mound as a Registered National Historic Landmark. The other shows William Becknell's first pack train over the SFT with the Wagon Mound in relief in the background. Made by the same sculptor who created a similar plaque for Pawnee Rock, it was installed in 1971 on the 150th anniversary of the opening of the trail.

Cross US 85 and continue on NM 120 through the town of Wagon Mound (the town was founded to serve the new A T and S F railroad). After a couple of blocks, turn right on Catron Street and go a short distance to the junction of Long Street. Here on the porch of the municipal building to the right is the displaced DAR marker for Wagon Mound. Return to NM 120 and turn right (east) toward Roy.

Continue driving past the Wagon Mound school complex on the right at the edge of town. Soon there is a dirt road to the right that leads to two cemeteries at the base of the Wagon Mound, easily seen from the highway. Follow the dirt road to the entrances. The Protestant Hillside Cemetery is on the left, while the Catholic Santa Clara Cemetery is on the right. In it is an extraordinary white marble tombstone of the SET freighter Charles Fraker. Of mixed German and Cherokee ancestry, Fraker was closely involved with the Santa Fe trade during its last days. He married Maria de Luz (Lucy), a daughter of Manuel LeFevre, a French Canadian trapper who settled in Taos in the 1820s. (Another of LeFevre's daughters, Dolores, married Uncle Dick Wootton of Raton Pass fame.) The tombstone, somewhat damaged by time or vandals, shows a magnificent ox team and covered wagon in bold relief.

Charles Fraker's tombstone.

At this location the Wagon Mound towers overhead behind the cemetery. From the high ground here, look north and a bit east to observe the route (though not the ruts) of the Cimarron Route coming from the Rock Crossing of the Canadian toward the Wagon Mound. In May 1850, a war party of Utes and Jicarilla Apaches used this same vantage point to watch the approach of the Santa Fe-bound stage carrying ten men and the U.S. Mail. They concealed themselves behind the low rounded hill just to the southwest of the cemetery, then suddenly attacked. After a furious battle, all the whites were killed and the stage destroyed. Days later a military patrol from Las Vegas found the human remains, scattered by wolves, and buried them. The Santa Clara Cemetery, established many years later, may be on the site of that earlier burial.

Return to NM 120 and turn left back toward the town. At a high point in the road before reaching the school complex, look in the distance to the west (straight ahead) for a good view of Santa Clara Canyon, the site of its spring surrounded by trees. At the interchange you have a choice. An interesting side trip can be made from here to the Ocaté Crossing on the Mountain Route, or you can head directly for Fort Union.

SIDE TRIP TO OCATÉ CROSSING

To get to Ocaté Crossing, drive west on NM 120. When you reach the top of the hill, you can see ruts on both sides of the highway. Many traders heading for Fort Union went west from Wagon Mound to connect with the Mountain Route rather than continuing south on the Cimarron Route to La Junta (present-day Watrous). One branch of the SFT kept close to the Turkey Mountains to the left of the highway and made it directly to Fort Union.

At about 14 miles look for the signed Mora Ranch Road on your right. Turn here and continue 1.5 miles to Ocaté Creek, parking on this side of the creek. The crossing, or ford, is to your right. Ruts can be seen leading down to the creek and up the south side. This route is a continuation of the one leading south from Rayado. From this point it was a straight trip south to Fort Union.

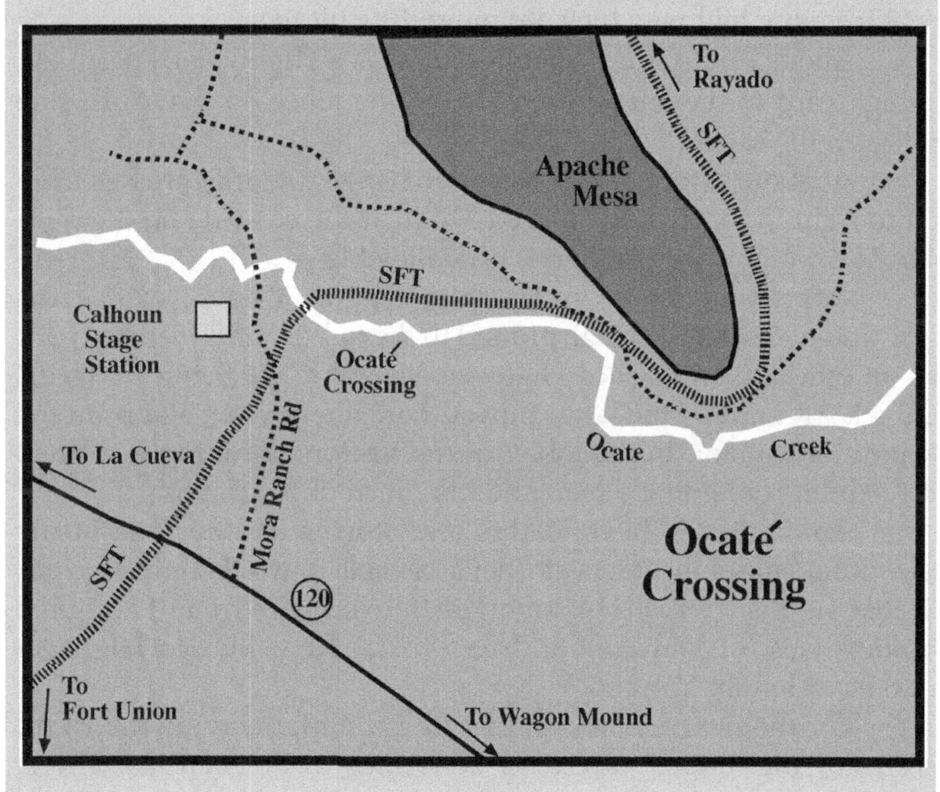

By 1860, there was a ranch at the crossing, established by A. J. Calhoun. By 1877, he had built a gristmill and a stage station at the site. He and other family members are buried in the small cemetery behind the corral. The corral and cemetery are a short (100-yard) walk west from the road. Today, the corral is just several lines of stones, the cemetery is fenced a few yards west.

From here you can continue on Mora Ranch Road over the creek another 6 miles, although the road is not always good. At 4 miles is Apache Mesa on your left. Trail ruts are evident on the left between the road and the mesa. Just past Apache Mesa it is advisable to turn and retrace your route to Wagon Mound. The SFT from here north to Rayado is not open to the public.

At the interchange, rejoin Interstate 25 headed toward Fort Union and Watrous. Just beyond Wagon Mound, to the left between the highway and the railroad tracks, are SFT swales, which are clearly visible. From the air they stand out boldly, but at ground level from the highway they are more difficult to see.

About 1 mile from Wagon Mound is a Highway Department storage yard to the left. There a dip in the fence on the south side indicates the route of the trail.

At about 6 miles from the interchange, the trail crosses from left to right. A rancher has placed a sign at the crossing on the right side of the highway. The sign is now illegible.

Approximately 13 miles from Wagon Mound, exit at the Fort Union Rest Stop on high ground to the right. In this roadside park are an official New Mexico Highway Marker, "The Santa Fe Trail," and a DAR marker, the latter moved here a few years ago from the vicinity of Colmor. In the lobby of the visitors' building is a small SFT exhibit containing a map and historical photographs.

About 1 mile beyond this rest stop is another one in the eastbound lane of the interstate, not accessible to westbound travelers. At that stop is another DAR marker (moved here from its original location west of Watrous) and an official New Mexico Highway Marker, "Capulin Volcano."

For the next 8 miles, paralleling the highway on the right, is one of the longest stretches of swales to be seen anywhere.

They are unsurpassed. At a high point about 2 miles beyond the last rest stop, the country falls away in a vast sweep, providing a spectacular vista rimmed by mountains in the distance. In this area it is possible to pick out a secondary trail (at 7 miles from the rest area) that diverges and heads right toward Tiptonville. For the past few miles the wooded Turkey Mountains have been visible to the right of the highway. Beyond them the Mountain Route of the SFT follows their western flank to Fort Union and its original junction with the Cimarron Route near the fort.

Chapter 6
THE MOUNTAIN ROUTE

From the Kearny County Historical Museum, drive west on Railroad Avenue (this road is on the south side of the museum. At approximately 5 miles is a pullout on the right, with a path over a bridge and continuing up to the summit of a hill. This small hill, rising conspicuously above the Arkansas floodplain, was known to traders as Chouteau's Mound, or later, Indian Mound. On the summit is a DAR marker, although sand-laden winds have nearly obliterated the inscription.

The mountain route west from Lakin.

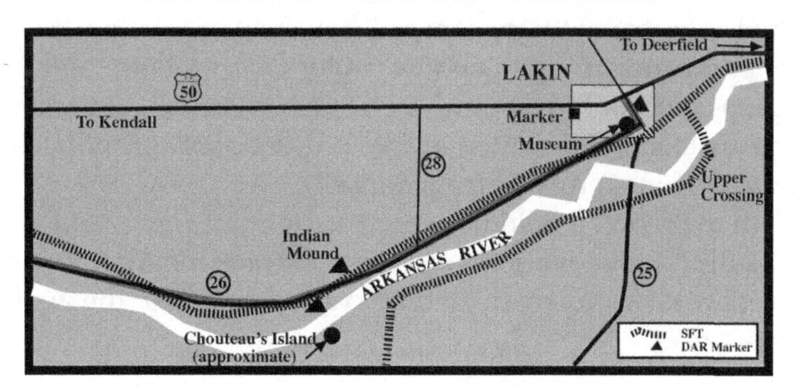

Indian Mound.

In trail days, Indian Mound was a prominent landmark since it denoted the location of Chouteau's Island immediately to the south. From the mound's summit, look south and slightly east to the tree-lined Arkansas River. The approximate location of the island was in a bend of the river, but with changes in the river, the island has long since disappeared. It was named after Auguste Chouteau, who with a band of approximately twenty trappers was returning from the upper Arkansas River in 1816 when they were attacked by 200 Indians near here. They took refuge on the island and held off the Indians with the loss of only one man.

During the summer of 1829, Bvt. Maj. Bennet Riley and two hundred infantry soldiers camped here after escorting the annual westbound caravan, captained by trader Charles Bent, to this point. The troops did not have permission to cross the Arkansas River into Mexico. Instead, they waited at the ford, fending off Indian attacks, until the wagons returned from Santa Fe.

In the plowed field between the railroad tracks and the river, was the Bluff Stage Station, of which no trace remains. Trees along the river are now mostly dead due to a drastic fall in the water table in recent years.

Wagon caravans taking the Cimarron Route either crossed the Arkansas several miles east at present-day Lakin and then followed the south bank of the river to Chouteau's Island or crossed the river here at the island. These two crossing points were considered the Upper Crossing of the Arkansas. The traders left the river at this point and started due south through a wide band of sand hills via Bear Creek Pass, which was merely a shallow valley whose level floor offered an easy route of travel.

Leaving Indian Mound, continue west on Railroad Avenue. The road here is almost directly on the SFT, which was at the very edge of the floodplain and next to the bordering hills. About 2 miles from Indian Mound, there is a DAR marker on the left (south) side. Continue west toward Kendall. Those who do not wish to drive on this gravel road should return to US 50 and turn left (west) on US 50 to Kendall.

At approximately 6 miles from Indian Mound, the Amazon Diversion Dam is on the left. Just before the dam site, traders left the floodplain and climbed the hills since the river was hard against the hills here, thus preventing passage near the floodplain. We witnessed the same situation west of the Middle Crossing. The trail returned to the edge of the floodplain after 1 mile.

Continue on the gravel road to Kendall, where there is a DAR marker directly across the road as you turn right toward US 50. Kendall was originally named Aubry in honor of famed SFT freighter and long-distance rider François (commonly called Francis) X. Aubry, but the Post Office Department later forced the change to Kendall because a town named Aubrey (misspelling of his name) already existed in eastern Kansas. Aubry is noted for opening the Aubry Route (also known as Aubry Cutoff) and his record-breaking 780-mile trip from Santa Fe to Independence in 1848, which took only five days and sixteen hours. Thereafter, he was called the "Skimmer of the Plains." Lovers of horses are not impressed with his accomplishment. Return to US 50 here.

West of Lakin and Chouteau's Island, at high points on the highway, modern drivers can look south across the Arkansas Valley and see long, undisturbed vistas that were familiar to wagon travelers. In this vicinity you get the sense that the crowded East has been left behind and that the spacious West has been reached. Many likely had this sense when they departed Council Grove.

Francis Aubry wanted to find a faster and easier way to get from the Arkansas River to Santa Fe. In 1851 he found a shorter route by about 50 miles. It left the SFT a few miles west of Kendall going almost due south until it met Bear Creek and then angling southwest through present Colorado and Oklahoma. The new Aubry Cutoff joined the Cimarron Route near Cold Spring, Oklahoma. A later version of the Aubry Cutoff was established in 1865 near Fort Aubry. This route went south and met the earlier route near Bear Creek. The Aubry Cutoff was much used as it was shorter than the Cimarron Route and had better access to water. When the railroad reached Sheridan, Kansas in 1868 and a wagon road was established south from Sheridan to Fort Lyon, this spelled the end for use of the Aubry Cutoff. Those wishing to follow the Aubry Cutoff for a short distance should consult Greg Franzwa's book *The Santa Fe Trail Revisited*. Franzwa covers the portion of the Cutoff just south of the Arkansas River.

About 8 miles west of Kendall on US 50 and 1 mile south of the highway, are traces of the remains of Fort Aubry, a temporary post used to guard the SFT in 1865-1866. However, the site is on private land and not accessible to the public. Fort Aubry guarded the northern end of the Aubry Cutoff and Camp Nichols in Oklahoma the southern end.

Continue west on US 50 to Syracuse. Approaching the one main intersection in the center of town, note the Hamilton County Museum on the right housed in an old commercial building. The museum contains nothing of interest about the SFT except the DAR marker in front. Beyond Syracuse there is a sign reminding travelers that the highway here lies on top of the SFT for 5 miles.

For those interested in visiting one spot on the Aubry Route you can turn south on Kansas 27 in Syracuse. Drive south 10 miles to Road 31, then east 4 miles to Road S. Here at the Ebenfleur Cemetery is a DAR marker for the Aubry Cutoff. Swales are still visible nearby.

The next town, 15 miles from Syracuse, is Coolidge, the last place in Kansas. Note the fine two-story stone building on the right, which lies immediately to the west of the post office. One block beyond, on the left (south) side of the highway, is a DAR marker, the last in Kansas on the Mountain Route.

GLO map of the Santa Fe Trail. If you look carefully you will see Ft. Aubry.

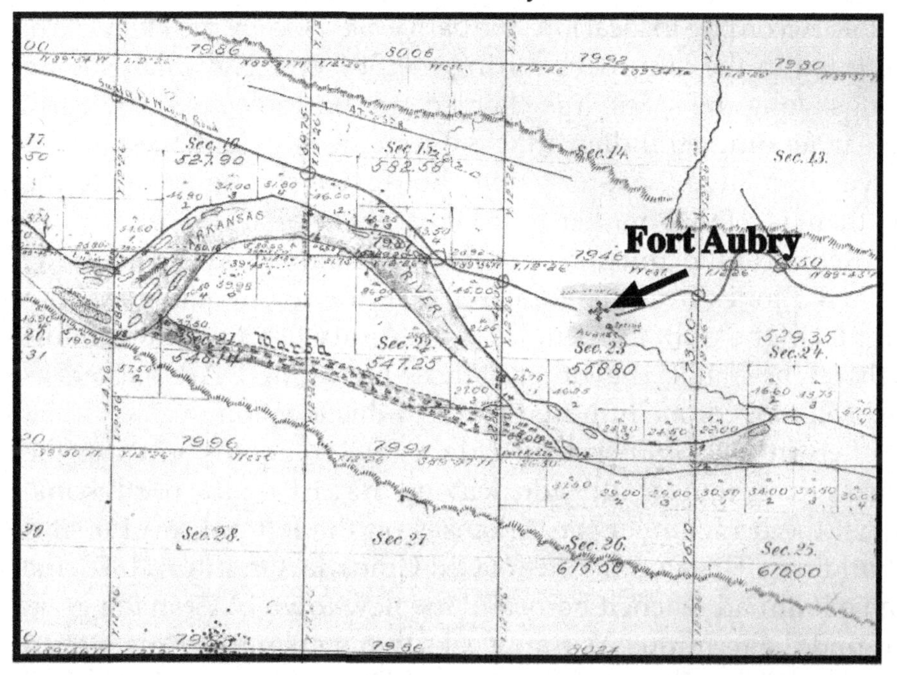

At the state line on the right (north) side of US 50, on the northeast corner of an intersecting dirt road, is the first DAR marker in Colorado. The marker is below a "Prowers County" sign. The word Kansas is incised on the east side of the base and Colorado on the west side. The Colorado markers are of gray granite, in contrast to the red ones in Kansas. The infamous Trail City was along the Kansas-Colorado border. Trail City was a "rest" stop for cowboys along a cattle trail that passed through here but after the SFT had closed.

Chapter 6

HOLLY TO GRANADA

In Colorado, Holly is the first town on US 50. At the intersection of Main Street, turn left (south) three blocks to the railroad tracks and depot. Straight ahead, and 100 feet beyond the tracks, is a large white limestone barn in beautiful condition with a fine arched opening in the loft. According to local lore, the barn, called locally the Holly Barn, was erected in the late 1860s during the SFT era. The small square openings along the sides, it is claimed, are portholes used by early settlers in fending off Indian attacks. From the barn look west up the driveway of a large two-story stone house. On the right side of the drive, there is a DAR marker in front of a lilac bush.

Return to the junction of Main Street and US 50 and continue west. At 4.3 miles from the junction, take the road coming in from the right. On the right at 1.1 miles is the Amity DAR marker, almost directly on the trail. It is another of those migrating DAR markers as it has been moved one hundred yards to this location.

Return to US 50 and turn right (west). Soon you cross the Arkansas River to its south side, leaving the SFT on the north bank. Just past the bridge over the Arkansas on the left are several silos and buildings. This was the site of Old Granada. On July 4, 1873, the Santa Fe Railroad reached here, and the new town of Granada grew up around the terminus. Within weeks two mercantile firms moved to this site (Chick, Brown, and Co. and Otero, Sellar, and Co.) and began sending goods by wagon to New Mexico. Soon three restaurants, two hotels, and three grocery stores were built. By 1875, however, the town was in decline because the railroad had extended its line to La Junta. Fred Harvey bought much of the nearby land here in the 1880s and raised beef for his many Harvey Houses along the country's railroads.

If you leave the highway and drive past the silos, you can see several decaying buildings, one of which, in the center, is an original building from trail days.

From here, the new SFT route heading southwest was called the Granada to Fort Union Military Road or sometimes the Two Buttes Branch. Although the route is unmarked, you can see a swale of this branch if you turn left .4 mile past the railroad bridge at

Road 27. At about 1 mile south on this road, ruts can be seen to the right (west). You can also follow this route on Google Earth. Return to US 50.

Laid out by the army, the Military Road was used by freighters going to Fort Union and Santa Fe. There was much traffic on it from 1873 to 1875, when Granada as a short-lived railhead was the actual beginning of the Santa Fe wagon road. The Military Road went southwest, passed near modern Folsom, New Mexico, and joined the Cimarron Route in the vicinity of the Rock Crossing of the Canadian River. You will have an opportunity to view a part of this route if you choose to take a side trip from Trinidad described below under the heading Tollgate Canyon. A good description of the route is provided by Stocking in his *Road to Santa Fe*.

Before rejoining the SFT, it is worthwhile driving 1.1 miles west of modern Granada on US 50 to Camp Amache, which was the only World War II Japanese-American internment camp in Colorado. At one time there were as many as 7,000 Japanese-Americans interned here. Many of the building foundations are still in place. The camp is named for Amache Ochinee Prowers, a Cheyenne Indian who met and married John Prowers in 1861. Prowers was an important SFT figure and you will visit his house at Boggsville later.

GRANADA TO LAMAR

To rejoin the original mountain route of the SFT (left where US 50 crosses the Arkansas east of Granada), take US 385, which goes north from the center of Granada. At just over 2 miles, the highway crosses the Arkansas River. At .4 mile beyond the bridge, is a DAR marker on the right. Continue 1 mile north on US 385 to a junction and turn left (west) on CO 196. At 5.5 miles from the junction, is an intersection with a sign for Road 19. Turn left (south) off CO 196 and drive .2 mile toward the river to a DAR marker on the left (east) side of the road. Good SFT swales existed in the field behind the marker until 1965, when they were silted over by a flood that covered the Arkansas Valley. Return to CO 196 and turn left (west). At 6 miles is an intersection with County Road 13 with a DAR marker on the northwest corner. After another 5.3 miles, you intersect with US 50 in Lamar.

SIDE TRIP TO SAND CREEK MASSACRE SITE

The National Park Service has located and documented the site and events of the 1864 Sand Creek Massacre. The site is approximately 8 miles north of Chivington, Colorado, which is reached by driving north from Lamar on US 287, then east on CO 96. It can also be reached from Granada by driving on US 385, then west on CO 96. The site is now developed and is well worth visiting.

Established in 2006, Sand Creek Massacre National Historic Site commemorates the tragedy along Sand Creek in southeast Colorado. The site just north of the Mountain Route of the SFT may be reached from CO 96 east of Eads, Colorado. Following gold discoveries traffic increased across the plains into Colorado Territory (1861) with miners using a number of routes through traditional lands of the Cheyenne and Arapaho. From 1851-1861 those tribes, assigned by treaty the territory between the North Platte and Arkansas Rivers, increasingly clashed with trail travelers. After territorial status plains tribes had their lands reduced with Sand Creek as the northernmost boundary. As tensions rose Governor John Evans of Colorado asked Cheyenne and Arapaho to move to a "designated place of safety" near Ft. Lyon on the Santa Fe Trail. When incidents continued the governor in 1864 directed the Third Colorado Cavalry commanded by Col. J.M. Chivington to Ft. Lyon to carry out an August proclamation, to "kill and destroy hostile Indians." Advancing under the cover of darkness, at dawn, November 29, the Colorado militia attacked Black Kettle's sleeping village at Sand Creek, killing about 200, many of whom were women and children, and scattering the camp along Sand Creek. Through wanton acts of cruelty, soldiers removed "private parts" of victims and paraded such in the streets of Denver. For years afterward the SFT and other plains locations suffered from retaliation by outraged tribes.
Jere Krakow, Retired Superintendant Long Distance Trails, NPS

Col. J. M. Chivington had enlisted his volunteers, called "hundred dazers," in Denver for short-term service. There were regular army troops along but they refused to join the attack. The Cheyennes had believed that they were under the protection of the U.S. Army.

Following the massacre, Chivington was hailed as a hero when he returned to Denver, and the event had a strong impact on the SFT. For years afterwards, travel on the trail proved very dangerous for traders and others since the outraged Indians retaliated.

LAMAR

At the intersection of US 50 and CO 196, turn left (south) and drive across the Arkansas River into the center of Lamar. On the east side at the corner of Main and Beech Streets is Colorado's DAR Pioneer Mother statue, or Madonna of the Trail. The statue is just past the railroad tracks, and there is a Colorado Welcome Center in the nearby depot. An inscription on the statue's base refers to the "Big Timbers," a 45-mile-long grove of cottonwoods extending up and down the Arkansas Valley. The grove served as a popular campground for Plains Indians and was a familiar landmark to SFT traders and mountain men since it was the first significant stand of timber on the trail west of Council Grove. The Welcome Center has many brochures that can prove helpful as you explore this area.

Return north on US 50 (Main Street) and recross the Arkansas River. Just past the bridge watch for a pullout on the right side of the highway where there is a DAR marker. Just beyond the pullout, US 50 curves to the left (west), but continue straight ahead to the large red brick building housing the Big Timbers Museum. To the left of the museum's main door, is a metal historical plaque with extensive text.

Traveling west on US 50, a little over 4 miles from the river bridge and DAR pullout there was a huge stone barn about .5 mile south of the highway. This structure has now fallen down. It was built in 1891 with sandstone hauled from the ruined walls of Old Fort Lyon a few miles upriver. The keystone in the giant arched door on the west end was inscribed: "1st Cavalry I860," the troops that established Fort Wise in 1860 that became Fort Lyon. That stone is now in private hands.

Stone keystone from Old Ft. Lyon.
Photo courtesy of Pat Palmer.

BENT'S NEW FORT

At 7.5 miles from the Arkansas River at Lamar, US 50 crosses the Bent-Prowers County line. One mile beyond the line is a gravel crossroad, County Road 35. Turn left (south) and go 1 mile, where the road ends in a T. From here look straight across the field to a stone monument barely visible on a hill-the site of Bent's New Fort.

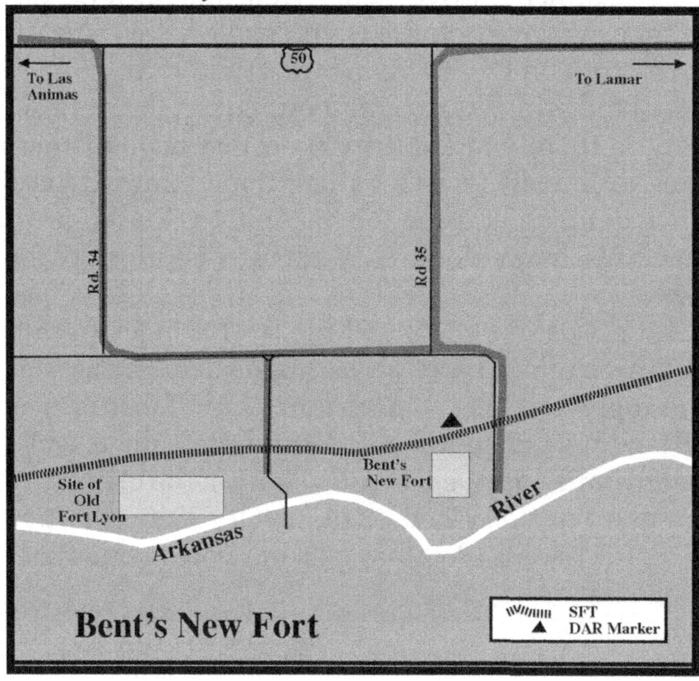

To get to the fort, turn left (east) at the T, drive .2 mile to the first road intersecting on the right (south), and follow it .5 mile to a wire gate on the right. Park at the gate, cross the fence, and hike .2 mile to the site, aiming for a telephone pole on top of the hill. Around the monument are the stone foundations of the fort, and a few feet north is a fine DAR marker.

The original Bent's Fort, completed by the Bent brothers and Ceran St. Vrain in 1833, was located about 30 miles west up the Arkansas River. In 1849, it was abandoned by the one surviving Bent, William, who in the winter of 1852-1853 began building a new stone fort in the Big Timbers on a bluff overlooking the Arkansas.

Like the earlier fort, the new one also served as a way station for SFT travelers, as well as a trading post and Indian agency. In 1860, William Bent leased his fort and surrounding land to the army, which soon built a new post on the Arkansas just to the west. The army first called its establishment Fort Wise, in honor of the governor of Virginia. In 1862, it was renamed Fort Lyon after Nathaniel Lyon, the first Union general killed in the Civil War. Following a flood in June 1867, this site was abandoned and Fort Lyon moved 20 miles upstream to its present site.

Return to the T and go straight ahead (west) to the first intersecting road from the left. Take it and start south toward the iron bridge over the Arkansas. At about .25 mile, an irrigation ditch crosses the road. Stop just beyond it, and in the distance to the left (east) you can see the monument at Bent's New Fort. Fort Lyon was to the right (west). In recent years a farmer has turned what remained of Fort Lyon into a hay field.

Return to US 50 and continue west about 4 miles, watching for the McClave junction. At that intersection, CO 196 goes right, and gravel County Road 34 turns left (south). Turn left (south) on County Road 34, and at 1.9 miles, where the road curves right and starts down toward the bridge over the Arkansas, watch for a DAR marker on the left in an open field near prominent SFT swales. Return to US 50.

RED SHIN'S STANDING GROUND

At the community of Hasty, turn left (south) off US 50 on CO 260 leading to John Martin Reservoir. Although the reservoir, completed in 1948 with the damming of the Arkansas River, has destroyed sections of the SFT, one patch of swales is preserved.

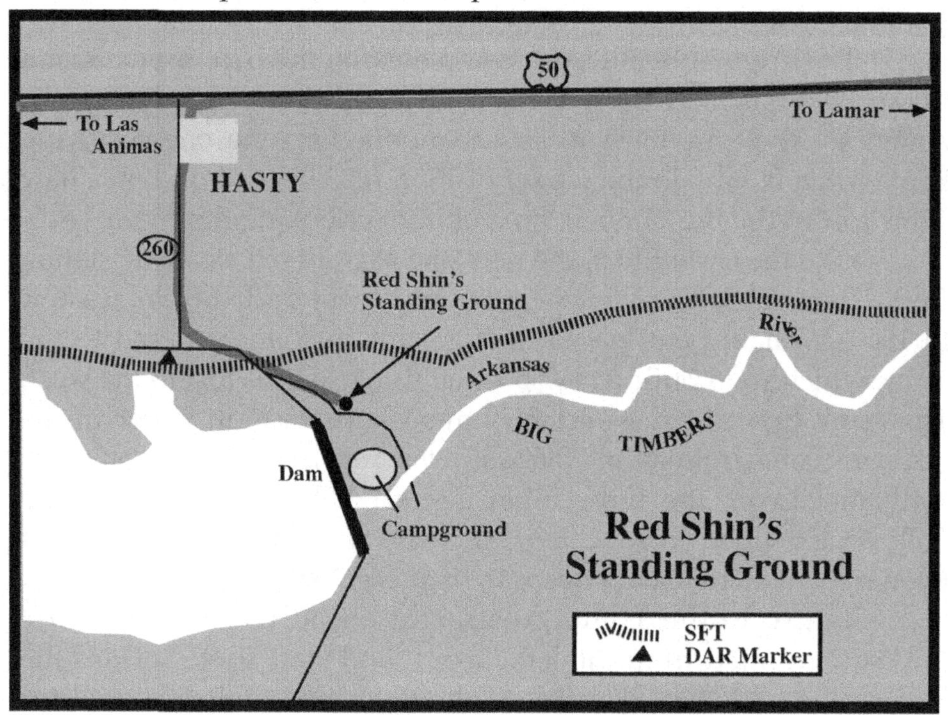

At 1.8 miles south of Hasty, CO 260 forks to the left and continues to the dam and a campground. There is a new "Welcome Center" before you enter the campground. If this center is open, they will extract a fee for visiting the area. Driving past the center, at the fork (with a wooden "Welcome to the Reservoir" sign in the middle of the Y), a dirt road goes straight ahead (the right fork of the Y). Follow it, and a short distance beyond a dirt road intersects. Turn right (west) and drive .1 mile to a small access road entering from the left (south). A wooden sign here calls attention to the SFT swales. Turn left (south) and follow the access road .2 mile to a fenced area with a turnstile at the entrance. Inside, there is a DAR marker on faint SFT swales.

Artist conception of Red Shin's Standing Ground
by Roger Balm.

Return to the Y and turn right .5 mile toward the dam on the paved road. Just before that road starts across the top of the dam, another road, leading to the picnic and camping area, intersects from the left. Take this road, which descends below the dam. Near the bottom where it makes a curve to the left, note on the left a toadstool-shaped rock formation with a flat top, a prominent trail landmark known as Red Shin's Standing Ground. In his The Old Santa Fe Trail, Stanley Vestal tells how the rock got its curious name (Vestal 1996). In 1833, Cheyennes were camped on the river below. A warrior named Red Shin got in an argument with some of his tribesmen over a woman. The quarrel became violent, and taking his weapons Red Shin fled to the top of the flat formation behind camp. Although his foes attacked him furiously, he successfully drove them off, and ever after the rock was known as Red Shin's Standing Ground. From a pullout, you can climb to the top and stand on the same spot where the Cheyenne warrior made his stand.

This interesting site narrowly missed destruction when the John Martin Dam was built immediately to the west. In fact, the location of Red Shin's rock had been lost until recently, when Paul Bentrup's speculation led to this formation's acceptance as the rock.

Return to US 50 at Hasty and continue west.

Chapter 6

NEW FORT LYON

At the intersection of CO 183 with US 50 (6 miles east of Las Animas), is a sign pointing left (south) to Fort Lyon. Fort Lyon is now the "Fort Lyon Supportive Residential Community," a location for homeless people. It was a State Hospital after it closed as a military post, then a State Prison before this new use. At mile .5 on CO 183, is a gray granite DAR marker on the right (west) side of the road, just past a faint intersecting dirt road leading west into a field. (In summer it may be hidden by weeds.)

At 1 mile from US 50, is the fort entrance gate. Drive straight through extensive grounds and turn left at C Avenue. That street leads east. The fort parade ground is on the right, while a row of two-story houses on the left comprises the original officers' quarters, now considerably remodeled, some of which date to the late 1860s. The middle house, in line with the flagpole in the center of the parade ground, was the commanding officer's house. Continue straight ahead past a main building with columns on the right. Behind this building was located the Kit Carson Chapel. The small structure was originally the residence of the post surgeon. An ailing Carson was brought here from his nearby home at Boggsville and died on May 23, 1868. The upper two-thirds of the building was dismantled in 1957 and the stones used to rebuild it in the form of a chapel, so the structure now has little historical integrity. It has since been relocated to the entrance to the Fort on the right.

Return to the junction of C Avenue and the entrance road (called Gate Street). Turn left (south) on Gate and follow it past the west side of the parade ground until it curves left to become A Avenue. To the right (south) of A Avenue, are two large buildings of cut limestone, the best-preserved original structures still standing. The one on the east (or left as you face south), Building 19, housed the Commissary Department. It has an incised stone in the west gable reading: "Capt. E. B. Kirk, 1867." The building on the west (right), Building 17, was the quartermaster storehouse. Return to US 50 and continue toward Las Animas. About 2 miles west of the

US 50 and CO 183 junction is a paved crossroad, County Road 13, marked by a small green street sign. On the northeast corner is a DAR marker.

Continue west. Near the eastern limits of Las Animas (at the intersection of US 50 and CO 194) there is a motel on the left called Bent's Fort Inn. In the parking lot of the motel there is another DAR marker.

BOGGSVILLE

Just past Bent's Fort Inn and before the bridge over the Arkansas River, CO 194 turns off US 50 to the right and goes 15 miles west (along the north bank of the Arkansas) to Bent's Old Fort. Before taking that road, however, continue south on US 50 across the bridge and down the main street of Las Animas. At the end of the street, US 50 curves right and a block farther intersects with CO 101. There are signs directing you to the Boggsville National Historic District. Turn left (south) on CO 101 and go about 1.2 miles to a Y. The left fork is CO 101, but drive straight ahead on a paved road that goes .5 mile south to the entrance of the Las Animas Cemetery on the left.

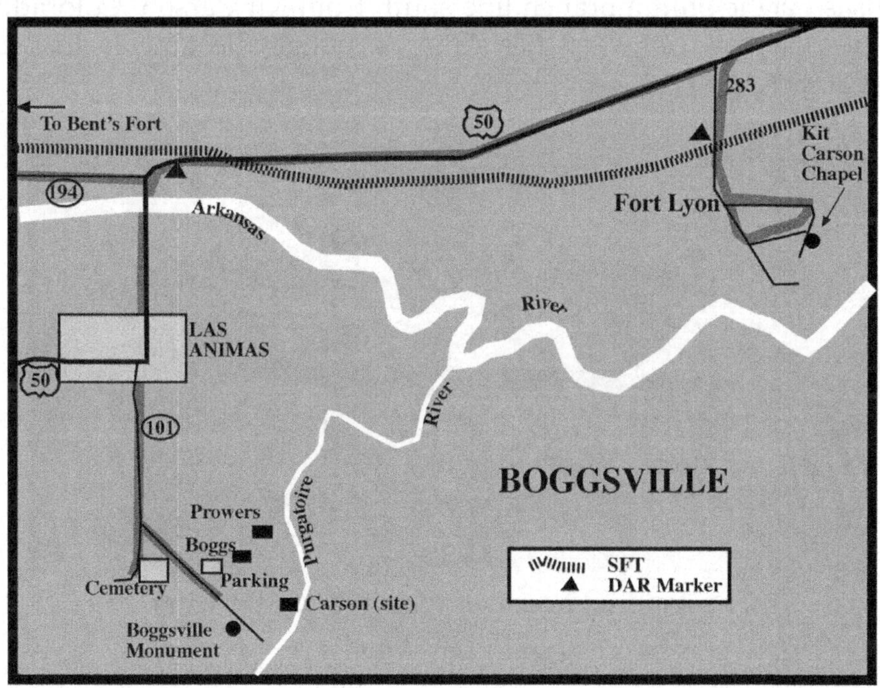

At the right-hand (southeast) corner of the cemetery, at the junction of the lanes marked 6th Street and South Drive, is a stone column with an urn on top marking the grave of William Bent (May 23, 1809-May 19, 1869), one of the most prominent men associated with the SFT. From this point go north on 6th Street one block to the next intersection. On the right at the corner is the tall marble monument, also with an urn on top, for the grave of John Wesley Prowers (1837-1884), who freighted for William Bent on the SFT and was later a station agent for Barlow, Sanderson and Company.

From the cemetery go back .5 mile to the Y and take the other fork, continuing south on CO 101 another .6 mile to a tall concrete monument, titled "Boggsville," on the left (east) side of the highway. Thomas 0. Boggs, long associated with the Bents and Kit Carson, settled near here in the early 1860s with local pioneer John Wesley Prowers. The monument provides information about the history of the place.

Return a few yards from the monument and enter the parking lot at Boggsville Visitors' Center. By 1871, Boggsville had a school and served as the county seat for Bent County but declined due to the western expansion of the railroads. In 1873, when the Kansas Pacific built a branch line south from Kit Carson, Colorado, to the new town of West Las Animas. Boggsville quickly lost its importance.

The restored house of John Wesley Prowers in Boggsville.

The Boggsville site is now being restored by the Boggsville Revitalization Committee and is one of the most interesting areas along the trail. Both the Boggs and Prowers Houses are registered historic sites, open to the public, during summer at least. Maps are available for a worthwhile walking tour of the site. The U-shaped adobe house belonged to Boggs. Behind that is the two-story house of Prowers, once a stage stop on the SFT. Furthermore, Kit Carson and his family lived in a primitive house, now gone, several hundred yards to the east, along the small Purgatoire River. It was there that Carson became ill in 1868 and was taken to nearby Fort Lyon, where he died. Tom Boggs took the Carson children to live in his own house and was the executor of Kit's will. It is said that Boggs himself planted the huge cottonwoods that still grow around the house.

Return to the junction of CO 101 and US 50 on the south side of Las Animas. From here, one option is to turn left (west) and follow US 50 to La Junta on the south side of the Arkansas. About midway there, at the Bent-Otero County line, is a roadside park on the left (south) side of the highway containing an exhibit with extensive text on the "Big Timbers" and referring to the SFT.

However, if you travel this route you will miss Bent's Old Fort, the pearl of the SFT. Therefore, it is preferable to turn right at the above junction on US 50 and follow it to the north side of Las Animas, where you can pick up CO 194 and follow it west to the fort. It is at the Bent-Otero County line on this route that traders had their first glimpse of the Spanish Peaks to the southwest.

BENT'S OLD FORT

Bent's Old Fort was the most renowned landmark on the Mountain Route of the SFT. Many travelers wrote about it, and its history has been ably presented by David Lavender in his book *Bent's Fort.* The place was a private, not a military, post and served as a center for the Indian and fur trade. Established by Charles and William Bent and Ceran St. Vrain in 1833, it was called Fort William by many traders because William Bent largely directed its operations. Faithfully reconstructed in the mid-1970s by the National Park Service, it is now a Registered National Historic Landmark and one of the most exciting points of interest on the entire SFT. Here one can feel the pulse of trail days.

The site of the fort was chosen for several reasons. First, it was on the north bank of the Arkansas and thus in United States territory rather than in Mexico. Second, it was a natural trading area. In 1821, Jacob Fowler reported from a location just upstream from the future site of Bent's Fort that his camp was among seven hundred lodges representing the Comanche, Arapaho, Kiowa, and Cheyenne tribes (Coues 1965).

Approaching the grounds from the east on CO 194, the first entrance gate (now closed) is seen on the left (south), a large stone arch with "Bent's Old Fort" at the top. One DAR marker is at the left of the gate, and a second, with a map of the fort, is under the gate. Continue west to the present entrance marked by a National Park Service sign.

At this point the imposing fort can be seen to the south in a loop of the Arkansas River. To preserve the historical atmosphere, visitors must leave cars in a parking lot near the entrance and walk a long path to the fort's front gate. Transportation is available for those unable to make the walk.

Bent's Fort.

Approaching the main gate, the path passes the Fort Cemetery, containing a historical marker. The only gravestone is that of Edward Dorris (d. 1865), but the plot contains twelve other unidentified graves. The cemetery was used after William Bent's abandonment of the fort and while the place was a stage station. Close to the fort's gate notice the marshy area to the left of the path. The Arkansas River flowed through here during trail days. The river was forded directly in front of the main gate as the traders headed for Timpas Creek and Raton Pass.

Inside, the storerooms, shops, and living quarters all have period furnishings. The Susan Magoffin Room is furnished with the type of things she carried in her wagon and installed for her comfort during a brief stopover here in 1846, when she suffered a miscarriage. A freight wagon is on display; a Mexican carreta can also be seen at the entrance to the fort. Used in New Mexico during the trail period, the turning wheels of these vehicles were so loud that they could be heard for miles. Individuals in period clothing give demonstrations, and a mountain man rendezvous is held in the spring. In addition, a sales shop offers publications on the fort and the SFT.

LA JUNTA

From Bent's Old Fort, drive 8 miles west on CO 194 to La Junta and pick up US 50 on the east side of town. (Note: This La Junta is not to be confused with the historical La Junta at Watrous, New Mexico.) Drive through the center of town and, at the railroad station (which will be on the right) turn left (south) on Colorado Avenue and go two blocks to 3rd Street. On the northwest corner is an unusual DAR marker on the Otero County Courthouse grounds.

From this marker go south to the Koshare Indian Museum located at 115 West 18th Street (at the corner of Santa Fe Street). This is the home of the famous Koshare Boy Scout dancers. The museum contains excellent exhibits of Plains Indian materials, some from the era of the SFT. The trail entered La Junta on its eastern edge, went up the slope, and passed just south of the Koshare Kiva before continuing southwest toward Trinidad.

Chapter 6

LA JUNTA TO TRINIDAD

On the west side of La Junta, pick up US 350, which runs almost 80 miles to Trinidad. This is a desolate stretch of road, but the country looks much as it did in trail times. (There are no gas stations along the way, and the only restroom facility is at the Timpas Picnic Area.) The earliest wagon road stayed close to Timpas Creek, a short distance to the right (west) of the present highway. Susan Magoffin had much to say about this route. A later stagecoach road followed parts of the highway or paralleled it on the left (east), while another route, the Purgatoire Stage Road, coming from Boggsville, was 10 or more miles to the east. There are some remains of stage stations along the latter route (described by Margaret Long in *The Santa Fe Trail*), but unfortunately much of the country east of US 350 has been condemned by the army for military use, and thus the station ruins are not accessible to the public. The many "Not For Sale" signs you will see in this part of Colorado are for the purpose of letting the government know the ranchers do NOT want the Army base expanded as threatened.

A little less than 4 miles from La Junta, there is a DAR marker against the fence on the right (west) side of US 350. It is on the spot where the trail crossed the present highway from east to west heading toward Timpas Creek, and ruts lie behind it. From this point on, watch for trail ruts to the west. Along here is a good view of the famed twin Spanish Peaks (Wahatoya [Two Peaks] in Ute) on the far horizon to the front right, about 70 miles away, a guiding landmark for trail travelers. Most traders would have reached this point in July when the peaks would still have been covered with snow, providing the hot, weary travelers with a refreshing sight.

At 13 miles from La Junta, CO 71 comes in from the right. Turn here and drive .5 mile to the Sierra Vista overlook. This area is in the Comanche National Grasslands, and the rangers have built this overlook to give visitors a sense of the trail. The trail is marked here, and hikers can walk a 3-mile section of it to the Timpas Picnic Area, the next stop.

Go back to US 350, turn right, and drive about 3 miles to the Timpas Picnic Area on the right (west). Traders used this route because in Timpas Creek they could always find water, which was foul but wet. Park at the picnic area, where there are informative signs, and walk the .5-mile nature trail, which begins on the west side of the fenced grounds. The trail goes to Timpas Creek and past a DAR marker. Interestingly, this site was homesteaded until drought drove the farmers out.

Approaching the ghost town of Timpas on US 350, observe the Three Buttes (really three pointed hills) to the left (east) of the highway. The stage route of the SFT passed through a gap between them and the adjoining hills on the west side. Deeply eroded ruts ascend the gap. A stage station was thought to be in this area, but recent research has provided no such evidence.

About 4 miles from Timpas a gravel road leading left from the highway is an alternate trail route to Iron Springs but becomes a private road and thus is not open to the public. Another mile past this road, there is a DAR marker located on the west side of US 350. Near mile marker 47 you will begin to see limestone marker posts on your right between the highway and the railway. These are in the swales of the SFT. The trail eventually crosses the highway and heads for Iron Springs.

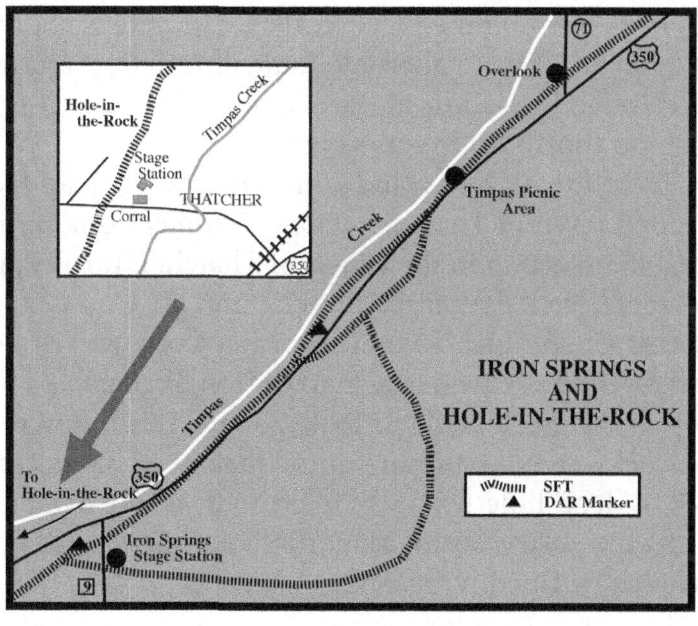

At 11 miles beyond Timpas, County Road 9 turns off US 350 to the left (south). This is a well-marked corner advising you of the Iron Springs Historic Area. Turn here and drive .4 mile to the marker on the right, which is located on the trail. There is a DAR marker 200 yards to the right. Continue another .6 mile to the parking area, close to the Iron Springs Stage Station site. In the parking area is a very good interpretive marker. Trail ruts can be seen just west of it, and beyond individuals with good eyes can see the DAR marker in the distance. It is an easy walk to it and the swales through low grass.

Leave the parking lot, turn right (east) on the county road, and cross over a small bridge. Just past it on the left are two low stock tanks. To the right of them is a concrete box which caps the original Iron Spring. Water from the box goes underground to one of the tanks. Near it is the stone foundation of what was once the station's small fortified barn.

The adobe station itself is marked only by a very low mound of dirt around which are fragments of colored glass. Stubs of cedar fence posts to the left of the stock tank outline the original rectangular stage corral. A protective wall was built around the station soon after its establishment in 1861, but that did not prevent hostile Cheyennes from burning the place in 1864. This site is about .5 mile east of the main SFT, but an alternate route reportedly came down to the station through the saddle at the end of the high bluff seen in the distance behind (north of) Iron Springs.

Return to the highway and continue toward Trinidad to the nearly deserted town of Thatcher, about 45 miles from La Junta. At the only real intersection in the center of Thatcher, turn right (west) on a gravel road, cross the railroad tracks, and go,.6 mile past a two-story deserted school. Just beyond the school you will drive across the dry bed of Timpas Creek (see map of Iron Springs).

Stop in the creek bed and look .25 mile north down it to the mouth of a rocky canyon, the site of the major SFT landmark Hole-in-the-Rock, a deep hole that was filled with water available even when the creek was dry. Susan Magoffin had much to say about the hole, which is now filled with sand.

The site of the Barlow, Sanderson and Company's Hole-in-the-Rock Overland Stage Station was west of the creek and north of the corrals. To reach the location, drive past the creek bed, and before the corrals you see a barbed wire fence with a sign warning you not to gather artifacts. There is a gate you can open and enter, but remember to close it behind you. This property was donated to the Archaeological Conservancy by Bob Jones of La Junta, hence the warning signs. Drive or walk straight ahead past the corrals, and in about 100 yards you will see the remains of the station. Although today it is basically a hole in the ground, the station was made of rock, and the basic outline of the foundations are still visible. The corrals near the road were there during trail days, noted in the original government survey of this area in 1869.

Further, early railroad maps show three pools, one south of the road crossing the creek and two north near the canyon. In addition, Margaret Long, who interviewed old-timers in the 1950s, speaks of a "fort" just north of the corrals that must have been the stone stage station (Long 1954).

Return to the highway and continue to Trinidad, keeping an eye on the looming Spanish Peaks just as wagon travelers once did. At 4.5 miles past Thatcher, there is a DAR marker on the right (west) almost across from the entrance to the U.S. Army's Piñon Canyon Maneuver Site. Straight ahead you will also see Fisher's Peak, which looms over Trinidad.

One-half mile past Model (59 miles from La Junta) turn right at County Road 52, a gravel road but one that should be avoided if it has recently rained. At 2.5 miles a DAR marker is on the right, and some very nice swales are on the left. Return to US 350.

TRINIDAD

From far out on the highway northeast of Trinidad, flat-topped Fisher's Peak (originally called Raton Peak) is visible. With Trinidad lying at its foot, it rises just to the left (east) of the entrance to Raton Pass and therefore served as a pilot point bringing wagon caravans to this important crossing of the mountains.

US 350 enters town from the east (after the intersection with US 160) and becomes Main Street, the actual route of the SFT, at least when it was part of the stagecoach route. The earlier trail route stayed on the west side of the Purgatoire River, where the swales west of Model were located.

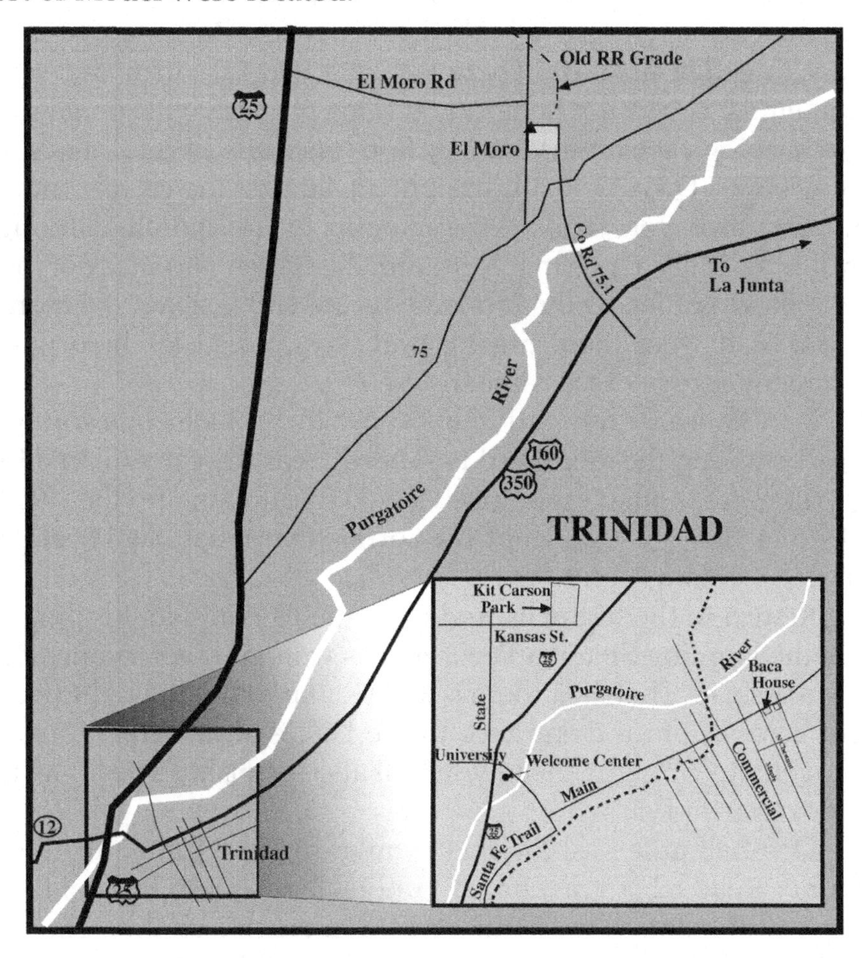

Approaching the edge of downtown, observe a two-story adobe house on the left at the southeast comer of Main and Chestnut Streets. This is the house of Don Felipe Baca, a rancher who was the principal founder of Trinidad in 1862. Dating from 1869, in the trail era, the Baca House is now a museum containing furnishings recently brought from New Mexico. It was originally built for John Hough, who moved here from Boggsville and later in 1873 sold it to Felipe Baca. Directly behind it is the interesting Santa Fe Trail Museum in an adobe building that was once the Baca servants' quarters.

On exhibit is a hunting coat reportedly given to Kit Carson by a Cheyenne chief.

Behind the Santa Fe Trail Museum on the southeast corner of the intersection of Chestnut and 1st Streets is a 1930s WPA building reportedly constructed to resemble Bent's Old Fort, although the resemblance is minimal.

Continue west on Main Street two blocks to the intersection with Commercial Street. On the northwest corner is the old Colombian Hotel, which has on the outside wall near the door, facing Commercial, a splendid metal plaque with an extensive text on the SFT.

Go one more block on Main Street and turn right (north) on Convent Street. This street leads down to the railroad tracks and just beyond, after a curve, to a bridge over the Purgatoire (or Purgatory) River. It was about here that the early trail crossed the river. Just before passing under the interstate, at University and Nevada Streets, is the Colorado Welcome Center, which has a wealth of information about southern Colorado. Continue under the interstate, turn right (north) on State Street, and follow it about six blocks to Kansas Street. Turn right (east) and go two blocks to Kit Carson Park.

At the park entrance at the intersection of San Pedro and Kansas is a fine archway. In addition, on the hill in the center of the park is a magnificent equestrian statue of Kit Carson showing the scout in mountain garb peering toward Raton Pass. Nearby is the largest DAR marker on the SFT in Colorado.

There were two railroad companies competing for the SFT trade here in Trinidad. The Santa Fe won the battle by obtaining the rights to Raton Pass from Uncle Dick Wootton in 1878. The other railroad, the Denver and Rio Grande, made it to this area before (1876) the Santa Fe but stopped at a location on the SFT called El Moro about four miles short of Trinidad. To get to El Moro drive north on Interstate 25 and exit at El Moro Road. Drive east to CO 75, turn right and go to Rd 32. There is a DAR marker at this corner telling about El Moro. There were still trains coming here as late as 1910 as photos of the dedication of the DAR marker at El Moro show coaches here on that day.

SIDE TRIP TO STONEWALL

Individuals who have been following the SFT journal of Marion Russell will want to make a side trip from Trinidad to her grave. Go west on CO 12 up the Purgatoire Valley about 40 miles to the small community of Stonewall. Ask directions to the local pioneer cemetery at the one store on the left. Entrance to the cemetery is through an unmarked wire gate (with a crosswire overhead) on the right (north) side of CO 12 about .5 mile past the Stonewall store, just beyond the western limits of the community. The dirt road, which crosses an irrigation ditch just inside the gate, is merely two tire tracks leading up a hill .5 mile to a pine clearing. All the immediate family of the Russells are buried in this inspiring place.

At Trinidad you have a choice of routes. You can either continue south over Raton Pass, the original trail route, or you can take an interesting, but longer, side trip to Tollgate Canyon and follow an alternate route to Raton, New Mexico.

SIDE TRIP TO TOLLGATE CANYON

From Trinidad (or Raton, New Mexico, in reverse) an interesting side trip can be made to visit parts of the Granada to Fort Union Military Road, a late and little-known section of the SFT. From Trinidad go back on US 350 about 6 miles to the junction with US 160. Take US 160 east 39 miles to CO 389. Turn right (south) on CO 389 at the junction and continue to the hamlet of Branson.

One mile beyond Branson is the New Mexico State line. This low exit is called Emery Gap. The Military Road came to this point from the northeast after leaving the Arkansas River at Granada. Stephen Long used this route in 1820 when he sought the headwaters of the Red River. This was also the route of Becknell's 1821 venture that opened the Santa Fe trade. Finally, the Jacob Fowler party passed nearby in 1822. A wagon road was not established until 1867 or 1868 by Madison Emery. As you pass south through the gap, note that Emery's route went down Gleason Canyon, which is 2 miles east of the highway. You can see faint ruts to the left of the highway leading to the canyon.

Freighters first used this trail in 1868, but its real importance dates from March 1870, when the Kansas Pacific Railroad reached

Kit Carson, Colorado. A new freighting road was established south from the railhead to Fort Lyon, where it connected with the Military Road going south to Emery Gap. Here traders encountered the road already established by Madison Emery. In summer 1873, the Santa Fe Railroad reached Granada, Colorado, and that town became the new trailhead.

The route down Tollgate Canyon was opened in the same year when Basil (Missouri Bill) Metcalf cleared a road there. Eventually, his toll road was easier and quicker than the Gleason Canyon road to the east, but it was a difficult route to construct, prompting Metcalf to charge tolls to recoup his costs. The roofless stone toll house is on your right as you descend the canyon, about 5 miles south of the state line. For the complete story of this road, see Richard Louden's article "The Military Freight Road" (Louden 1993).

At the bottom of the canyon, NM 551 intersects NM 456. You are now in the valley of the Dry Cimarron River, likely first used by wagons in the 1850s. (This is the same Cimarron River that you visited at Wagon Bed Spring).

Turn right at the junction onto NM 456 and continue 1.2 miles. There, on the left, are the remains of the town of Madison, named for Madison Emery. Emery arrived in 1862 and shortly thereafter established his town. In trail days, this was a thriving community with a gristmill, ruins of which can still be seen, store, saloon, blacksmith shop, and post office. From the road you can see some stone ruins about 200 yards toward the river. Since the site is on private property, you can only view it from the road.

Continue on NM 456 up the Cimarron Canyon, and at 3.5 miles Folsom Falls is on the left. Between the falls and the town of Folsom, ruts can be seen along the road. Mostly on the right side of the road, they are particularly evident in open fields as you reach the top of the canyon.

At the town of Folsom continue south on NM 325 toward Capulin. The Military Road is now several miles to the east, but continue on to the Capulin Volcano National Monument and drive to the summit of the cinder cone. From the east side of the paved road ascending the cone, you can get an aerial view of the ruts of the Military Road several miles to the east. They came down the distant

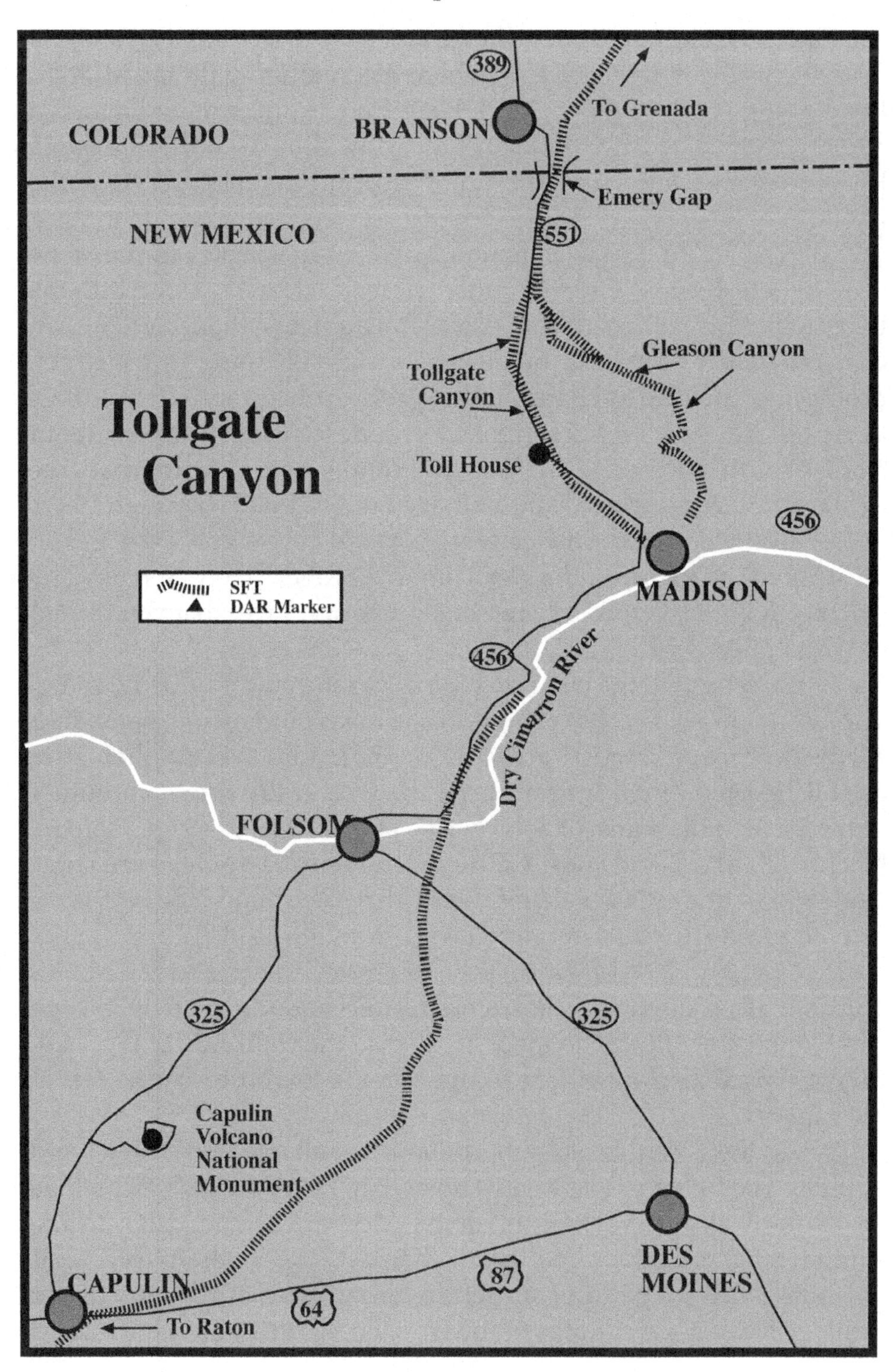
389
To Grenada
COLORADO
BRANSON
Emery Gap
NEW MEXICO
551
Gleason Canyon
Tollgate
Canyon
Tollgate
Canyon
Toll House
456
MADISON
SFT
DAR Marker
456
Dry Cimarron River
FOLSOM
325
325
Capulin
Volcano
National
Monument
DES
MOINES
CAPULIN
87
64
To Raton

creek before turning west toward Capulin (see map for help locating the ruts). The monument is worthwhile visiting even if you cannot spot the ruts.

Return to NM 325 and drive to the hamlet of Capulin. The Military Road passed through here and then headed south to the Canadian River. From this point drive to Raton by way of US 64/US 87.

RATON PASS

From Trinidad take Interstate 25 south over Raton Pass. This route, now an easy twenty-minute drive, was a major obstacle for the wagon trains. It took the caravan, in which Susan Magoffin traveled, five days to get through the pass. Her comment on the road was: "worse and worse the road" (Magoffin 1982). The trail followed Raton Creek (on your right as you drive south), purportedly crossing it fifty-three times in the ascent. At Exit 6 (Gallinas), is a DAR marker, just behind the exit sign accessible only from the southbound lane of Interstate 25.

Several miles beyond, just past the Wootton Exit, watch for a little valley that opens on the right (west) side of the interstate. A billboard facing the highway, placed by the Santa Fe Railroad, reads: "Dick Wootton Ranch and Old Santa Fe Trail." In 1865, "Uncle" Dick opened a toll road for wagons over the pass. His ranch had a stage station as well as a tollgate, although the present owner of the ranch claims that none of the original Wootton buildings remain. In 1878, Wootton's toll road was purchased by the Santa Fe Railroad, and the tracks were laid on the road for much of its route.

Follow Interstate 25 to the summit, take Exit 460, and proceed to the right of the weigh station. At a small pullout behind the weigh station is a stone marker indicating a National Historic Landmark, Old Raton Pass. The actual Old Raton Pass is about .5 mile west of this location, but the Highway Department moved the marker to this spot. If you look back toward the northwest, you have a fine view of the Spanish Peaks.

While facing the marker, look to your left to see a bridge over Interstate 25. You may want to drive across this bridge and turn left on the frontage road to view a four-panel interpretive display on the

SFT. To get back on Interstate 25 south bound, retrace your steps to the weigh station and take the Interstate 25 south ramp toward Raton, New Mexico.

As you enter the interstate you have a remarkable view of flat-topped Tinaja Peak ("water tank" or "water jar") and to its right Eagle Tail Peak. The trail is now on your right, and just past mile marker 459 you will see a welcome sign and then an informal turnout. From the turnout, looking back to your right you will see a valley coming in from the northwest. The trail came down this valley and followed the present route of the train tracks into Raton.

RATON

Leave the interstate at Exit 454, cross the tracks, and follow the highway (Business Interstate 25) into Raton. On the northern outskirts of town, watch for a service station on the right, and a block beyond is Moulton Street. Turn right to follow the Old Raton Pass Highway (also called the Ocean-to-Ocean Highway), the principal auto highway in 1910. Although this road only goes 5 miles now, it is worth following at least as far as Goat Hill. As Moulton Street climbs toward Goat Hill, motor courts associated with the old highway are on the right just as the road turns left. The overlook at Goat Hill provides an excellent panorama of Raton and surroundings, from which you can see the route of the SFT approximately along the railroad tracks. The City of Raton is preparing to develop a new SFT park just to the east of the tracks near the old train terminal.

Brave individuals may want to continue up the old highway to get a feel for turn-of-the-century roads. Nancy Robertson, a Raton historian, reports that young men in Raton would offer to drive cars over the pass for the fainthearted. Five wrecked cars at the bottom of one ravine are evidence of the dangers involved.

Returning to the corner of Moulton Street and Business Loop 25, turn right, and drive one block, then turn left and go under the railroad tracks. After passing under the tracks, take the first left turn and drive along the east side of the tracks to 545 Railroad Avenue, a building on the site of the Willow Spring forage station established in 1860. Stagecoaches began stopping here the following year when

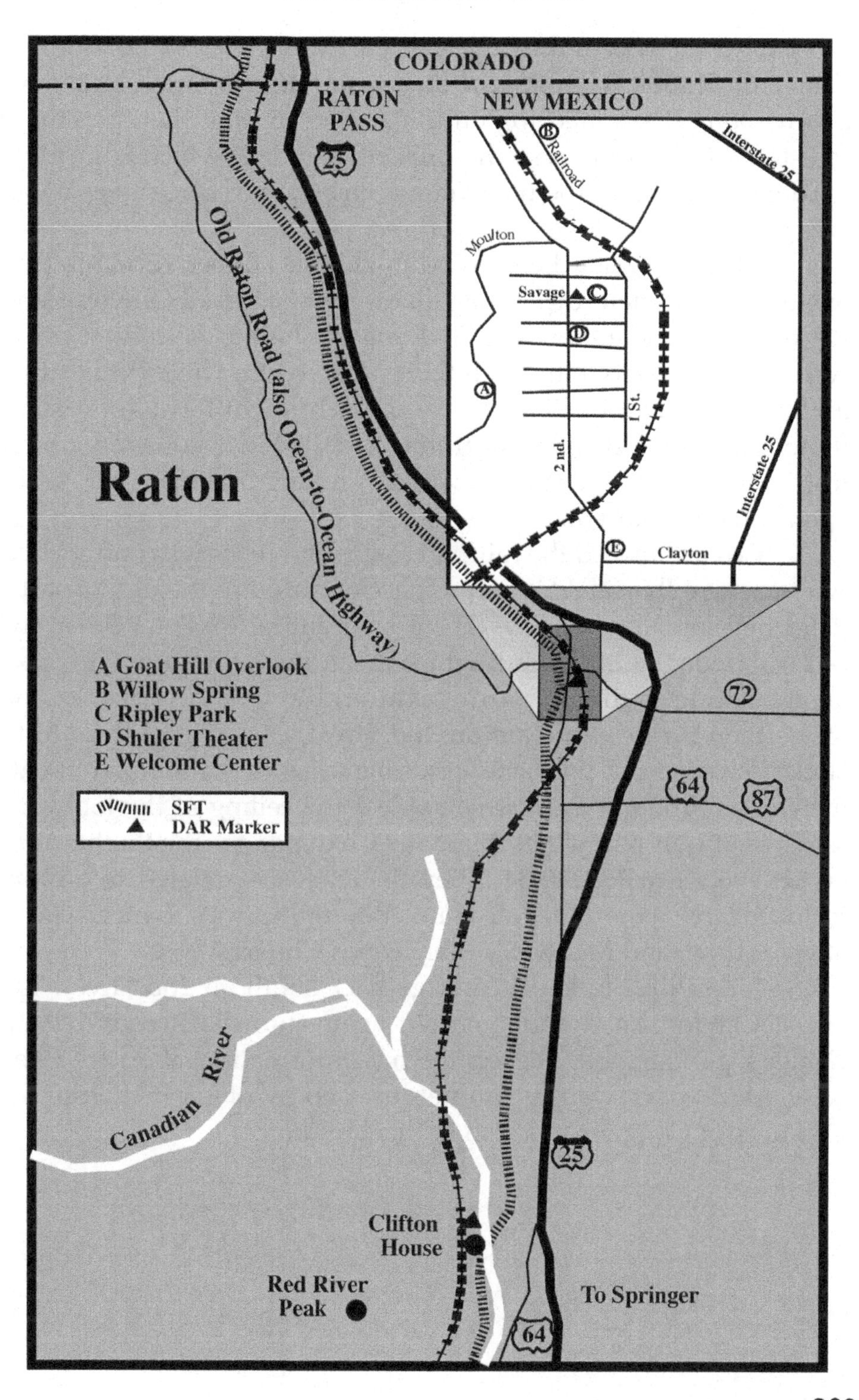
COLORADO
NEW MEXICO
RATON PASS
25
Old Raton Road (also Ocean-to-Ocean Highway)
Raton
Railroad
Interstate 25
Moulton
Savage
2 nd.
1 St.
Clayton
A Goat Hill Overlook
B Willow Spring
C Ripley Park
D Shuler Theater
E Welcome Center
SFT
DAR Marker
72
64
87
Canadian River
25
Clifton House
Red River Peak
To Springer
64

the U.S. Mail was rerouted over the Mountain Route from the Cimarron Route. By 1870, the stage station and ranch house was a four-room, flat-roofed log building. A portion of that structure is said to be incorporated in the present building, which is a private residence. Behind it, the old Willow Spring, later dug out as a well, is capped and still flows.

Go back under the railroad to East 2nd Street, turn left, drive one block, and then turn left again on Savage Street. On your left is Ripley Park, where there is a DAR marker on the southwest corner. Although unrelated to the SFT, there are two other historical features in this park: a pair of Civil War cannons brought from Rock Island, Illinois, in 1911 and an air porthole, installed in a stone monument, from the battleship Maine, whose sinking in 1898 led to the Spanish-American War.

Go east toward the railroad tracks and turn right on 1st Street. As you drive this street, you are passing through the oldest part of Raton built just after trail days. There is a beautiful Mission Revival-style railroad depot and other buildings, including a museum with a few items relating to the SFT. Turn right on Rio Grande Street, go one block, then turn right again on 2nd Street, continuing north to the Shuler Theater on the right side. Inside the entrance of the Shuler Theater (between Clark and Park streets), near the ceiling of the lobby, is a series of murals painted by Manville Chapman for the Public Works of Art Project in 1933-1934. They depict scenes related to the SFT, including the Wootton Toll Gate, Willow Springs Ranch, Clifton Stage Station, and Maxwell's Mansion in Cimarron.

From the Shuler Theater go back south on 2nd Street. Turn left at Clayton Road and then left again into the Raton Welcome Center's parking lot. The center has information about northern New Mexico, as well as numerous photos of early Raton. The Chamber of Commerce is also in this building.

CLIFTON HOUSE

Return to 2nd Street and drive south to rejoin Interstate 25. Leave the interstate at Exit 446, which is the intersection with US 64 to Cimarron and Taos. Leaving the intersection, just past the frontage road on the right, stop at a turnout, where there is an official New Mexico Historical Marker for Clifton House, an important way station on the SFT.

The site of the Clifton House is on private land, about .75 mile to the west of the turnout. To visit it, you need to request a guided tour at the Welcome Center in Raton. The Clifton House is on the far side of the Canadian River beyond the open field and a row of cottonwood trees seen from the turnout. At the location are a DAR marker and scattered foundation stones, all that remains of the historic structure.

Located where the SFT crossed the Canadian River on its way to Cimarron, the three-story adobe Clifton House with promenade balconies around the upper levels was built between 1866 and 1870 by rancher Tom Stockton. Barlow, Sanderson and Company soon leased most of the building for a "home station" where its passengers could get meals and stay overnight. Barns, outbuildings, and a blacksmith shop were installed nearby. The food and lodging here were considered the best along this section of the trail. With the establishment of the railroad in 1879, the stage line was abandoned and the Clifton House closed down. In 1885, the fine mansion, with woodwork and windows that had been freighted over the SFT from Fort Leavenworth, was gutted in a fire believed to have been started by hoboes.

From the turnout look west past the Clifton House to the highest mountain on the horizon, which is Red River Peak, a well-known landmark for all SFT travelers. The name, Red River, reminds us that many early explorers sought the headwaters of the Red River as this river was part of the boundary between Mexico and the United States after 1819. It really is understandable how Stephen Long and others might think the Canadian was the Red. It was the first major stream they came to south of the Arkansas.

Chapter 6

CLIFTON HOUSE TO CIMARRON

A couple of miles beyond the Clifton House pullout on US 64, the highway crosses the Canadian River then goes under a railroad trestle. Just beyond on the right begin the grounds of the NRA Whittington Center. There are a number of interesting SFT attractions in this location. Admission is free and the Center is open to the public. About .5 mile after passing through the gate house you come to a pullout. This is where the SFT crosses the paved road and the NPS has several waysides here.

There is a boulder with a bronze plaque and four smaller stones representing the four trail states. All of this is topped off with a life size bronze statue of a plainsman on a horse. Return to the visitors center next to the gate house and you can visit the Frank Brownell Museum of the Southwest. In this museum you will see a 100 foot long mural by artist Ron Kil depicting the history of northeast New Mexico. Many of the scenes are of SFT events.

From the Whittington Center to the town of Cimarron, identifying trail traces is difficult. There are several abandoned railroad beds along here that once served various coal mines. Also, the old highway, which was parallel to the present one, has left its marks: culverts, bridge abutments, and roadbeds.

At high points along the highway in this vicinity watch to the left front for occasional glimpses of the silhouette of the Wagon Mound on the far horizon, 60 to 70 miles away. At 8.7 miles from the Clifton House pullout, is the Hoxie Junction, a mere Y in the highway on the bald prairie. The left fork, old US 85, continues to Maxwell and rejoins Interstate 25. The right fork, US 64, goes to Cimarron.

The Mountain Route of the SFT divided in this area. The right fork stayed close to the foot of the ridge of mountains seen on the north and headed for Cimarron. Continuing west on US 64, swales of this fork can be detected from time to time on the right. The left fork struck off across the rolling plain in a direct line for a point below Rayado, a small community south of Cimarron. From the air these two forks are plainly visible, as well as a number of crossovers connecting them at various points. The trail can be seen about 100 yards to the right as you approach the Y. The actual location where the Mountain Route split is past the Hoxie Junction near a relay tower on the right. The trail can be seen to the left of the highway just as you pass the tower.

The next point of interest on US 64 is at the crossing of the small Vermejo River. Approaching two bridges here-one concrete, the second steel-a paved road enters from the right (north). Take this Vermejo Creek Road and at .9 mile is a trail crossing marked with Santa Fe Trail crossing signs. If you continued up this road, it would lead to the now-closed coal mining town of Dawson. Return to US 64 and turn right. Past the second bridge and just across the railroad tracks on the right are the remains of the ghost town of Colfax. At this crossing there was also a stage station, the adobe ruins of which are in the center of the Colfax site.

Beginning at about mile marker 319, you may see buffalo on both sides of the highway since the local rancher (Ted Turner at the time of writing) has a very large herd. If you look carefully, you can see the electrified fence that keeps them where they belong.

CIMARRON

Settlers, including Kit Carson, first entered this area in the mid-1840s. Later, Cimarron became the home of frontiersman Lucien Maxwell and headquarters for his 1.7 million-acre Maxwell Land Grant. He acquired the grant through his father-in-law Charles Beaubien, who had been an associate of the Bents. In 1870, Maxwell sold the grant to a group of investors. Afterward Cimarron became an outlaw hangout and the center of the bloody Colfax County War (1875-1878).

As early as the 1850s, Cimarron was an important stop for wagon and stage traffic on the Mountain Route of the SFT. A dozen buildings and sites associated with trail days can be visited. The Cimarron River [not the Dry Cimarron] divides the community into a new town and old town, with the trail sites all in the latter, a National Historic District.

Entering from the east on US 64, there is a pullout with an official Scenic Historic Marker and several National Park Service waysides. One side of the marker describes Cimarron, the other the Colfax County War. Continue toward the center of Cimarron to the junction with NM 21. Just before the junction are two official New Mexico highway markers referring to the SFT, both on the left side of US 64. Approaching this junction, a sign reading "National

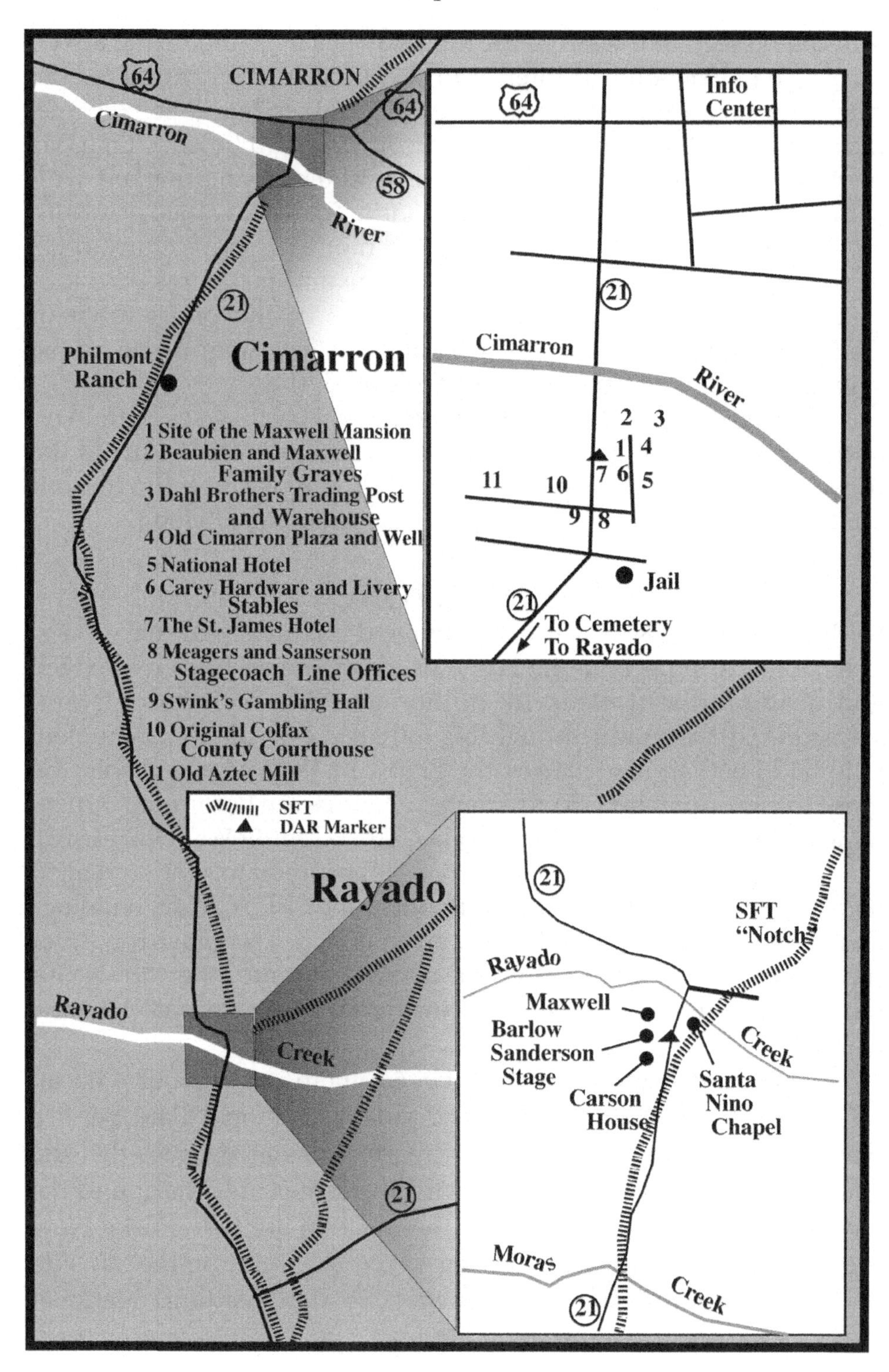
64
CIMARRON
64
Cimarron
58
River
21
Philmont
Ranch
Cimarron
1 Site of the Maxwell Mansion
2 Beaubien and Maxwell
Family Graves
3 Dahl Brothers Trading Post
and Warehouse
4 Old Cimarron Plaza and Well
5 National Hotel
6 Carey Hardware and Livery
Stables
7 The St. James Hotel
8 Meagers and Sanserson
Stagecoach Line Offices
9 Swink's Gambling Hall
10 Original Colfax
County Courthouse
11 Old Aztec Mill
SFT
DAR Marker
Info
Center
Cimarron
River
Jail
To Cemetery
To Rayado
Rayado
Rayado
Creek
21
SFT
"Notch"
Rayado
Creek
Maxwell
Barlow
Sanderson
Stage
Carson
House
Santa
Nino
Chapel
Moras
Creek

Historic District" points left (south) on NM 21 to old Cimarron. Before following that route, however, turn north one block off US 64 and view a concrete enamel-painted statue of Lucien Maxwell in a park next to the small City Hall.

At the intersection of US 64 and Lincoln, is the bright yellow Chamber of Commerce Visitors' Center. The staff can provide you with information about Cimarron and maps of a walking tour of the historic district.

Go south an NM 21, crossing the rushing Cimarron River to the old part of town in the National Historic District. Find the St. James Hotel, which is on your left (east) after you enter old town, and park somewhere nearby. The SFT sites, all clustered within a small area, are listed below. The Historical Society has provided very nice informative signs at these locations, which can be visited by referring to the accompanying map.

1. Site of the Maxwell Mansion

The historic St. James hotel in Cimarron.
The DAR marker is partially visible under the flag.

The entire block across from the St. James Hotel to the north was once the location of Lucien Maxwell's huge mansion, which was built about 1858 and burned down in 1885. Today, part of the site is occupied by a brown frame dwelling. Maxwell's mansion faced the west side of the plaza and had two sections, divided by an inner courtyard. Adobe and stone walls surrounded the rear section, where the cooking was done and the many employees fed. A remnant of the original stone wall foundation can be seen at the southwest corner. Local tradition has it, that it was the first structure built on the site of Cimarron.

2. Beaubien and Maxwell Family Graves

From the Maxwell Mansion site, walk to the east and then north at the corner. There are two graves here of interest to trail buffs.Behind an iron fence lie Pabla Lovato Beaubien (d.1864), wife of Charles and mother-in-law of Lucien, and Verenisa Maxwell (d. 1864), little daughter of Lucien. This site was originally a part of the Lucien Maxwell property on the south.

3. Dahl brothers Trading Post and Warehouse

This long building is immediately east of the graves and runs along the north side of the plaza. Allegedly begun in 1847 or 1848, the structure has been extensively remodeled so that it is difficult to get any idea of its original character, despite the fact that it contains some of the orginal adobe walls.

4. Old Cimarron Plaza and Well

The SFT crossed the Cimarron River about 50 yards northeast of the plaza. Perhaps as early as the 1870s over the river there was a log bridge which later burned. Wagons entered the open east end of the plaza, in the center of which was a well, said to have been dug in 1871. It is now covered by a white well house with a red roof. A SFT sign is nailed to an adjacent tree.

5. National Hotel

Located to the south of the plaza behind the St. James Hotel, the National Hotel reputedly dates from 1858. It is thought to have become a hotel some time after 1871, and if so, trail travelers would have stayed there. It also served as home office for Maxwell Land Grant officials. Today, it is a well-kept white building with bright blue trim used as a private residence.

6. Carey Hardware and Livery Stables

Constructed in 1872, this building also housed the Cimarron News.

7. The St. James Hotel

Formerly called the Don Diego Hotel, this two-story structure was built in the 1870s by the French immigrant Henri Lambert, who was once a chef for General Grant and President Lincoln. For a while it was a hangout for outlaws, including the notorious Clay Allison. Pancho Griego was one of Allison's shooting victims in the hotel. In the room that served as a saloon, twenty-six bullet holes still show in the pressed-tin ceiling. In addition, Buffalo Bill may have been a guest, and a room is named for him. The hotel and restaurant are open for business. A DAR marker is on the northwest corner of the block facing NM 21.

8. Meagers and Sanderson Stagecoach Line Office

The building to the south of the St. James Hotel recently served as a store but is now closed. We can find no historical reference to Meagers, but Jared Sanderson was of the stagecoach firm of Barlow, Sanderson and Company, which operated the Southern Overland Mail line on the SFT. In 1870, the firm is known to have maintained a station with a stock tender at Cimarron. It was one of the last major stagecoach companies in the country.

9. Swink's Gambling Hall

Across the street from the stage station, Swink's was the most notorious gambling hall and saloon in northern New Mexico. Originally built as a brewery in 1854, it served as a gas station in recent years but is now closed. An interesting bronze plaque giving a brief history is attached to the front of the building.

10. Original Colfax County Courthouse

Located on the right as you approach the Old Aztec Mill, this one-story building, constructed in 1872, now houses a Masonic Hall. It served as the local courthouse from 1872 to 1882.

11. Old Aztec Mill

A noted SFT landmark, the Old Aztec Mill was operated as a gristmill by Lucien Maxwell between 1864 and 1870. Trail travelers bought flour here for the last push to Santa Fe, and Ute and Jicarilla Apaches were issued government flour rations purchased from Maxwell. The building is now owned by the CS Cattle Company, which allows the Cimarron Historical Society to operate it as a museum. The museum opens in early May on Saturday and Sunday only, but is open from Memorial Day through Labor Day.

Two more sites related to the SFT can be seen as you leave town to the south on NM 21. At the first road beyond the old stagecoach office (8 on the map), turn left and then right into a little lane. On your left is a stone building with a pitched roof, originally the county jail. Return to NM 21 and turn left.

As you leave town, look for a sign directing you to the Mountain View Cemetery to the right. Established in 1870, it contains the grave of Rev. F. J. Tolby, who was assassinated in 1875 during the Colfax County War. This war was between the investors who purchased the Maxwell Land Grant (1.7 million acres) and those many families who had settled on the grant to ranch and farm. The war began in 1875 and persisted for decades.

From Cimarron a side trip can be made 55 miles across the Sangre de Cristo Mountains via US 64 to Taos and its SFT sites. However, since the excursion requires an entire day, the trip is better made from Santa Fe, after completion of your main tour.

From the Cimarron Historic District, go south on NM 21 toward the Philmont Boy Scout Ranch. Watch to the left of the road for swales of the Cimarron to Rayado section of the SFT. In the open pasture to the right (west) of the road, you may catch a glimpse of the Philmont's large buffalo herd or occasionally antelope.

NM 21 goes through the center of the ranch headquarters. The huge Mediterranean mansion, Villa Philmonte, once owned by Waite Phillips, who donated the ranch to the Scouts, can be seen on the left (east). Just past it, also on the left, is the library and museum named in honor of famed naturalist Ernest Thompson Seton, a founder of the Boy Scouts of America, whose collections are housed here. The exhibits are open to the public. A DAR marker is in front of the facility near the road.

Just beyond Philmont, NM 21 climbs a hill and makes a curve to the left. Below the check dam on the inside of this curve (to the left) are deeply eroded trail ruts. Continue on to the hamlet of Rayado, about 10 miles from Cimarron.

RAYADO

This small community was begun in 1848 by Lucien Maxwell and others on land belonging to his father-in-law, Charles Beaubien. Kit Carson also had a farm and house here. In 1850, a small military post was established at Rayado (using Maxwell's buildings) to escort caravans along the SFT between Raton Pass and Las Vegas. Later, the community was designated a "home station" by Barlow, Sanderson and Company. Rayado was also on the Taos pack trail that branched off the SFT at Point of Rocks and came directly west to this point. From here pack trains went over the mountains to Taos. Dr. Willard used this route in 1825 (Poole 2015).

Deeply eroded SFT ruts sweep into Rayado from the northeast. To see the cut through which they came, turn left on the ranch road just before Rayado Creek. At about 200 yards, you can observe the route that early stagecoaches used to come over this ridge; the driver blew a bugle signaling the station ahead as to the number of passengers so that enough places could be set at the table.

Entering Rayado from the north, note the small, private Santo Niño Chapel on the left (east). Directly across the road on the west is Lucien Maxwell's long adobe house with white wooden posts and railing on the veranda. Constructed in the early 1850s, it originally had a flat roof. Late in the decade Maxwell moved north to Cimarron, where he built his larger mansion on the plaza. Afterwards, the Rayado house came into the possession of Jesus Abreu, another son-in-law of Beaubien.

Just past the Maxwell House on the right, facing the road, is a restored building of brown stucco with a red pitched roof. This was the combination stage station and store operated by Jesus Abreu. Several hundred yards beyond, also on the right (west) side of the road, is the restored house of Kit Carson with a DAR marker in front. The large building with interior courtyard incorporates some of the walls of the original, but the plan and design bear little resemblance to what Kit built. The place is operated as a museum by the Philmont Scout Ranch and is usually open only in summer. Inquire at the Seton Museum and Library back at the scout ranch. Inside are a stagecoach and covered wagon, as well as other exhibits relating to the SFT. The wagon is reputed to have been used on the SFT by Ceran St. Vrain, a partner of the Bents.

About 1 mile south of the Carson House, NM 21 crosses Moras Creek. Looking to the right (west), note that a wide canyon forms a bay in the mountains. This is the gap mentioned by Commissioner George Sibley in 1825 as the one through which a "trace," or rough trail, passed then ascended Grulla Mesa and crossed the mountains to Taos. Pack trains heading for Taos rather than Santa Fe left the Cimarron Route of the SFT at Point of Rocks, about 30 miles to the east, and steered for the Moras Gap, visible in the distance. Sibley, however, did not go west here but instead continued south and used the Ocaté Crossing.

Continuing on several miles, the road makes a sharp turn to the left (east), while a gravel road continues straight ahead. The gravel road, closed to traffic now, eventually becomes a primitive jeep road. That is its way around several mesas to the Ocaté Crossing and eventually on to Fort Union. This is the route that George Sibley followed in 1825 to the Ocate´ Crossing and then over Osha Pass to Taos. We will pick up the Mountain Route later at the Ocaté Crossing.

At this corner you can look back toward Rayado and see deep ruts just to the east of NM 21. Continue east here on what is now NM 199, until, at .3 mile, you can see more ruts to the right of the highway. This is the branch of the trail we left at Hoxie Junction.

Stay on NM 21 about 20 miles to Springer. Here you have joined the Cimarron Route of the SFT. For details from here to Fort Union you should look at the Cimarron Route chapter (Chapter 5). In that chapter there is a side trip to Ocaté Crossing which is on the Mountain Route.

Chapter 7
NEW MEXICO

FORT UNION

Approaching the interchange on the north side of Watrous, SFT swales can be seen on both sides of Interstate 25. Exit here, and at the end of the off-ramp, turn right onto NM 161 for the 8-mile drive to Fort Union.

At about .5 mile after entering this road, a grassy lane intersecting from the left leads down to the small Tiptonville Cemetery. Stay on the highway, and at .7 mile a narrow gravel road intersects from the left. Follow it .5 mile, and where the road bends sharply to the right the ghost town of Tiptonville begins.

To the left front of the intersection, is a large well-preserved adobe and rock quadrangle, once the Tiptonville store and reputedly a stage stop. Although it is private property, you can get a good view of two sides of the complex from the road. The SFT passed directly along the road in front of the store. Today, there is a line of trees marking its route to the south. When the trail reached the Mora River about 1 mile below, it crossed to Barclay's Fort (described below).

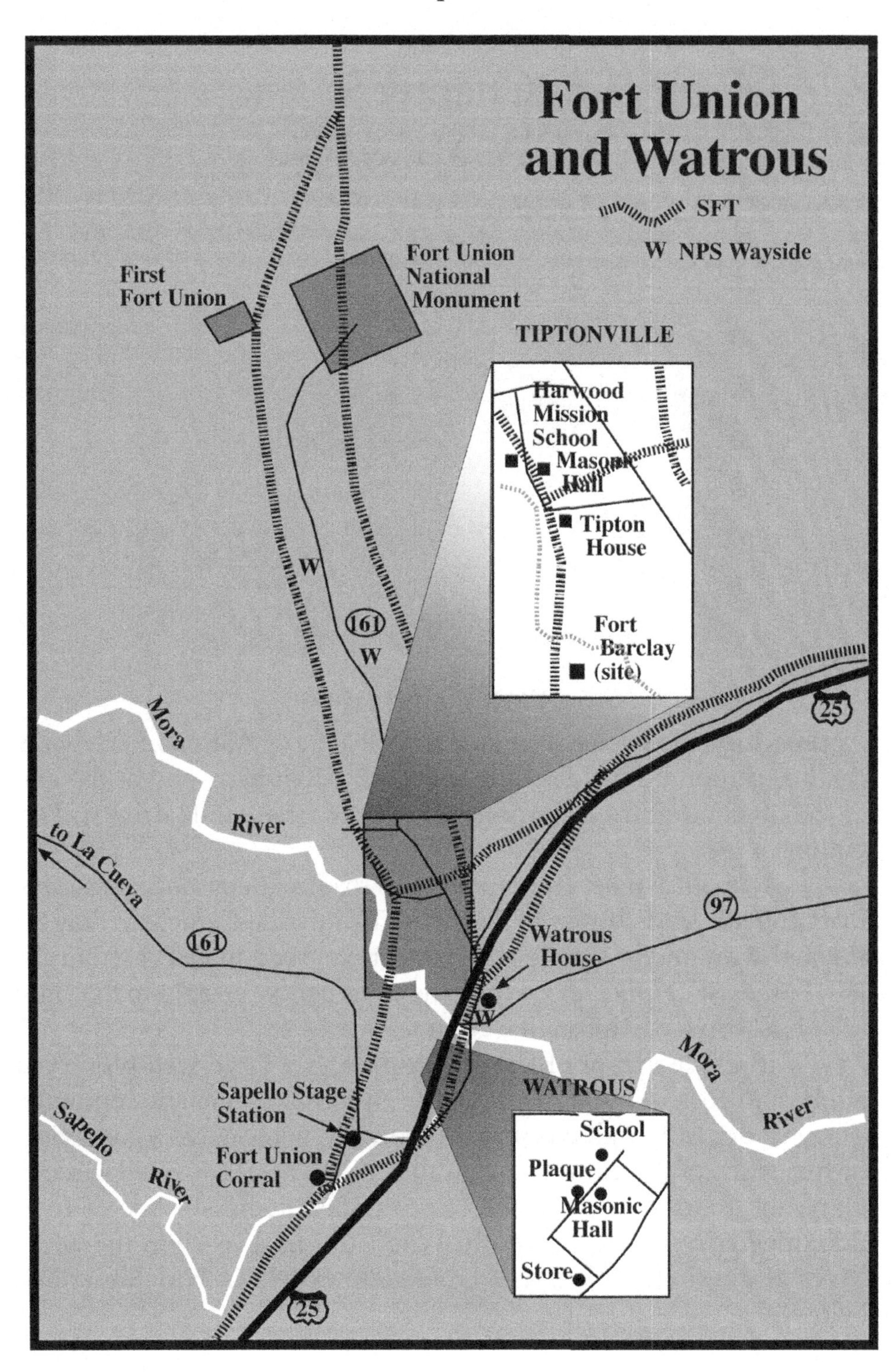
Fort Union and Watrous
SFT
W NPS Wayside
First Fort Union
Fort Union National Monument
TIPTONVILLE
Harwood Mission School
Masonic Hall
Tipton House
Fort Barclay (site)
161
W
Mora River
to La Cueva
161
25
97
Watrous House
W
WATROUS
School
Plaque
Masonic Hall
Store
Mora River
Sapello Stage Station
Fort Union Corral
Sapello River
25

From the road bend at the Tiptonville store, you can see the ruined walls of a house close by on the left. This was the residence of William Tipton (1825-1888), who came over the SFT and was prominent in the territory during the Civil War and after. The son-in-law and business partner of trail figure Samuel Watrous, Tipton settled 2 miles north of his in-laws, founding Tiptonville on the trail leading down from Fort Union. His large two-story house burned in 1957.

Continue a short distance past the bend and a large cottonwood on the right. Immediately inside the fence is a dirt bank and behind it the ruins of the old Tiptonville Masonic Lodge, whose membership included soldiers from Fort Union. Just past the lodge on the left side are the remains of the Rev. Thomas Harwood's Methodist mission school, built in 1869. After his arrival via the SFT, Harwood became a circuit preacher using Tiptonville as his headquarters.

Drive straight ahead .5 mile past other deserted buildings until the road ends in a T. Turn right and go .25 mile to rejoin NM 161. Turn left toward Fort Union once again. Very soon, notice a deep notch in a low ridge to the right of the highway representing some of the many SFT ruts in this area. There is a pullout on the right with several NPS wayside exhibits. The SFT is obvious at this point. A network of alternate trails led from Fort Union to Tiptonville and Watrous, and from here on traces can be observed on both sides of the road.

NM 161 ends in the parking lot of Fort Union National Monument. The approach to the fort and the site itself offer superlative views of a landscape that has experienced only minor changes since the days of the wagon caravans. Herds of antelope can often be seen grazing on the surrounding plains, and rangers warn visitors, at least in the summer, to watch for rattlesnakes. The monument is one of the most exciting places along today's trail, and there is so much to be seen that several hours should be allotted for a tour.

A small but excellent visitors' center and museum, with very helpful National Park Service personnel, introduce the fort and its history. In addition, publications relating to the site and to the SFT are also for sale.

The long self-guided tour around the parade ground and through the ruins is furnished with interpretive signs and audio speakers. At the rear of the fort, a marker calls attention to the ruts of the Mountain Route of the SFT coming down from the northwest side of the Turkey Mountains.

Fort Union was established in 1851 to replace Santa Fe as Military Department headquarters because the New Mexico territorial capital was regarded as "a sink of vice and extravagance." Soldiers from the new post patrolled the western end of the SFT to protect it from the kind of Indian raids that had led to the stagecoach massacre at Wagon Mound in 1850. The army also maintained a large quartermaster depot from which military supplies, freighted over the SFT, were dispersed to forts all across the southwestern frontier.

Over the years three separate forts were constructed. The first was located about 1 mile west of the visitors' center. Looking across the open plain, its few scattered ruins can be seen near the foot of a long wooded ridge. A ranch road leads to the location, but it is closed to the public except for one day a year. Check at the monument headquarters for the date if you are interested in visiting this site. Marion Russell described that first fort in her trail memoirs as in part having palisade walls. Individuals traveling with her book may wish to read her vivid account of life at Fort Union.

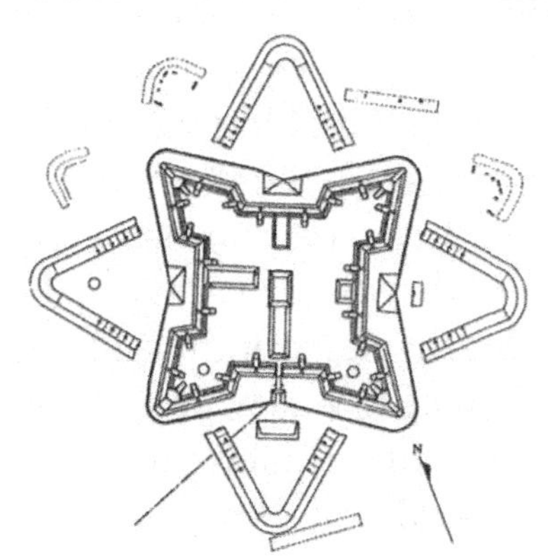

This sketch is of the fieldwork constructed in anticipation of a Confederate attack in 1862 often called a Star Fort. It really was octagonal in shape.

In August 1861, a second installation, the fieldwork, was begun. It was not a star fort as is often said, but a square earthwork with demilunes. It was constructed on the plain east of the original post. An earthwork in the form of an octagon, it was built to repel an anticipated Confederate attack, which never materialized. Its location is west of the visitors' center, well marked on the walking tour.

The last site of Fort Union, begun in 1863, adjoined the fieldwork on the north. The ruins of its large adobe buildings are the central feature of today's monument. Arrival of the railroad in Watrous in 1879 lessened the fort's importance, but it was not closed until 1891. This is one trail stop worth visiting again, particularly to catch some of the fort's summer events when reenactment groups in period uniforms put on exhibitions.

Fort Union Hospital.

Return via NM 161 to the interchange at Interstate 25.

WATROUS (LA JUNTA)

Cross Interstate 25 on the overpass, following the sign to Watrous, and enter old US 85. Note that the highway is lined with huge black willow trees. Homer Hastings, former superintendent at Fort Union, claimed that the original cuttings were brought in wagons over the SFT by Samuel B. Watrous. Watrous arrived in this area in 1849 and built a large adobe store and residence. This structure is now incorporated into the beautiful white building with a pitched roof. It faces US 85 on the left about .75 miles from the Interstate 25 interchange.

Watrous traded with soldiers from Fort Union and travelers on the SFT. One of his daughters was married to William Tipton, founder of nearby Tiptonville, and another wed George Gregg, manager of the Sapello Stage Station (described below). Watrous and his son died mysteriously in 1886, probably murder victims.

There is a pullout just north of the Watrous house with a NPS marker describing the area. This marker barely mentions the Watrous house.

Watrous house.

Just beyond the Watrous house, NM 161 crosses bridges, first over the Mora River and then over the Sapello River. To the left of the highway, the two small streams come together at what the Spaniards called La Junta, meaning the junction. That name became doubly applicable later when the Mountain Route and the Cimarron Route of the SFT united nearby to again form a single trail on the final stretch to Santa Fe.

About 1 mile north and west up the Mora River, British-born Alexander Barclay, a former employee of the Bents, built an adobe fort in 1849 that served as a major stopping place on the SFT and a relay station for the Independence to Santa Fe mail. The ruins were washed away in a flood in 1904, and the site, now on a private ranch, is not open to the public.

By the late 1840s, individuals eastbound for Missouri had begun using the La Junta area as a rendezvous site where travelers camped until a caravan large enough to ensure safety could be formed. Here officers were elected and regulations adopted that would govern the wagon train on its trip to Independence or Westport.

In this respect La Junta was the counterpart of Council Grove, the main rendezvous point on the eastern end of the trail. When the Santa Fe Railroad tracks reached this vicinity in 1879, the railroad changed the name of the small community from La Junta to Watrous, mainly to honor Samuel B. Watrous, who reportedly donated land for the right-of-way, but also because there was another place called La Junta on the main line in southeastern Colorado.

Continue on US 85 a short distance to the tiny, post-trail community of Watrous. Turn onto the second dirt lane that intersects the highway from the right. Go one block toward the park, passing on the right a tiny church built by Reverend Harwood from Tiptonville, said to be the oldest Protestant church still standing in New Mexico.

The lane ends in a T at a ball field. Turn left on the gravel street. To the right in the park is the Registered National Historic Landmark plaque for La Junta. Across the street from the plaque is the abandoned Masonic Lodge with a beautiful stone front containing an arched doorway and windows. Like the lodge in Tiptonville, it included among its original members soldiers from Fort Union.

Continue straight ahead on the street in front of the park for another two blocks. Then turn left and go one block to rejoin US 85. At that intersection on the right is the old Schmidt and Reinkens General Store, which postdates the SFT but is a nice stone structure.

Turn right (south) on US 85 and go a mile or so out of town to the (south) Watrous interchange on Interstate 25. An official New Mexico Highway Marker, "Watrous," is on the right. Go under the overpass and enter NM 161 toward Las Golondrinas. Go .5 mile to the first gravel road intersecting the paved road from the left and turn onto it.

Ahead and to the left, you will see a vine-covered house with a pitched roof and stone chimney. This is the Sapello Stage Station once operated by Barlow, Sanderson and Company as a "home station" where coaches made half-hour meal stops. The manager, George Gregg, must have sold alcohol as well because the place was known locally as Gregg's Tavern. In 1868, a stagecoach driver got into a fight with the station employees and was stabbed to death. It was a private residence in the recent past but now appears to be abandoned. The station is well preserved.

The Sapello Stage Station.

Across the road on the right beyond the fence, good trail swales lead close to the station. The actual union of the Mountain Route and Cimarron Route is believed to have been at the Sapello Crossing in the valley behind the station.

There is a corral about a third of a mile beyond the Stage Station but the road to it is now closed. The corral, a large enclosure of native stone now on private property, was reportedly built after the arrival of the railroad in Watrous. Army horses were off-loaded from stock cars and held here briefly before being driven the approximately 8 miles to the fort.

Return to the interchange and continue on Interstate 25 south toward Las Vegas. For the first several miles after rejoining the interstate watch for SFT swales along the high ground to the right. At the first rise, the trail crosses from the right side to the left and remains south of the highway to Las Vegas.

LAS VEGAS

At the Onave exit about 8 miles from Watrous, is an important water divide. To this point, traders were in the drainage of the Mississippi and Arkansas Rivers and their tributaries, but after this point they were in the drainage of the Pecos and Rio Grande Rivers.

About halfway between Watrous and Las Vegas, Hermit's Peak can be noted in the range of mountains that fill the horizon on the west. It is the tallest peak in the chain, hump-shaped with a sheer face of pink granite. However, the color is only evident in the early morning hours when the slanting sun strikes it. The peak is named in honor of Giovanni Maria Augustini (or Agostini), the hermit whose cave at Council Grove has already been described. He arrived in Las Vegas in 1863 with a freight caravan of the Romeros, who with the Bacas were one of the two leading merchant families of the town. Augustini reputedly performed a number of cures and miracles, but the crowds he attracted caused him to flee to the flat-topped mountain 14 miles west of Las Vegas and resume his life as a hermit. He remained there three years and then headed for southern New Mexico, where he was murdered in the Organ Mountains near Las Cruces in 1867. A few pilgrims from the Las Vegas area still climb Hermit's Peak to visit a shrine honoring Augustini.

About 4 miles from Las Vegas, Interstate 25 curves to the left heading almost due south. Along here, the wide valley of the little Gallinas River begins to parallel your route on the right (west), forming a trough between the highway and the foothills of the mountains beyond. In the valley were the well-watered meadows (las vegas in Spanish) that gave the area its name. Here SFT caravans camped to give their stock a good feed and rest before braving the pass through the mountains on the last leg of the trip to Santa Fe.

Until 1835, there were no permanent settlers in the area, the first New Mexican town encountered by the wagoners was San Miguel on the Pecos River, 20 miles farther. However, about 1835 a group of San Miguel residents moved to the grassy valley, establishing Las Vegas.

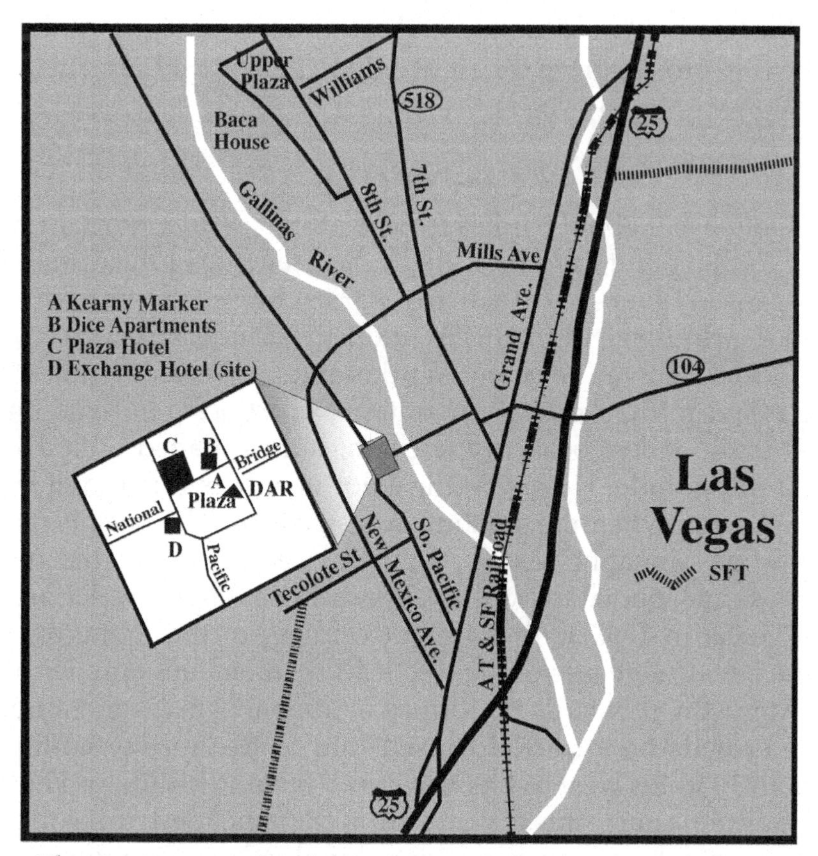

The town actually had two small communities, or plazas. The first, Upper Plaza, was on an east side bench above the Gallinas River, while Lower Plaza was 2 or 3 miles downstream on the west bank, which is now near the center of present-day Las Vegas. Sometimes wagon trains that had no business in either plaza skirted the valley on the east (to the left of Interstate 25) and swung west through Kearny Gap south of the modern city.

To see traces of the trail as it entered town, continue past the first interstate exit to the second (Exit 345). Get off here and turn left, cross over the freeway, and take the entrance back on to Interstate 25 toward the north. At about 2 miles on the right, you will see dramatic ruts, one deeply-cut swale, and another less pronounced to its right. At the bottom of the hill, to your left, the trail forded the small creek and headed for Lower Plaza. Mike Olsen, now retired historian at Highlands University, believes that caravans either stayed low and followed the route of today's Grand Avenue or went up the hill to connect with a trail from Mora.

Continue north on the interstate to the next exit (Exit 347) and get off headed south. Drive toward the city on old US 85, which parallels the interstate. At the first major intersection, Mills Avenue joins US 85 from the right (west).

Turn right (west) on Mills, go .8 mile to the intersection of 7th Street (also NM 518 here), and turn right (north). After about 1 mile turn left on Williams Drive, and go about .7 mile to 8th Street. Turn right here and drive .5 mile (just past a Mennonite Mission on the right) to a dirt road coming in from the left. Take this road, and in one block, you will be at old Upper Plaza. The plaza is in good shape, with several old adobe houses and the trail-era church still intact. The plazas were planned as rectangles, and you can see that shape.

At the stop sign in front of the church, turn left and proceed a few hundred yards to a house on the right (number 505 on the mailbox). This is the home of Jose Albino Baca, now a private residence closed to the public. Baca, a prominent SFT trader, built a large three-story adobe mansion in the 1850s for his family and the headquarters of his freighting and mercantile business. However, only about half of the second story remains, as the house has been much remodeled in recent years. Along the road and around the rear of the house, is a beautiful stone wall, inside of which SFT wagons once parked.

A photo of the Jose´ Albino Baca house from the Smithsonian archives.

Return to NM 518 (7th Street), where you may elect to turn left (north) and make a 60-mile round-trip to SFT sites at La Cueva and Mora. If not, turn right (south) on 7th Street toward the center of Las Vegas. After describing the trip to Mora, our narrative will pick up again in Las Vegas.

SIDE TRIP TO LA CUEVA AND MORA

Several miles north of Las Vegas, NM 518 crosses the small dam that Impounds Storrie Lake. At about 5 miles after the dam, is a pullout on the east (right) side of the highway with an official New Mexico Highway Marker, "Hermit's Peak." From this location, there is a good view of the peak directly to the west.

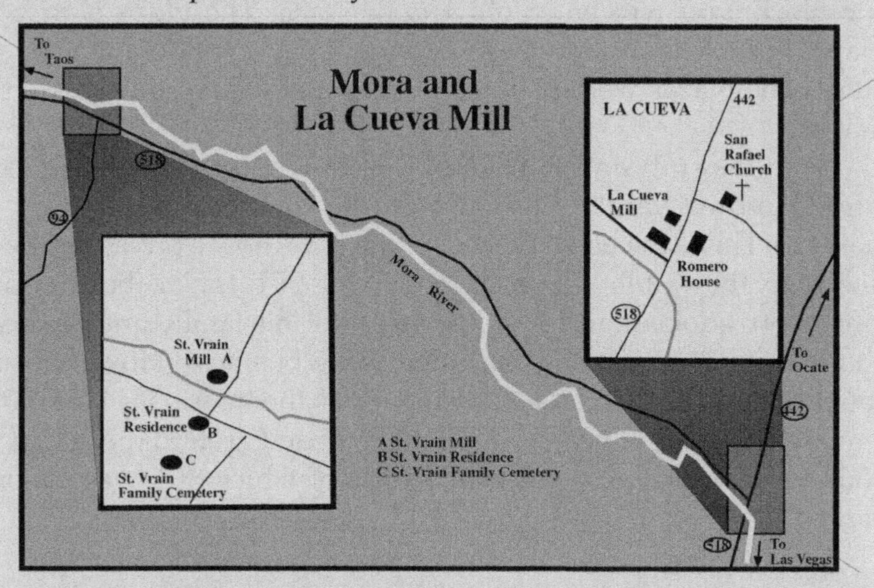

Behind the pullout immediately to the east are superb swales of the old Mora to Las Vegas wagon road, which may be regarded as a branch of the SFT. Some caravans coming from the States left the main SFT in the vicinity of Fort Union and struck almost due west 15 miles to the town of Mora, located in the valley of the Mora River at the eastern foot of the Sangre de Cristo Mountains. Mora was then an important place, a distribution center for communities lying in the high country beyond and a producer of surplus farm products, particularly wheat. From Mora, the caravans would turn south to Las Vegas, their route completing two sides of a triangle, with the main SFT from Fort Union to Las Vegas forming the third side.

Just beyond the Hermit's Peak pullout, NM 518 tops a ridge and goes down into a small valley. A wide swath of fine trail ruts, some deeply eroded, stretch along the east side of the road from this point on. At about 10 miles from the Hermit's Peak pullout, the ruts are exceptional, first on the right side of the highway and then crossing to the left.

After another 2 miles, NM 161 to Watrous intersects NM 518 from the right (east). The eye can follow the route of NM 161 as it leads through a gap in a ridge of hills about 1 mile away, also the course of the Mora River. Fort Union is approximately 12 miles due east. The trail from there traversed the gap, following the north bank of the river on its way to La Cueva and Mora. From NM 518, you can see the deserted adobe buildings of the ghost town of Buena Vista strung along the riverbank for quite a distance, all private property.

At 3 miles beyond, NM 518 forks to the left as it enters the Mora Canyon. The right-hand fork is NM 442 to Ocate´. At this junction, in a pullout to the left, is an informational sign "La Cueva National Historic District."

To the right, along NM 442, are the magnificent ruins of La Cueva Mill. An extensive stone and adobe complex includes the well-preserved mill with its wheel and race, store building, storage structures, and large stone-walled corral. The site is part of the William Salman Ranch. Although it is private property, there is a small store at the north end of the complex, and you can wander through the gardens in the old stone corral. A great deal can be seen from the road, and the complex is a photographer's dream. Today, this is one of the most interesting and scenic places in the entire SFT network.

A sketch of La Cueva Mill by artist Roger Balm.

A sign facing NM 442 gives a brief history of the mill. Shortly after the opening of Fort Union in 1851, Vicente Romero established a ranch with mill at La Cueva to grow grain and forage for the new post. At one time he controlled some 3,000 acres, much of it in the bottomlands along the Mora River. He developed an intricate irrigation system to water his vast fields of wheat and corn, and reportedly engineers came from Europe to study his use machinery freighted over the SFT. His operation supplied a huge quantity of flour to Fort Union, from which it was distributed to other military posts in the Southwest. Although the sign says the mill was established in the 1870s, it probably was in operation by the 1850s or at the latest the 1860s.

Directly across the road from the mill, on the east side of NM 442, the rear of Vicente Romero's large two-story adobe house is visible through the trees. Now authentically restored, it is a private residence and the headquarters of the Salman Ranch. A long double veranda with white trim runs across the front of the building. By continuing up NM 442 a short distance past the mill and taking the road intersecting from the right that leads to San Rafael Church (an adobe structure with pitched roof and arched windows), it is possible to catch a glimpse of the front of the Romero House just past the church. Soldiers from Fort Union were frequent guests at the many parties given by the Romeros when the house was a center of social activity.

San Rafael church.

From La Cueva, continue west on NM 518 about 5 miles to Mora. Early in 1847, a revolt against the newly established U.S. rule that began in Taos and resulted in the death of Charles Bent spread across the mountains to Mora. Eight members of a SFT caravan were killed here, including L. L. Waldo, a younger brother of traders William and David Waldo. In retribution, the American army leveled much of the town with artillery.

In 1855, Ceran St. Vrain, noted SFT figure and longtime associate of the Bents, moved to Mora from Taos and established a store and mill. The following three points of interest in town associated with the SFT relate to him:

A. St. Vrain Mill

Drive to the center of Mora on NM 518. Take NM 434, which intersects from the right (north) and go one block to cross the Mora River. Just beyond the bridge the highway curves, and on the left is the large three-story stone St. Vrain Mill. It is boarded up but still roofed and from the front looks to be in fair condition, although major cracks at the rear indicate that the beautiful building is in a precarious state. The mill is thought to have been built in 1855. At least one account suggests that the original mill was a frame structure that afterward burned and the current stone building, which replaced it, was constructed in 1864. In any case, the St. Vrain Mill as it now stands is an impressive sight. Like the present La Cueva Mill downriver, it furnished flour to the quartermaster at Fort Union.

St. Vrain Mill.

B. St. Vrain Residence

Return one block to the intersection of NM 434 and NM 518. Turn right, and stop immediately. On the left (south) side of NM 518 is the St. Vrain residence, a long adobe building with brown stucco, unmarked. The room at the extreme east end is a tavern and liquor store. A wing extends back along the west side so that the building now appears to be L-shaped. Probably when St. Vrain lived there (until his death in 1870), the other two sides were enclosed, in traditional New Mexican style, to form an open courtyard, or placita, in the center.

St. Vrain house.

C. St. Vrain Family Cemetery

Return on NM 518 east one block, then turn right on NM 94. After approximately 1 mile, NM 94 ascends a hill, and there is a pullout on the right, adjacent to a small cemetery. Walk to the cemetery and look east to a small hill with a monument, which is in the St. Vrain Cemetery, on private land. Ceran's grave is in the center of the little cemetery, surrounded by those of his family. Just outside the fence on the north side is a marker for Col. George W. Cole, 2nd U.S. Cavalry.

Return to Las Vegas via NM 518.

LAS VEGAS TOUR CONTINUED

Follow 7th Street into the center of Las Vegas. At the intersection with National Avenue, turn left and go east on National several blocks to the intersection of Grand (US 85). On the southwest corner (to the right) in the stone municipal building, is the Rough Riders Memorial and City Museum. The Chamber of Commerce and some municipal courts are also in this building.

Although not primarily focused on the SFT, the museum is worth a visit. Teddy Roosevelt recruited members of his famous Rough Riders unit from this area to fight in the Spanish-American War of 1898. For many years, Las Vegas held an annual Rough Riders Reunion. The collection contains mementos of the unit as well as other historical artifacts. Moreover, there are plans to make one room of the museum into a SFT exhibit.

Go west on National Avenue to the intersection of 8th Street and the beginning of New Mexico Highlands University campus. Traders camped here at what became the university grounds. On the north edge of the campus, are apartments for students, one called Gregg House. There are interesting plaques in an open hallway in front of this building commemorating the SFT and Josiah Gregg. Return to National Avenue.

Continue on National and after one block University Avenue enters from the left. The short segment of University going up the hill to your left is on top of the SFT. Drive straight ahead through the campus two blocks to the bridge over the small Gallinas River. Here National Avenue (now Bridge Street after crossing the river) is on the exact route of the SFT as it heads for the old Lower Plaza just beyond. On the northeast bridge abutment at about knee level, is an inscription commemorating stagecoaching on the SFT, while the northwest abutment is dedicated to the Coronado Expedition, which crossed the Gallinas River in this vicinity in 1541. The southeast abutment has an inscription honoring Gen. Stephen Watts Keamy and his march over the SFT. Keamy entered Las Vegas a colonel and left a general since his promotion papers arrived while he was here.

Cross the bridge and continue one block west to the historic Las Vegas Plaza, where there is a DAR marker in the park near the gazebo. In the northeast corner of the plaza, is a tall petrified log to which is attached a marker with historical text about Kearny's proclamation to the citizens of Las Vegas. The most historic building on the plaza is the cream-colored, flat-roofed adobe with white trim located in the row of units along the north side at numbers 210 to 218. Now known as the Dice Apartments, it is actually a series of stores, reportedly the location a platform from which Kearny read a proclamation annexing New Mexico. After his march over the SFT from Bent's Fort, Keamy camped on the ridge to the east at the site of Highlands University. Kearny went to the plaza for the ceremony; he and the alcalde (town mayor) used a ladder to climb to the flat roof, from which Kearny spoke to the townspeople assembled in the plaza below. Kearny's words follow:

PROCLAMATION OF
BRIGADIER GENERAL STEPHEN W. KEARNY,
to the PEOPLE of LAS VEGAS
August 15th 1846

Mr. Acalde, and people of New Mexico: I have come amongst you by the orders of my government, to take possession of your country, and extend over it the law of the United States, we consider it, and have done so for some time, a part of the territory of the United States. We come amongst you as friends- not as enemies; as protectors not as conquerors, We come among you for your benefit- not for your injury, "Henceforth I absolve you from all allegiance to the Mexican government, and from all obedience to General Armijo. He is no longer your govenor I am your govenor. I shall not expect you to take up arms and follow me to fight your own people, who may oppose me; but I now tell you, that those who remain peaceably at home, attending to their crops and their herds, shall be protected by me, in their property, their persons, and their religion; not a pepper nor an onion, shall be disturbed or taken by my troops without pay, or by the consent of the owner. But listen! He who promises to be quiet, and is found in arms against me, I will hang. From the Mexican government you have never received protection. The Apaches and Navajoes come down from the mountains and carry off your sheep, and even your women, whenever they please. My government will correct all this. It will keep off the Indians, protect you and your persons and property; and I repeat again, will protect you in your religion. I know you are all great Catholics; that some of your priests have told you all sorts of stories- that we should ill-treat your women, and brand them on the cheek as you do your mules on the hip. It is all false. My government respects your religion as much as the Protestant religion, and allows each man to worship his Creator as his heart tells him best. The laws protect the Catholic as well as the Protestant the weak as well as the strong; the poor as well as the rich. I am not a Catholic myself- I was not brought up in that faith; but at least one-third of my army are Catholics and I respect a good Catholic as much as a good Protestant. There goes my army- you see but a small portion of it; there are many more behind- resistance is useless Mr. Acalde, and you two captains of militia, the laws of my country require that all men who hold office under me shall take the oath of allegiance I do not wish, for the present, until affairs become more settled, to disturb your form of government If you are prepared to take oaths of allegiance, I shall continue you in office, and support your authority.

The crowd listening to the Kearny Proclamation.

The Plaza Hotel, established in 1880 soon after the arrival of the railroad and closing of the SFT, played host to numerous dignitaries in the past. The hotel is at the northwest corner of the plaza.

On the west side of the plaza, National Avenue exits in the middle of the block. Entering National, on the left is a one-story professional building, the site of the Exchange Hotel, built in 1850 by Dr. Henry Connelly and a partner named Mitchell. Connelly was heavily involved in the Santa Fe trade. In the first year of the Civil War, he was appointed territorial governor. With the advance of the Confederates in early March 1862, Connelly and other officials fled Santa Fe for Las Vegas, where they set up a temporary capital in the Exchange Hotel. After the Battle of Glorieta later in the month, Santa Fe again became the seat of government.

Behind the hotel on the west a large corral served SFT travelers. Stagecoaches also stopped here and used the livery facilities. A narrow wing of the hotel ran along the north side of the corral, its rooms facing on present-day National Avenue. The Exchange Hotel survived until 1959, when a fire destroyed the main building facing the plaza. However, part of the wing behind, a small building with pink stucco and brown trim bordering the street, escaped damage and is now used for storage.

In addition, of interest is the Plaza Antiques building on the corner where National enters the plaza. This is the site of the original church. When towns were laid out in colonial times, the church was always given a prominent place on the plaza. Inside the store is the "footprint" of the church. The owner often lets visitors see where the church was.

Take Pacific, which leaves the southwest corner of the plaza, and drive south. Pacific is on top of the SFT for several blocks leaving the plaza. Continue on Pacific to Socorro, turn right and in a few yards left onto Chavez. As you start along Chavez, you will pass a Presbyterian church on your right. The Presbyterians came to New Mexico early in the U S period and this was their first church in Las Vegas. It was built in 1871. Continue on Chavez to Perez, turn right and drive two blocks to US 85 Alternate (also called New Mexico Avenue). Turn left here and drive past a creek to Tecolote Street. Go right on Tecolote (the road to the community of Tecolote) and continue to where it turns to gravel and on your left front, climbing the hill there are parallel swales of the SFT. We will see the continuation of this piece of the SFT at Kearny Gap.

Return to New Mexico Avenue, turn right, and continue to US 85. Turn right here and follow US 85 to its junction with Interstate 25. An on-ramp straight ahead leads to the interstate, however veer left under the overpass and beyond it turn right (south) on to NM 283 at the sign pointing to Mineral Hill.

Continue on NM 283, which for the next mile parallels the interstate on the right. Then NM 283 makes a turn and passes over the interstate pointing west toward Kearny Gap, a natural pass in the high ridge ahead. Before reaching the pass, you will see a pullout on the right with a marker, "Puertocito de la Lumbre." This is the approximate location of the meeting between Capt. William Becknell and five companions with about four hundred soldiers under the command of Capt. Pedro Gallego. Becknell spoke no Spanish and Gallego no English so there wasn't much communication here. Becknell and companions were taken to San Miguel del Vado and then to Santa Fe. In Santa Fe they met with governor Facundo Melgares, the same man who befriended Zebulon Pike in 1807. Melgares may not have known of Mexican independence at that moment but he welcomed Becknell anyway. Mike Olsen and the late Harry Myers related the story of the meeting at the gap in an article in Wagon Tracks (Olsen 1992). There is also a new DAR marker at the site.

Approaching the gap, ruts of the SFT curve toward it from the right, the route leading from Tecolote Street in Las Vegas. If you look carefully up the valley to the right, you will see the deeply cut washouts on the side of the hill (to see these swales you must drive a few hundred yards past the Becknell pullout). The main route of the SFT, used by General Kearny and his troops in August 1846, went through the pass. Before Kearny's time, the gap was called Puerto del Norte (North Pass) to distinguish it from Puerto del Sur (South Pass), which is about 2 miles farther south and is now threaded by Interstate 25.

Just after passing through the gap, the old road climbs a low ridge. At its top Spanish or Mexican settlers once had a round defensive

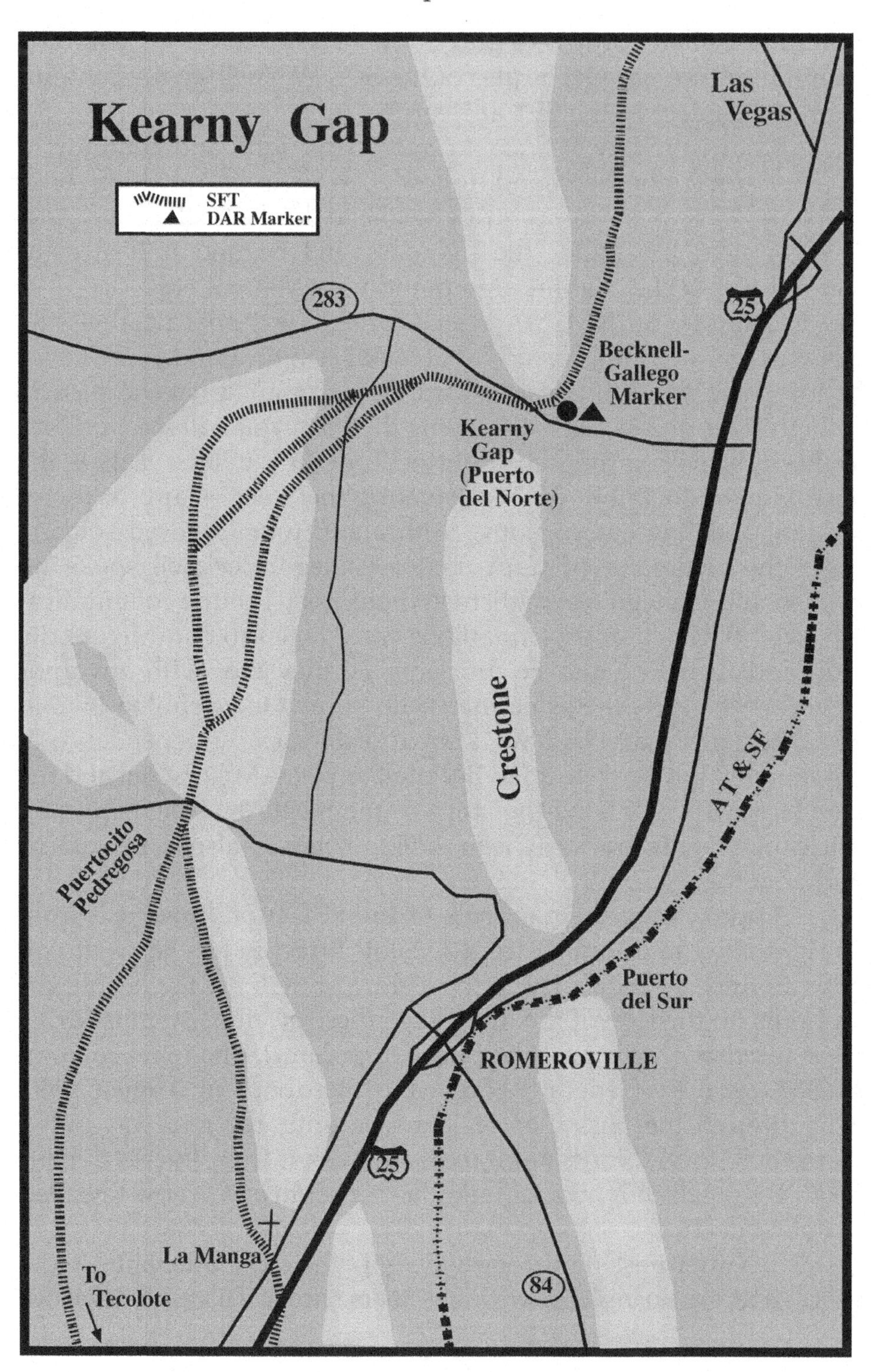
Kearny Gap
SFT
DAR Marker
Las Vegas
283
25
Becknell-Gallego Marker
Kearny Gap (Puerto del Norte)
Crestone
A T & SF
Puertocito Pedregosa
Puerto del Sur
ROMEROVILLE
25
La Manga
To Tecolote
84

tower (torreon), to control access through the pass. Just inside Kearny Gap, the SFT split into several branches, which are clearly shown on Lt. George Wheeler's geographical survey map of the mid-1870s.

The principal routes, led from Kearny Gap in a southwesterly direction up a long valley but very quickly veered to the right, crossing through a small pass in the long wooded ridge on the west.

One branch may have paralleled the first branch, but where that trail turned west through the pass, the south branch continued up the valley another mile or so to Puertocito Pedregosa (Little Rocky Gate).

To view the ruts of the middle and south branches, continue on NM 283 .4 mile. Take an unmarked dirt road on the left. Caution here as this road can be treacherous in the rainy season, impassable when wet. Just after climbing the gentle hill (at about .2 mile) you will see a series of five swales in the valley to the right front, two deepened by erosion. One is to the left of the gravel road, while another four are to the right of the road. They all climb the ridge to the right and head for a pass leading to Tecolote.

You can either follow this poor road (in good weather) to Puertocita Pedregosa or return to the frontage road paralleling the interstate, If you decide to return to the frontage road, retrace your steps and after passing over the Interstate, turn right on the frontage road headed for Romeroville.

PUERTOCITA PEDREGOSA

South of Las Vegas, Interstate 25 makes a sweeping curve to the west and passes through Puerto del Sur along with the railroad tracks. The frontage road lies between the interstate and the tracks and goes through Puerto del Sur (South Pass) just before Romeroville. This was a secondary route for still another branch of the SFT, used by a portion of Kearny's army in 1846, although the main force went through the gap 2 miles north that now bears his name. Once inside Puerto del Sur, this branch of the SFT moved off in a northwesterly direction to join the main trail at Puertocito Pedregosa. There is no sign for this gap. A note here about Romeroville. US Route 66 entered Romeroville on a narrow dirt road in the center of town.

Looking at it today it is hard to imagine this was a major east to west highway in 1935.

To reach Puertocito Pedregosa, continue past Romeroville to US 84. If you turn left here, you would go to Santa Rosa, but instead turn right and cross over the interstate to the stop sign. Turn right on County Road A-20 that starts back toward the east, parallel to the interstate. Shortly it turns to the left north, making a couple of curves before pointing west toward Puertocito Pedregosa.

Approaching the mouth of the gap, a road intersects from the right (north) at a junction about two miles from Interstate 25, where there is a sign reading "Ojitos Frios Ranches." This is a new subdivision road in good condition (at least as far as the cattle gate), and some signs of the trail can be seen along it. This is the south end of the road you left near Kearny Gap.

Back at the junction, continue west into Puertocito Pedregosa, which is a winding canyon for about .5 mile. Just before exiting the pass you can see two valleys converging to your right, where the several routes of the SFT passed. As you exit the pass on the west side, well-defined ruts are on the left, leading off in a southwesterly direction. Just out of sight the trail splits: the left branch went toward the interstate and on to Tecolote, while the right branch went just to the left (east) of Tecolote Peak and then threaded its way to Tecolote.

From this point return to the frontage road paralleling the interstate and turn right toward Tecolote.

TECOLOTE

The frontage road immediately climbs a hill, and when it descends, you see a small church on the right in the distance, the site of La Manga (the "sleeve" or edge). If you look just to the left of the church, you can see ruts of the trail descending the hill toward the frontage road. This is a continuation of the left fork of the trail that branched at Puertocito Pedregosa.

Continuing on the frontage road, Tecolote Peak looms to your right. The other branch of the trail passes by its base. At a high point in the road, a break in the trees and an open valley on the right provide a panoramic view of the distant mountains to the north, with

Hermit's Peak being the most prominent. From this perspective, it presents the outline of two huge tilted and connected blocks, quite unlike the shape observed from the plains approaching Las Vegas.

Turn right into Tecolote on a dirt road that leads two blocks to the plaza. Facing the plaza is an interesting adobe church, while opposite it is an old, unpaved highway going toward Tecolote Creek. Since Romeroville, you have been following old Route 66 that came from Santa Rosa (this is the famous Chicago to Los Angeles Highway and before that it was the Ocean-to-Ocean Highway). If you walk to Tecolote Creek here, you can see the broken bridge that formed part of the old highway. On the corner of the plaza and this road, is a DAR marker, behind a wire fence and inside the yard of a deserted adobe house.

Tecolote (which means "owl" in Spanish) retains the historical flavor of an earlier day. Readers of Marion Russell's journal will recall her account of the trading post she and her husband operated here after he left the service at Fort Union. In his book *The Road to Santa Fe,* Hobart Stocking says he saw their building being demolished in the late 1960s (Stocking 1971). In later trail days, Tecolote was maintained as a U.S. Army forage station, and reportedly large stables and a headquarters building were in evidence as late as the 1930s.

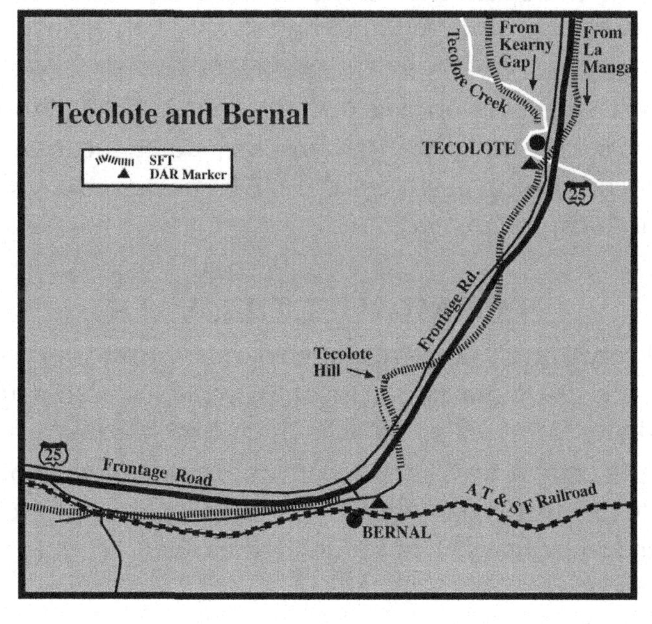

BERNAL

Return to the frontage road and turn right toward Bernal. After 1.5 miles, you will be in a small valley, where the SFT crossed from right to left. In another mile, the trail passes back to the right of the road. As you continue, you will see Tecolote Hill, a major hurdle for traders looming in front that was anticipated with apprehension. Ascending the hill required traders to double the teams to 12 yoke of oxen, and even then, it was a full day's work. We discovered the route they used by finding the old paved highway (Route 66), which used the same path to climb the hill. About 3.2 miles from Tecolote the valley is to the right, and approximately .5 mile up that valley is the narrow pass they used.

Stay on the frontage road to where you can turn left, cross the interstate, and enter Bernal. The road is not marked but is the very next left turn. The road ends in a T, turn left (east) and go about 50 yards to a clump of junipers on the right (south) side of the road. Here is a DAR marker, easily missed.

To the right rear in the distance is Starvation Peak, a flat-topped butte properly called Bernal Hill. According to legend, though unverified, a band of travelers, either colonial Spaniards or Santa Fe traders depending on the version, was attacked by Indians and fled to the summit, where they starved to death after a long siege.

A SFT stage station was once located in the vicinity of nearby Ojo de Bernal (Bernal Spring), but the exact location is open to debate. By continuing east past the DAR marker, the village's interesting church can be visited.

SAN MIGUEL DEL VADO

Instead of returning to the frontage road, continue west on the road on which the DAR marker is located, which was old Route 66, at least until the late 1930s. As you drive for the next 3 miles, look for trail ruts only a few yards from the road, mostly on the right. At 3.2 miles from Bernal, about where the railroad tracks cross on the left, the trail splits. The left branch, the older, went to San Miguel, while the right branch (a later variant) stayed up high and headed for San José.

Continue on the gravel road under the interstate, where it rejoins the frontage road. Drive to NM 3 a few miles ahead. Turn left (south) on paved NM 3 to Ribera, at the railroad crossing, then San Miguel, about 3 miles south of the interstate.

In the initial years of the Santa Fe trade, San Miguel del Vado was the first New Mexican community encountered by caravans arriving from the States. William Becknell received a warm welcome here in 1821 on his inaugural journey. Entering the village, established in the mid-1790s, a large adobe church with its twin towers is on the right (west). The church was built in 1805, and although it has been remodeled many times, the outline of the facade remains the same as it was in 1846 when SFT traveler Lt. J. W. Abert captured it in a watercolor.

Near the church door is a bell whose casting indicates that it was made in Ohio in 1861. It was freighted over the SFT to San Miguel del Vado and according to popular belief was one of the last bells cast in the East before foundries were converted to making cannons at the outbreak of the Civil War. (A bell with a similar inscription, now in the Catholic church at Belen, south of Albuquerque, apparently was brought over the SFT at the same time.) Also, on the bell, note the name of the priest, Don Juan Guerin, and the names of the two padrinos, literally godparents, who were sponsors of the bell.

During the Mexican period, San Miguel del Vado was a port of entry, where the Missouri merchants had their first dealings with Mexican customs officials. Close to the river is a sprawling building that some claim is the old customs house. However, it was more a place where soldiers stayed while waiting to escort wagon trains. Escorts roamed far out on the trail to keep traders from caching goods to avoid customs duties, which actually were probably paid in Santa Fe.

The old village with its several hundred inhabitants had a defensive plaza-contiguous adobe houses forming a large rectangle with an open area in the center and a single gate that could be closed

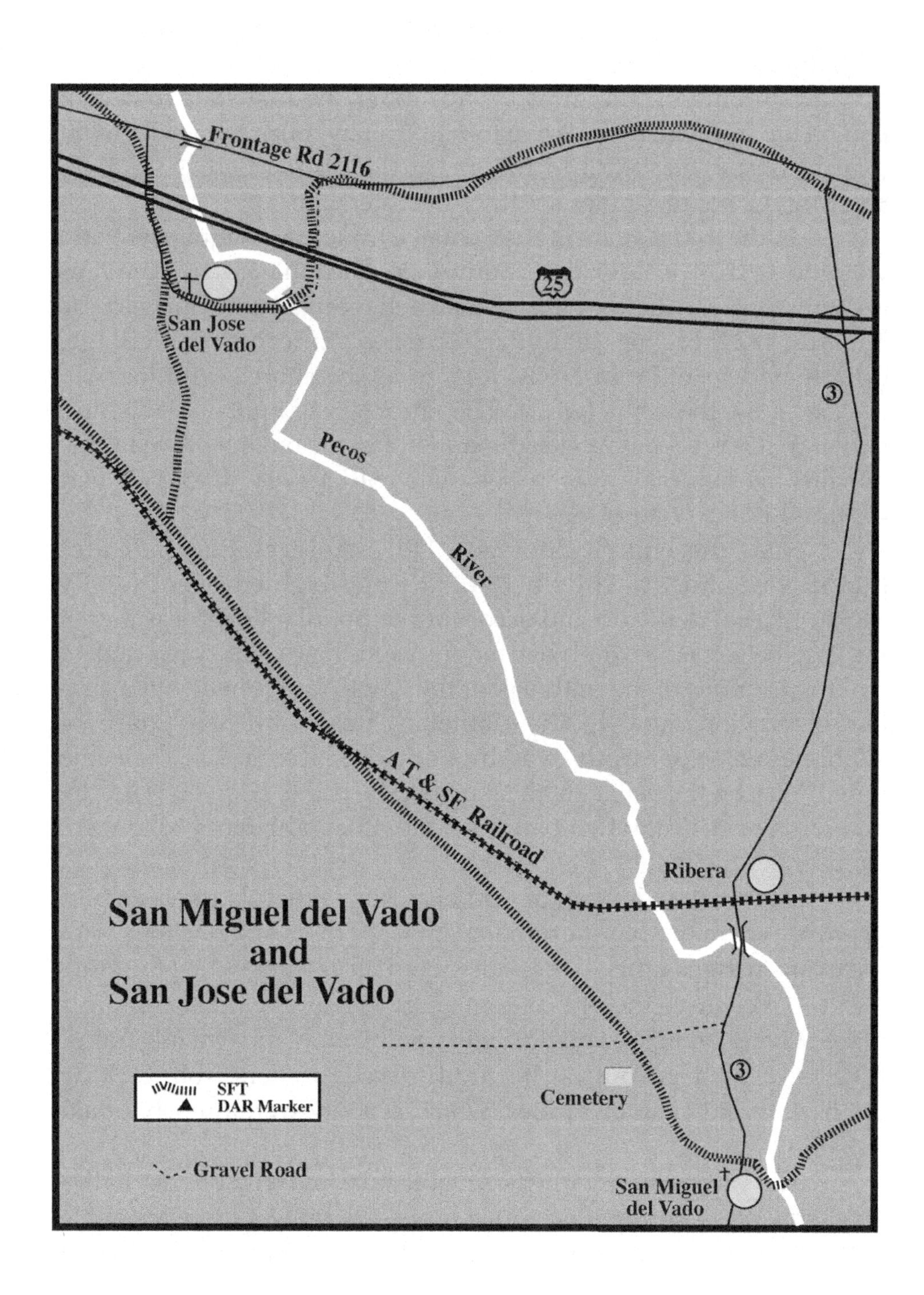

Frontage Rd 2116
25
San Jose
del Vado
3
Pecos
River
A T & SF Railroad
Ribera
San Miguel del Vado
and
San Jose del Vado
3
SFT
DAR Marker
Cemetery
Gravel Road
San Miguel
del Vado

during Indian attack. Just past the church, the road cuts through the center of the old plaza. Although many of the houses on the plaza have disappeared, enough remain to outline the original rectangle. Behind the church are the ruins of a number of stone and adobe houses outside the plaza area, which date from trail days. The SFT forded the Pecos River just east of the main plaza (vado means ford in Spanish). Standing at the entrance of the church, look straight ahead (due east) across NM 3 to a small lane that leads down to the Pecos River a block away. Take a walk there to see traces of the ford. See map for details of exactly where the crossing was.

Return on NM 3, cross under the interstate, and continue to the frontage road, which is now about .5 mile straight ahead. Turn left at the stop sign and follow the frontage road, and in .5 mile on the right, you can spot ruts of the later trail headed for San Jose. Continue on the frontage road across the Pecos River and turn left at the first road past the river, which will take you into San Jose del Vado.

SAN JOSE´ DEL VADO

Several miles up the Pecos River at San Jose del Vado was an alternate ford for the SFT on a shorter cutoff with a rougher approach. San Jose del Vado began to assume more importance as San Miguel declined after the 1835 founding of Las Vegas farther east. San Miguel then was no longer the first community encountered by wagon trains.

San José was built around a fortified plaza like San Miguel, but more of the houses survive here making the arrangement clearer. A large church, post-dating the SFT, is in the center of the plaza.

Follow a road that leaves the southeast corner of the plaza. About a block later, there is a DAR marker on the right side of the road. Continue several more blocks to an abandoned steel girder bridge over the Pecos. This may have been the site of the original ford, but we have not been able to verify that. However, you should know that this road and the bridge were part of the old Route 66.

Return to Interstate 25.

San José del Vado.

PECOS

At San José begins Glorieta Mesa (or Rowe Mesa), whose towering escarpment remains on the left for the next 20 or 25 miles. Maps of the 1870s show that the SFT (by that date often labeled the Fort Leavenworth Road) roughly followed the route of present-day Interstate 25 and the Santa Fe Railroad tracks, which are to the left. The earlier SFT probably took this same path since the country to the right is very rough, broken by arroyos leading down to the deep canyon of the nearby Pecos River.

At just over 11 miles from the San Juan/San Jose interchange, leave Interstate 25 at the Rowe/Pecos exit (Exit 307). Take NM 63 leading toward Pecos National Historical Park. Within a mile or two, SFT ruts can be seen to the left of the highway, where the clearing of piñon timber has left a grassy pasture. After 1.4 miles, you will enter Pecos National Historical Park.

At about 3.4 miles from the exit ramp of Interstate 25, NM 63 passes the old headquarters of Greer Garson's Forked Lightning Ranch. It is on the right (east) side of the road, a salmon-colored adobe building with bright blue trim, now part of the park. An ox yoke hangs from the top of the porch, while near the corner of the porch, next to a blue wagon wheel, is a DAR marker. In addition, there is a marker attached to the front claiming that this building is a "Historic Stagecoach Stop and Trading Post Built in 1810," although the source of this date is unknown to us.

The headquarters is on the site of Kozlowski's Ranch and Stage Station. It incorporates some of the original walls of the station. Martin Kozlowski, a Polish immigrant, entered New Mexico after 1846. Later he acquired this site on the SFT and constructed ranch buildings using materials scavenged from the ruined Pecos mission and Indian pueblo 1 mile away. Meals provided to stage passengers by his wife, including fresh trout from the Pecos River, were said to be the best on the western end of the trail.

Just past the ranch house, NM 63 crosses a bridge. Kozlowski's Spring, the reason he located here, can be seen on the right, down in the creek bed. This was also the site of the Union headquarters in late March 1862, when the Blue and the Gray fought the Battle of Glorieta several miles to the west.

At .6 mile ahead is the entrance to Pecos National Historical Park on the left (west) side of NM 63. Here are extensive Indian ruins and the remains of a huge Spanish colonial mission church. Buddy Fogelson and his wife the actress Greer Garson donated the land immediately around the ruins to the park many years ago. After they died, the park acquired additional land, including Kozlowski's Ranch and the Greer Garson summer house.

Pecos, located on the east side of Glorieta Pass at the gateway to the plains, has a long and fascinating history, beginning with a visit by members of the Coronado Expedition in 1541. It was a major landmark on the SFT, mentioned in practically all trail journals, including those of Josiah Gregg and Susan Magoffin. Excellent publications on Pecos are available at the visitors' center, and a film shown there focuses, in part, on the SFT. You can also drive to a picnic ground near the park headquarters, where ruts can be seen behind the headquarters building. In addition, although the Greer Garson summer house has nothing to do with the SFT, if you are interested in viewing it check at the visitors' center.

Continue north on NM 63 to the center of the modern community of Pecos. At a service station on the right, NM 50 intersects from the west. Turn left onto it, and immediately on the right is an official New Mexico Highway Marker, "Pecos." Follow winding NM 50 toward Pigeon's Ranch and stage station.

PIGEON'S RANCH

At 4.3 miles from the junction of NM 63 and NM 50, is a roadside pullout on the right. To the right rear of the pullout are two markers, both commemorating the Battle of Glorieta, between Union and Confederate forces, that occurred on March 28, 1862, often described as the Gettysburg of the West. One marker, placed by the Texas Division of the United Daughters of the Confederacy, remembers the Confederate dead. The second, placed later, is for the Colorado Volunteers who made up a significant portion of the Union forces. Union troops advancing from Fort Union on the east and Confederates coming from Santa Fe on the west both followed the SFT. This area is now part of the Pecos National Historical Park, which eventually hopes to move the present highway to a ridge on the left, making it possible to show where the various actions took place during the battle.

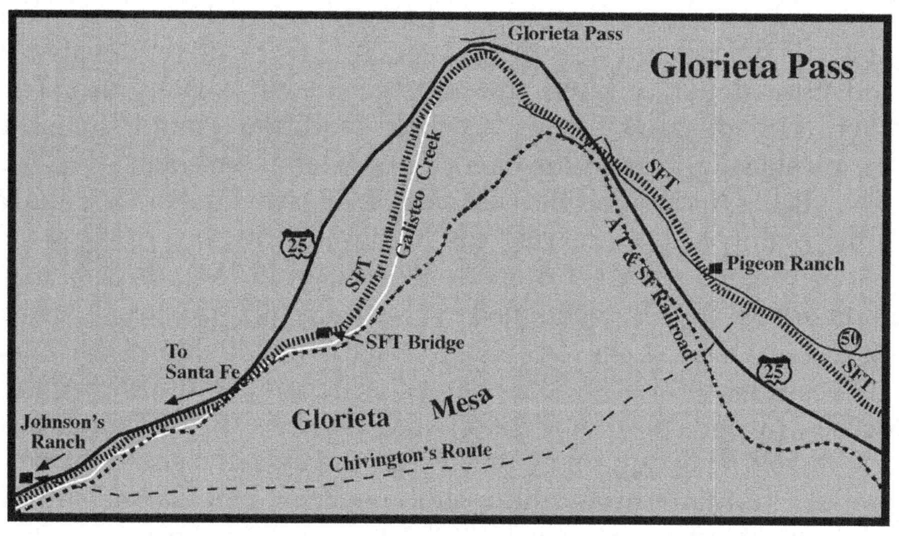

At .5 mile beyond the pullout, on the right side of NM 50, are the remains of Pigeon's Ranch. In the 1850s, Alexander Valle, of French background from St. Louis, established a ranch and SFT hostelry on the site. The place was universally referred to as Pigeon's Ranch. Only three adobe rooms adjacent to the highway survive of what was once a twenty-three-room complex. Mounded ruins are behind the building, and the stone footings of a corral are attached on the west end. A porch on the front, now gone, bordered the SFT. Across the road to the left are a few fruit trees from the earlier orchard.

During the Battle of Glorieta, the ranch alternately changed hands between Union and Confederate forces. Briefly, it served as a makeshift hospital, where bodies of dead soldiers were stacked to the ceiling in one room. Most of the fighting occurred in the open area to the west, beyond the present highway bridge and on both sides of the road. There is an official Scenic Historic Marker "Glorieta Battlefield" on the left .3 mile beyond Pigeon's Ranch.

In June 1864, Kit Carson spent a night at Pigeon's Ranch telling stories of his exploits to members of the Doolittle Commission, a U.S. Senate investigative body sent west to study the condition of the Indians. However, for reasons not readily apparent few latter-day SFT travelers mentioned stopping at Pigeon's Ranch. However, the ranch building can be seen in early twentieth century tourist post cards as it was on U S Route 66 until 1937.

TO JOHNSON'S RANCH SITE

One mile beyond Pigeon's Ranch, NM 50 reaches an interchange that leads back onto Interstate 25 to Santa Fe. The high point on the interstate directly ahead is the unmarked summit of Glorieta Pass, where the highway curves to the left. Traces of the SFT are hidden in the trees on the left.

Between mile markers 296 and 295 on the left, is an informal pullout, accessible only from eastbound lanes. Behind the pullout, on private property, you can see a memorial that commemorates the Battle of Glorieta, as well as a skirmish at Apache Canyon two days before the major battle at Pigeon's Ranch.

At 5 miles from entry onto the interstate is Cañoncito at Apache Canyon. Here blasting for the railroad and Interstate 25 has widened what was once a narrow wagon gap on the SFT. In August 1846, Governor Manuel Armijo fortified the gap with the intention of opposing Kearny's advance on Santa Fe, but he abandoned the position before any hostilities occurred.

As Interstate 25 passes out of the gap, take the off-ramp at Exit 294. Turn right at the stop sign, and immediately to your left will be Scenic Historic Marker "Cañoncito at Apache Pass." Adjacent to the marker is a DAR marker, which disappeared in the 1950s and was found and restored in 1988. From the marker drive east past the small, quaint Cañoncito church with its bright red roof. You are now heading back toward the mouth of the gap, parallel to the interstate.

Continue past a stucco house down to the bottom of the hill, where a dirt road intersects from the left. At this intersection on the left is an old corral adjacent to the site of Johnson's ranch house and stage station. Large gray logs inside the corral are the vigas, or roof beams, from the old station, which was leveled in the 1950s by the owner.

Anthony P. Johnson of St. Louis came to New Mexico in the late 1840s. Afterward he worked as a teamster out of Fort Union. From an officer there he borrowed $400 to purchase this ranch in 1858. His adobe and rock residence with a porch across the front became a stop for stagecoaches on the last stretch of trail before Santa Fe. Johnson was absent in March 1862 when Confederate troops occupied his ranch, using it as a headquarters and supply depot for several days before the Battle of Glorieta. He sold the ranch in 1869 and was murdered by outlaws in 1879.

At this point, you can either return to Interstate 25 and continue to the end of the SFT in Santa Fe or stay on the road passing the church and take it to Santa Fe. The latter way more closely follows the SFT, and is the route described below.

SANTA FE

At 9 miles from the Cañoncito church, turn right on Gaucho Way. (If you took Interstate 25, take Exit 284, turn right at the stoplight, and continue to this same point.) Soon you will see the New Mexico Academy on the left and come to Old Santa Fe Trail. Turn left on Old Santa Fe Trail, and look immediately to the right to view a DAR marker, about 15 yards behind a barbed wire fence and difficult to see.

Continue on Old Santa Fe Trail 3 miles, passing the Southwest Headquarters for the National Park Service on the left just after a turn in the road. Just past the Park Service there will a road to your left leading to Museum Hill. At this corner is a portrayal of a wagon train and traders on the SFT. (Sonny Rivera is the artist). The next road entering from the right here is Monte Sol. Turn right onto it, and immediately you will see one of the new SFT "XING" markers on your right. The trail crossed here and then went on toward the Santa Fe Plaza, paralleling Old Santa Fe Trail.

Go back and follow Old Santa Fe Trail to where it joins Old Pecos Trail at a stop sign. After you turn right here, you are on the SFT the remaining ten blocks to the plaza. One block after the stop sign East Buena Vista joins from the left, and on the southwest corner of that intersection is a marker, with the barely discernible words "Santa Fe Trail." The sponsor of this marker and its placement date remain a mystery. Continue on Old Santa Fe Trail to the center of Santa Fe.

Santa Fe's maze of streets requires that you obtain a city map. Many hotels, shops, galleries, and restaurants have free maps and historical brochures. In summer there is usually a tourist information booth maintained on the porch, or portal, of the First National Bank of Santa Fe on the west side of the plaza. Moreover, Santa Fe has a visitors' center located in the Lamy Building, adjacent to the San Miguel Chapel on Old Santa Fe Trail.

The End of the Trail Chapter of the SFTA has developed a fine guide to Santa Fe entitled Santa Fe: A Walking Tour (Self-Guided), which can be found at the information booth on the plaza or the Santa Fe Visitors' Center in the Lamy Building.

In addition, the many local bookstores sell a variety of city guides that provide directions to numerous points of historical interest not associated with the SFT. Especially recommended is the magazine shop in the lobby of La Fonda Hotel on the plaza, or the Museum Shop of the Palace of the Governors, which has a good selection of books about the SFT. The new state history museum also has a wide selection of books. It is just off the plaza and adjacent to the Palace of the Governors.

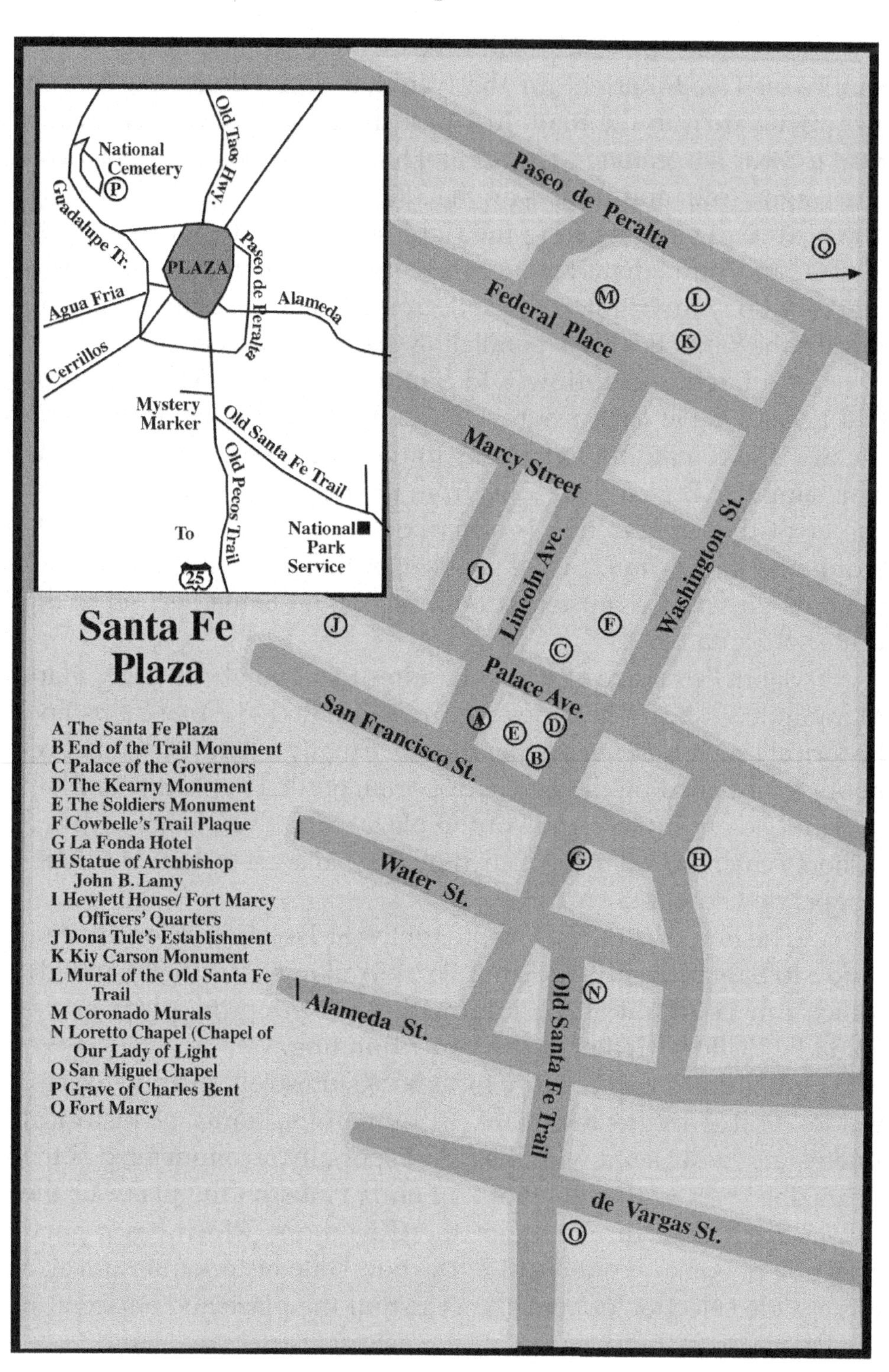
Santa Fe Plaza
A The Santa Fe Plaza
B End of the Trail Monument
C Palace of the Governors
D The Kearny Monument
E The Soldiers Monument
F Cowbelle's Trail Plaque
G La Fonda Hotel
H Statue of Archbishop John B. Lamy
I Hewlett House/ Fort Marcy Officers' Quarters
J Dona Tule's Establishment
K Kiy Carson Monument
L Mural of the Old Santa Fe Trail
M Coronado Murals
N Loretto Chapel (Chapel of Our Lady of Light
O San Miguel Chapel
P Grave of Charles Bent
Q Fort Marcy
Paseo de Peralta
Federal Place
Marcy Street
Lincoln Ave.
Washington St.
Palace Ave.
San Francisco St.
Water St.
Alameda St.
Old Santa Fe Trail
de Vargas St.
National Cemetery
Old Taos Hwy.
Guadalupe Tr.
PLAZA
Agua Fria
Alameda
Cerrillos
Mystery Marker
Old Pecos Trail
To
25
National Park Service

Individuals visiting Santa Fe for the first time should be aware that it is crowded during the height of the tourist season, from mid-June to Labor Day weekend. The Santa Fe Opera draws thousands at this time, and on many weekends there are special events, including fiestas, craft shows, Santa Fe Rodeo, Spanish Market, and, in August, the famed Indian Market. Thus during the high season accommodations may not be available without reservations, and parking may be scarce. Downtown hotels and the finer restaurants charge big city prices. In fact, they are exorbitant! However, more modestly priced motels and restaurants can be found along Cerrillos Road, which begins four blocks south of the plaza and eventually joins Interstate 25 going to Albuquerque. The best times to visit are in April and May, and September through mid-October.

A tour of SFT sites should begin at the plaza. Points of interest A through P, described below, are within a three to four block radius of the plaza and are best reached by walking. The remaining sites are a little farther out, and all but experienced walkers will probably prefer to reach them by car. Consult our map or inquire locally for directions.

THE PLAZA AREA

A. The Santa Fe Plaza

The Santa Fe Plaza marks the official end of the 1,000-mile SFT. As one of the oldest historic sites in America, dating back to the founding of the city by the Spaniards in 1610, it has been designated a Registered National Historic Landmark marked by a bronze plaque mounted just inside the entrance to the Palace of the Governors.

In the earliest days of the Santa Fe trade, Missouri merchants unloaded and sold their wares here in the open air. But soon they began to rent space for stores in the rambling adobe buildings surrounding the plaza. Before 1846, traders occupied one end of the historic Palace of the Governors. In Chapter One we wrote about the shift from individual traders to commercial trading about 1830. At this date much of the traffic went on to Chihuahua and beyond.

Josiah Gregg does a good job describing the travel south. Also, Max Moorhead's fine book *New Mexico's Royal Road: Trade and Travel on the Chihuahua Trail* covers the Santa Fe to Chihuahua section of the Camino Real.

B. End of the Trail Monument

Located on the southeast corner of the plaza, this historic granite stone is the last of the approximately 170 DAR markers that travelers have been finding along the trail since Franklin. It signals the completion of a journey that commenced at the Beginning of the Trail Monument, in New Franklin near the Missouri River. The Santa Fe marker was dedicated in special ceremonies on August 21, 1911. A map of the trail incised on its face has an error. Can you find it?

C. Palace of the Governors

This building, dating from the early Spanish colonial period, was closely associated with the SFT. For many years before 1846, it was the residence of Governor Manuel Armijo, who was deeply involved in overland trade. Gen. Stephen Watts Kearny, after crossing the Mountain Route of the SFT and occupying New Mexico for the United States, raised the American flag over the palace and took up temporary quarters inside.

Today, the Palace of the Governors is a part of the Museum of New Mexico. Although the exhibits change, there are usually some relating to the SFT. On display is a stagecoach that was used on the trail for many years, labeled "Mud Wagon." In addition, New Mexico's bicentennial covered wagon, which traveled part of the SFT in 1976, can be seen in the patio. The new Museum of New Mexico on the west side of the Palace has a section on the SFT.

D. The Kearny Monument

A small stone monument on the plaza facing the entrance to the Palace of the Governors honors Gen. Stephen Watts Kearny and his famous 1846 march over the trail.

E. The Soldiers Monument

Dedicated in 1867, this 33-foot column, surrounded by an iron fence in the center of the plaza, honors Union soldiers who died at the Battle of Glorieta (March 28, 1862) on the SFT near Pigeon's Ranch. Another inscription honors pioneers (among them many trail travelers) who died in battles with hostile Indians. The marker originally called these Indians "savages," but that word was later "edited off" by a vandal. The monument can be seen in early photographs showing ox caravans arriving in the plaza.

F. Cowbelle's Trail Plaque

Located on Washington Avenue at the east end of the Palace of the Governors, under an iron hitch rail, this bronze plaque honors early trail drivers.

G. La Fonda Hotel

On the outer corner of the plaza, opposite the End of the Trail Monument, this historic hostelry, entirely rebuilt in the 1920s, was known as the Inn at the End of the Trail. The hotel, whose fame extended to Missouri and beyond, was host to some of the best-known individuals who came over the trail.

Facing the La Fonda Hotel, across Old Santa Fe Trail and about 12 yards east of that street's junction with San Francisco Street, is one of the DAR's special bronze trail plaques set into the wall of a commercial building.

H. Statue of Archbishop John B. lamy

This statue, which inspired Willa Cather's famous novel *Death Comes for the Archbishop,* is located at the entrance to St. Francis Cathedral, built by Lamy at the east end of San Francisco Street just past La Fonda Hotel. Lamy made numerous trips over the SFT by wagon train and stagecoach. In a famous crossing of 1867, his caravan was attacked by Comanches, and though it was first erroneously reported that he and the priests and nuns accompanying him had been massacred, all (except for those who died of cholera) eventually reached Santa Fe safely.

NORTH OF THE PLAZA

Leave the plaza by the Fine Arts Museum (on the site where Marion Russell's mother, Eliza Mahoney, ran a boardinghouse in the 1850s) and walk north on Lincoln Avenue.

I. Hewett House/Fort Marcy Officers' Quarters

Located behind the Museum of Fine Arts Museum at 116 Lincoln, this extensively remodeled building is one of two surviving officers' quarters of old Fort Marcy. The other one is a block northwest at 135

Grant Avenue. General Kearny ordered construction to begin on Fort Marcy in August 1846. A blockhouse was built on a prominent hill about 600 yards northeast of the plaza, but it was never garrisoned. (Inquire locally if you want to visit that site.) Instead, decaying Spanish military installations behind the Palace of the Governors were used for barracks and warehouses. In the 1870s, during the last decade of the SFT, seven two-story gabled officers' quarters were built along Lincoln and Grant Avenues. When Fort Marcy was abandoned in 1894, these quarters passed into private hands, and five were demolished. The one now on Lincoln was purchased in 1916 by Frank Springer (publisher of the Cimarron News and attorney for the Maxwell Land Grant Company, both closely identified with the trail). Springer remodeled the structure in the Spanish-Pueblo architectural style. Springer gave the building as a residence for Museum of New Mexico Director Edgar L. Hewett, who occupied it until his death in 1946. Today, the building houses offices of the Museum of New Mexico Foundation.

J. Doña Tules's Establishment

Doña Tules maintained a gambling establishment at 142 West Palace in what is now the Palace Restaurant. Many trail diaries and journals mention this noteworthy place of diversion for the traders. She was also engaged in the trade as an investor and knew many traders. She is buried at the cathedral.

K. Kit Carson Monument

This tall stone column is located at the end of Lincoln Avenue in front of the main entrance to the U.S. Courthouse. Carson (1809-1868), a mountain man, scout, and soldier, was perhaps the most famous person associated with the SFT. He traveled it many times and, although his home was in Taos, he was a frequent visitor to Santa Fe and a member of this city's Masonic Lodge, which still preserves his rifle.

L. Mural of the Old Santa Fe Trail

Located immediately on the left just inside the main door of the U.S. Courthouse behind the Kit Carson Monument, the mural was painted by Santa Fe artist William Penhallow Henderson as part of the New Deal federal art projects in the early 1930s. It shows a wagon train from Missouri approaching Santa Fe through the eastern hills. Other historical and scenic murals of interest are located in the building.

M. Coronado Murals

Located in the lobby of the U.S. Post Office just west of the Carson Monument and the U.S. Courthouse, the two murals show explorer Francisco Vasquez de Coronado and the Pueblo Indians in 1540. Local artist Gerald Cassidy painted them in 1921.

SOUTH OF THE PLAZA

Return to the plaza and follow the street signs for Old Santa Fe Trail, beginning on the west side of La Fonda Hotel, the route by which you came to the plaza.

N. Loretto Chapel (Chapel of Our Lady of Light)

The building faces Old Santa Fe Trail behind La Fonda Hotel. In the early 1850s, Archbishop Lamy brought six nuns of the Order of Loretto over the SFT to establish a girls' academy surrounding this site. The Gothic chapel was begun in 1874 and completed in 1878, while freight wagons still rumbled past.

0. San Miguel Chapel

Located on Old Santa Fe Trail, one block beyond the Santa Fe River Bridge, this chapel, destroyed in the Pueblo Revolt of 1680, was rebuilt in 1710 and is sometimes referred to as "the oldest church in the U.S.A." In 1859, Lamy brought the Christian Brothers over the trail to manage the chapel and found a school for boys on adjacent lands. Both this structure and the so-called "Oldest House" next door were familiar sights to travelers on the SFT. Next to the chapel is the Lamy Building, which contains the Information Center for New Mexico and the City of Santa Fe.

NORTHWEST OF THE PLAZA

P. Grave of Charles Bent

General Kearny appointed celebrated SFT trader Charles Bent first civil governor of New Mexico after the conquest in 1846. The following January he was killed in an uprising while at his home in Taos. His body was brought to Santa Fe for burial. His grave can be found in the National Cemetery ten blocks northwest of the plaza (see map for directions from the plaza).

Entering the main gate of the National Cemetery, drive straight ahead to the office. Turn right, then right again, continuing past an adobe service building. The grave is about 50 yards beyond the adobe building, with an oversized white marble stone on the left toward the back of the cemetery. Next to it is a tall brown sandstone marker for Maj. Lawrence Murphy, one of the figures in the notorious Lincoln County War in which Billy the Kid was a participant. Behind Bent's grave is the grave of William F. Amy, who came over the SFT by stagecoach in 1861 to become Indian agent for the Utes and Jicarilla Apaches at Cimarron. He succeeded Kit Carson as the agent for those tribes and while at Cimarron became closely associated with Lucien Maxwell. Amy also served a term as secretary for the New Mexico Territory.

SIDE TRIP TO TAOS

In 1825, Commissioner George C. Sibley and his trail survey party reached Taos, which he had intended should serve as the official end of the SFT. Even though Taos had the disadvantage of being locked in by mountains and virtually inaccessible by wagon from either the east or south, it had advantages. It was becoming a resort for American trappers operating in the Southern Rockies and a center of the fur trade. The Mexican government maintained a port of entry there. In addition, because of its location in the northeast part of the province, Taos was the closest settlement to both Raton Pass on the Mountain Route and the Rock Crossing of the Canadian on the Cimarron Route. Notwithstanding, Taos failed to become a major trail terminus.

From Santa Fe drive north on US 84/US 285 to Española, about 20 miles. From there, take NM 68 north to Taos, approximately 75 miles from Santa Fe. At Velarde, the highway enters the scenic canyon of the Rio Grande and some 10 miles south of Taos emerges onto a high plateau that extends to the foot of the Sangre de Cristo Mountains. If you look carefully to your left after you crest the hill, you can see the deeply-eroded canyon cut by the Rio Grande.

Boasting eighty art galleries, Taos is a smaller version of Santa Fe, with a helpful Chamber of Commerce. Historic Taos Plaza in the center of town is the site where formerly all mountain trails converged. Nearby are at least four points of interest associated with the SFT:

A. Kit Carson Home and Museum
Located on US 64 East, one block east of the plaza on Kit Carson Road, this structure was built about 1825 and was owned by Carson from 1843 to 1868; serving as both residence and office during the years he was agent for the Utes and Jicarilla Apaches. In addition to fine exhibits, there are several furnished period rooms that impart the flavor of trail days. The only portion of the building that is original is the front section facing the road. There is an admission fee.
B. Governor Bent Home and Museum
Located one block north of the plaza on Bent Street this house is where SFT trader Charles Bent spent more of his time during his last years than at Bent's Fort on the Arkansas River. He was assassinated here in January 1847 while serving as the first appointed civil governor under United States rule. It is difficult to ascertain which part of the house is original. There is a hole punched through an interior wall, said to resemble the one through which Bent's family and friends escaped. There is an admission fee.
C. Kit Carson Park and Cemetery
On Pueblo del Norte Road, N M 68, at one block north of the plaza on the east is Kit Carson Park. The graves of Kit Carson, his wife Josefa, and other notables are enclosed within a fenced cemetery at the rear of the park. Padre Antonio Jose Martinez, who married Kit and Josefa and was a foe of the Bents, has a fine carved headstone that was made in the East and freighted over the SFT. A number of excellent historical markers have recently been added to the cemetery.
D. Southwest Research Center of Northern New Mexico
After following Ledoux Street from the southwest corner of the plaza one long block, the center is on the left next to the Harwood Foundation. It houses the combined libraries of the Harwood Museum, the Millicent Rogers Museum, and the Kit Carson Museum. The latter, of interest to trail buffs, has some resources pertaining to trail research. Nearby is the Blumenschein House, the entrance fee for which is included with the entrance fee for the Kit Carson House. Blumenschein was a prominent Taos artist.

E. Taos Pueblo

From the entrance of Kit Carson Park, continue north several blocks to a Y. In the center of the Y, is an official New Mexico Historical Marker, "Taos Pueblo." Take the right-hand fork 2 miles to the pueblo. There is an entrance fee.

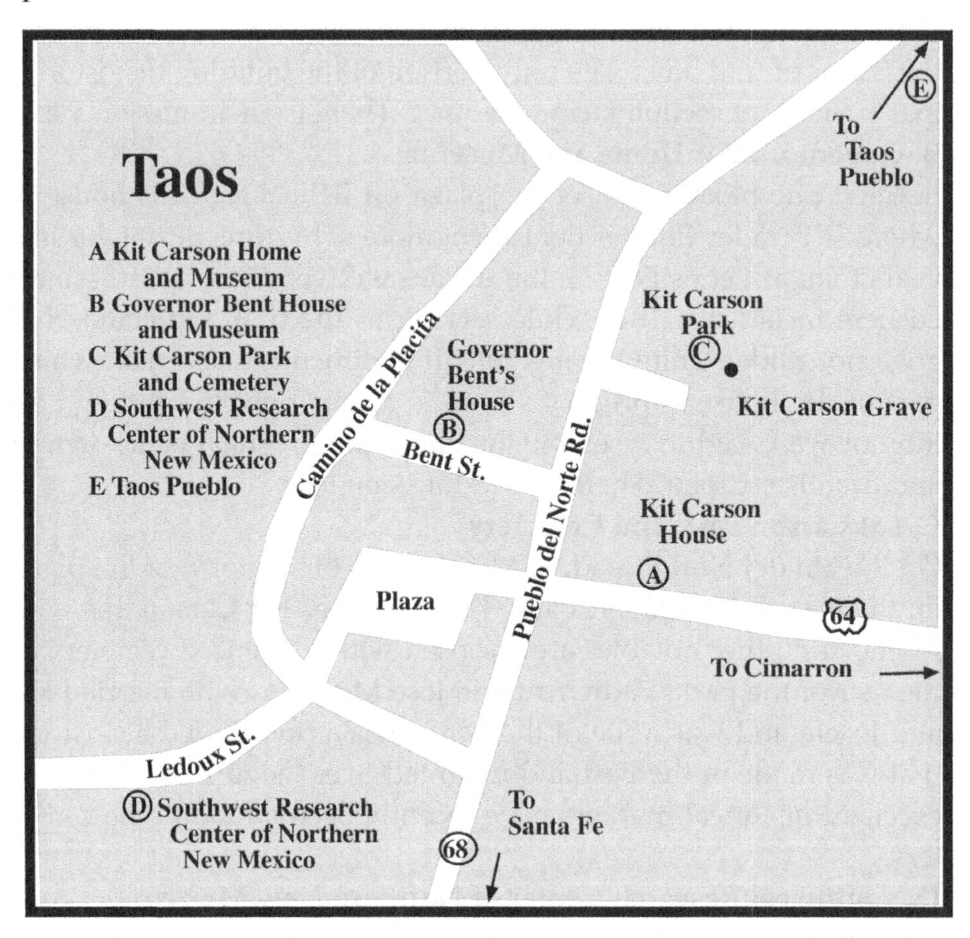

This spectacular adobe pueblo played a prominent role in the history of the Southwest, but its association with the SFT is only marginal. In 1843, Governor Manuel Armijo took a large force from Santa Fe over the Cimarron Route to escort the annual SFT caravan westward. At Cold Spring in the present-day Oklahoma Panhandle, he sent ahead a party of one hundred Taos militiamen under Capt. Ventura Lobato, including many Taos Pueblo Indians.

In southwestern Kansas, Lobato was attacked by raiders from the Texas Republic, who killed or captured almost all his command. The severe losses sustained in the incident embittered Taos Indians against U.S. citizens as well as Texans. This enmity is believed to have led them to participate in the murder of Charles Bent and others four years later. At the edge of the pueblo, you can still see ruins of the church that became a refuge for the rebels and was battered down by Col. Sterling Price's artillery during the U.S. Army's assault in February 1847.

Another victim of the Taos Revolt was Simeon Turley. Turley and others were engaged in making whisky at his distillery at Arroyo Hondo (a few miles north of Taos) since 1832. There is ample evidence that much of his product was sold on the Arkansas River and mostly to Indians. The sale of alcohol to Indians was against the law but many took advantage of lax enforcement to continue in the business. Details of this trade are found in William Unrau's book *Indians, Alcohol, and the Roads to Taos and Santa Fe*. Turley lost his life in the Revolt and the distillery was destroyed.

SIDE TRIP TO ALBUQUERQUE

While Albuquerque, on the Rio Grande 60 miles southwest of Santa Fe, was not situated on the SFT, many Missouri traders passed through it on their way south to El Paso and Chihuahua City. This route, beginning at Santa Fe, became known to SFT merchants as the Chihuahua Trail but was really the old Camino Real of colonial days. Several individuals prominent in the Santa Fe trade settled in Albuquerque and opened stores on or near the plaza. Most important among them was German-born Franz Huning, whose wagons were attacked at the Plum Buttes and whose trail journal has been published.

From Santa Fe take Interstate 25 south to Albuquerque. About halfway there is a large stone monument with a plaque dedicated to the Mormon Battalion. Leave the interstate at Exit 257, and take the frontage road on the west side of the freeway. The marker is about 1 mile south on this road. After arriving in Santa Fe, the Battalion followed this route south to pick up what was to become the Gila Trail leading to California.

The small city of Bernalillo is just off the interstate at Exit 242. One of New Mexico's wealthiest merchants, Jose Leandro Perea, lived here. He was the most prominent Hispanic merchant in 1860 and 1870 according to Susan Boyle in *Los Capitalistas: Hispano Merchants and the Santa Fe Trade*. From Bemalillo, Perea's caravans went east to the village of Placitas and continued northeast to connect with the SFT at Johnson's Ranch. Hispanic merchants such as Perea carried out a substantial portion of the trade on the SFT. Many of the wealthy Hispanic families sent their sons to schools in Missouri as well.

Continue to the main interchange in Albuquerque, where Interstate 25 intersects with Interstate 40. Exit to Interstate 40 heading west to Grants. After about a mile take the Rio Grande Boulevard exit and turn left (south) on Rio Grande to Old Town Plaza, the former center of Albuquerque. There are numerous historical markers in the center of the plaza, some of which relate to the period of the SFT. On the northeast edge of Old Town, at 2000 Mountain Road N.W., is the Albuquerque Museum, whose splendid historical exhibits include sections on Coronado and the Chihuahua and Santa Fe Trails.

The fourth and last Madonna of the Trail statue (or Pioneer Mother) on the SFT is located near the courthouse between 3rd and 4th Streets at Lomas, a major street that enters Old Town from the east joining Central Avenue one block south of the plaza. Follow Lomas to 3rd Street, turn left (north), and go to the next corner. Located to your right, the Madonna of the Trail statue was supposed to have been placed in Santa Fe in 1927, but artists and writers there rejected it as being ugly and not representative of the region's Spanish pioneer women, so the DAR moved the statue to Albuquerque.

SELECTED BIBLIOGRAPHY

Boyle, Susan Calafate. *Los Capitalistas: Hispano Merchants and the Santa Fe Trail.* Albuquerque: University of New Mexico Press, 1997.

Brown, Joseph C. *Survey of the Western Boundary of the State of Missouri, 1823.* Originals located in Missouri State Department of Natural Resources, Rolla, Missiouri.

Coues, Elliott, ed. *The Journal of Jacob Fowler.* Minneapolis, Minn.: Ross and Haines, 1965.

Crease, Craig. "Lone Elm and Elm Grove: A Case of Mistaken Identity?" *Wagon Tracks* (August 1991): 10-13.

Duffus, Robert L. *The Santa Fe Trail.* Albuquerque: University of New Mexico Press, 1999.

Field, Matt. *Matt Field on the Santa Fe Trail,* edited by John E. Sunder. Norman: University of Oklahoma Press. 1995.

Franzwa, Gregory M. *The Santa Fe Trail Revisited.* St. Louis, Mo.: Patrice Press, 1989.

_________. *Maps of the Santa Fe Trail.* St. Louis, Mo.: Patrice Press, 1989.

Gardner, Mark L. *Wagons for the Santa Fe Trade: Wheeled Vehicles and Their Makers.* Albuquerque: University of New Mexico Press, 2000.

Gregg, Josiah. *Commerce of the Prairies,* edited by Max L. Moorhead. Norman: University of Oklahoma Press, 1990.

Gregg, Kate L., ed. *The Road to Santa Fe: The Journal and Diaries of George Champlin Sibley.* Albuquerque: University of New Mexico Press, 1995.

Hafen, LeRoy R. *The Mountain Men and the Fur Trade of the Far West.* 10 volumes. Glendale, Calif.: Arthur H. Clark Co., 1965-1972. Hoegan, Paul. *Lamy of Santa Fe.* New York:Farrar, Straus, and Giroux, 1975.

Hughes, John Taylor. *Doniphan's Expedition.* College Station: Texas A and M University Press, 1997.

Jackson, Hal. *Boone's Lick Road: A Brief History and Guide to a Missouri Treasure.* Trails Press, Woodston, KS. 2012

Kirwan, John S. "Patrolling the Santa Fe Trail: Reminiscences of John S. Kirwan." *The Kansas Historical Quarterly* (Winter 1955): 569-87.

Lavender, David. *Bent's Fort*. Lincoln: University of Nebraska Press, 1972.

Long, Margaret. *The Santa Fe Trail*. Denver, Colo.: Kistler Company, 1954.

Louden Richard. "The Military Freight Route." *Wagon Tracks* (May 1993):7-10.

Lowe, Percival G. *Five Years Dragoon*. Norman: University of Oklahoma Press, 1965.

Magoffin, Susan Shelby. *Down the Santa Fe Trail and into Mexico, 1846-1847: The Diary of Susan Shelby Magoffin*, edited by Stella M. Drumm. Lincoln: University of Nebraska Press, 1982.

Marmaduke, Meredith Miles. "Santa Fe Trail: M. M. Marmaduke Journal." *Missouri Historical Review* (October 1911): 1-10

Olsen, Michael L., and Harry C. Myers. "The Diary of Pedro Ignacio Gallego Wherein 400 Soldiers Following the Trail of Comanches Met William Becknell on His First Trip to Santa Fe," *Wagon Tracks* (November 1992):1, 15-20.

Parks, Ronald D. *The Darkest Period: The Kanza Indians and Their Last Homeland 1846-1873*. Norman, OK.: University of Oklahoma Press, 2014.

Poole, Joy L. (ed). *Over the Santa Fe Trail to Mexico: The Travel Diaries and Autobiography of Dr. Rowland Willard*. Norman, OK:University of Oklahoma Press. 2015

Quaise, Milo, ed. *Narrative of the Adventures of Zenas Leonard*. Chicago: Lakeside Press, 1934.

Russell, Mrs. Hal, ed. *Land of Enchantment: Memoirs of Marian Russell Along the Santa Fe Trail*. Albuquerque: University of New Mexico Press, 1993.

Sappington, John. *The Theory and Treatment of Fevers*. Arrow Rock, Mo.: Friends of Arrow Rock, 1993.

Simmons, Marc, ed. *On the Santa Fe Trail*. Lawrence, Kansas: University Press of Kansas, 1986.

Slusher, Roger. "Lexington and the Santa Fe Trail." *Wagon Tracks* (1991): 6-9.

Stocking, Hobart E. *The Road to Santa Fe.* New York: Hastings House, 1971.

Taylor, Morris. *First Mail West: Stagecoach Lines on the Santa Fe Trail.* Albuquerque, NM: University of New Mexico Press, 1971.

Unrau, William E. *Indians, Alcohol, and the Roads to Taos and Santa Fe.* Lawrence, KS.: University Press of Kansas, 2013.

Vestal, Stanley. *The Old Santa Fe Trail.* Lincoln: University of Nebraska Press, 1996.

Wetmore, Alphonso. "Major Alphonso Wetmore's Diary of a Journey to Santa Fe, 1828." *Missouri Historical Review* 8 (July 1914): 177-97.

Wright, Robert M. *Dodge City: The Cowboy Capital.* Wichita, Kansas: Wichita Eagle Press, 1913.

INDEX

Page numbers in bold type indicate maps.

Made in the USA
Middletown, DE
29 June 2022